THE MENTAL HEALTH FOUNDATION

The *Mental Health Foundation* (MHF) is Britain's leading grant-making charity concerned with promoting and encouraging pioneering research and community care projects in the field of mental health and disorder.

The Foundation aims to prevent mental disorders by funding and encouraging research into the causes of mental illness and mental handicap, and to improve the quality of life for the mentally disordered by funding and supporting pioneering and innovative care schemes.

The MHF has three professional committees which meet at regular intervals to decide upon the allocation of funds to priority areas. One of these committees is the research committee, the Honorary Secretary of which is currently Professor Peter McGuffin, co-editor of this book. Dr Paul Bebbington was his predecessor in this post.

In 1987, the MHF hosted a major conference to assess the future of research into schizophrenia. The aim of the conference was to examine the concern of various scientific disciplines about the state of research into schizophrenia. Many of the ideas and revelations from the meeting are highlighted and expanded upon in this book, a parallel venture.

SCHIZOPHRENIA
The Major Issues

Edited by

PAUL BEBBINGTON
MB, PhD, MRCP, MRCPsych

Medical Research Council, Social Psychiatry Unit, Institute of Psychiatry, London

and

PETER McGUFFIN
MB, PhD, FRCP, MRCPsych

Professor, Department of Psychological Medicine, University of Wales College of Medicine, Heath Park, Cardiff

Heinemann Professional Publishing
in association with

The Mental Health Foundation

Heinemann Medical Books
An imprint of Heinemann Professional Publishing Ltd
Halley Court, Jordan Hill, Oxford OX2 8EJ

OXFORD   LONDON   MELBOURNE   AUCKLAND

First published 1988

© Mental Health Foundation and individual contributors as cited 1988

British Library Cataloguing in Publication Data

A CIP catalogue record for this book is available
from the British Library.

ISBN 0 433 00045 7

Typeset by Latimer Trend & Company Ltd, Plymouth and
printed by Dotesios (Printers) Ltd, Bradford-on-Avon, Wiltshire

Contents

Contributors

Heidelinde A. Allen
CRC Division of Psychiatry, Northwick Park; Psychiatry Department, Chase Farm Hospital, Enfield, Middlesex

Paul E. Bebbington
Medical Research Council, Social Psychiatry Unit, Institute of Psychiatry, London

Gordon Claridge
University of Oxford Department of Experimental Psychology, Oxford

T. J. Crow
CRC Division of Psychiatry, Northwick Park, Middlesex

J. F. W. Deakin
University Department of Psychiatry, Withington Hospital, Manchester

Lars Farde
Department of Psychiatry and Psychology, Karolinska Hospital, Stockholm, Sweden

Anne E. Farmer
Department of Psychological Medicine, University of Wales College of Medicine, Heath Park, Cardiff

Alice Foerster
Institute of Psychiatry, London

Christopher D. Frith
CRC Division of Psychiatry, Northwick Park; Psychiatry Department, Chase Farm Hospital, Enfield, Middlesex

Håkan Hall
Department of Psychiatry and Psychology, Karolinska Hospital, Stockholm, Sweden

A. Jablensky
WHO Collaborating Centre for Mental Health, Institute of Neurology, Psychiatry and Neurosurgery, Medical Academy, Sofia, Bulgaria

D. A. W. Johnson
University Hospital of South Manchester, Manchester

Liz Kuipers
District Services Centre, Maudsley Hospital, London

P. L. Lantos
Department of Neuropathology, Institute of Psychiatry, London

J. Leff
Medical Research Council Social Psychiatry Unit, Institute of Psychiatry, London

Shôn W. Lewis
Institute of Psychiatry, London

Peter McGuffin
Department of Psychological Medicine, University of Wales College of Medicine, Heath Park, Cardiff

A. V. P. Mackay
Argyll and Bute Hospital, Lochgilphead, Argyll

Robin M. Murray
Institute of Psychiatry, London

Michael J. Owen
Institute of Psychiatry, London

Göran Sedvall
Department of Psychiatry and Psychology, Karolinska Hospital, Stockholm, Sweden

Geoff Shepherd
Department of Psychology, Fulbourn Hospital, Cambridge

Stephen M. Stahl
Neuroscience Research Centre, Merck Sharp and Dohme Research Laboratories, Harlow, Essex

Kathleen M. Wets
Neuroscience Research Centre, Merck Sharp and Dohme Research Laboratories, Harlow, Essex

Frits-Axel Wiesel
Department of Psychiatry and Psychology, Karolinska Hospital, Stockholm, Sweden

1 *Schizophrenia at the crossroads*

PAUL BEBBINGTON AND PETER McGUFFIN

INNOVATION IN SCHIZOPHRENIA RESEARCH

Albeit the heartland of psychiatry, schizophrenia remains a will o' the wisp landscape, full of shadows and chimeras. Explorers here have laboured hard to define the territory, establish landmarks, and to discover the cause and meaning underlying what they have seen. Alas, this journey of discovery has been painstakingly slow, for it is now 80 years since Bleuler first coined the term.

Nevertheless, at the meeting in Balliol College, Oxford in September 1987, organized by the Mental Health Foundation in parallel with this volume, there was a palpable excitement. The inadequacy always apparent in our theories is gradually giving rise to new appraisals of a more radical kind. These reappraisals enshrine what we have always known, that schizophrenia is a most subtle and challenging disorder, but, in addition, they are accompanied by a new determination to meet the challenge with a whole range of sophisticated techniques.

Many of the chapters in this book are concerned with far-reaching aetiological theories. They concern the mode of genetic transmission, the neurochemical and histopathological basis, and the nature of psychological abnormality. Other chapters are perhaps more modest in their aims, but are complementary, identifying contributory influences and issues of management.

DEFINING THE FIELD

However, underlying all of these concerns, there is still the ancient preoccupation with the 'what' of schizophrenia—what is it? how can we best identify it? which bits of it are central, and which accessory? There is always that tension, which Popper (1963) has described, between wanting to be quite sure of what we are talking about and wanting to get on with the job of finding out about it. Nevertheless, our views on the circumscription of schizophrenia seem to be undergoing a change, and one which may be extremely beneficial to the progress of study.

Recognizing that the question 'what do we mean by schizophrenia' does not, even now, have a universally satisfactory answer, we devoted a session of the Oxford conference to a panel-led discussion of phenomenology. We have chosen not to attempt to record this verbatim or even to paraphrase the proceedings. Instead, Chapter 4 provides a summary of some of the issues of current interest and, we think, captures the flavour of the important points of the discussion. It is worth noting that much recent work has been devoted to providing definitions of schizophrenia and its subtypes which can be described explicitly and which provide good inter-rater reliability. This has meant that certain well delineated positive features, such as Schneider's first rank symptoms, have often been emphasized at the expense of less easily rated signs and symptoms. The re-emergence of interest in negative symptoms is apparent not only in Chapter 4, but also elsewhere in this volume, for example in Chapter 13. These authors also focus our attention on other phenomena which have recently been comparatively neglected, such as disorder of the form of thought, and reintroduce the almost forgotten concept of impairment of the will in schizophrenia.

THE EPIDEMIOLOGICAL CONTRIBUTION

Definition of the disorder is thus a recurrent theme throughout this book. Nowhere is this more important than in epidemiology. As Jablensky points out in Chapter 3, epidemiological studies of schizophrenia have a long history. They have always been hampered by the non-availability of a ready, reliable, and epidemiologically feasible test for the presence of the disorder. For the time being, detection must therefore rely purely on the recognition of symptom patterns. However, the recent WHO studies have consolidated our knowledge, such that we can now make certain assertions with confidence, and Jablensky lists these. He divides them into 'findings of the first rank', which almost certainly reflect something about the nature of the condition itself, and less specific 'findings of the second rank'.

In general, the value of epidemiology is in setting up hypotheses: it is less useful in testing them. However, Jablensky feels that the evidence from epidemiological studies is sufficient to make certain aetiological hypotheses highly implausible, e.g. a horizontally transmissible virus infection, an autoimmune disease, or a purely social agent. It also suggests useful analogies, for instance, with diabetes mellitus or, more convincingly perhaps, with epilepsy.

DOPAMINE

The research described by Sedvall and his colleagues in Chapter 5 may well in future years be seen as a turning point in our understanding of schizophrenia. For over 20 years, we have been enamoured of the dopamine hypothesis of schizophrenia. This was based on inference from the dopamine-inhibiting actions of effective antipsychotic drugs, and from abnormalities such as increased D2 dopamine binding in the brains of schizophrenic patients examined post-mortem. However, it has never been clear whether or not the latter are artefacts of long-term neuroleptic treatment. This is known to produce such effects in laboratory animals and almost certainly in humans, too. Post-mortem studies are virtually guaranteed to be contaminated by the consequences of treatment, but until recently there was no ethical means of assessing receptor binding in the brains of early 'drug naive' cases.

Inference from the mechanisms of action of effective antischizophrenic medication is also extremely rash, as an analogy will underline. MacKay points out in Chapter 2 that the impressive link between neurochemistry and pharmacology in Parkinson's disease actually represents inference in the opposite direction—an effective treatment was established from a knowledge of the neurochemical abnormality. The current state of knowledge in schizophrenia is more like our knowledge of Parkinson's disease in, say, the late 1950s. If we had made a corresponding pharmacological inference at that time, we would have concluded that parkinsonism was due to abnormalities of the cholinergic system, since the known effective drugs all possessed anticholinergic actions.

The emergence of a technique for assessing dopaminergic function in the living brain, i.e. through positron emission tomographic (PET) screening, gave the prospect of a more secure basis for the dopamine theory. However, the findings of Sedvall and his group (Chapter 5) in recent onset drug-naive schizophrenic patients showed no abnormalities of D2 dopamine receptor characteristics in the basal ganglia.

This is a startling result, and must be confronted by the adherents of the dopamine theory. Parallel studies by Wong *et al.* (1986) did show results more in keeping with the dopamine theory, but their techniques lacked the simplicity and directness of the Swedish group; moreover, the patients in the American study had been ill twice as long as the Swedish sample. Clearly, confidence in the drug-naive status of patients must decline with increasing prior duration of illness. It must be acknowledged that the technique is limited by its powers of resolution, currently around 7 mm, and it is possible that dopaminergic abnormalities exist in areas of the brain that the Swedish group were not able to visualize.

However, such reservations should not detract from the impact and importance of these studies. They at least leave the ball firmly in the court of the protagonists of the dopamine theory, and they may initiate an unprejudiced and productive evaluation of alternatives. Similar reservations about the theory are apparent in Chapters 2, 6 and 11.

Deakin (Chapter 6), however, points out that there may be a far more complex set of processes underlying the involvement of dopamine in schizophrenia than has been previously recognized. For example, it has usually been assumed that the two types of dopamine receptor, D1 and D2, function synergetically. However, they appear to have opposed actions on cyclic AMP formation. The possible role of peptides in modulating dopamine neurotransmission continues to provoke interest (and the part played by substances such as cholecystokinin and neurotensin is a theme which recurs in Chapter 11). Consideration also has to be given to recent findings which suggest that dopaminergic abnormalities in schizophrenia may be both localized and lateralized. Chapter 6 recognizes the further fact that neurochemical theories must take account of cerebral atrophy in some schizophrenics and proposes an ingenious method for investigating degeneration and dysplasia in limbic areas using radio-labelled ligand binding with glutamate and gamma-aminobutyric (GABA) receptors. Such techniques have already yielded noteworthy preliminary results which may tie in well with neuropathological findings reviewed by Lantos (Chapter 7).

In retrospect, then, our preoccupation with the dopamine theory may have become counter-productive, or even a cul-de-sac, as Murray puts it in Chapter 8. Although this sounds a pessimistic note, the prospect of new ideas and new searches is an exciting one.

THE NEW NEUROPATHOLOGY

The struggles of the science of neuropathology to get to grips with the disease of schizophrenia epitomize research into the subject. Early studies were bedevilled by problems of method and design, such that very little consensus was possible. Recently, developments in electron microscopy, quantitative morphometry, histochemistry and immunochemistry have made possible the identification of subtle and localized changes in both structure and function. In Chapter 7, Lantos reviews the results of this new neuropathology. As yet, they are not dramatic: there is good evidence of hippocampal involvement for the first time; it is clear that in many cases of schizophrenia, the medial aspect of the temporal lobe is bilaterally affected; there is also evidence of abnormal cells in the medial temporal lobe and frontal lobe. Lantos' review identifies the reasons for this slow progress, and he particularly warns against conceptual errors that are likely to hinder advances in the subject.

Paramount are the dangers of 'false localization'—the too ready identification of a local abnormality as a 'cause' of the disorder. Even if such a localization were of central pathogenetic significance, no brain area can be studied in isolation from its afferent and efferent connections. Moreover, changes like neuronal loss and gliosis are non-specific, and may represent damage elsewhere. It may indeed be abnormalities of the *surviving* neurons that contribute to the development of the schizophrenic syndrome. These difficulties sound remarkably like those of the cognitive neuropsychologists, as described by Frith and Allen in Chapter 13.

Nevertheless, a start has been made: the difficulties of the subject are far from insuperable, and if research workers respond to the guidelines suggested by Lantos, the discipline of neuropathology will assume a proper and central position in the elucidation of schizophrenia. Advancement may depend on a readiness to follow-up the results of new techniques, e.g. the suggestion from PET scan studies of abnormalities in the left globus pallidus of those with schizophrenia (Early *et al.*, 1987).

TOWARDS A NEW NEUROPSYCHOLOGY

Another area in which quite radical changes have occurred recently is in cognitive neuropsychological studies of schizophrenia. In the past, psychologists were concerned to devise cognitive tests that would serve to distinguish between the 'functional' disorder of schizophrenia and 'organic' deficits. This now seems a little odd in view of accumulating evidence of the neuropathological changes in schizophrenia. There is considerable irony in the fact that psychologists are now more interested in using tests to demonstrate the similarities between schizophrenia and localizable organic deficits.

The object of this neuropsychology is to relate psychological performance to supposed deficits in the neurophysiological substrate, a deliberately reductionist approach. However, in Chapter 13 Frith and Allen argue that much of this work is based on a flawed assumption: similar impairments in psychological function *cannot* be taken to indicate neurological and pathological similarities, a point also made strongly by Miller (1986).

To put it another way, much of the work in the neuropsychology of schizophrenia has been and is 'data-driven' rather than 'theory driven', and for this reason has failed in its task of providing new insights into the underlying pathology. The neutral observer can be forgiven for seeing the current situation in the cognitive neuropsychology of schizophrenia as something of a log-jam.

Frith and Allen emphasize the need for testable theories linking psychological and neurophysiological function. Their own work is a reflection of this, and also a recommendation, in that their model of language dysfunction leads to exactly the sort of radical and indeed surprising postulates that might break the log-jam.

They argue that 'positive' and 'negative' speech disorders in schizophrenia are *not* dichotomous, but are the consequences of the same dysfunction. Moreover, both linguistic and cognitive knowledge structures remain intact, and the deficiency is therefore one of performance. The common antecedent to the positive and negative disorders is a restriction in the production of willed intentions.

The authors adduce considerable evidence for this position, although some findings have been contrary to prediction. The relationship with underlying and localized brain mechanisms remains speculative. However, the attractiveness of the model is that it leads to testable hypotheses.

The conative defects that the authors postulate would suggest the value of comparative studies, not only in manic, but in depressive, subjects. Manic patients have lots of drive, and circumstantial speech, with its considerable degree of clausal embedding, would seem to be the converse of poverty of content in schizophrenia. However, manic patients can be conceptualized as showing impaired cohesion devices in the same manner, if not in the same degree, as schizophrenic patients (Wykes and Leff, 1982). At first sight counterintuitive, Frith and Allen's thesis accounts for much of the data, and surely deserves serious attention. As we have mentioned earlier, it is interesting to reflect upon the return of the will to psychiatry.

GENETICS AND THE AETIOLOGICAL CONTROVERSY

In a volume such as this, where authors attempt to highlight recent developments and foreshadow future prospects, one does not expect unanimity. It will not surprise our readers therefore that some of the contributors disagree with each other. This is perhaps most apparent in Chapters 8, 9 and 10. Yet all three essentially adopt the same basic premise, that an understanding of the genetics of schizophrenia provides the most potentially useful set of clues for unravelling its complex aetiology. McGuffin's position (Chapter 9) is perhaps closest to accepted orthodoxy in viewing schizophrenia as a disorder or group of disorders which, despite the clumsiness of the phenotype, can be accommodated (like other common familial non-Mendelian diseases) within the concepts and methods of study of modern genetic epidemiology. Murray *et al.* (Chapter 8) are more perturbed by the observation of a high proportion of schizophrenics who do not have affected relatives (even though this is not out of keeping with the models of transmission discussed by McGuffin), and favour a more explicit account of environmental involvement.

Schizophrenia is usually a disease of adulthood, occasionally of adolescence: it is very rare indeed before puberty. In this sense it might be seen as a developmental disorder, as a certain degree of maturity is almost a necessary condition of its efflorescence. Murray *et al.*, while acknowledging the genetic component, argue strongly for another distant cause in terms of early neurological damage. A full explanation of aetiology must account not only for the causes of the disease, whether genetic or environmental, but for the mechanisms that lie behind the timing of onset. Murray *et al.* speculate that early damage occasions neural dysplasia that results in premorbid cognitive deficits and abnormal personality, negative symptoms, and an abnormal computed tomographic (CT) scan. As the brain matures in adolescence, it is possible that the known processes of myelination or neuronal retraction permit the emergence of changes in stimulus handling that lead in turn to florid symptoms such as delusions and hallucinations.

As Murray *et al.* freely admit, they are engaged in an exercise of speculation. They rely fairly heavily on the claim that schizophrenia is not a disease characterized by a degenerating performance, and not all would agree with this. For instance, in Chapter 12, Johnson is clearly of the opinion that degeneration is the consequence of acute episodes, which should therefore be treated energetically. There are certainly alternative interpretations of the evidence regarding the significance of obstetric complications in schizophrenia, and it is not clear why women, who mature earlier, develop the disease relatively later than men (Loranger, 1984). Nevertheless, as they say, the theory is eminently testable, and such speculations are the stuff of progress.

Crow's position (Chapter 10) is similarly provocative, but from a quite different angle. He argues that schizophrenia is a disease wholly attributable to a component of the human genome, albeit one which behaves in a way which is more complex than that of other single locus disorders. Crow proposes that a virogene incorporated into the human genome has the capacity to disrupt local brain function, but that it has survived the process of evolutionary selection by providing a contribution to cerebral development. He suggests that this element interacts with a cerebral dominance gene in a symbiotic relationship which confers flexibility and a *specifically human* potential for brain growth. Like Murray *et al.*, Crow considers that his views are speculation, but such conjectures may provide a necessary starting point for embarking on the exploration of schizophrenia at a molecular level.

THE PHARMACOLOGICAL CONTRIBUTION

We have seen that the dopamine theory of schizophrenia is under attack. This could also be true of the pharmaceutical industry's preoccupation with neuroleptics that act on dopaminergic neural transmission. There is little doubt that a dopamine theory is the best we have to explain the actions of neuroleptic drugs on schizophrenia (Iversen, 1987; Crow, 1987), although even this has been questioned (e.g. Dinan, 1987). Johnson points out in Chapter 12 that we do not fully understand how the dopaminergic actions of neuroleptics produce their side-effects. What is certain is that clinicians may be forgiven for failing to notice great therapeutic progress following the introduction of 'me too' drugs in the long years since the introduction of chlorpromazine.

However, as Stahl and Wets argue in Chapter 11, we may be about to emerge into a new pharmaceutical era. The advances in immediate prospect are likely to arise from drugs with 'atypical' behavioural effects in animal models. These drugs still act on dopamine systems, but may do so more selectively, being effective in the treatment of psychosis without extrapyramidal side-effects. The great hope from such drugs would be the avoidance of tardive dyskinesia.

Stahl and Wets also describe a very different group of drugs. These include cholecystokinin-8 and neurotensin, peptides that appear to modulate dopaminergic systems. Research is also directed at sigma opiate site inhibitors and at 5-hydroxytryptamine (5HT3) antagonists. These new drugs, which are in the early stages of investigation, are all based on novel pharmacological mechanisms. It is from such novel approaches that a breakthrough in the treatment of schizophrenia is most likely to come, and the more we know about neurochemical and neuropathological abnormalities in schizophrenia, the more likely we are to identify alternative targets for pharmacological innovation.

SCHIZOPHRENIA IN THE SOCIAL DOMAIN

The search for radical aetiological theories of schizophrenia is not the only focus in this volume. A consensus is probably now established that such radical theories are most likely to be corroborated in the biological realm, although it is clear that we are as yet far from a convincing account. Social theories, as suggested in Chapters 14 and 15, are more likely to account for the timing and course of schizophrenia rather than for its emergence in particular individuals. McGue *et al.* (1985) pointed out the difference between schizophrenia and tuberculosis. Analogies have sometimes been drawn between the two since both are familial and show substantial concordance in identical twins. However path analysis shows that tuberculosis is a much less genetic, much more environmental condition. Nevertheless, cultural transmission probably accounts for around 30% of the variance in schizophrenia. Moreover, this 30% is important because it opens the door to strategies of management that have a major impact on the course of schizophrenia and on the lives of patients and their relatives (Kuipers and Bebbington, 1988).

These strategies operate at the interface between stresses and skills. People with schizophrenia tend to relapse in the face of stress. Some of this stress is occasioned by maladaptive behaviour on the part of those with whom they live, and there are now several examples of interventions aimed at improving the adaptation of relatives in order to ameliorate the environment of patients.

Patients may also experience stress because they themselves lack essential skills. Shepherd argues persuasively in Chapter 16 that early attempts to train such skills may have failed to generalize because they operated at a very specific level. He prefers to 'turn the skills model on its head', by finding out what the patient wants to be able to do and attempting to help through enhancing behaviour at a more integrated level. This avoids problems both of motivation and of generalization.

While we continue to await further advances in psychopharmacological treatment, the social consequences of schizophrenia remain to be dealt with by the clinician. The social management of schizophrenia is now a rationally based set of flexible strategies that can be applied to the established requirements of individual patients (Wing, 1987). The effective dissemination of this knowledge and skill among general psychiatric teams would have a considerable impact on the well-being of schizophrenia sufferers.

DELIVERING THE GOODS

Treatments are always provided within the context of the overall service offered to patients. Since the early 1960s, service provision in mental health has been dominated in the UK by the ideology of community care. This encouraged the run-down of the old-established mental hospitals that was happening anyway, and indeed enshrined it. As a result, by the 1980s regional health authorities (RHAs) felt themselves in a position to consider the closure of certain hospitals, ostensibly by replacing them with community-based services.

This change in venue must have an enormous impact on the well-being of patients with chronic schizophrenia previously cared for in long-stay hospital wards. The requirements arising from the disabilities consequent on the condition, and from the principles of treatment and management, will together determine whether the move into the community will be for good or ill. However, the policy has been implemented with little consideration of these issues. It is typical that the evaluation, described by Leff in Chapter 17, was initiated well after the original decision to close Friern and Claybury hospitals. This would be less remarkable if the closure formed an organized and coherent experiment from which other RHAs were waiting to learn, but it is not.

Leff describes an individual study, but in doing so, he illustrates very important principles underlying this type of evaluation: the need to frame the questions that are right for the population to be studied; the construction of adequate questionnaires; and, most basically, a consideration of the problems surrounding the conceptualization and measurement of ideas like 'need' and 'quality of life'. Only when such issues are clarified is it possible to decide if all our clever treatments and strategies of management can be delivered for the real benefit of patients with this tragic condition.

REFERENCES

Crow T. J. (1987). The dopamine hypothesis survives, but there must be a way ahead. *British Journal of Psychiatry*; **151**: 460–5.

Dinan T. G. (1987). Calcium-activated potassium conductance: an alternative to the dopamine hypothesis of neuroleptic action. *British Journal of Psychiatry*; **151**: 455–9.

Early T. S., Reiman E. M., Raichle M. E., Spitznagel E. L. (1987). Left globus pallidus abnormality in never-medicated patients with schizophrenia. *Proceedings of the National Academy of Science (USA)*; **84**: 561–3.

Iversen L. L. (1987). Commentary on Dinan's hypothesis. *British Journal of Psychiatry*; **151**: 459–60.

Kuipers L., Bebbington P. E. (1988). Expressed emotion research in schizophrenia: theoretical and clinical implications. *Psychological Medicine*: (in press).

Loranger A. W. (1984). Sex difference in age of onset of schizophrenia. *Archives of General Psychiatry*; **41**: 157–61.

McGue M., Gottesman, I. I., Rao D. C. (1985). Resolving genetic models for the transmission of schizophrenia. *Genetic Epidemiology*; **2**: 99–110.

Miller T.. (1986). 'Narrow localisationism' in psychiatric neuropsychology. *Psychological Medicine*; **16**: 729–34.

Popper K. R. (1963). *Conjectures and Refutations*. London, Routledge and Kegan Paul.

Wing J. K. (1987). Psychosocial factors affecting the long-term course of schizophrenia. In: *Psychosocial Treatment of Schizophrenia* (Strauss J. S., Boker W., Brenner H. D., eds.), pp. 13–29. Toronto: Huber.

Wong D. F., Wagner H. N., Tune L. E., *et al.* (1986). Positron emission tomography reveals elevated D2 dopamine receptors in drug-naive schizophrenics. *Science*; **234**: 1558–63.

Wykes T., Leff J. P. (1982). Disordered speech: differences between manics and schizophrenics. *Brain and Language*; **15**: 117–24.

2 *A clinician's view of research*

A. V. P. MACKAY

My aim in this brief chapter is to reflect a clinician's view of the current state of research into schizophrenic illness. Schizophrenia has been aptly described by Kendell as the 'heartland of psychiatry', a position earned as much by the enigmatic nature of the illness as by its fearful toll of morbidity, and one which reflects an ongoing problem rather than a success story. Priorities for research can only be framed in terms which are governed by existing clues and available technology, and I propose to argue below for one particular priority. Clinical priorities are easy to define by anyone involved in the diagnosis and management of schizophrenic illness. Cure, or better still prevention, are self-evident goals. There is at present no reasonable prospect of either, and the clinician must lower his sights and ask for palliative treatment which is relatively safe, and rules by which he can grade prognosis. Even these more modest requirements are largely unmet, a slightly embarrassing admission on the part of practitioners and researchers alike in the face of the most common seriously disabling disorder of adult life in the UK.

TAKING STOCK

Present ignorance is not a symptom of neglect. Schizophrenic illness has been a focus for clinical and biological research for many decades. Progress has indeed been made, but probably more in the realm of setting the scene for the right questions to be asked, rather than providing answers which can be used by the clinician in the management of his patients.

The original naturalistic research of Emil Kraepelin and Eugen Bleuler provided us with both the concept and the name of the illness. Diagnostic rules have now been introduced, an enormously important step, and a logical prerequisite for serious and applicable research. Epidemiological patterns for the illness have been documented and refined, and have prompted excellent work on the strength, if not the precise nature, of the genetic endowment. Epidemiology has also demonstrated how silly was the question 'nature or nurture?'. The spectrum of environmental insults required to interact with faulty genetic programming has also been greatly expanded in recent years. Indeed it has recently been said (Reveley and

Reveley, 1986) that theories of causation have become almost desperate in their inventiveness, and extend from cryptic viral infection, through perinatal birth injury, and disordered family dynamics, to circulating psychotogenic peptides.

This is all very interesting, but the most important landmark of this century in relation to schizophrenia emerged in 1952 with the revelation of chlorpromazine. A typical case of medical serendipity, this modest phenothiazine was so effective that clinicians did not need persuasion by *t*-tests to start prescribing it. The important pharmacological action of the drug in relation to the amelioration of psychotic symptoms, that of antagonism at central dopamine receptors, bred an era of clinical neurobiological research into dopamine systems. Preoccupation with this transmitter was justifiable for a time, but extrapolation from the fact that dopamine antagonists ameliorate psychotic symptoms to the proposition that schizophrenic illness was due to overactivity at dopamine synapses was always logically shaky. Understandable, certainly; it was undoubtedly clinically effective, and the appealing precedent in the use of L-dopa in Parkinson's disease no doubt also played a part. If one seriously disabling disorder could be cured by manipulating one transmitter system, why couldn't this also prove to be the case with schizophrenia? The essential difference between Parkinson's disease and schizophrenia was that, in the former the neurochemical abnormality was first identified and then the chemical remedy was deduced. The reverse process for dopamine antagonists and schizophrenia simply has not worked. We cannot shake our fingers free of the inescapable fact that we do not know the nature of the brain dysfunction(s) which underlies the symptoms.

Another major milestone, albeit of lower profile, has been a renaissance of the distinction between 'positive' or florid symptoms and the 'negative' symptoms or defect state in schizophrenic illness. Although chlorpromazine may turn out to have limited heuristic value in relation to the aetiopathology of the illness, it certainly throws into relief the neurochemical distinction between the florid psychoses and the defect state. In the former, blockade of central dopamine synapses ameliorates the syndrome, in the latter this pharmacological strategy is at best impotent and is arguably detrimental to the quality of life. Viewed simply as a chemical probe, chlorpromazine tells us that the two syndromes are neurochemically different (Mackay, 1980; Crow, 1980; Andreasen, 1985). Recent reconsiderations of the contribution by gross brain pathology to the schizophrenic syndrome have tended to associate gross pathology with the defect state. The pathological relationship between florid symptoms and negative symptoms remains something of a conundrum, but the idea that the florid syndrome is a pathological precursor of the chronic defect state may still have some face validity (Kay and Opler,1987).

The last 40 years have, therefore, given the clinician a set of diagnostic rules and a series of pharmacologically related drugs which can ameliorate some of the symptoms, but only at the risk of inducing neurological disorder which can be distressing, disfiguring and irreversible. Non-chemical environmental therapies have also been developed through careful and systematic research in the sphere of rehabilitation, and these techniques provide a welcome glimmer of hope in an otherwise desolate predicament for sufferers whose florid symptomatology has responded to the dopamine antagonists. The negative symptom complex or defect state is arguably the single most serious impediment to successful rehabilitation, and a condition in which pharmacological therapy provides little more than a permissive background for painstaking nursing care and re-education. Lowering our sights even more, therefore, the most urgent and reasonable priority for the practising clinician must be the provision of a chemical remedy for the defect state.

But surely, in all this, one has the feeling of groping in the dark, hoping to stumble across practical remedies for immediate clinical problems, in total ignorance of those brain mechanisms which are responsible for schizophrenic symptoms, florid or negative.

TERMINOLOGY

While of trivial importance in terms of the practical management of patients, the terminology associated with schizophrenic illness is nonetheless a reflection of attitudes about the nature of the illness. We have all been taught that schizophrenia is one of the 'functional psychoses'. Most textbooks of psychiatry define the term thus: 'changes in functioning not attributable to known organic alteration' (Kaplan *et al.*, 1980). The term is usually taken to imply a dysfunction of such subtlety that it might be considered as much a physiological reaction to stress as a disorder arising out of constitutional flaws. Genetic, morphological, psychological, electrophysiological, and neurochemical evidence (for review *see* Andreasen, 1986) now surely makes it appropriate to include schizophrenia within the group of organic psychoses. Many psychiatrists still find this notion dangerously premature, and while the point may well be trivial, at least it serves to draw attention to the most obvious gap so far in the schizophrenia story. We do not have the vaguest notion of the nature of the brain dysfunction(s) which produces delusions and hallucinations, and only vague notions of the anatomical loci for these dysfunctions.

HORSES WORTH BACKING?

It is natural for us to believe that if we 'knew what caused schizophrenia' we would be in a powerful position to respond to some of the requirements of the clinician stated above. There are various ways of approaching this intimidating question, a question which has been asked of many diseases and for which a clear answer has historically only been possible in the case of a disorder caused by an infective agent. Once the answer is provided, an antibiotic largely removes the need for further discussion and questions relating to the mechanism of dysfunction caused by the organism become of academic interest. However, schizophrenic illness, in company with disorders such as diabetes or ischaemic heart disease, is probably different. When the problem is that of a fault in the mechanism itself, the elucidation of the precise nature of the dysfunction becomes of primary importance.

Certain areas of research impinge on the description of the fault in the mechanism, and the following seem worthy of particular mention.

Genetic

Given that the aetiopathology of schizophrenic illness includes a programmed element, then it is logically predictable that the precise definition of the defective genes and subsequent demonstration of their protein products will eventually lead to the identification of some of the aetiological components. This is very much easier said than done: with probable polygenic inheritance (but *see* Chapters 9 and 10) the definition of the suspect genes is horrendously complex but logically feasible. The subsequent steps are equally feasible but time-consuming. Thus, it is no brave prediction to state that molecular biology will eventually contribute significantly to the debate. Whether an answer which will suggest improved treatment techniques will emerge from this area of research is at present unpredictable.

Morphology

Recent years have seen impressive research which has revealed a level of gross and histological abnormality in schizophrenia which was never accepted throughout the middle decades of this century. There is now undeniable evidence that ventricular enlargement and a variety of disturbances of fine structure exist in the brains of a high proportion of sufferers (*see* Chapters 7 and 10). Further work is likely to be rewarding, but again, the likelihood that findings will suggest improved treatment is hard to predict.

Epidemiology

Observation of the patterns of incidence of schizophrenia has always had a rather dry feel to it, and has been associated with much less drama than reports of dopamine receptor densities or big ventricles. However, with a disease such as schizophrenia, with an apparently multifactorial aetiology, the value of epidemiological research is that it may point the way, not necessarily to more effective management, but to prevention. This becomes especially pertinent if one accepts the view that schizophrenic illness is an essentially neurodevelopmental disorder (*see* Chapter 8).

Neurochemistry

The examination of biochemical variables in post-mortem brain tissue is attractive in the directness of the approach. For several years, the present author derived great excitement and satisfaction out of measuring the concentrations of dopamine and its binding sites in brain tissue derived from patients who had in life been diagnosed as suffering from schizophrenia. The stimulus to this research has already been mentioned and, in a sense, dubious logic was rewarded. Abnormalities in dopamine concentration and the density of dopamine binding sites have consistently been shown in at least some cases of schizophrenic illness (Mackay *et al.*, 1982). However, even if one neglects the suggestion that some of these changes may reflect chronic treatment with neuroleptic drugs, the clinician is left with the unavoidable thought 'so what?'.

Increased concentrations of dopamine and an increased density of dopamine binding sites have suggested to some that central dopamine systems may be overactive in the illness. Already we have pharmacological agents such as chlorpromazine which should be able to counteract such overactivity. Even if the dopamine abnormality is asymmetrical (Reynolds, 1983), there is biological evidence to suggest that dopamine antagonists could correct a unilateral abnormality (Bradbury *et al.*, 1985). Despite the availability of potent and specific dopamine receptor antagonists, the treatment of the florid syndrome is by no means dramatic and the defect state is as unassailable as ever. It has been suggested that dopamine binding site proliferation and increased dopamine concentrations have been misinterpreted and that these abnormalities reflect chronic reduction in traffic at dopamine synapses (Mackay, 1980). However, even the opposite strategy of pharmacological potentiation of dopamine systems in chronic schizophrenia has so far failed to produce consistent evidence of benefit. Pharmacological inference from the known mode of action of chlorpromazine has led us into a cul-de-sac. A way out is to go beyond the dopamine systems to those systems with which they have dialogue, and the best way to achieve this may be to concentrate on developing techniques for catching these system disorders 'in the act' in the living brain.

LIVING MAPS

The technology for describing brain dysfunction in relation to the cardinal signs and symptoms of schizophrenia is all but with us. Breathtaking advances have occurred in functional imaging techniques such as single photon emission tomography (SPET), positron emission tomography (PET) and nuclear magnetic resonance (NMR). For the first time it is possible to visualize, in the living patient, the work of sets of neurons and to specify the identity of neurotransmitters and the receptors with which they interact.

The importance of terminology was alluded to above. In this instance the importance of language is greater, and here the language with which to frame the right questions seems lacking. Schizophrenia is a reflection of brain dysfunction and the function of the brain is to create consciousness and to control behaviour through the interaction of nerve cells which communicate by chemical messages. When the brain does not work properly to an extent that leads to the cardinal features of schizophrenia, it is unlikely that a useful understanding of the dysfunction will come from asking questions about individual cells, individual transmitter systems or even individual anatomical nuclei. The question therefore arises of the level at which an understanding of brain function can be said to be useful. Understanding can occur at numerous levels, and the appropriate level must be defined by need. In the case of the clinician, the need is to understand neuronal activity in such a way that particular clinical phenomena can be labelled as belonging to distinctive patterns of neuronal activity and in terms which can inform therapeutic intervention. Cognitive and perceptual activity is likely to be the product of very high order neuronal interactions that are neither specific to one cell type nor confined to one neuroanatomical sector. Chemical intervention is the category to which most clinical therapeutic activity presently belongs.

However, given that it is highly dubious that even complete knowledge of molecular or electrochemical events in and around the neuron will ever allow the translation of clinical phenomena into brain phenomena by a language that has any use, a higher order of description is needed. It is important that the modality to which the description refers is nonetheless able to sustain a reduction, when necessary, to molecular processes in order to inform the design of appropriate drugs. Thus, the most useful, perhaps the only way to understand the relationship between neuronal activity and the sorts of clinical phenomena encountered in schizophrenic illness may be at the level of neurochemical behaviour patterns exhibited by sets of neurons in complex rhythm, perhaps analogous to those observed in sheets of cardiac muscle cells (Brown, 1986). Pattern recognition will be the descriptive level at which translation can take place, and this will require moving visual displays. One way of putting it might be to predict that normal brain function has a characteristic signature of neuronal activity, visible as patterns and sequences of energy utilization. For schizophrenic illness most interest would be in abnormal patterns of neuronal activity over the frontal cerebral cortex and associated limbic structures. Already there have been intriguing, yet crude, demonstrations of altered neuronal work in the dorsolateral prefrontal cortex in schizophrenic illness during the performance of a specific psychological task (Weinberger *et al.*, 1986).

The description of brain dysfunction at the level of patterns of neuronal activity through techniques such as PET scanning has the immediate and seductive attraction of 'seeing is believing' but the value is much more fundamental. As already stated, the means at our disposal for intervening in demonstrated brain dysfunction are, by and large, pharmacological.

Drugs either act on physiological receptors which mediate interneuronal communication or act directly to modify the energy utilization of these cells, and techniques such as PET allow both the quantitative and qualitative analysis of how patterns of neuronal behaviour are related to energy consumption, neurotransmitter turnover, and receptor plasticity. The demonstration of disordered patterns of neuronal interaction can therefore be specified in terms of transmitter identities, verified and expanded if necessary by reference to post-mortem neurochemistry. To borrow the term of Iversen, an abnormality can then be described which is 'chemically addressed', and it is at this stage that the most helpful pharmacological goals may be defined.

CONCLUSIONS

Go to any academic meeting of the various societies for sufferers and their families and the most important question will be patently obvious: 'yes, but what causes schizophrenia?'. Patient and genuine interest is shown in erudite accounts of inheritance patterns, seasonality of birth, still photographs of brain structure and dopamine receptor subtypes. Disappointment is often only partly concealed over the fact that the neurosciences still have not revealed what is wrong with the brain when the schizophrenic patient suffers symptoms. This is surely the most urgent area for investment in response to the question about the 'cause' of schizophrenia, to which we all like to give different interpretations. An all too rare attempt to relate clinical phenomena to brain pathology in schizophrenia has recently appeared in the literature (McKenna, 1987) but severe limitations are at present imposed by the morphological and neurochemical data which derive largely from dead brain tissue.

Imaging technology offers the brightest prospect for an understanding of mechanisms and for the development of rational drug therapy. The answers may not be encouraging; the complexity of transmitter incrimination may be so great that crude intervention with alien chemicals will always create as many problems as it solves, but at least the nature of the challenge will be evident. What has been said above about the impact of chemically addressed dysfunction intuitively applies more to the florid syndrome than to the defect state. A degree of nihilism has accompanied the demonstration that gross neuropathology may be associated with the defect state, but here the analogy with Parkinson's disease might actually prove beneficial. Although certain brain structures may be grossly atrophic, restoration of function by chemical intervention may still be feasible. Again, it will only be by appreciating the nature of the brain dysfunction which actually accompanies (and therefore 'causes') features such as poverty of affect and disordered form of thought that the potential for intervention can be properly evaluated.

Imaging technology has been referred to in very general terms, and it must be recognized that at the moment of writing the level of time fidelity and topographical specificity of techniques such as PET scanning are inadequate. Nonetheless, it is reasonable to expect that these limitations will diminish in the near future to allow a visual representation, in real time, of patterns of neuronal activity during states of normal and disordered consciousness. That is what this clinician wants, while recognizing the continued but secondary value of genetic, epidemiological and morphological research. Together these approaches promise to give the pharmacologist a valid list of requirements on behalf of the clinician, and may eventually point toward the higher aim of prevention.

REFERENCES

Andreasen N. C. (1985). Negative syndrome in schizophrenia: strategies for long term management. In: *Chronic Treatments in Neuropsychiatry. Advances in Biochemical Psychopharmacology Vol 40* (Kamli D., Racagni G., eds.), pp. 1–7. New York: Raven Press.

Andreasen N. C. (1986). (ed.) *Can schizophrenia be localised in the brain?* Washington, DC: American Psychiatric Press, Inc.

Bradbury A. J., Costal B., Domeney A. M., Naylor R. J (1985). Laterality of dopamine function and neuroleptic actions in the rat amygdala. *Neuropharmacology*; **24**: 1163–70.

Brown D. (1986). Acetylcholine and brain cells. *Nature*; **319**: 358–9.

Crow T. J. (1980). Positive and negative schizophrenic symptoms and the role of dopamine. *British Journal of Psychiatry*; **137**: 383–6.

Kaplan H. I., Freedman A. M., Sadock B. J. (1980). *Comprehensive Textbook of Psychiatry* 3rd edn. Vol 3, p. 3328. Baltimore: Williams and Wilkins.

Kay S. R., Opler A. (1987). The positive-negative dimension in schizophrenia: its validity and significance. *Psychiatric Developments*; **2**: 79–103.

Mackay A. V. P. (1980). Positive and negative schizophrenic symptoms and the role of dopamine. *British Journal of Psychiatry*; **137**: 379–83.

Mackay A. V. P., Iversen L. L., Rossor M., *et al.* (1982). Increased brain dopamine and dopamine receptors in schizophrenia. *Archives of General Psychiatry*; **39**: 991–7.

McKenna P. J. (1987). Pathology, phenomenology and the dopamine hypothesis of schizophrenia. *British Journal of Psychiatry*; **151**: 288–301.

Reveley A. M., Reveley M. A. (1986). Can schizophrenia be localised in the brain? A genetic approach. In: *Can Schizophrenia be Localised in the Brain?* (Andreasen N. C., ed.), pp. 77–87. Washington, DC: American Psychiatric Press, Inc.

Reynolds G. P. (1983). Increased concentrations and lateral asymmetry of amygdala dopamine in schizophrenia. *Nature*; **305**: 527–9.

Weinberger D. R., Berman K. F., Zec R. F. (1986). Physiological dysfunction of dorsolateral prefrontal cortex in schizophrenia. *Archives of General Psychiatry*; **43**: 114–24.

3 *Epidemiology of schizophrenia*

A. JABLENSKY

Seen in the broad context of human pathology, schizophrenia exhibits features so extraordinary that one is strongly tempted to assign it to a class of its own. Imagine a population survey in which a powerful screening battery including all kinds of modern clinical and pathological tests is applied on a mass scale to detect objectively diagnosable disorders and dysfunctions. It is very likely that, apart from many common diseases and abnormalities, such a comprehensive investigation will also pick up some rare disorders and subclinical conditions, such as inborn errors of metabolism, chromosome abnormalities, neurodegenerative disease, occult congenital malformations, and viral infections.

If we add to the screening battery a few suitable psychometric tests and self-administered instruments like the general health questionnaire (Goldberg, 1972), our survey will also identify cases of mild mental retardation, learning disabilities, incipient dementia, and a good deal of the neurotic and affective illnesses in that population. However, even a survey of this power will certainly miss most cases of schizophrenia. On practically every 'objective' index of morphological structure or physiological function schizophrenic individuals will either appear perfectly normal, or the deviations that may be detected in a minority will be so non-specific as to preclude any diagnostic inference. In spite of advances in the technology of biological research, no disease marker nor laboratory test is yet available for the identification of schizophrenia, and its diagnosis remains entirely dependent on clinical judgement and convention.

Yet on average in most populations, 5 out of every 1000 adults 'have' the hypothetical disease, and schizophrenia accounts for no less than one-fifth of all chronic and severe disability. Its economic cost to society is almost half as much as that of myocardial infarction (Andrews *et al.*, 1985), and it is the cause of immeasurable personal suffering.

Nearly a century has elapsed since the original formulation of the concept of dementia praecox by Kraepelin (1899), and this year marks the 80th anniversary of the invention of the term 'schizophrenia' (Bleuler, 1908). However, despite several decades of research ranging in perspective from histopathology to psychoanalysis, and from genetics to sociology, the nature of the condition remains elusive, and schizophrenia still represents the central riddle of psychiatry. Its refractory character has naturally given rise to eclectic theoretical approaches, and to the practice of applying every conceivable new technology to its investigation. Thus, the situation in which we find ourselves today is reminiscent of Lewis Carroll's hunters of the Snark:

> 'For the Snark's a peculiar creature, that won't
> Be caught in a commonplace way.
> Do all that you know, and try all that you don't:
> Not a chance must be wasted to-day!'

This description of the current situation in schizophrenia research need not imply any underestimation of the complexity of the phenomenon of the disease. However, some reservation seems to be warranted *vis-à-vis* the current trend of adopting multifactorial or 'biopsychosocial' explanatory models of schizophrenia, as if such models were of self-evident validity. Two methodological considerations are important in this respect:

1. In spite of the advances in the technology of investigation, much of the present clinical and biological research in schizophrenia is plagued by the 'law of small numbers' (Tversky and Kahneman, 1982) and by the insufficient statistical power of research designs, to ward off type II errors, i.e. the invalid rejection of hypotheses that may be true.
2. Although the multi-domain strategy of research, and the resulting multiaxial or 'biopsychosocial' schemes for organizing the data do justice to the complexity of the issues, a 'catch-all' approach is not conducive to the establishment of mutually exclusive testable concepts and propositions. This explains why so few of the currently coexisting theories and models of schizophrenia can be discarded.

THE ROLE OF EPIDEMIOLOGY

Such considerations bring up the question of the role and place of epidemiology in modern schizophrenic research. In its dual function as a data base and as an analytical tool, epidemiology should provide us with some means of triangulation in this exceedingly complex area.

Indeed, epidemiological studies have been carried out since the inception of the nosological concept of dementia praecox. In 1895 at the suggestion of Kraepelin, Jenny Koller surveyed the occurrence of psychotic disorders in two random community samples in the Swiss canton of Zurich and, in the period up to and including the First World War, much of the clinical and population genetics research carried out at the Kaiser Wilhelm Institute in Munich was epidemiological in nature (Rudin, 1916). A closely linked development was the birth of 'comparative psychiatry', the forerunner of the cross-cultural approach, which was proposed by Kraepelin after his trip to Java in 1904. These early developments were followed by the German population studies of the 1920s and 1930s; the Scandinavian surveys of the pre- and post-World War II period; the social ecology research in North America; and the great variety of cross-sectional, case control, longitudinal, and intervention studies of basically epidemiological design of the last 20 years (Jablensky, 1986a). Thus, a broad spectrum of possible epidemiological approaches to the study of a disorder has already been applied to schizophrenia over several decades. Fragments of this vast collection of data have been reviewed, from a varying perspective, by a number of authors (Lemkau *et al.*, 1943; Strömgren, 1950; Cooper and Morgan, 1973; Gottesman *et al.*, 1982; Warner, 1985; Häfner, 1987).

However, the majority of the epidemiological studies have been of the descriptive type, i.e. with a main focus on 'persons, place, and time', on distributions by age, sex, social class, geographical and cultural location, and on 'natural history'. Few epidemiological inquiries have been explicitly designed as hypothesis-testing studies and, considering the formidable demands of case-finding, sample size, and statistical power needed, it is not surprising that studies of the analytical epidemiology of schizophrenia are rare.

Nevertheless, even the descriptive data from past and current epidemiological research in schizophrenia are, as a rule, under-utilized for hypothesis building, because of hesitation about their methodological soundness. Doubts have been raised repeatedly about the representativeness of populations studied and about the comparability of findings reported by investigators applying different, or unspecified, rules of diagnosis and of measurement of natural history variables. As a result, the phantom of unreliability has been invoked, perhaps more often than it should, to discourage conceptual generalizations. Such generalizations are, of course, only possible if data from many investigations and from different locations can be pooled for the purpose of formulating, if not for testing, hypotheses.

Retrospectively, much of the earlier descriptive epidemiological research in schizophrenia can be validly criticized for methodological imperfections which rule out an unambiguous interpretation of the findings. As pointed out recently by one of the contributors to the Heidelberg Symposium 'Search for the Causes of Schizophrenia' (Häfner *et al.*, 1987):

'It is now clear that the design of a study aiming to elucidate the natural history of schizophrenia must take account of at least four factors: (1) the identification of all cases in a defined population during a fixed period of time; (2) the application of standardized diagnostic procedures with criteria of known reliability; (3) prospective follow-up procedures, preferably from the onset of first attachment for at least 5 years, with interim as well as endpoint assessments and, preferably, uniform treatment regimes throughout the follow-up period; (4) standardized and independent clinical and social measures of outcome.' (Shepherd, 1987)

WORLD HEALTH ORGANIZATION STUDIES OF SCHIZOPHRENIA

These requirements, as well as the demand that the patient population should be representative, in a specifiable sense, of the clinical universe of the disorder, have been met to a large extent by the World Health Organization research programme on schizophrenia. The programme which now spans nearly two decades has involved psychiatrists and other investigators in 20 centres in 17 countries. The strategy of the WHO programme has been characterized by: (1) simultaneous data collection, according to a uniform design and methodology, in a number of geographically defined areas in different countries and cultures; (2) use of standardized instruments; (3) data collection by highly trained psychiatrists whose performance was monitored by means of intra- and inter-centre reliability exercises: (4) a system of diagnostic classification which takes into account clinical judgement, but adds to it a computer-based reference categorization of the cases; and (5) multiple follow-up assessments at intervals of one, 2 and 5 years.

The WHO programme comprises three major studies (Table 3.1). The first (1969–1977) was the International Pilot Study of Schizophrenia (IPSS) which included nine centres in Africa, Asia, Europe, Latin and North America, with a total of 1202 patients selected from consecutive admissions to the services and meeting specified criteria. Each patient had a detailed standardized clinical assessment and a complete re-assessment 2 years and 5 years later (some of the centres have now accomplished a 10-year follow-up) (WHO, 1973, 1979).

The second study (Assessment and Reduction of Psychiatric Disability) was focused primarily on the manifestations and course of behavioural impairments and social disabilities in patients with schizophrenia of a recent onset (Jablensky *et al.*, 1980). It included 520 patients in five European and one African country who were investigated initially and again at one-year and 2-year follow-up assessments.

The third, most recent study (1978–1986), on Determinants of Outcome of Severe Mental Disorders, included 1379 patients assessed at 12 research centres in 10 countries. The core component of the study was an epidemiological case-finding investigation in which, during 2 consecutive years, all individuals making a first-in-lifetime contact with various 'helping agencies' in specified geographical areas were identified and screened for symptoms of functional psychosis. Those meeting criteria for possible schizophrenic illness were further examined with standardized instruments and followed-up for 2 years, with re-examinations. The design, methodology, and part of the findings of this study have been published (Sartorius *et al.*, 1986; Jablensky, 1987); the publication of further, more detailed data is under way (Jablensky *et al.*, 1988).

The WHO programme has succeeded in building up a unique data base comprising over 3000 clinically and socially well documented cases of

Table 3.1 The WHO programme of cross-cultural research in schizo₁ (1967–85)

	International pilot study of schizophrenia (IPSS)	*WHO collaborative study on psychiatric disability*	*Determinants of outcome of severe mental disorders*
Number of centres	9	7	12
Countries	China (Taiwan), Colombia, Czechoslovakia, Denmark, India, Nigeria, UK, USA, USSR	Bulgaria, Federal Republic of Germany, Netherlands, Sudan, Switzerland, Turkey, Yugoslavia	Colombia, Czechoslovakia, Denmark, India, Ireland, Japan, Nigeria, UK, USA, USSR
Number of patients	1202	520	1379
Main areas assessed	Mental state (PSE), past history, social description, course and outcome	Mental state (PSE), past history, sociodemographic description, disability in social roles, behavioural impairments, pattern of course	Mental state (PSE), past history, course and outcome, disability in social roles, stressful life events, expressed emotion, perception of illness, family functioning
Diagnosis	Clinical (ICD-8), computer (CATEGO), statistical clusters	Clinical (ICD-9), computer (CATEGO)	Clinical (ICD-9), computer (CATEGO), DSM-III (some centres)
Follow-up	2 years, 5 years	1 year, 2 years, 5 years	1 year, 2 years

ICD: International Classification of Diseases; DSM: Diagnostic and Statistical Manual of Mental Disorders

schizophrenia in different cultures. This material should permit certain general conclusions and the formulation of specific hypotheses on the nature of the condition. Before outlining the findings of greatest theoretical interest, it should be said that none of the results and conclusions of the WHO investigations are either entirely unprecedented or breaking radically new ground. Many of the new data generated by the WHO complex of studies confirm, or add a new significance to earlier findings or conjectures derived from smaller or less representative samples, or based on less well standardized observations. This fact suggests that, despite all the methodological deficiencies and difficulties, the epidemiological literature on schizophrenia is consistent enough to sustain informed speculation on the nature of the disorder, or even provide hypotheses to guide further research.

THE EPIDEMIOLOGICAL CONSENSUS

Agreeing that the 'search for a kind of inviolable Platonic entity is most unlikely to succeed' (Wing, 1987) if schizophrenia is *a priori* construed as a single disease entity, it is proposed that, on the basis of data already available, a fairly distinct epidemiological profile of the syndrome of schizophrenia can be constructed. If valid, such a profile may make the diversity of its manifestations less protean and perplexing, and help to distinguish fact from artefact in this complex area.

There are good reasons to try to establish a hierarchy of epidemiological findings describing schizophrenia. On one hand, there are data which not only have been sufficiently replicated to be regarded as 'robust' but, on the strength of general principles of the epidemiology of human disease can be regarded as plausible indicators of underlying essential processes or mechanisms. By analogy, such findings could be termed 'first-rank epidemiological phenomena' because, in the absence of clearly established disease markers to distinguish schizophrenia from other pathological processes of the personality, they can tentatively perform a demarcating function. On the other hand, there will be a variety of 'second-rank' epidemiological data which are either less firmly established, or contribute to the completion of the epidemiological picture without reflecting essential or necessary features of the condition.

First-rank findings

The findings which are strong candidates for a first-rank status are as follows.

1. *The syndrome of schizophrenia is universal.* To date, no known human population, demographic or cultural group, has been convincingly demonstrated to be free of schizophrenia. The psychopathological syndromes thought to be characteristic of schizophrenia since its delimitation by Kraepelin and Bleuler were found to occur in all the cultures and geographical areas covered by the WHO investigations. Although no single symptom was identified as invariably present in every patient and in each setting, the overall clinical configuration of the disorder was remarkably constant across the cultures. The similarity of the clinical pictures was

confirmed by the CATEGO program which classified the cases according to strict rules, based on explicit definitions of symptoms and syndromes. Even more significantly, the subjective experiences of individuals suffering from schizophrenia and their verbal expression are remarkably similar in patients belonging to very different cultures and of hardly comparable educational background. Patients in the tropical rainforest of Nigeria and in the fishing villages of Denmark feel and report alike that their innermost thoughts are being stopped, taken away, 'read' by some alien agency, or 'broadcast' at large. Considering the differences in cultural beliefs, social norms, and language, this similarity in the subjective experience of the 'core' schizophrenic symptoms is quite striking.

2. *There is only a modest variation in the incidence rates of schizophrenia in different cultures.* In the WHO study, annual incidence rates (based on the definition of a 'first-in-lifetime contact') were determined for seven of the research centres in different cultures (Fig. 3.1). The seven centres selected were those in which complete, or nearly complete, coverage of the catchment area was maintained throughout the case-finding period. The rates were calculated separately for cases meeting a 'broad' definition of schizophrenia (i.e. patients with disorders that would either be classified as schizophrenic according to the International Classification of Diseases (ICD-9) glossary, or fall into one of the CATEGO classes S, P, or 0), and for cases satisfying the 'restrictive' criteria for the 'central' or 'nuclear' schizophrenic syndrome represented by the CATEGO class S + . For the 'broad' definition of schizophrenia, the combined incidence rates for males and females varied from 1.5/10 000 in Aarhus (Denmark) to 4.2/10 000 in the rural area of Chandigarh (India). The differences across the study areas were highly significant ($P < 0.001$ for males and $P < 0.0001$ for females). However, the application of the 'restrictive' definition of CATEGO class S + not only resulted in lower mean rates, ranging from 0.7 in Aarhus to 1.4 in Nottingham, but also led to a disappearance of the significant differences between the areas which was not the result of a loss of statistical power.

This finding lends support to the validity of earlier attempts at determining a 'standard' incidence rate for schizophrenic disorders. In eight epidemiological surveys, carried out in several European countries between 1946 and 1977, and using different methods and case definitions, the range of the incidence rates per 10 000 population was between 1.7 and 5.7 (Jablensky, 1986b). There were few, if any, comparable incidence data from developing countries, prior to the WHO study.

It should be noted that a case can be made for the existence of significant geographical variation in the frequency of schizophrenia if point prevalence, and not incidence, rates are compared. Evidence for this is forthcoming from studies of pockets of unusually high prevalence in several small areas in the north of Sweden (Böök, 1953); the north of the USSR (Gainullin *et al.*, 1986); the west of Ireland (Torrey *et al.*, 1984); and the coastal area of Croatia, Yugoslavia (Crocetti *et al.*, 1971). Conversely,

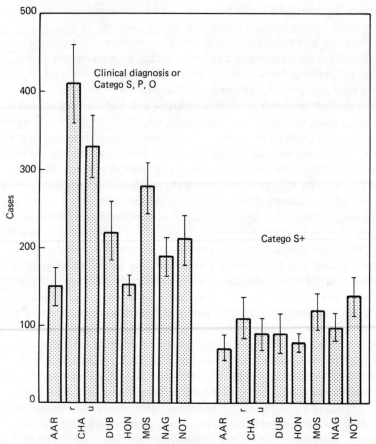

Fig. 3.1.   *Incidence rates per million population age 15–54 (both sexes) for the 'broad' and 'restrictive' definitions of schizophrenia. AAR = Aarhus (Denmark); CHA = Chandigarh (India); DUB = Dublin (Ireland); HON = Honolulu (USA); MOS = Moscow (USSR); NAG = Nagasaki (Japan); NOT = Nottingham (UK); r = rural area; u = urban area*

claims of unusually low prevalence rates have been made for population groups in Papua New Guinea (Torrey *et al.*, 1974), the Solomon Islands (Dohan *et al.*, 1983), and a low incidence has been found in a coastal area of British Columbia (Bates and van Dam, 1984). Even if we disregard the methodological difficulties in ascertaining such high or low rates, and assume that the reported findings are valid, their existence would be an illustration of the exception, rather than the rule. To date, there is no evidence to refute the conclusion that in most human populations schizophrenia typically occurs at a rate between 1 and 4 cases per 10 000 population at risk per annum. Since this is a low incidence rate, the three- to fourfold difference that may be observed between areas and populations (even if statistically significant, when based on large samples), could be regarded as trivial from an epidemiological point of view.

3. *There is a characteristic gender effect on the age-specific incidence rate of schizophrenia*. Although the total cumulative risk of developing schizophrenia up to the age of 54 is about equal for males and females, the mean age of onset—especially in the period of peak incidence between 15 and 34—is higher in females. This means that in the critical age period of reproduction the rate of 'consumption' of the total risk of developing the disorder is slowed down in females (or, since the reference point is an arbitrary one, speeded up in males). Whatever the biological and social significance of this phenomenon, it is cross-culturally robust and replicable in societies that differ considerably with regard to the attributes of the male and female roles. Sex differences in the incidence, manifestations, and prognosis of schizophrenia are becoming a focus of increasing interest (Lewine, 1979; Seeman, 1982; Loranger, 1984).

4. *The epidemiological evidence points to a significant genetic component in the transmission of schizophrenia* (*see* Chapter 9). This point hardly needs elaboration, since much of the genetic research that has established a sufficient (though not absolutely necessary) role for hereditary factors in the occurrence of schizophrenia has been epidemiological in design. Even in studies which have not been designed with a view to elucidating a genetic mechanism, the strength of genetic factors can be demonstrated indirectly, by using simple statistical tests of vertical transmission of the disorder. Thus, in the WHO study, the proportion of index cases of schizophrenia who had at least one sibling with psychotic disorder was shown to be significantly higher if one or both parents had a history of psychotic illness than if no such problem is reported for either parent.

5. *Two major subtypes within the schizophrenic syndrome explain much of the variance: schizophrenia of acute onset and schizophrenia of gradual (insidious) onset*. In each of the three WHO studies, the mode of onset, defined in terms of the time elapsed since the first appearance of an unequivocally psychotic manifestation and the point at which a recognizable clinical syndrome or symptom-complex is established, emerged consistently as the strongest predictor of the subsequent pattern of course, i.e. of the likelihood that a patient would develop a remitting or a continuous type of illness. The strength of this relationship was of the same order in both the developing and the developed countries, although the proportion of patients with an acute onset and hence, with a higher probability of a remitting course, was higher in non-European settings (Table 3.2).

Moreover, the follow-up demonstrated that patterns of course, significantly predicted by the mode of onset, tended to cluster at two extremes. On the one hand, there were cases of acute onset, in which the cumulative duration of psychotic episodes amounted to less than 15% of the length of the follow-up period. On the other hand, the majority of the cases of an insidious onset tended to be severely psychotic for more than 75% of the follow-up period. Relatively few cases fell between these two extremes, and the statistical distribution was strongly suggestive of bimodality. It must be

Table 3.2 Pattern of course (2-year follow-up) by type of onset and setting (percentages)

Setting	Type of onset	Pattern of course		
		Mild	Inter- mediate	Severe
Developed countries	Acute	52.1	25.1	22.6
$X^2 = 40.3$	Subacute	41.3	23.9	34.7
$P < 0.001$	Gradual	29.8	17.5	52.6
	All types	38.9	21.1	39.8
Developing countries	Acute	62.0	21.0	16.9
$X^2 = 26.4$	Subacute	58.7	23.8	17.4
$P < 0.001$	Gradual	40.2	16.3	43.4
	All types	55.7	20.2	24.0

emphasized that at the height of the initial psychotic episode the two groups could not be distinguished from one another in terms of symptomatology, and that CATEGO class membership was not predictive of one or other pattern of course. There was no evidence from the clinical presentation or from background factors to support the view that the acute onset/remitting course group of cases might represent a separate class of 'acute transient psychoses', nosologically different from the rest of the schizophrenic disorders.

6. *Schizophrenic illnesses all over the world have a strong tendency to respond therapeutically to drugs interfering with dopaminergic neurotransmission.* Strictly speaking, this is not an epidemiological finding, and the statement is not based on results of the WHO schizophrenia studies (although the data collected by WHO indicated that 96% of the patients in the total study sample were prescribed neuroleptic drugs and 41% of them were on antipsychotic medication for 76–100% of the length of the follow-up period). Nevertheless, one would be justified in regarding the response of the majority of schizophrenic patients to neuroleptics, regardless of any other factors that may influence the course of symptoms and impairments, as an important epidemiological 'constant'.

Second-rank findings

Another group of epidemiological findings can be seen as constituting the second rank in the hierarchy, not because of a lower consistency or replicability than those enumerated above, but as a function of their less certain specificity. These findings may eventually contribute to a better understanding of the features of the disorder that could be termed pathoplastic, or secondary; but it is rather unlikely that they would reveal cardinal causative or pathogenetic mechanisms.

7. *Culture and the social environment have an effect on the course and outcome of schizophrenia* (*see* Chapter 15). One of the most striking findings of the WHO studies was that schizophrenic patients in traditional cultures (i.e. in the developing countries) had a significantly better 2-year and 5-year prognosis than patients in the industrialized world. This was true for several different and independent measures of course and outcome, and the results of repeated multivariate statistical analyses demonstrated beyond doubt that the differences could not be explained by sampling bias, diagnostic variation, or unequal proportions of patients with acute and insidious onset in the centres in the developing and the developed countries. It should be admitted that, in spite of the increasing refinement of the research design and instruments in succeeding WHO studies, the exact nature of the effect could not be fully explained. A modest but consistent impact of stressful life events could be demonstrated in relation to the acute onset of psychotic episodes in different cultures, and differential levels of 'expressed emotion' within the family were found to be associated with differences in the relapse rates in schizophrenic patients in India and Denmark. However, a more general effect of culture seems to exist, which at present cannot be reduced to single explanatory variables. Together with the observation that schizophrenic disorders may follow a great variety of patterns of course, the effects of culture reinforce other evidence that the syndrome of schizophrenia is highly responsive to environmental influences. The reason for attributing a second rank to this impressive and consistent finding is in its presumed lack of aetiological implications and in the lack of certainty that it is specific to schizophrenia. In all likelihood, the social environment of traditional cultures favours the symptomatological recovery and the restoration of function in other mental disorders as well.

8. *Schizophrenia can occur as a symptomatic disorder in association with a variety of cerebral and physical diseases.* Disorders with schizophrenic features occur in association with no less than 12 major groups of neurological, endocrine and infectious diseases, intoxications, and space-occupying intracranial lesions (Davison and Bagley, 1969). Epilepsy is the most notable example (Flor-Henry, 1983), but recent additions to the list include idiopathic basal ganglia calcification (Francis and Freeman, 1984) and aqueduct stenosis (Roberts *et al.*, 1983). Many genetic disorders, ranging from XXX karyotype to acute intermittent porphyria, are associated with a significantly increased risk of schizophreniform psychosis (Propping, 1983). Some genetic conditions, such as metachromatic leuko-dystrophy, are sometimes discovered, by chance or through screening, in patients diagnosed as schizophrenic.

Unfortunately, the search for cerebral or somatic pathologies which can cause schizophrenic symptoms has not been systematic and few of the observations collected so far lend themselves to epidemiological analysis. However, if the clinical characteristics of psychotic illness secondary to cerebral or physical disease eventually prove to be indistinguishable from 'true' schizophrenia, then in the long run a number of discrete entities of genetic or exogenous causation may be identified, resulting in a progressive shrinkage of the share of 'idiopathic' forms.

9. *Schizophrenia shows both positive and negative associations with other conditions and abnormalities.* The Oxford Record linkage study (Baldwin, 1979) has demonstrated an increased relative risk in schizophrenics for arteriosclerotic heart disease, for the malabsorption syndrome associated with coeliac disease, and for myxoedema. In addition, minor physical abnormalities and malformations seem to be more frequent in schizophrenic patients than in the general population, but the relationship has not been statistically demonstrated. More interesting, however, are the negative associations. Among the diseases reported to occur with significantly reduced incidence in schizophrenic patients, the best documented evidence pertains to rheumatoid arthritis (Osterberg, 1978) which, at least in northern Europe, where the disorder is frequent, appears to be extremely rare in individuals with a diagnosis of schizophrenia. In contrast, ankylosing spondylitis and uroarthritis, both associated with the HLA B-27 antigen, are frequent among schizophrenics. These data suggest an area for investigation of possible disease markers, which should be based on record linkage and large samples, in order to explore the relations among schizophrenia, joint disease, and the major histocompatibility complex.

In a recent WHO study, based on a record linkage between the Danish national psychiatric case register and the cancer registry (comprising a total of nearly 100 000 person-years), a significant reduction of the relative risk for cancer of different localization was found for schizophrenic patients (Dupont *et al.*, 1986). Subsequent data analyses (Mortensen, 1986) indicated that cancer risk reduction was positively correlated with the length of neuroleptic treatment, thus suggesting a protective effect of phenothiazines with regard to malignant neoplasia.

10. *There is a consistent seasonality effect on the distribution of births of persons who subsequently develop schizophrenia.* The seasonality phenomenon has attracted much attention, and the findings have been subjected to a good deal of statistical analysis and re-analysis. There seems to be a significant but modest excess of births in the season with the lowest average temperatures, regardless of latitude. It should be noted that seasonality of births has been described in other disorders too, e.g. in diabetes mellitus, malformations of the cardiovascular system, anencephaly, congenital hip dislocation, Down's syndrome, and bipolar affective disorder (Christy *et al.*, 1982; Jongbloet *et al.*, 1982; Boyd *et al.*, 1986). The finding, therefore, does not seem to be specific to schizophrenia and, regardless of the different causal explanations proposed, is unlikely to be of cardinal importance for understanding the nature of schizophrenia.

CONCLUSIONS

What tentative conclusions can be drawn from the evidence, if we assume that the proposed hierarchy of the epidemiological findings according to their theoretical significance has some validity?

First, the evidence can rule out, or at least make highly implausible, certain models and theories of schizophrenia. For example, it appears rather unlikely that the schizophrenic syndrome is a manifestation of a horizontally transmissible viral or other infection, or of an autoimmune disease. At the other end of the aetiological spectrum, we can probably quite safely reject theories of a pure psychogenic or sociogenic causation. As regards the genetic evidence, single dominant gene, or recessive transmission models, do not seem to fit the empirical data. However, if genetic heterogeneity is assumed, such models could have partial explanatory power.

Second, although the evidence does not point unequivocally to a single explanatory model, it raises the question whether possible analogies to schizophrenia could be found in disorders which are at present better understood and 'behave' epidemiologically in ways similar to schizophrenia. One such disorder, which offers a tempting analogy to schizophrenia, is diabetes mellitus. It has been pointed out (Shepherd, 1985) that until recently, 'little was known about its pathogenesis apart from the facts that the syndrome was hereditary, the genetics was probably multifactorial, and more than one disease process was represented by the clinical picture ... The recent work on auto-immunity, HLA systems, and virology has led to a more searching mode of classification which, though still speculative, maps the complexity of the condition. If the promise of current biological research in psychiatry is eventually fulfilled, a model of this type may point the way to a more fundamental approach to the classification of the schizophrenias ...'.

However, even if the scientific progress in understanding diabetes can serve as a model for research in schizophrenia, it is unlikely that the nosology of diabetes could offer a prototype for the nosology of schizophrenia. Epidemiologically, the incidence and prevalence distribution of diabetes across populations is quite different from that of schizophrenia. For example, while the differences between the incidence rates of schizophrenia between populations as distant from one another as Denmark and India are relatively minor, the difference in the rate of occurrence of diabetes between areas in these two countries may be as large as 500-fold.

A much closer analogy may be found in conditions which exhibit comparable levels of incidence, are ubiquitous in human populations and, as far as we know today, are multifactorial in their causation. Such conditions, for example, are moderate and severe mental retardation and, in particular, epilepsy. Epilepsy, apart from its well known pathophysiological affinity to psychosis of a schizophreniform type, is one of the relatively small number of disorders occurring at similar rates in different populations. Although a major proportion of the variance in the total risk of developing epileptic seizures can be explained by a genetic predisposition (which, presumably, is multifactorial), there are subgroups of 'symptomatic' epilepsies due to exogenous insults and lesions, or to the effects of dominant or recessive genes. The ictal discharge appears to be a response modality of a certain type of neurophysiological organization that can be activated by a variety of lesions and stimuli.

Similarly, if schizophrenia is not a single disease but a 'common final pathway' for a variety of pathological processes and neurodevelopmental anomalies, the similar rates of its incidence in different populations could be seen as the expression of a more or less uniformly distributed liability for a 'schizophrenic' type of reaction to different causes, mediated by the dopaminergic system.

Such a model would be in good agreement with the epidemiological facts. In a way, it would bring us back to Kraepelin who, towards the end of his career, saw the problem of schizophrenia in a new perspective, radically different from his earlier views. In his article 'Die Erscheinungsformen des Irreseins' (1920), he proposed that 'the affective and schizophrenic forms of mental disorder do not represent the expression of particular pathological processes but rather indicate the areas of our personality in which these processes unfold ... It must remain an open question whether hereditary factors make certain areas more susceptible and accessible to pathological stimuli ... The various syndromes of illness may be compared to the different registers of an organ, any of which may be brought into play according to the severity and extent of the pathological changes involved. They impart a characteristic tone to the illness quite irrespective of the mechanism which has brought them into play ... Schizophrenic symptoms are by no means limited to dementia praecox. We find them also in varying degrees in many morbid processes in which there is widespread destruction of nerve tissue ... There is no doubt, however, that schizophrenic symptoms may also occur without any damage to cerebral tissue ...'.

However, whether a neurodevelopmental, a 'common final pathway', or any other reductionist model will provide us with the ultimate understanding of the phenomenological reality of schizophrenia, must remain an open question. After all, the essential subjective experience of schizophrenia, which remains the cornerstone of its diagnosis, is a reflection of events which occur, to use the metaphor of Popper and Eccles (1977), at the interface between the self-conscious mind and the mechanisms of the brain. Until the nature of that interface becomes more transparent to neuroscience, it will be premature to expect a radical solution of the riddle of schizophrenia.

REFERENCES

Andrews G., Hall W., Goldstein G., Lapsley H., Bartels, R. and Silove, D. (1985). The economic costs of schizophrenia. *Archives of General Psychiatry*; 42: 537–43.

Baldwin J. A. (1979). Schizophrenia and physical disease. Editorial. *Psychological Medicine*; 9: 611–18.

Bates C. E., van Dam C. H. (1984). Low incidence of schizophrenia in British Columbia coastal Indians. *Journal of Epidemiology and Community Health*; 38: 127–30.

Bleuler E. (1908). Die Prognose der Dementia praecox (Schizophreniegruppe). *Allgemeine Zeitschrift für Psychiatrie*; 65: 436–64.

Böök J. A. (1953). A genetic and neuropsychiatric investigation of a North Swedish population (with special regard to schizophrenia and mental deficiency). *Acta Genetica*; 4: 1–100.

Boyd J. H., Pulver A. E., Stewart W. (1986). Season of birth: schizophrenia and bipolar disorder. *Schizophrenia Bulletin*; 12: 173–86.

Christy M., Christau B., Molbak A. G., Nerup J. (1982). Diabetes and month of birth. Letter to editor. *Lancet*; ii: 216.

Cooper B., Morgan H. G. (1973). *Epidemiological Psychiatry*. Springfield, Ill.: Thomas.

Crocetti G. J., Lemkau P. Y., Kulcar Z., Kesic B. (1971). Selected aspects of the epidemiology of psychoses in Croatia, Yugoslavia. III. The cluster sample and the results of the pilot survey. *American Journal of Epidemiology*; 94: 126–34.

Davison K., Bagley C. R. (1969). Schizophrenia-like psychoses associated with organic disorders of the central nervous system: a review of the literature. In : *Current Problems in Neuropsychiatry* (Herrington R. N., ed.). British Journal of Psychiatry Special Publication No. 4, pp. 113–84. Ashford: Headley Brothers.

Dohan F. C., Harper E. H., Clark M. H., Rodrigue, R., Zigas V. (1983). Where is schizophrenia rare? *Lancet*; ii: 101.

Dupont A., Moeller-Jensen O., Strömgren E., Jablensky A. (1986). Incidence of cancer in patients diagnosed as schizophrenic in Denmark. In: *Psychiatric Case Registers in Public Health* (ten Horn G. H. M. M., Giel R., Gulbinat W., Henderson J. H., eds.), pp. 229–39. Amsterdam: Elsevier.

Flor-Henry P. (1983). *Cerebral Basis of Psychopathology*. Boston: John Wright.

Francis A., Freeman H. (1984). Psychiatric abnormality and brain calcification over four generations. *Journal of Nervous and Mental Disease*; 172: 166–70.

Gainullin R. G., Shmaonova L. M., Trubnikov V. I. (1986). Clinico-demographic characteristics and features of the social and occupational adjustment of schizophrenic patients in three population groups inhabiting the North-Eastern region of the USSR (a clinical epidemiological investigation). *Zhurnal nevropatologii i psihiatrii* (Korsakov); 86: 713–19.

Goldberg D. P. (1972). *The Detection of Psychiatric Illness by Questionnaire*. London: Oxford University Press.

Gottesman I., Shields J., Hanson D. R. (1982). *Schizophrenia: The Epigenetic Puzzle*. New York: Cambridge University Press.

Häfner H. (1987). Epidemiology of schizophrenia. In: *Search for the Causes of Schizophrenia* (Häfner H., Gattaz W. F., Janzarik W., eds.), pp. 47–74. Heidelberg: Springer.

Häfner H., Gattaz W. F., Janzarik W. (eds.) (1987). *Search for the Causes of Schizophrenia*. Heidelberg: Springer.

Jablensky A. (1986a). Epidemiologic surveys of mental health of geographically defined populations in Europe. In: *Community Surveys of Psychiatric Disorders* (Weissman M. M., Myers J. K., Ross C. E., eds.), pp. 257–313. New Brunswick, NJ: Rutgers University Press.

Jablensky A. (1986b). Epidemiology of schizophrenia: a European perspective. *Schizophrenia Bulletin*; 12: 52–73.

Jablensky A. (1987). Multicultural studies and the nature of schizophrenia: a review. *Journal of the Royal Society of Medicine*; 80: 162–7.

Jablensky A., Sartorius N., Ernberg G. *et al.* (1988). *Schizophrenia: Manifestations, Incidence, and Course in Different Cultures*. Geneva: A World Health Organization Ten-Country Study (in press).

Jablensky A., Schwarz R., Tomov T. (1980). WHO collaborative study on impairments and disabilities associated with schizophrenic disorders. *Acta Psychiatrica Scandinavica*; 62 (Suppl. 285): 152–63.

Jongbloet P. H., Mulder A., Hamers A. J. (1982). Seasonality of pre-ovulatory non-disjunction and the etiology of Down syndrome: a European collaborative study. *Human Genetics*; 62: 134–8.

Koller J. (1895). Beitrag zur Erblichkeitsstatistik der Geisteskranken im Kanton Zurich. *Archiv für Psychiatrie*; 27: 268–94.

Kraepelin E. (1899). *Psychiatrie: Ein Lehrbuch fur Studierende und Aerzte.* Leipzig: Abel.

Kraepelin E. (1904). Vergleichende Psychiatrie. *Zentralblatt für Nervenheilkunde und Psychiatrie*; 27: 433–7.

Kraepelin E. (1920). Die Erscheinungsformen des Irreseins. *Zeitschrift für die gesamte Neurologie und Psychiatrie*; 62: 1–29.

Lemkau P., Tietze C., Cooper M. (1943). A survey of statistical studies on the prevalence and incidence of mental disorders in sample populations. *Public Health Reports*; 58: 1909–27.

Lewine R. R. J. (1979). Sex differences in schizophrenia: a commentary. *Schizophrenia Bulletin*; 5: 3–7.

Loranger A. W. (1984). Sex difference in age at onset of schizophrenia. *Archives of General Psychiatry*; 41: 157–61.

Mortensen P. B. (1986). Environmental factors modifying cancer risk in schizophrenia. Paper presented at the World Psychiatric Association Symposium, August 1986, Copenhagen.

Osterberg E. (1978). Schizophrenia and rheumatic disease. *Acta Psychiatrica Scandinavica*; 58: 339–59.

Popper K. R., Eccles J. C. (1977). *The Self and Its Brain. An Argument for Interactionism*. Berlin: Springer International.

Propping P. (1983). Genetic disorders presenting as 'schizophrenia'. Karl Bonhoeffer's early view of the psychoses in the light of medical genetics. *Human Genetics*; 65: 1–10.

Roberts J. K. A., Trimble M. R., Robertson M. (1983). Schizophrenic psychosis associated with aqueduct stenosis in adults. *Journal of Neurology, Neurosurgery and Psychiatry*; 46: 892–3.

Rudin E. (1916). *Zur Vererbung und Neuentstehung der Dementia Praecox*. Berlin: Springer.

Sartorius N., Jablensky A., Korten A. *et al.* (1986). Early manifestations and first-contact incidence of schizophrenia in different cultures. *Psychological Medicine*; 16: 909–28.

Seeman M. V. (1982). Gender differences in schizophrenia. *Canadian Journal of Psychiatry*; 27: 107–12.

Shepherd M. (1985). Contributions of epidemiological research to the classification and diagnosis of mental disorders. In: *Mental Disorders, Alcohol- and Drug-related Problems. International Perspectives on Their Diagnosis and Classification*, pp. 337–341. Amsterdam: Excerpta Medica International Congress Series No. 669.

Shepherd M. (1987). Formulation of new research strategies on schizophrenia. In: *Search for the Causes of Schizophrenia* (Häfner H., Gattaz W. F., Janzarik W., eds.), pp. 29–38. Heidelberg: Springer.

Strömgren E. (1950). Statistical and genetical population studies within psychiatry: methods and principal results. *Proceedings of the First International Congress of Psychiatry*, vol. VI, pp. 155–92. Paris: Herman & Cie.

Torrey E. F., McGuire M., O'Hare A., Walsh D., Spellman M. P. (1984). Endemic psychosis in western Ireland. *American Journal of Psychiatry*; 141: 966–70.

Torrey E. F., Torrey B. B., Burton-Bradley B. G. (1974). The epidemiology of schizophrenia in Papua New Guinea. *American Journal of Psychiatry*; 131: 567–73.

Tversky A., Kahneman K. (1982). Judgment under uncertainty: heuristics and biases. In: *Judgment Under Uncertainty: Heuristics and Biases* (Kahneman D., Slovic P., Tversky A., eds.), pp. 3–20. Cambridge: Cambridge University Press.

Warner R. (1985). *Recovery from Schizophrenia: Psychiatry and Political Economy*. London: Routledge & Kegan Paul.

Wing J. K. (1987). History, classification, and research strategies: discussion. In: *Search for the Causes of Schizophrenia* (Häfner H., Gattaz W. F., Janzarik W., eds.), pp. 39–43. Heidelberg: Springer.

World Health Organization (1973). *Report of the International Pilot Study of Schizophrenia, vol. I*. Geneva: WHO.

World Health Organization (1979). *Schizophrenia. An International Follow-up Study*. Chichester: Wiley.

4 *The phenomena of schizophrenia*

ANNE E. FARMER, PETER McGUFFIN
and PAUL BEBBINGTON

'[The phenomena of schizophrenia] are not only the starting point and motivation for enquiry but also the ultimate goal, since the point of research is to understand their causes and modes of production well enough to correct the underlying abnormalities or, better still, prevent them from occurring' (MRC, 1987).

Throughout this volume there are discussions of research into the aetiological basis of schizophrenia, its biochemistry, genetics, and neuro-pathology, and into its psychological and social management. All of these, if they are to be successful, must start with the assumption that there is a reasonable degree of consensus about how to define schizophrenia. At present, we identify schizophrenia by means of (and only by means of) the signs and symptoms which characterize the disorder and serve to discriminate it from other types of mental illness. This presents us with a problem in deciding, not so much what symptoms may be found, but which are most discriminating and where most emphasis should be laid.

The recent history of psychopathology has been concerned less with novel descriptions of mental phenomena than with deriving standard ways of eliciting them and evolving explicit rules for their interpretation. There is, in short, a general preoccupation with reliability and precision. This in itself can hardly be criticized, but an unfortunate side-effect is that the utility and validity of the definition of schizophrenia have sometimes been ignored. Furthermore, the recent introduction of many explicit but different definitions of schizophrenia has meant, as Brockington *et al.* (1978) have put it, that the previous state of inarticulate confusion in the diagnosis of schizophrenia has been replaced by a 'babble of precise but differing formulations of the same concept'. In this chapter, we attempt to review briefly the present state of play regarding the diagnosis and subtyping of schizophrenia, and the possible ways in which, with luck, the game might eventually be brought to a triumphal conclusion.

PHENOMENOLOGY:
APPEARANCES AND THE THING IN ITSELF

Although it is usual to commence a discussion on current concepts in the diagnosis of schizophrenia by tracing the origins back to Kraepelin and Bleuler, much recent thinking in the UK, Germany and some other parts of Europe (but to a lesser extent in the USA) has been influenced by the phenomenological approach of Karl Jaspers (1963). Indeed, the term *phenomenology* is now used in some circles virtually interchangeably with *descriptive psychopathology*. This is probably a mistake. Although phenomenology is difficult to define tersely, it is subtly different from and more ambitious than the earlier descriptive psychopathology of, for example, Kraepelin. The development of phenomenology as a school of philosophy is largely due to Husserl, but it also owes a debt to earlier writers, particularly Kant, who explored the limits of what can be known about the objective world, and drew attention to the necessary distinction between the thing as it appears and the thing in itself. Jaspers, before he eventually forsook psychiatry for the Chair of Philosophy at Heidelberg, incorporated many of the ideas and techniques of academic philosophy into his work as a psychopathologist.

For Jaspers the task of phenomenological psychiatry was not merely to describe appearances, i.e. the signs and symptoms of mental illness, in accurate detail, but to achieve a genetic understanding of how mental states arise. Jaspers' use of the word *genetic* has, of course, little to do with the way it is used in Chapter 9 and elsewhere in this book. It was his view that the clinician should, by empathy, be able to deduce meaningful connections between what the patient experiences and the emotions, thoughts and perceptions that he describes. This psychology of understanding is central to the Jasperian view of psychosis. Thus, for Jaspers, there was a clear discontinuity between the psychotic process as manifested in schizophrenia and mental states that are accessible by means of genetic understanding. The sensitive and well trained clinician can think himself into the position of the patient and achieve an empathic insight into most mental phenomena. However, it is the distinguishing characteristic of schizophrenic symptoms that they remain impenetrable by such methods. This is not to say that the schizophrenic cannot be understood, but merely that the phenomena which characterize the illness are non-understandable.

It is interesting that writers as different as Sigmund Freud and Hans Eysenck have been fundamentally in agreement with the Jasperian proposition that there is something qualitatively distinct about the schizophrenic process which demarcates it from normal experience. The most notable attacks on this position in the recent past have come from authors such as Laing (1961) who have maintained that the very core of schizophrenic thought and experience can be understood in existential-phenomenological terms. However, a less obvious and more recent challenge comes from modern North American classifications such as the Diagnostic and Statistical Manual of Mental Disorders (DSM-III) which allow that 'mood incongruent' symptoms, non-understandable in the Jasperian sense, may form part of an affective illness.

It could be argued that the greatest impact of Jaspers' phenomenological approach has come via Kurt Schneider (1959) who, in his *Clinical Psychopathology*, listed the 'first rank symptoms' (FRS). According to Schneider, the presence of one or more of these in the absence of coarse brain disease allows a confident diagnosis of schizophrenia. The absence of FRS does not exclude schizophrenia, and Schneider acknowledged that a small proportion of schizophrenic patients never exhibit FRS. Schneider maintained that he arrived at his list of FRS in a purely empirical way in the course of his clinical practice. However, Fish (1974) has pointed out that Schneider's FRS consist entirely of symptoms which Jaspers regarded as quintessentially non-understandable.

The appeal of first rank symptoms, and the important influence which they have had on recent diagnostic practice, probably owes more to the clear-cut way in which they can be reliably described and identified, than to any more theoretical appeal. Indeed, the most discernible trend in recent clinical practice and research has been towards an emphasis on what can be objectively elicited and provide high levels of inter-rater agreement. The history of this tendency is by now familiar. Disappointment with the poor reliability of psychiatric diagnosis shown in studies such as those of Beck *et al.* (1962) and Kreitman *et al.* (1961), and the realization that there were disquieting cross-national differences in the way diagnostic terms were used, eventually culminated in the development of reliable diagnostic instruments and their use in such important studies as the US/UK Diagnostic Project (Cooper *et al.*, 1972). The triumph of an explicit, carefully defined diagnostic approach over the problems of international and intercultural differences was indeed impressive. We therefore find ourselves in a time when explicit rules for diagnosis and operational diagnostic criteria have won widespread acceptance as the 'remedy for diagnostic confusion' (Kendell, 1975).

OPERATIONAL DEFINITIONS

The comparatively recent introduction of operational definitions of schizophrenia has markedly improved the reliability of diagnosis and facilitated the communication between researchers. The concept of the operational definition was originally introduced, not in medicine or the behavioural sciences, but in physics, by Bridgman in 1927. An operational definition of a scientific term S is the stipulation to the effect that S is to apply to all and only those cases for which performance of test operation T yields the specific outcome O (Bridgman, 1927). Hempel (1961) suggested that operational definitions could be used to overcome classification problems in psychiatry, although he did concede that 'in the context of psychiatric diagnosis the term "operation" has to be interpreted very liberally to include mere observation'. Thus Hempel suggested the following modification of the notion of operational definitions for use in psychiatric classification: 'the diagnosis S should apply to all those and only those manifesting the characteristic or satisfying the criterion O, subject only to the proviso that O should be objective and intersubjectively certifiable and not simply something experienced intuitively or empathically by the examiner'.

In psychiatric classification, a range of clinical features, none of which are sufficient in their own right, are usually required to make a diagnosis. Hempel suggested that these be reduced (or amalgamated) into a single criterion O, and that to facilitate this, graded signs or symptoms would need to be converted to dichotomous variables by imposing arbitrary but explicit cut-offs. Thus the diagnostician using Hempel's operational definition would need to enquire of a graded symptom, X: 'does the subject exhibit *this much* of X?' Typically, the 'this much' of the symptom would refer to its severity or duration or both. Hempel also proposed that typical features of each disorder should be combined algebraically so that those combinations which satisfy criterion O and those which do not are distinct and unambiguously separated.

In practice, most authors seeking to produce operational definitions have adopted the approach described (somewhat disparagingly) as resembling a Chinese menu. Thus a typical format would be that the subject must exhibit X or more of a list of features A, Y or more of a list B, Z or more of a list C, etc. to 'meet criteria' for the disorder.

As we have mentioned, Schneider's FRS have proved attractive to many modern clinicians because of their (apparently) highly explicit nature. The Schneiderian definition can be readily cast into an operational format; i.e. schizophrenia can be diagnosed if A and B are fulfilled:

A: absence of coarse brain disease
B: one or more FRS present.

Many authors published operational definitions for schizophrenia in the 1970s, culminating in 1980 with the criteria set out in the Diagnostic and Statistical Manual, third edition (DSM-III) produced by the American Psychiatric Association (APA). The introduction of the DSM-III criteria was a landmark for clinicians as well as researchers, since the APA required all practising psychiatrists within the USA to use the criteria for guidance in their clinical practice.

A number of other operational definitions preceding the DSM-III criteria for schizophrenia have been widely used in research. Among the first were those of the St Louis group (Feighner *et al.*, 1972). Their definition of schizophrenia requires that as well as exhibiting delusions, hallucinations or communication difficulties, the subject must have been ill for at least 6 months and have certain premorbid characteristics. The authors also proposed 'probable' and 'definite' categories as a means of quantifying the certainty of diagnosis.

The 'flexible' criteria for schizophrenia were published in 1973 by Carpenter *et al.* and originated from a somewhat different standpoint. The authors used ratings from present state examination (PSE) (Wing *et al.*, 1974) of 1121 patients and entered the signs and symptoms as variables in a discriminant function analysis to select 12 major discriminators for schizophrenia. These were chosen as the basis for the 'flexible' system of diagnosis. The authors showed that five or more of the 12 items were present in 80% of their schizophrenic sample. By using a higher 'cut-off' of six or more items for the diagnosis, fewer false positive cases were found. Thus the Carpenter 'flexible' system allows both 'broad' (five or more items required for the diagnosis) and 'narrow' (at least six items required) definitions of the disorder.

Similarly, the research diagnostic criteria (RDC) (Spitzer *et al.*, 1978) enable the disorder to be defined in both 'broad' and 'narrow' forms, depending on the number of symptoms present from a specified list. Originally derived for use in a collaborative study on the psychobiology of depression, the RDC and the associated interview, the schedule for affective disorder and schizophrenia (SADS), have been widely used in research. Although there are similarities between the RDC and earlier definitions like that of Feighner, there are also important differences, one of which is illness duration. The Feighner and DSM-III criteria both require that the subject be ill for at least 6 months before the diagnosis of schizophrenia can be made, whereas the RDC require an illness duration of only 2 weeks. It is clear that such a difference in illness duration will have an impact on the type of case defined by each classification. The Feighner and DSM III-criteria define a narrow group with persistent symptoms, while the RDC definition is broader, including short-lived episodes of psychosis. Also within symptoms there are allowances for a gradation in the certainty or narrowness of definition. Except for DSM-III criteria, the systems mentioned above include such a grading: Feighner 'broad' and 'narrow', Carpenter '5 cut-off' and '6 cut-off' and RDC 'broad' and 'narrow'.

Definitions also differ in the relative emphasis placed on the presenting mental state and information about course. Thus items such as premorbid work and social adjustment and a family history of schizophrenia are included in the Feighner criteria, whereas Carpenter's 'flexible' criteria consist of cross-sectional psychopathological items only. The CATEGO classification (Wing *et al.*, 1974; Wing and Sturt 1978) is perhaps the most sophisticated example of an algorithm based on the cross-sectional ap-proach. The CATEGO computer program processes data from the PSE (Wing *et al.*, 1974) or its associated syndrome check list (SCL), and applies a series of algorithms, based on a hierarchical ordering of symptoms, to arrive at a classification. The PSE used in the conventional way provides a detailed assessment of mental state over the preceding month, although it may be used to describe a whole episode. Because this is a based on evidence restricted to symptom items, it is not a diagnosis, as Wing (1983) makes clear. The SCL can be used to rate written accounts such as hospital case notes of current and previous episodes, and the PSE itself can be used reliably in a 'lifetime ever' fashion (McGuffin *et al.*, 1986). However, the information gathered still concerns symptoms and signs and does not include considerations of cause.

The CATEGO system, because of its explicitly hierarchical structure is necessarily more complex than the 'Chinese menu' classifications, and the output from the CATEGO program can provide a description from different levels of the classification process. Thus ratings of a large number of symptoms yield progressively smaller numbers of 'descriptive groups' and finally a single CATEGO class. The hierarchy regarding psychotic symptoms is constructed so that schizophrenia 'trumps' all other categories except for organic psychosis. Typical (or nuclear) symptoms, i.e. FRS, carry particular weight and so in this respect CATEGO is faithfully Schneiderian.

A tenth edition of the PSE is now being developed which will form the basis of a new version of the CATEGO program and will include consideration of course and aetiology. The classification provided will thus resemble the process of diagnosis more closely, and algorithms will permit the use of more than one classification system, in particular DSMIII-R and the International Classification of Diseases (ICD-10).

Current North American classifications, among which DSM-III (now DSMIII-R) occupies pride of place, do not have a comprehensive or explicit structure, but in some places implied hierarchies are incorporated. Interestingly, the tendency has been to reverse the order of the hierarchy concerning schizophrenia and affective illness, so that prominence of mood disturbance heavily favours a diagnosis of affective disorder—sometimes even when FRS or the 'typical' schizophrenic features are present. Thus a patient who experiences thought insertion and motor passivity for the first time, but who in all other respects fulfils the criteria for major depressive episode, may be diagnosed as having 'major depression with mood incongruent psychotic features'. It is tempting to see this elastic concept of affective disorder as a reaction against past profligacy in the diagnosis of schizophrenia.

THE LIMITS OF OPERATIONALISM AND THE PROBLEMS OF VALIDITY

There is no doubt that using operational criteria greatly improves inter-rater reliability, providing diagnostic agreement at a far better than chance level. Even so, DSMIII-R and ICD-10 both deal only with part of the problem of unreliability, as neither provides definitions of the constituent symptoms. Nevertheless, they confer major benefits from a research viewpoint by enhancing the comparability of results. However, we are left with the problem of a plurality of competing definitions of schizophrenia and, as various studies have shown (e.g. Brockington *et al.*, 1978; Stephens *et al.*, 1982), the agreement between different, equally reliable, methods of diagnosing schizophrenia is poor. Which definition should the researcher choose? From the clinician's viewpoint the 'babble of precision' is perhaps even more perplexing than it is for the researcher. Even if the choice of operational criteria is laid down by some professional body such as the American Psychiatric Association, the doctor is faced with the dilemma of what to do with patients who do not quite 'meet criteria' when clinical intuition says that they should. What, for example, should be done with a patient who has all the hallmarks of schizophrenia but whose illness is some weeks short of a 6-month duration, or with the one who fits the bill on every other count, but only has one rather than two of a list of five symptoms? It is tempting to suspect that some doctors will feel they really *know* that certain patients ought to fit the bed, and will perform a sort of Procrustean exercise to make sure that they do. It certainly seems unreasonable to expect psychiatrists in clinical practice to carry a manual around in their pockets which dictates their diagnostic decisions and over-rules the mental template which they carry in their heads. A possible solution is to have two sets of definitions, as will probably be the case with ICD-10, one purely descriptive and used for clinical practice, and the other in an operational format to be used for research.

Another unfortunate aspect of definitions of schizophrenia of high reliability is that the appearance of scientific precision may disguise a lack of validity. It is possible to add measures in an arbitrary way which enhance reliability but have little to do with the intrinsic nature of schizophrenia (whatever that may be). A slightly preposterous example: we could concoct a definition of schizophrenia whereby, in addition to certain characteristic symptoms such as delusions and hallucinations, all male patients are required to be 1.8 m (6 feet) tall or greater. This would provide a 'narrow' definition, and one which ought to be reliably rated, but would clearly be clinically inappropriate. Most operational definitions have better face validity than this, but still differ considerably from each other both in their constituent items and in the combinatorial rules which are applied.

The central difficulty with operational definitions of psychiatric conditions is that they are considerably cruder than the process by which a psychiatrist arrives at a diagnosis. The 'Chinese menu' system in particular falls down because it imposes a fake and largely atheoretical rigidity upon the variability of mental phenomena. The Schneiderian hierarchy at least has the benefit of a theoretical basis in the Jasperian concept of under-standability: it can say what is schizophrenia, even though it cannot say for certain what is not. By making it easier to classify, operational definitions may change the nature of the classification away from the concept which led us to attempt the classification in the first place. Thus the instigation of DSM-III may produce a generation of American psychiatrists who know all about the classification rules for schizophrenia but have mislaid the concept the rules attempt to capture.

The problem of placing validity on a firmer footing is not straightforward in the absence of a demonstrable and specific pathological agent or process. Robins and Guze (1970) have suggested five phases by which diagnostic validity can be established less directly. The first and second of these, clinical description and the attempted exclusion of other disorders, we have already touched on. However, it is now worth considering the three remaining phases: laboratory investigation, follow-up studies, and family-genetic studies. At present, the state of laboratory investigation, as will be clear from other chapters in this book, particularly Chapter 6, are not at a stage where they can be used convincingly to validate diagnosis. Similarly, the response of patients to pharmacological agents (Murray and Murphy, 1979) has yet to realize its theoretical potential. The biological finding which has been most widely replicated in recent investigations of schizophrenia, that of enlarged lateral cerebral ventricles on computed tomographic (CT) brain scan, is too non-specific and inconstant to be of any use as a diagnostic aid. A 'polydiagnostic' study which applied multiple definitions of schizophrenia to patients who had had CT brain scans, found no firm association between abnormalities in brain morphology and any single definition (Farmer *et al.*, 1987a).

Clinical outcome studies have provided interesting results in the evaluation of a wide range of operational definitions of schizophrenia (e.g. Brockington *et al.*, 1978; Helzer *et al.*, 1981; Stephens *et al.*, 1982). We have found that there is considerable variability, not only with respect to which subjects are classified as schizophrenic, but also with respect to the prediction of short- and long-term outcome. In general, criteria that incorporate longitudinal variables such as duration of illness in their definitions (e.g. the criteria of Feighner *et al.* (1972) and DSM-III) fare better than those relying purely on cross-sectional psychopathology.

There is evidence that the DSM-III criteria also predict outcome satisfactorily in terms of persisting symptoms/lack of recovery when the 6-months' duration criterion is omitted (Helzer *et al.*, 1981). However, the original DSM-III criteria unlike the revised version, DSMIII-R, did require that the patient had failed to return to a premorbid level of functioning.

If we take the analogy of physical diseases, predictability and uniformity of outcome have limitations for validating diagnosis. A genetic basis is perhaps the best established aetiological factor in schizophrenia, and so Brockington *et al.* (1978), in agreement with earlier authors such as Robins and Guze (1970) and Gottesman and Shields (1972), suggested that high heritability is a necessary attribute of a satisfactory definition. The Maudsley twin series, previously described by Gottesman and Shields (1972), have recently been re-examined using a variety of operational definitions. Some of the results and the underlying concepts are discussed in Chapter 9. Essentially, it was found that the definitions of Feighner *et al.*

(1972) and the Research Diagnostic Criteria (Spitzer *et al.*, 1978) identified conditions with a high degree of genetic determination. In both cases, about 80% of the variance in liability to schizophrenia was accounted for by genes (McGuffin *et al.*, 1984). Other definitions such as that of Carpenter *et al.* (1973) proved over-restrictive, and the use of Schneider's FRS produced a syndrome with an estimated heritability of zero.

The approach might not have provided a fair test of the Schneiderian classification, since the investigators were working from detailed abstracts which had not been 'purpose-built' for a study of this type and a rather strict approach to the definition of FRS was taken. This resulted in perfect inter-rater reliability for the presence of FRS, possibly at the price of being over-exclusive. In a subsequent study, the DSM-III criteria were again found to define a form of schizophrenia with heritability of more than 80% (Farmer *et al.*, 1987b). These authors explored further the effects of repositioning the boundaries of the disorder, and found that the mono-zygotic/dizygotic concordance ratio here (a somewhat cruder index than heritability) could be raised by including certain other categories, such as affective disorder 'with mood incongruent psychosis', under the heading of schizophrenia (*see* Chapter 9).

We can conclude that not only is the reliability of recent North American definitions of schizophrenia such as DSM-III satisfactory, but their validity is supported by follow-up and genetic studies. However, such definitions do have their draw-backs from a clinical perspective, and do not completely satisfy the more limited needs of the researcher.

Concepts such as schizotypal personality and schizoaffective disorder are central to the question of the 'spectrum' of schizophrenic disorders, discussed elsewhere in this volume (e.g. Chapter 14). Our focus, however, is upon the centre of schizophrenia rather than the periphery. We must now consider whether recent attempts to examine the heterogeneity within schizophrenia can further our understanding of the syndrome as a whole.

NUCLEAR FISSION: SPLITTING THE CORE SYNDROME

Positive and negative symptoms of schizophrenia

The notion of dividing symptoms of a neurological or neuropsychiatric disorder into positive and negative categories is an old one which has its origins in the writings of nineteenth century authors such as Reynolds and Hughlings-Jackson (Berrios, 1985). The original idea was that certain neurological symptoms due to loss of function (e.g. paralysis) could be classed as negative while others due to excess of function (e.g. muscular spasms) could be classed as positive. Jackson introduced the more sophisticated conceptual framework of a hierarchical model of the central nervous system. Here negative symptoms occur after the loss of higher centre function, which in turn facilitates a release of lower centres. The uninhibited, but otherwise healthy, functioning of lower centres then leads to 'positive symptoms'. It is central to such a model that positive symptoms cannot occur in the absence of negative ones (Berrios, 1985).

Some authors have employed the terms 'positive' and 'negative' as if there were a dichotomy, and have even suggested that positive and negative symptoms of schizophrenia represent two distinct syndromes (Mackay and Crow, 1980). As Berrios (1985) pointed out, this is certainly at variance with Jackson's hierarchical model. Wing (1988) suggested that the two groups of symptoms are not immutable and that either may become prominent in chronic patients depending on certain environmental factors. Thus, if the patient is placed in an over-stimulating milieu where there is pressure to perform to high social or occupational standards, there may be exacerbation of positive symptoms with an increase in delusions and hallucinations. On the other hand, an impoverished or under-stimulating environment, whether on a poorly staffed hospital 'back ward' or within a community facility, can lead to the development of more negative symptoms. Therefore, Wing's view is that both types of symptoms are present to a greater or lesser extent in all chronically ill subjects and fluctuate largely in response to environmental factors.

Crow (1980) has used positive and negative symptoms as the basis for a subtyping scheme which incorporates an aetiological hypothesis. Crow has suggested two subtypes (which to some extent may overlap). The type I syndrome is associated with abnormalities in brain dopaminergic systems, and is characterized by positive symptoms and a good response to neuroleptics. The type II syndrome is associated with cognitive impairment, cerebral ventricular enlargement demonstrable on CT scan, and negative symptoms. The type II syndrome shows poor response to neuroleptic drugs and, Crow suggested, has a different aetiology which may even be infective in origin. For Wing, negative symptoms are defined behaviourally and are notably mutable. For Crow, the real negative symptoms are those which are effectively immutable. In subsequent descriptions, Crow has suggested that movement disorder of the tardive dyskinesia type may be associated with the type II syndrome. Thus we have negative psychological symptoms (flattening of affect, social withdrawal, poverty of thought, and so on) associated with positive motor disturbance. This fits with the Jacksonian view of the necessary coexistence of negative and positive symptoms. It is also worth noting in this context that one recent study, using operational criteria for the Crow classification, found that a 'pure' type II syndrome was much less common than a mixed type I/type II picture in which there were both positive and negative features (Farmer *et al.*, 1987a).

A rather different concept of negative symptoms emerges from the aetiological hypothesis of Murray *et al.* (Chapter 8) that early cerebral insults contribute to the later development of schizophrenia. The view of Crow and his colleagues is essentially neo-Kraepelinian, with negative symptoms of the defect state developing after the positive symptoms of the acute illness and with the defect state becoming steadily worse, at least for the first several years after onset. Johnstone *et al.* have referred to this as the 'dementia of dementia praecox' (Johnstone *et al.*, 1976). However, Murray's argument is that negative symptoms precede the positive ones (as Hughlings-Jackson suggested), perhaps by many years. The 'schizoid' personality characteristics which have commonly been observed to precede the onset of illness are therefore early negative symptoms, and their later re-emergence is mistakenly construed as decline into a defect state. Social factors may contribute to other negative features, but there is no cognitive decline nor any continuing morphological changes in the brain, since the damage has all been done at a much earlier stage. Some support for the theory comes from the finding that enlargement of cerebral ventricles is already present in first-admission cases of schizophrenia (Turner *et al.*, 1987). The relationship between positive and negative symptoms is of major significance for the future study of schizophrenia. Both types occur commonly in the course of most schizophrenic disorders, and thus probably reflect related underlying processes.

Paranoid and non-paranoid subtypes

The division of schizophrenia into more 'traditional' Kraepelinian-Bleulerian subtypes has waned in popularity. The genetic findings are reviewed in Chapter 9. These suggest that the separation of paranoid and hebephrenic or other non-paranoid subtypes is an imposition on a continuity of severity, and that there are not two or more qualitatively distinct categories. However, recent studies using multivariate statistical methods (Farmer *et al.*, 1983, 1984) have produced categories which, in some respects, closely resemble paranoid and hebephrenic subtypes. Two mathematically quite different methods of performing cluster analysis showed highly significant agreement in producing two non-overlapping groups of chronic schizophrenic patients. That this represented some true structure within the data was corroborated by reanalysing 100 data sets composed of computer simulated cases of schizophrenia in which the pattern of symptoms was generated randomly. For every trial, the reliability of the two methods of clustering the simulated data was markedly poorer than when the real data were used. Further analysis showed that the clusters remained stable when extra cases were added, and that affected pairs of relatives tended to show the same subtype of disorder. However, the analyses also indicated that the fundamental differences between the two subtypes are again probably quantitative on a reliability continuum rather than qualitative (Farmer *et al.*, 1984).

IS THERE A WAY AHEAD?

To the outsider, discussions among psychopathologists about how best to define, identify, and classify the phenomena of schizophrenia, and about how best to plot out the boundaries of the syndrome or to divide subgroups, must sound arcane and even a little like theological debate. The exact configuration of symptoms that are required to make a diagnosis is a less obscure and other-worldly issue than how many angels can dance on a pinhead, but the arguments sometimes have a similar flavour of knowledge through faith. Yet informed debate and continued research on how schizophrenia should be defined are vital. On them depends every statement about incidence, prognosis, response to treatment and the nature of neuropathological or biochemical changes. The introduction of operational criteria must, as we have already stated, be regarded as advantageous. However, there is a multiplicity of competing criteria, and even if one particular system gains ascendancy for research purposes, the partially arbitrary nature of operational definitions will prevent it being a panacea for diagnostic difficulty.

Ideally, choosing the most satisfactory definition should be fairly straightforward. After the establishment of reliability, competing definitions can be tested against a range of validating criteria. The most satisfactory definition can then be refined by an iterative process where components of the definition are added, removed, or rearranged, until optimal validity is achieved. This is, in effect, the strategy employed by Farmer *et al.* (1987b), albeit in a crude sort of way, with the DSM-III definition of schizophrenia applied to a twin sample. The strategy seems theoretically sound and can, as this preliminary study shows, be put into practice. However, the range of useful validating criteria is at present very limited. Predictions of outcome and heritability are unlikely on their own to produce definitive answers. Treatment response is currently even less precise as an aid to classification, and so far characteristic neuropathological or biochemical lesions have yet to be demonstrated.

It is probably advisable, therefore, for researchers to use more than one definition of schizophrenia. In practice this will mean taking a definition with which the researchers are familiar as the primary basis of a diagnosis, but collecting the data in such a way that analyses can subsequently be performed using other definitions. At the very least researchers should probably employ two definitions, one broad and one fairly narrow, with the narrow definition nested within the broad.

The recent concern with reliability of diagnosis has meant an emphasis on positive symptoms, particularly the more readily definable forms of delusions and hallucinations. There has now been a reawakening of interest in negative symptoms, but this has largely been focused on the 'more objective and inter-subjectively verifiable' behaviours, such as social withdrawal and affective flattening. Many of the negative symptoms observed in clinical practice, and perceived as so distressing and disabling by relatives, are concerned with lack of volition. Kenneth Rawnsley remarked on chairing one of the sessions at the Oxford conference that the Kraepelinian concept of a disturbance of the will has virtually disappeared from current discourse on schizophrenia. (But there are perhaps beginnings of a reappearance in Chapter 13.) This may be because the rating of a defect in will is almost as hard to objectify as the 'praecox' feeling.

Difficulties in assessment have also led to the neglect of formal thought disorder as a feature of schizophrenia. Clinical methods of describing abnormalities of the form of speech rely on metaphors such as 'knight's move' and 'word salad' or in vague terms such as 'tangentiality' and 'derailment'. The more comprehensive schemes for describing formal thought disorder such as those of Cameron (1944) or C. Schneider (1930) take us little further than the broad Bleulerian description of loosening of associations. Although psychiatrists talk of formal thought disorder, the inference that thinking is disordered rests on the observation of syntactical and structural abnormalities of speech. Linguistic analysis has recently developed into an elaborate and methodologically exacting science. Recent studies of schizophrenics' speech (Morice and Ingrams, 1982; Fraser *et al.*, 1986) were able to demonstrate clear differences in the speech of schizophrenics compared with manic patients or normal controls. Subordinate and imbedded clauses were fewer in number, and there were many grammatical errors of various types. The accuracy of discrimination between schizophrenia and other disorders was at least as good as that achieved with any biological variables. It would seem that studies of this type need to be pursued more widely.

In conclusion, real progress has been made in recent years and we need make no apology for the process of continual re-examination and re-evaluation of basic concepts. Indeed, although much has been achieved in the production of reliable definitions of schizophrenia, it is important to recognize that the task is not complete. In improving our definitions we go through a process of refining our working hypotheses, no more and no less. To set out to encapsulate schizophrenia, the thing in itself, within the framework of a set of explicit diagnostic rules is an attractive but ultimately illusory quest.

ACKNOWLEDGEMENTS

The stimulus for this chapter was the discussion on the same title at the Oxford Conference led by a panel chaired by Sir Martin Roth and consisting of Tim Crow, Bob Kendell, Robin Murray and John Wing. Our thoughts were provoked and our ideas shaped by this debate. However, the responsibility is ours for the views expressed here.

REFERENCES

American Psychiatric Association (1980). Committee on Nomenclature and Statistics. *Diagnostic and Statistical Manual of Mental Disorders*, 3rd edn. Washington, DC: American Psychiatric Association.

Beck A. T., Ward C., Mendelson M., Mock J., Erbaugh J. (1962). Reliability of psychiatric diagnoses: a study of consistency of clinical judgement and ratings. *American Journal of Psychiatry*; **119**: 351–7.

Berrios G. E. (1985). Positive and negative symptoms and Jackson. A conceptual history. *Archives of General Psychiatry*; **42**: 95–7.

Bridgman P. W. (1927). *The Logic of Modern Physics*. New York: Macmillan.

Brockington J. F., Kendell R. E., Leff J. P. (1978). Definitions of schizophrenia: concordance and prediction of outcome. *Psychological Medicine*; **8**: 387–98.

Cameron N. (1944). Experimental analysis of schizophrenic thinking. In: *Language and Thought in Schizophrenia* (Kasamin J., ed.), pp. 50–65. Berkeley: University of California Press.

Carpenter W. T., Strauss J. S., Bartko J. J. (1973). Flexible system for the diagnosis of schizophrenia: a report from the WHO Pilot Study of Schizophrenia. *Science*; **182**: 1275–8.

Cooper J. E., Kendell R. E., Gurland B. J., Sharpe L., Copeland J. R. M., Simon R. (1972). *Psychiatric Diagnosis in New York and London*. Maudsley Monograph. London: Oxford University Press.

Crow T. J. (1980). The molecular pathology of schizophrenia: more than one disease process. *British Medical Journal*; **280**: 66–8.

Farmer A. E., Jackson R., McGuffin P., Storey P. (1987a). Cerebral ventricular enlargement in schizophrenia: consistencies and contradictions. *British Journal of Psychiatry*; **150**: 324–30.

Farmer A. E., McGuffin P., Gottesman I. I. (1984). Searching for the split in schizophrenia: a twin study perspective. *Psychiatry Research*; **13**: 109–18.

Farmer A. E., McGuffin P., Gottesman I. I. (1987b). Twin concordance for DSM-III schizophrenia: scrutinising the validity of the definition. *Archives of General Psychiatry*; **44**: 634–41.

Farmer A. E., McGuffin P., Spitznagel, E. L. (1983). Heterogeneity in schizophrenia: a cluster analytic approach. *Psychiatry Research*; **8**: 1–12.

Feighner J. P., Robins E., Guze S. B., Woodruffe R. A., Winokur G., Munoz R. (1972). Diagnostic criteria for use in psychiatric research. *Archives of General Psychiatry*; **26**: 57–67.

Fish F. (1974). *Clinical Psychopathology: Signs and Symptoms in Psychiatry* (Hamilton M., ed.). Bristol: John Wright and Sons Limited.

Fraser W. I., King K. M., Thomas P., Kendell R. E. (1986). The diagnosis of schizophrenia by language analysis. *British Journal of Psychiatry*; **148**: 275–9.

Gottesman I. I., Shields J. (1972). *Schizophrenia and Genetics: a Twin Study Vantage Point*. New York and London: Academic Press.

Helzer J. E., Brockington I. F., Kendell R. E. (1981). Predictive validity of DSM-III and Feighner definitions of schizophrenia: a comparison with Research Diagnostic Criteria and CATEGO. *Archives of General Psychiatry*; **38**: 791–7.

Hempel C. G. (1961). Introduction to problems of taxonomy. In: *Field Studies in the Mental Disorders* (Zubin J., ed.), pp. 3–22. New York: Grune and Stratton.

Jaspers K. (1963) translated. *General Psychopathology*. Manchester: Manchester University Press.

Johnstone E. C., Crow T. J., Frith C. D., Husband J., Kreel L. (1976). Cerebral ventricular size and cognitive impairment in chronic schizophrenia. *Lancet*; **ii**: 924–6.

Kendell R. E. (1975). *The Role of Diagnosis in Psychiatry*. Oxford: Blackwell Scientific Publications.

Kreitman N. (1961). The reliability of psychiatric diagnosis. *Journal of Mental Science*; **107**: 876–86.

Laing R. D. (1961). *The Divided Self*. London: Penguin Books.

McGuffin P., Farmer A. E., Gottesman I. I., Murray R. M., Reveley A. (1984). Twin concordance for operationally defined schizophrenia. Confirmation of familiality and heritability. *Archives of General Psychiatry*; **41**: 541–5.

Mackay A. V. P., Crow T. J. (1980). Positive and negative schizophrenic symptoms and the role of dopamine. *British Journal of Psychiatry*; **137**: 379–86.

McGuffin P., Katz R., Aldrich J. (1986). Past and Present State Examination: the assessment of 'lifetime ever' psychopathology. *Psychological Medicine*; **16**: 461–5.

Medical Research Council (1987). *Research into Schizophrenia: Report of the Schizophrenia and Allied Conditions Committee to the Neurosciences Board.* London: MRC.

Morice R., Ingrams J. C. L. (1982). Language analysis in schizophrenia: diagnostic implications. *Australian and New Zealand Journal of Psychiatry*; **16**: 11–21.

Murray R. M., Murphy A. E. (1979). Drug response and psychiatric nosology. *Psychological Medicine*; **7**: 667–81.

Robins E., Guze S. B. (1970). Establishment of diagnostic validity in psychiatric illness: its application to schizophrenia. *American Journal of Psychiatry*; **126**: 983–7.

Schneider C. (1930). *Psychologie der Schizophrenen*. Leipzig: Thieme.

Schneider K. (1959). *Clinical Psychopathology* (translated by Hamilton, M. W.). London and New York: Grune and Stratton.

Spitzer R. L., Endicott J., Robins E. (1978). Research diagnostic criteria: rationale and reliability. *Archives of General Psychiatry*; **35**: 773–82.

Stephens J. H., Astrup C., Carpenter W. T., Shaffer J. W., Goldberg J. (1982). A comparison of nine systems to diagnose schizophrenia. *Psychiatry Research*; **6**: 127–43.

Turner S., Toone B., Brett-Jones A. (1986). Computerised tomography scan changes in early schizophrenia—preliminary findings. *Psychological Medicine*; **16**: 219–25.

Wing J. K. (1983). Use and misuse of the PSE. *British Journal of Psychiatry*; **143**: 111–17.

Wing J. K. (1988). The concept of negative symptoms. *British Journal of Psychiatry*; (in press).

Wing J. K., Cooper J. E., Sartorius N. (1974). *The Measurement and Classification of Psychiatric Symptoms*. Cambridge: Cambridge University Press.

Wing J. K., Sturt E. (1978). *The PSE-ID-CATEGO System Supplementary Manual*. London: Institute of Psychiatry.

5 Application of the PET scan to the study of schizophrenia

GÖRAN SEDVALL, LARS FARDE, HÅKAN HALL and
FRITS-AXEL WIESEL

For more than two decades, the possible role of central dopaminergic mechanisms in the pathophysiology of schizophrenia has been a focus of discussion. Several studies have indicated the occurrence of increased D2 dopamine receptor densities in the major basal ganglia of deceased schizophrenic patients (Seeman *et al.*, 1984). Long-term antipsychotic drug treatment has been shown to increase D2 dopamine receptor densities in experimental animals, but it has still not been ascertained whether the increased dopamine receptor density in deceased schizophrenic patients is related to their previous drug treatment or is a genuine feature of the schizophrenic disorder. Recent developments in positron emission tomography (PET) has allowed the determination of neuroreceptor characteristics in the brains of living human subjects. This approach is based on the intravenous injection of tracer concentrations of selective drugs (ligands) that bind to specific neuroreceptor systems (Wagner *et al.*, 1983; Sedvall *et al.*, 1986a). Recently Wong *et al.* (1986), using [^{11}C]-N-methylspiperone as the ligand, claimed that drug-naive schizophrenic patients have a two- to threefold elevation of the D2 dopamine receptor densities in the major basal ganglia. This finding is unexpected, since previous measurements *in vitro* have not disclosed such a degree of D2 dopamine receptor elevation in the brain post-mortem. Moreover, previous studies *in vitro* indicated that the majority of drug-naive schizophrenic patients had D2 dopamine receptor densities within the normal range (Seeman *et al.*, 1984).

In an attempt to develop further methods *in vivo* for the quantitative characterization of subtypes of dopamine receptors in the living human brain, we have developed [^{11}C]-SCH 23390 and [^{11}C]-raclopride as selective ligands *in vivo* for PET studies on D1 and D2 dopamine receptors respectively (Farde *et al.*, 1985; Sedvall *et al.*, 1986b). The present chapter gives a brief outline of these studies.

DEVELOPMENT OF SELECTIVE LIGANDS FOR PET ANALYSIS OF D1 AND D2 DOPAMINE RECEPTORS IN THE LIVING HUMAN BRAIN

N-methylspiperone and other spiperone analogues have high affinities for D2 dopamine receptors, but they also bind to 5-hydroxytryptamine (5HT2), alpha-1, dopamine Dl and spirodelanone sites. Therefore, more selective ligands are required for the quantitative analysis of subtypes of dopamine receptors. SCH 23390 is the most potent and selective D1 dopamine receptor antagonist developed so far (Billard *et al.*, 1984). [¹¹C]-raclopride, a substituted benzamide, was recently described as the most potent and selective D2 dopamine receptor ligand (Hall and Wedel, 1986). These compounds were labelled with ¹¹C, using desmethylated analogues that were subsequently methylated using ¹¹C-labelled methyliodide. The kinetics of these compounds in the living human brain were subsequently examined by PET in healthy volunteers and patients with neuropsychiatric disorders (Farde *et al.*, 1987a).

IN VIVO BINDING OF [¹¹C]-SCH 23390 AND [¹¹C]-RACLOPRIDE IN THE LIVING HUMAN BRAIN

After the intravenous administration of [¹¹C]-SCH 23390 and [¹¹C]-raclopride to healthy volunteers, we were able to demonstrate a high degree of both D1 and D2 dopamine receptor binding in the major basal ganglia, the caudate and the putamen (Farde *et al.*, 1987a). In the neocortices, there was a significant accumulation of radioactivity after administration of [¹¹C]-SCH 23390 but not [¹¹C]-raclopride. Subsequent analysis *in vitro* of the binding of [³H]-SCH 23390 to human brain tissue indicated that the neocortical binding of this ligand is related to the presence of both D1 and 5HT2 receptors (Hall *et al.*, 1987).

DEMONSTRATION OF STEREOSELECTIVITY AND SATURABILITY OF [¹¹C]-SCH 23390 AND [¹¹C]-RACLOPRIDE BINDING IN THE LIVING HUMAN BRAIN

Using the biologically inactive stereoenantiomers of SCH 23390 and raclopride labelled with ¹¹C, we demonstrated that most of the binding of the active enantiomers is stereoselective. Thus, the biologically active enantiomers of both these ligands accumulated markedly in the caudate putamen in the living human brain. On the other hand, the inactive enantiomers showed no, or only an insignificant accumulation in the basal ganglia (Farde *et al.*, 1987b; Sedvall *et al.*, unpublished data).

We were also able to demonstrate that the binding of [¹¹C]-raclopride to central D2 dopamine receptors is saturable. By giving tracer doses of the ligand in the presence of increasing doses of non-labelled raclopride in a series of experiments, the saturability of D2 dopamine receptor binding of raclopride could be demonstrated (Farde *et al.*, 1986). This saturation approach allowed the estimation *in vivo* of the maximal number of binding sites (B_{max}), and the affinity *in vivo* (K_d) for D2 receptors in the caudate and putamen (Farde *et al.*, 1986).

DETERMINATION OF D2 DOPAMINE RECEPTOR DENSITIES IN DRUG-NAIVE SCHIZOPHRENIC PATIENTS

Using the saturation approach *in vivo* with [^{11}C]-raclopride, B_{max} and K_d values for central D2 dopamine receptors were determined in young healthy volunteers and in completely drug-naive, first admission schizophrenic patients (DSM-III) of the same age range. As shown in Table 5.1, there were no significant differences with regard to B_{max} or K_d values in the two groups of subjects. There was an almost complete overlap of values for both these variables. Although the healthy volunteers were slightly older than the schizophrenic patients, previous studies on the effect of age on D2 dopamine receptor densities do not indicate that the lack of difference might be related to age.

Table 5.1 D2 dopamine receptor density (B_{max}) and affinity (K_d) in healthy controls and drug-naive schizophrenic patients

	n	*Sex (M/F)*	*Age (years)*	*B_{max} (pmol/ml)*	*K_d (nM)*
Controls	14	10/4	29.1 ± 4.6	24.6 ± 6.0	7.1 ± 1.3
Schizophrenics	15	9/6	24.3 ± 3.7	25.1 ± 7.0	7.1 ± 1.3

SUMMARY AND CONCLUSIONS

The studies briefly outlined above demonstrate the feasibility of performing analysis of dopamine receptor characteristics in the living human brain. [^{11}C]-SCH 23390 and [^{11}C]-raclopride appear to be suitable ligands for the selective analysis of central D1 and D2 dopamine receptor characteristics in the major basal ganglia. Both these ligands show a high degree of selectivity for the two subtypes of dopamine receptors compared to previously used ligands for PET scan studies. Moreover, these ligands bind in a reversible manner that is stereoselective, thus fulfilling two of the criteria conventionally required for suitable receptor ligands. [^{11}C]-raclopride has a much higher degree of selectivity for D2 dopamine receptors than [^{11}C]-N-methylspiperone. The advantage conferred by the reversibility of [^{11}C]-raclopride binding also allowed the performance of the saturation analysis *in vivo* using an *in-vivo* equilibrium model for calculating B_{max} and K_d values. The [^{11}C]-raclopride equilibration model is less complex than the quantitative procedure for the determination of D2 receptors previously developed by Wong *et al.* (1986). Thus, it is not based on the competition of binding with a different compound as in the model developed by Wong (haloperidol). Moreover, assumptions with regard to the protein binding of the ligand and of the competitor are not required.

The obviously very different results obtained for D2 dopamine receptor densities in drug-naive schizophrenic patients using [^{11}C]-N-methylspiperone and [^{11}C]-raclopride should call for a careful comparison of the two methods. It seems possible that differences between drug-naive patients and healthy volunteers in plasma protein binding of [^{11}C]-N-methylspiperone and haloperidol in the study by Wong *et al.* may have resulted in erroneous conclusions concerning receptor densities. However, it is possible that the fairly weak binding of [^{11}C]-raclopride compared to [^{11}C]-N-methylspiperone may have precluded the demonstration of increased D2 dopamine receptors densities by our own group if some of our schizophrenic patients had an increased endogenous dopamine release.

It is also obvious that the patient characteristics are different in the studies of Wong *et al.* (1986) and Farde *et al.* (1987a, b). The duration of the schizophrenic disorder in the study by Wong *et al.* was more than twice that in the Scandinavian study.

The obvious methodological differences between the studies and their inconsistent results make it pertinent to analyse further the possible role of altered dopamine receptor densities in the pathophysiology of schizophrenia.

ACKNOWLEDGEMENTS

This study was supported by grants from the National Institute of Mental Health (MH 41205-01) and the Swedish Medical Research Council (03560).

REFERENCES

Billard W., Ruperto C., Crosby C., Iorio L. C., Barnett A. (1984). Characterization of the binding of ^{3}H-SCH 23390, a selective D1 receptor antagonist ligand, in rat striatum. *Life Sciences*; 35: 1885–93.

Farde L., Ehrin E., Eriksson L. *et al.* (1985). Substituted benzamides as ligands for visualization of dopamine-D2 receptor binding in the human brain by positron emission tomography. *Proceedings of the National Academy of Science (USA)*; 82: 3863–7.

Farde L., Hall H., Ehrin E., Sedvall G. (1986). Quantitative analysis of D2 dopamine receptor binding in the living human brain by PET. *Science*; 231: 258–61.

Farde L., Halldin C., Stone-Elander S., Sedvall G. (1987a) PET analysis of human dopamine receptor subtypes using ^{11}C-SCH 23390 and ^{11}C-raclopride. *Psychopharmacology*; 92: 278–84.

Farde L., Pauli S., Hall H. *et al.* (1987b). Stereoselective binding of ^{11}C-raclopride and ^{11}C-FLB 472—a search for extrastriatal central D2-dopamine receptors by PET. *Psychopharmacology*; (in press).

Farde L., Wiesel F-A., Hall H., Halldin C., Stone-Elander S., Sedvall G. (1987c). PET determination of striatal D2-dopamine receptors in drug-naive schizophrenic patients. *Archives of General Psychiatry*; 44: 671.

Hall H., Farde L., Sedvall G. (1987). Human dopamine receptor subtypes—*in vitro* binding analysis using ^{3}H-SCH 23390 and ^{3}H-raclopride. *Journal of Neural Transmission*; (in press).

Hall H., Wedel I. (1986). Comparisons between the *in vitro* binding of two substituted benzamides and two butyrophenones to dopamine D2 receptors in the rat striatum. *Acta Pharmacologica et Toxicologica*; 58: 368–73.

Sedvall G., Farde L., Persson A., Wiesel F-A. (1986a). Imaging of neurotransmitter receptors in the living human brain. *Archives of General Psychiatry*; 43: 995–1005.

Sedvall G., Farde L., Stone-Elander S., Halldin C. (1986b). Dopamine D1-receptor binding in the living human brain. In: *Neurobiology of Central D-1 Dopamine Receptors. Advances in Experimental Medicine and Biology* vol 204 (Breese G. R., Creese I., eds.) pp. 119–24. New York: Plenum Press.

Seeman P., Ulpian C., Bergeron C. *et al.* (1984). Bimodal distribution of dopamine receptor densities in brains of schizophrenics. *Science*; 225: 728–31.

Wagner H. N., Burns H. D., Dannals R. F. *et al.* (1983). Imaging dopamine receptors in the human brain by positron tomoraphy. *Science*; 221: 1264–6.

Wong D. F., Wagner H. N., Tune L. E. *et al.* (1986). PET reveals elevated D2 dopamine receptors in drug-naive schizophrenics. *Science*; 234: 1558–63.

6 *The neurochemistry of schizophrenia*

J. F. W. DEAKIN

Any theory of the aetiology of schizophrenia has to accommodate the following facts:

1. there is a major genetic contribution to causation
2. neuroleptic drugs are effective in treating the symptoms
3. cerebral atrophy is associated with schizophrenia
4. there is a small excess of winter births
5. onset occurs in the late teens and twenties
6. schizophrenic psychoses in temporal lobe epileptics are more likely to occur when the focus is on the left hand side.

Facts (2) and (3) have the most immediate neurochemical implications.

The hypothesis that neuroleptic drugs exert their antipsychotic effect by dopamine receptor antagonism has no serious competitors. It has given rise to the complementary hypothesis that schizophrenia is due to excessive dopaminergic neurotransmission. The dopamine theory has been the major stimulus to neurochemical studies in schizophrenia for the last 20 years and current issues are discussed below.

There is no doubt that schizophrenia is associated with cerebral atrophy as indicated by enlargement of the ventricular system in pneumoencephalographic and computed tomographic (CT) scan studies. Neuropathological and neurochemical studies are beginning to bear on the issue of whether particular groups of neurons are involved or whether the atrophy is generalized. The answer is likely to have implications for possible causes of the atrophy and possibly for new approaches to treatment.

The remaining facts are of uncertain neurochemical significance. A molecular understanding of the genetic mechanisms (1) may well have neurochemical implications in the future, but this may be many years off especially if major gene effects do not operate in the transmission of schizophrenia. The significance of the winter birth effect (4) is entirely a matter of speculation. The characteristic age of onset (5) is surely trying to tell us that late developmental changes in the brain are important to aetiology. Whether these changes are aberrant in schizophrenia or simply necessary for the production of symptoms is obviously an important issue. The probable association of left-sided temporal lobe epilepsy with schizophrenic psychoses (6) suggests that lateralized abnormalities of neurochemical function may occur in endogenous schizophrenia.

THE DOPAMINE THEORY

Dopamine neurons

There is little evidence from neurochemical studies of post-mortem brain tissue that there is a generalized overactivity of dopamine neurons in schizophrenia. Homovanillic acid (HVA) is a stable end-product of dopamine metabolism and HVA concentrations are an index of dopamine release and turnover. Unfortunately, changes in HVA concentrations in cerebrospinal fluid or post-mortem brain from schizophrenics are difficult to interpret because of the powerful and persistent effects of neuroleptics on dopamine metabolism. In schizophrenic post-mortem brain there are no marked or consistent changes in HVA concentrations in subcortical areas which receive a dopaminergic innervation—nucleus accumbens, striatum, putamen (*see* Haracz, 1982). Certain frontal and temporal cortical areas are innervated by dopamine in the rat but much less is known about cortical dopamine systems in humans. Homovanillic acid concentrations are much lower in cortical than subcortical areas (Reynolds, 1987). Two studies suggest that cortical HVA concentrations are normal in unmedicated schizophrenic post-mortem brain (Bacopoulos *et al.*, 1979; Reynolds, 1987). However, these studies do not rule out the possibility that there may be localized or subtle abnormalities in dopamine neurons, e.g. in hippocampal or entorhinal dopamine terminals.

Concentrations of dopamine itself have been compared in schizophrenic and control post-mortem brain samples and in some studies the differences are significant. In one study increased dopamine concentrations in the nucleus accumbens occurred in patients with a young age of onset (Mackay *et al.*, 1980b). This is an interesting finding since recent studies from the Clinical Research Centre at Northwick Park (*see* Chapter 9) suggest that schizophrenics with an early age of onset show some clinical and CT scan differences from patients with an older age of onset. Other studies have failed to observe increases in nucleus accumbens dopamine content, although increases in the caudate and putamen have been described (Crow *et al.*, 1978; 1979; 1980). These studies did not divide patients according to age of onset. Differences in drug history and in the method of dissection, particularly of the accumbens, are but two of many possible factors contributing to the conflicting results.

The more recent and novel findings of Reynolds (1983, 1987) suggested that reports of increased dopamine content should not be ignored because they are inconsistent. He has found in two post-mortem brain series that dopamine concentrations are markedly increased in the left but not right amygdala in schizophrenic brain. No changes were seen in the caudate nucleus. In his 1987 study, Reynolds found these small increases in HVA accompanied the increases in dopamine content. One explanation of these results is that dopamine terminals are more densely packed in the left amygdala because other afferents, perhaps from temporal cortex, have degenerated. Indeed, shrinkage of the amygdala and left-sided thinning of temporal cortex have been reported in schizophrenic brains (*see below*).

It is not possible to know whether lateralized increases in dopamine content indicate an increase in functional dopamine neurotransmission. The finding could be due to some asymmetric effect of neuroleptic drugs. Nevertheless, the possible significance of the finding is heightened by recent animal experiments. Bradbury *et al.* (1985) reported that long-term infusions of dopamine into the left-hand amygdala of rats cause a phasic hyperactivity which is not seen with right-sided infusions. If dopamine function is lateralized in animals, the same may be true in humans. Reformulations of the dopamine theory may need to take laterality into account. At present, Reynolds' findings raise the possibility that three apparently separate strands in the biology of schizophrenia are in fact closely related—dominant hemisphere dysfunction, cerebral atrophy and the dopamine theory.

Dopamine receptors

All studies agree that the numbers of dopamine D2 receptors in striatum, putamen and accumbens are increased in schizophrenic post-mortem brains (Lee and Seeman, 1978; Owen *et al.*, 1978; Mackay *et al.*, 1980). The issue is whether this is some adaptive response to neuroleptic medication or whether increased D2 receptors are part of the disease process. Reports that the increase is seen in drug-free patients have not been confirmed (Mackay *et al.*, 1980; Cross *et al.*, 1981). Further post-mortem studies seem unlikely to resolve this issue. A definitive answer is likely to come soon from new imaging studies which enable radioligand-binding studies to be carried out in living patients during their first illness and before they have received neuroleptics. As discussed in Chapter 5, early studies suggest that D2 receptors are not increased in never-treated patients. If this is true, it presents a severe difficulty for the dopamine theory. Other straightforward mechanisms by which increased dopamine (D2) neurotransmission might come about have been excluded. However, it remains possible to imagine more indirect ways in which dopaminergic actions are enhanced in schizophrenia in the absence of changes in dopamine release or D2 receptors.

One possibility is that there is a change in the balanced functioning of D1 and D2 receptors. The development of highly selective D1 and D2 receptor agonists and anatagonists has rekindled interest in the D1 receptor and its interactions with D2 mechanisms. Animal studies suggest that the expression of behaviours evoked by D2 agonists is enhanced by D1 agonists (Waddington, 1986). Enhanced D1 neurotransmission is therefore a potential pathogenic mechanism in schizophrenia. Memo *et al.* (1983) found that addition of a D1 receptor agonist to brain membranes evoked exaggerated increases in cyclic AMP concentration in samples from schizophrenics. Sodium fluoride also evokes increases in cyclic AMP formation by an action beyond the dopamine receptor. Cyclic AMP responses to fluoride were increased in schizophrenic post-mortem brain and Memo *et al.* (1983) concluded that an increased coupling of the D1 receptor to the cyclase occurs in schizophrenia. However, the Northwick Park group have not observed increased cyclic AMP responses to fluoride in their studies of schizophrenic brains (Owen, personal communication).

D1 receptor binding sites in schizophrenic post-mortem brains were not changed in three studies (Cross *et al.*, 1981; Pimoule *et al.*, 1985; Czudek and Reynolds, 1988). Hess *et al.* (1987) reported reduced binding of the selective D1 antagonist [^{3}H]-SCH 23390. There is therefore little evidence for a generalized increase in D1 receptor function in schizophrenia. However, the cascade of post-synaptic consequences of dopamine receptor activation is poorly understood and an abnormality beyond the dopamine receptor may yet prove to be relevant to the pathogenesis of schizophrenia. As with all post-mortem studies, the possibility cannot be excluded that some highly localized but critically important change has been missed. The likelihood of this is reduced by investigating neurochemical parameters in structurally intact brain tissue using the techniques of autoradiography in sections of post-mortem brain (*see below*) and positron emission tomographic (PET) scanning in living subjects (*see* Chapter 5).

Neuropeptides and dopamine function

The finding that mesolimbic dopamine neurons contain cholecystokinin (CCK) as a co-transmitter (Hokfelt *et al.*, 1980) has excited considerable interest in peptide modulation of dopaminergic neurotransmission. Neurotensin may be another dopamine co-transmitter. Both CCK and neurotensin have remarkable neuroleptic-like properties in their ability to counteract behaviours mediated by mesolimbic dopamine neurons and receptors (Nair *et al.*, 1986; Nemeroff, 1986). Drug analogues of CCK and neurotensin are of obvious interest as potential antipsychotics which lack undesirable actions on basal ganglia function. Neurotensin and CCK do not have affinity for dopamine receptors but are capable of attenuating the behavioural effects of directly-acting dopamine receptor agonists. Such actions beyond the dopamine receptor are a potential mechanism of enhanced dopaminergic function in schizophrenia. A loss of these neuroleptic-like peptides in schizophrenia might be predicted.

Neurotensin concentrations appear to be normal in dopamine terminal areas in schizophrenic post-mortem brains (Biggins *et al.*, 1983; Ferrier *et al.*, 1983; Nemeroff *et al.*, 1983). Two studies report increased numbers of neurotensin receptors in the substantia nigra but not elsewhere (Uhl and Kuhar, 1984; Farmery *et al.*, 1986). Changes in neurotensin receptor binding are almost certainly a consequence of neuroleptic therapy since they are reproduced by neuroleptic therapy in experimental animals.

Kleinman *et al.* (1983) reported that CCK concentrations in accumbens, amygdala and caudate were normal in samples from schizophrenics. Ferrier *et al.* (1983) found no changes in CCK in putamen but, in a subgroup of patients with deficit symptoms, amygdalar CCK concentrations were reduced.

It can be seen that the few studies of dopamine co-transmitter peptides in schizophrenic post-mortem brain reveal little support for deficits in CCK or neurotensin in dopamine terminal areas. Loss of these neuroleptic-like peptides or their receptors seems an unlikely mechanism for the positive symptoms of schizophrenia.

Dopamine dysregulation

A persistent theme of speculation is that dopamine neurotransmission is unstable in schizophrenia. The common element is the idea that dopamine neurons are underactive resulting in supersensitive dopamine receptors. Reduced dopamine release gives rise to chronic deficit symptoms. Relapses into positive symptoms result from small increases in dopamine release which play upon supersensitive receptors to cause a breakthrough into a state of heightened dopamine neurotransmission (Chouinard and Jones, 1978; Mackay, 1980; Wyatt, 1986).

A recent variation on this theme has been proposed by Weinberger *et al.* (1987) who suggest that frontal cortical dopamine release is reduced in schizophrenia resulting in an avolitional frontal lobe syndrome. Pycock *et al.* (1980) showed that destruction of frontal cortical dopamine terminals with 6-hydroxydopamine resulted in increased dopamine release, and increased D1 and D2 receptor binding in the rat striatum. Weinberger *et al.* suggest that psychosocial stressors precipitate unstable increases in subcortical dopamine neurotransmission resulting in relapses.

There are several difficulties with these speculations. In the first place there is little evidence from post-mortem brain studies that dopamine release is reduced in schizophrenia. There are some inconsistent reports that HVA concentrations in cerebrospinal fluid are reduced in schizophrenics and studies of plasma HVA present an equally ambiguous picture (*see* Haracz, 1982 and Meltzer, 1987 for reviews). Furthermore, animal studies suggest that profound (> 80%) reductions in dopamine release are required to induce post-synaptic receptor supersensitivity and no changes of this magnitude have been described in schizophrenia. So far as the Weinberger variant is concerned, the few relevant studies do not suggest a widespread loss of cortical dopamine terminals in schizophrenia. Evidence for increased subcortical dopamine neurotransmission is confined to increased D2 receptor binding and, as we have seen, this may be consigned to the history books by isotope scan studies.

THE NEUROCHEMICAL BASIS OF CEREBRAL ATROPHY

Computed tomographic scan studies have unequivocally established that schizophrenia is associated with cerebral atrophy. The key area of debate is whether the atrophy is the outcome of a variety of non-specific perinatal insults to the brain or represents more specific developmental abnormality. The demonstration that anatomically and neurochemically specific populations of neurons are involved would seem incompatible with the non-specific nature of perinatal birth injury.

Anatomical and neurochemical specificity?

Evidence that specific areas of the brain are affected by the atrophic process is beginning to emerge. Both Bogerts *et al.* (1985) and Brown *et al.* (1986) reported that the parahippocampal gyrus is thinner in schizophrenic post-mortem brain, whereas other cortical areas are not affected. The para-hippocampal gyrus includes entorhinal cortex and this is one of the main sources of afferent projections to the hippocampus. Interestingly, Bogerts *et al.* (1985) reported that the hippocampus is atrophic in schizophrenic post-mortem brains. The parahippocampal gyrus has reciprocal connections with parietal and frontal association areas (Van Hoesen, 1982) (Fig. 6.1). Perhaps interruption of these temporal—neocortical connections

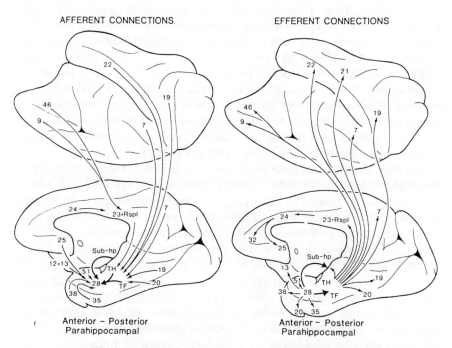

Fig. 6.1 *Cortical connections of the parahippocampal gyrus*

underlies the splitting of mental functions described by Bleuler, particularly the dissociation between affective and cognitive processes.

There are few studies of biochemical markers of intrinsic cortical neurons in schizophrenia. Ferrier *et al.* (1983) measured concentrations of several cortical neuropeptides in schizophrenic post-mortem brains. The patients had been rated in life and were subdivided into a group with predominant positive symptoms and a group with negative symptoms. Few significant differences emerged. Patients with the deficit symptoms of schizophrenia had reductions in hippocampal and amygdalar CCK content and reductions in somatostatin in the hippocampus. Perry et al. (1981) and Kleinman *et al.* (1983) did not find reductions in CCK but the patients were not clinically subdivided. In a later study, the Northwick Park group found reductions in CCK receptor binding sites in frontal cortex and hippocampus from schizophrenics (Farmery *et al.*, 1985). If confirmed, these findings suggest that neurons which contain CCK and others which bear CCK receptors degenerate or fail to develop in schizophrenia. Somatostatin-containing neurons may also degenerate in schizophrenia, but if so, the loss is much less marked or generalized than in Alzheimer's disease.

There are many other neurochemical markers of cortical neurons that should be studied in schizophrenia to address the specificity issue. Paramount among these are markers for glutamate neurons. Glutamate is probably the major cortical neurotransmitter. There is evidence that large pyramidal cells are glutaminergic and that glutamate is a neurotransmitter in association fibres (Fonnum, 1984). Glutamate is involved in cell metabolism and it is not possible to distinguish this from neurotransmitter glutamate. One way round this problem is to use ligand binding techniques to label the glutamate uptake site.

The Manchester neuroscience group have shown that $[^3H]$D–aspartate is a high affinity ligand for the glutamate uptake site and thus a marker for the integrity of glutamate nerve terminals (Cross *et al.*, 1986). We have also shown that $[^3H]$D–aspartate binding is reduced in Alzheimer's disease and this is compatible with the loss of pyramidal neurons which is known to occur in this condition (Cross *et al.*, 1987) (Fig. 6.2).

We have now made a start in determining whether cortical glutamate terminals degenerate in schizophrenia. Our first small series of post-mortem brains consisted of six brains from schizophrenics (five Feighner positive) and 12 control brains. Schizophrenic and control brains were not well matched for post-mortem delay and so the results (Fig. 6.3) are necessarily tentative. It can be seen that cortical and subcortical $[^3H]$D–aspartate binding is not significantly different in the two groups. In the schizophrenics, cortical $[^3H]$D–aspartate binding was lower on the left side than on the right, whereas binding was equal on the two sides or lower on the right in the control brains. However, none of these differences approaches statistical significance. If a loss of glutamate terminals from the left temporal lobe is confirmed in our larger series of brains, this may

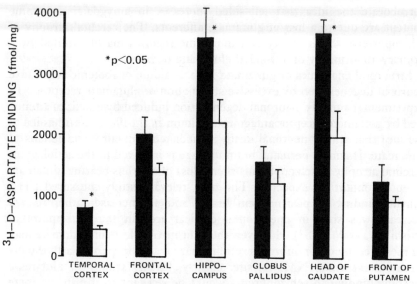

Fig. 6.2 [³H]-*D-aspartate binding (control + Alzheimer).* □ *Alzheimer;* ■ *control*

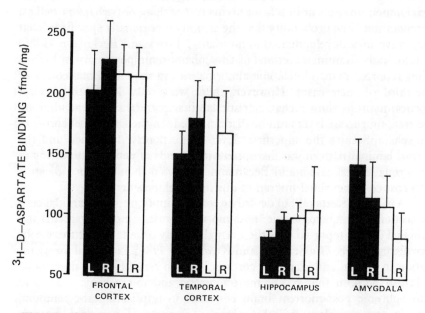

Fig. 6.3 [³H]-*D-aspartate binding in schizophrenia and control.* ■ *Schizophrenia;* □ *control*

corroborate the idea that left-sided increases in amygdalar dopamine content are due to a loss of glutamate afferents. The cerebral atrophy of schizophrenia, the laterality and dopamine theories may be united by a primary abnormality of left-sided glutamate neurons.

Structural analogues of glutamate such as kainic or ibotenic acid cause neuronal degeneration by excessive stimulation of glutamate receptors. In experimental animals, neuronal degeneration induced by anoxia is attenuated by glutamate receptor antagonists (Simon *et al.*, 1984). This has led to the idea that anoxic neuronal death is mediated by neurotoxic actions of glutamate. If anoxic perinatal brain damage is involved in the aetiology of cerebral atrophy in schizophrenia then a loss of neurons bearing glutamate receptors might be expected. The only relevant study measured [^{3}H]-kainate binding in post-mortem brains and an increase rather than a decrease was seen in one frontal cortical area in the schizophrenics (Nishikawa *et al.*, 1983). However, the neurotoxic effects of glutamate may be mediated by other subtypes of glutamate receptor, particularly the N-methyl-D-aspartate (NMDA) site. Clearly, further studies of glutamate receptor binding in schizophrenia would be relevant to the anoxia issue and, since glutamate receptors are widely distributed on cortical neurons, such studies would also be relevant to the question of identifying which cortical cells degenerate in schizophrenia.

Dysplasia or degeneration?

Several recent neuropathological studies suggest that aberrant neuronal development may occur in schizophrenia rather than, or perhaps as well as, degeneration. The probability that the atrophy is regionally specific is itself suggestive of a developmental abnormality. Jakob and Beckmann (1986) histologically examined sections of 64 schizophrenic post-mortem brains. They reported cytoarchitectonic abnormalities in the entorhinal cortex of one-third of their cases. However, there were only 10 control brains. Cortical neurons show a characteristic laminar pattern and, depending on the area, four to six layers can be distinguished. In the entorhinal cortex of the schizophrenics the superficial layers were poorly developed and the normal laminar pattern was disrupted with islands of neurons appearing in the wrong layers. Jakob and Beckmann suggested their results indicate a disturbance of neuronal migration during development.

Falkai and Bogerts (1986) described loss of hippocampal pyramidal cells in sections of schizophrenic post-mortem brains and Kovelman and Scheibel (1984) reported that the normal orderly orientation of these cells was disrupted (*see also* Scheibel and Kovelman, 1981). Neuronal disorganization in frontal and cingulate cortices has also recently been described.

It can be seen that recent morphometric and microscopic studies of schizophrenic post-mortem brain converge in implicating the temporal lobe in the pathology of schizophrenia. Reports of neuronal disarray suggest disturbances in the normal pattern of development particularly of entorhinal cortex and hippocampus.

Neurochemical neuropathology

Many neurotransmitter receptors show a highly ordered laminar distribution in cerebral cortex. This is revealed by autoradiography in which sections of brain are incubated with a radioactive ligand for the receptor of interest. After washing, the section is pressed against photographic emulsion for a period of weeks. Radioactivity associated with bound ligand causes deposition of silver grains in the emulsion thus revealing the distribution of receptors.

Neurotransmitter receptors in the hippocampus show a remarkable degree of laminar organization. Figure 6.4 shows the distribution of [^{3}H]-kainate-labelled glutamate receptors in monkey hippocampus. The dense band in the dentate gyrus corresponds to the band of nerve terminals which arise from pyramidal cells in the entorhinal cortex. Removal of the entorhinal cortex in rats is followed by sprouting of other afferents to the dentate and there is a corresponding increase in the thickness of the kainate receptor band in autoradiographic studies. The same autoradiographic changes have been described in Alzheimer's disease, which involves severe neuronal degeneration in entorhinal cortex (Geddes *et al.*, 1985). If the entorhinal cortex is atrophic or dysplastic in schizophrenia then changes in the laminar organization of dentate glutamate receptors could be revealed by autoradiography.

Dysplasia in entorhinal cortex or elsewhere can thus be studied neurochemically using autoradiography. Figure 6.5 shows an autoradiograph of 5-hydroxytryptamine (5HT) receptor subtypes in the human

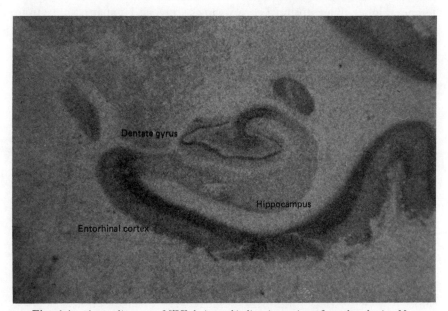

Fig. 6.4 *Autoradiogram of [^{3}H]-kainate binding in section of monkey brain. Note characteristic laminated appearance of glutamate receptors in cortex and hippocampus*

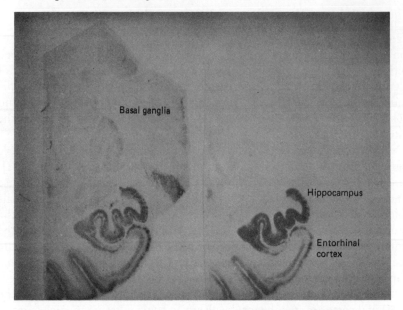

Fig. 6.5   *Autoradiogram of [³H]-5HT (5HT1A and B receptors) binding in section of human post-mortem brain on left and of [³H]-8 OHDPAT (selective for 5HT1A receptors) in adjacent section. Note lamination and clustering of binding sites in entorhinal cortex and hippocampus. The basal ganglia and substantia nigra are only visible with [³H]-5HT and not with [³H]-8 OHDPAT, indicating that these receptors are of the 5HT1B subtype*

temporal lobe. The entorhinal cortex shows a precise laminar organization of 5HT receptors and the clumping of receptors is reminiscent of the clumping of neurons in this cortical area. However, it is not known whether the 5HT receptors are located on cortical neurons or on afferent nerve terminals, e.g. on association fibres or on callosal fibres from the opposite hemisphere. Furthermore, it is not known how the laminar pattern arises during development. For example, does it arise early or late in development and is it associated with the arrival of a particular set of neurons or terminals? The same questions apply to most other receptor systems. There is thus a need for more information about the anatomical location of binding sites and mechanisms of their development before autoradiography is fully informative on the question of dysplasia in schizophrenia.

It can be seen that autoradiography is a potentially powerful tool in the study of neuronal organization in particular neurochemical systems. The availability of ligands for uptake sites means that chemically identified nerve terminals as well as receptors can be visualized in structurally intact brain. There is no loss of information as in conventional neurochemical studies where areas of brain are homogenized or not studied at all. Furthermore, with the incorporation of appropriate standards, the technique yields quantitative information about number and affinity of binding sites.

Laterality

The idea that schizophrenia involves left hemisphere dysfunction arose from the association of left-sided temporal lobe epileptic foci with schizophrenia-like psychoses. This theory has generated a large but inconsistent literature attempting to demonstrate left hemisphere dysfunction, e.g. using neuropsychological tests, psychophysiology and blood flow studies (Flor-Henry and Gruzelier, 1983). Recent findings have now widened interest in the idea. These include:

1. increased amygdalar dopamine content on the left-hand side (Reynolds, 1983)
2. left-sided hypodensity on CT scans (Reveley *et al.*, 1987)
3. left-sided thinning of entorhinal cortex (Brown *et al.*, 1986).

Left-sided atrophy or dysplasia of temporal lobe structures occurring early in development could give rise to aberrant patterns of interhemispheric communication. Goldman-Rakic (1983) showed that removal of a target area of cortex *in utero* caused callosal fibres destined for that area to innervate nearby areas of cortex instead. Thus non-homologous areas of cortex became interconnected by callosal fibres.

Callosal projections to cortex are abundant at birth (Ivy *et al.*, 1979; Ivy and Killackey, 1981). The adult pattern of a discontinuous columnar and laminar distribution of callosal neurons and terminals comes about by the elimination of transient callosal projections (O'Leary *et al.*, 1981). A failure in this remodelling process is another way in which aberrant patterns of interhemispheric communication and of cerebral dominance could arise.

It has been suggested that a disturbance in interhemispheric communication could underlie some of the symptoms of schizophrenia. One idea is that disturbed cerebral dominance results in the perception of right hemisphere generated speech, thoughts and emotions as auditory hallucinations and passivity phenomena (Green *et al.*, 1983).

Glutamate is a probable neurotransmitter in callosal fibres and there may be others. Little is known about the neurochemistry of cortical synapses, of how afferent and intrinsic neurons interact. For example, the neurochemical identity of cells receiving a callosal or association fibre innervation is unknown; nor is it known whether neurotransmitter release from callosal terminals is modulated by other neurotransmitters acting on presynaptic receptors. Could it be that cortical dopamine modulates interhemispheric communication and that antagonism of D1 or D2 receptors on callosal terminals contributes to the antipsychotic effect of neuroleptics? Could pharmacological interference with callosal mechanisms be an entirely new way of treating schizophrenia? These ideas are highly speculative but new ideas are badly needed. Better ideas may arise from comparatively straightforward studies of the development and anatomy of neurochemical systems in limbic cortical areas.

NEUROCHEMICAL STUDIES: THE FUTURE

Hypotheses

1. The dopamine hypothesis requires continuing investigation, whether or not PET scan studies rule out increased D2 receptors as the mechanism. Other ways in which enhanced dopaminergic function could occur in schizophrenia have been discussed and are worthy of investigation. These include abnormalities in: dopamine receptor subtype interactions; neuropeptide/dopamine mechanisms; and in dopamine receptor transduction. Cortical dopamine terminals and receptors need further exploration in human brain.
2. There is a pressing need to establish the location and neurochemical identity of neurons that are involved in the cerebral atrophy of schizophrenia. In particular, the integrity of the major cortical neurotransmitter, glutamate, and its receptors is a critical issue.
3. The idea that abnormalities in the development of cortical connectivity (callosal, intracortical) are aetiologically involved in schizophrenia needs to be elaborated and investigated. It is acknowledged that a precise hypothetical formulation is lacking at present.

Techniques

1. Positron emission tomography will revolutionize neurochemical studies in schizophrenia. The advantages and limitations of this technique are discussed in Chapter 5. However, PET does not yet provide the anatomical resolution nor the range of neurochemical parameters available with autoradiographic studies of post-mortem brain, and the two techniques are complementary.
2. Autoradiography adds a neurochemical dimension to neuropathology; it enables neurochemical studies to be carried out in structurally intact tissue. Thus the neurochemical identification of dysplastic pathways in schizophrenia is possible. Radioligands are available for both receptors and terminals. It is also possible to study dynamic neurochemical function in anatomical detail, e.g. second messenger responses to receptor activation. It can be seen that autoradiography will be a useful tool in the investigation of the three hypotheses above.
3. The continuing collection of post-mortem brains is essential to future neurochemical studies. Brains need to be stored in such a way that autoradiographic and neuropathological studies *in vitro* can be performed on both left and right hemispheres. The value of relating

detailed clinical assessments in life to post-mortem neurochemical parameters has already been demonstrated. The task is made more difficult by the declining numbers of long-stay patients. However, it should be possible to organize systems for rating patients and collecting brains in a few regional centres. This needs active collaboration between patients, relatives, voluntary organizations and researchers.
4. There is a need for basic science studies of cortical synaptic arrangements. There is a dearth of knowledge about how different neurotransmitter terminals and receptors interact and how these arrangements develop. Such information is likely to aid our understanding of the mechanisms of cerebral atrophy in schizophrenia, and may lead to the development of entirely new treatment strategies.

REFERENCES

Bacopoulos N. G., Spokes E. G., Bird E. D., Roth R. H. (1979). Antipsychotic drug action in schizophrenic patients: effects on cortical dopamine metabolism after long-term treatment. *Science*; **205**: 1405–7.
Biggins J. A., Perry E. K., McDermott J. R., Smith I. A., Perry R. H., Edwardson J. A. (1983). Post-mortem levels of thyrotropin-releasing hormone and neurotensin in the amygdala in Alzheimer's disease, schizophrenia and depression. *Journal of Neurological Science*; **58**: 117–22.
Bogerts B., Meertz E., Schonfeldt-Bausch R. (1985). Basal ganglia and limbic system pathology in schizophrenia: a morphometric study of brain volume and shrinkage. *Archives of General Psychiatry*; **42**: 784–91.
Bradbury A. J., Costall B., Domeney A. M., Naylor R. J. (1985). Laterality of dopamine function and neuroleptic action in the amygdala in the rat. *Neuropharmacology*; **24**: 1163–70.
Brown R., Colter N., Corsellis J. A. N. *et al.* (1986). Post-mortem evidence of structural brain changes in schizophrenia. Differences in brain weight, temporal horn area, and parahippocampal gyrus compared with affective disorder. *Archives of General Psychiatry*; **43**: 36–42.
Chouinard G., Jones B. D. (1978). Schizophrenia as a dopamine deficiency disease. *Lancet*; **ii**: 99–100.
Cross A. J., Crow T. J., Owen F. (1981). ^{3}H-Flupenthixol binding in post-mortem brains of schizophrenics: evidence for a selective increase in dopamine D2 receptors. *Psychopharmacology*; **74**: 122–4.
Cross A. J., Skan W. J., Slater P. (1986). The association of [^{3}H]D-aspartate binding and high-affinity glutamate uptake in the human brain. *Neuroscience Letters*; **63**: 121–4.
Cross A. J., Slater P., Simpson M. *et al.* (1987). Sodium dependent D-[^{3}H]aspartate binding in cerebral cortex in patients with Alzheimer's and Parkinson's diseases. *Neuroscience Letters*; **79**: 213–17.
Crow T. J., Baker H. F., Cross A. J. *et al.* (1979). Monoamine mechanisms in chronic schizophrenia: post-mortem neurochemical findings. *British Journal of Psychiatry*; **134**: 249–56.
Crow T. J., Cross A. J., Johnstone E. C., Longden A., Owen F., Ridley R. M. (1980). Time course of the antipsychotic effect in schizophrenia and some

changes in post-mortem brain and their relation to neuroleptic medication. *Advances in Biochemistry and Psychopharmacology*; 24: 495–503.

Crow T. J., Johnstone E. C., Longden A. J., Owen F. (1978). Dopaminergic mechanisms in schizophrenia: the antipsychotic effect and the disease process. *Life Sciences*; 23: 563–8.

Czudek C., Reynolds G. P. (1988). Binding of (^{3}H)SCH 23390 to post-mortem brain tissue in schizophrenia. *British Journal of Pharmacology* (in press).

Falkai P., Bogerts B. (1986). Cell loss in the hippocampus of schizophrenics. *European Archives of Psychiatry and Neurological Science*; 236: 154–61.

Farmery S. M., Crow T. J., Owen F. (1986). (3-(125 1)-iodotyrosyl 3) neurotensin binding in post mortem brain: a comparison of controls and schizophrenic patients. *British Journal of Psychiatry*; 88: 380.

Farmery S. M., Owen F., Poulter M., Crow T. J. (1985). Reduced high affinity cholecystokinin binding in hippocampus and frontal cortex of schizophrenic patients. *Life Sciences*; 36: 473–77.

Ferrier I. N., Roberts G. W., Crow T. J. *et al.* (1983). Reduced cholecystokinin-like and somatostatin-like immunoreactivity in limbic lobe is associated with negative symptoms in schizophrenia. *Life Sciences*; 33: 475–82.

Flor-Henry P., Gruzelier J. (1983). (Eds.) *Laterality and Psychopathology.* Amsterdam: Elsevier.

Fonnum F. (1984). Glutamate: a neurotransmitter in mammalian brain. *Journal of Neurochemistry*; 42: 1–11.

Geddes J. W., Monaghan D. T., Cotman C. W., Lott I. T., Kim R. C., Chang Chui H. (1985). Plasticity of hippocampal circuitry in Alzheimer's disease. *Science*; 230: 1179–81.

Goldman-Rakic P. S. (1982). Neuronal development and plasticity of the association cortex in primates. *Neuroscience Research Progress Bulletin*; 20: 520–32.

Green P., Hallett S., Hunter M. (1983). Abnormal interhemispheric integration and hemispheric specialization in schizophrenics and high risk children. In: *Laterality and Psychopathology* (Flor-Henry P., Gruzelier J., eds.), pp. 443–69. Amsterdam: Elsevier.

Haracz J. L. (1982). The dopamine hypothesis: an overview of studies with schizophrenic patients. *Schizophrenia Bulletin*; 8: 438–69.

Hess E. J., Bracha H. S., Kleinman J. E., Creese I. (1987). Dopamine receptor subtype imbalance in schizophrenia. *Life Sciences*; 40: 1487–97.

Hokfelt T., Skirboll L., Rehfield J. F., Goldstein M., Markey K., Dann O. (1980). A subpopulation of mesencephalic dopamine neurones projecting to limbic areas contains a cholecystokinin-like peptide: evidence from immunohisto-chemistry combined with retrograde tracing. *Neuroscience*; 5: 2093–124.

Ivy G. O., Akers R. M., Killackey H. P. (1979). Differential distribution of callosal projection neurons in the neonatal and adult rat. *Brain Research*; 173: 532–7.

Ivy G. O., Killackey H. P. (1981). The ontogeny of the distribution of callosal projection neurons in the rat parietal cortex. *Journal of Comparative Neurology*; 195: 367–89.

Jakob H., Beckmann H. (1986). Prenatal developmental disturbances in the limbic allocortex in schizophrenics. *Journal of Neural Transmission*; 65: 303–26.

Kleinman J. E., Iadarola M., Govoni S., Hong J., Gillin J. C., Wyatt R. J. (1983). Post-mortem measurement of neuropeptides in human brain. *Psychopharmacology*; 87: 292–7.

Kovelman J. A., Scheibel A. B. (1984). A neurohistological correlate of schizo-phrenia. *Biological Psychiatry*; 19; 1602–21.

Lee T., Seeman P. (1980). Elevation of brain neuroleptic/dopamine receptors in schizophrenia. *American Journal of Psychiatry*; 137: 191–7.

Mackay A. V. P. (1980). Positive and negative symptoms and the role of dopamine. *British Journal of Psychiatry*; 137: 379–83.

Mackay A. V. P., Bird E. D., Iverson L. L., Spokes E. G., Creese I., Snyder S. H. (1980b). Dopaminergic abnormalities in post-mortem schizophrenic brain. *Advances in Biochemistry and Psychopharmacology*; 24: 325–33.

Mackay A. V. P., Bird E. D., Spokes E. G. *et al.* (1980a). Dopamine receptors in schizophrenia: drug effect or illness? *Lancet*; ii: 915–16.

Meltzer H. Y. (1987). Biological studies in schizophrenia. *Schizophrenia Bulletin*; 13: 77–111.

Memo M., Kleinman J. E., Hanbauer I. (1983). Coupling of dopamine D1 recognition sites with adenylate cyclase in nuclei accumbens and caudatus of schizophrenics. *Science*; 221: 1302–4.

Nair N. P. V., Lal S., Bloom D. M. (1986). Cholecystokinin and schizophrenia. *Progress in Brain Research*; 65: 237–57.

Nemeroff C. B. (1986). The interaction of neurotensin with dopaminergic pathways in the central nervous system: basic neurobiology and implications for the pathogenesis and treatment of schizophrenia. *Psychoneuroendocrinology*; 11: 15–37.

Nemeroff C. B., Youngblood W. W., Manberg P. J., Prange A. J. Jr., Kizer J. S. (1983). Regional brain concentrations of neuropeptides in Huntington's chorea and schizophrenia. *Science*; 221: 972–5.

Nishikawa T., Takashima M., Toru M. (1983). Increased [³H]kainic acid binding in the prefrontal cortex in schizophrenia. *Neuroscience Letters*; 40: 245–50.

O'Leary D. D. M., Stanfield B. B., Cowan W. M. (1981). Evidence that the early postnatal restriction of the cells of origin of the callosal projection is due to the elimination of axonal collaterals rather than to the death of neurons. *Developmental Brain Research*; 1: 607–17.

Owen F., Cross A. J., Crow T. J., Longden A., Poulter M., Riley G. J. (1978). Increased dopamine receptor sensitivity in schizophrenia. *Lancet*; ii: 223–6.

Perry R. H., Dockray G. J., Dimaline R., Perry E. K., Blessed G., Tomlinson B. E. (1981). Neuropeptides in Alzheimer's disease, depression and schizophrenia. *Journal of Neurological Science*; 51: 465–72.

Pimoule C., Schoemaker H., Reynolds G. P., Langer S. Z. (1985). (³H)SCH-23390 labelled D1 dopamine receptors are unchanged in schizophrenia in rats. *European Journal of Pharmacology*; 114: 235–7.

Pycock C. J., Kerwin R. W., Carter C. J. (1980). Effects of lesions of cortical dopamine terminals on subcortical dopamine in rats. *Nature*; 286: 74–7.

Reveley M. A., Reveley A. M., Baldy R. (1987). Left cerebral hypodensity in discordant schizophrenic twins. *Archives of General Psychiatry*; 44: 625–32.

Reynolds G. P. (1983). Increased concentration and lateral asymmetry of amygdalar dopamine in schizophrenia. *Nature*; 305: 527–9.

Reynolds G. P. (1987). Post-mortem neurochemical studies in schizophrenia. In: *Search for the Causes of Schizophrenia* (Häfner H., Gattaz W. F., Janzarik W., eds.), pp. 236–40. Berlin: Springer-Verlag.

Scheibel A. B., Kovelman J. A. (1981). Disorientation of the hippocampal pyramidal cell and its processes in the schizophrenic patient. *Biological Psychiatry*; 16: 101–2.

Simon R. P., Suran J. H., Griffiths T., Meldrum B. S. (1984). Pharmacologic blockade of excitatory amino-acid neurotransmission attenuates the neuropathological damage of ischaemia. *Annals of Neurology*; **16**: 112.

Uhl G. R., Kuhar M. J. (1984). Chronic neuroleptic treatment enhances neurotensin receptor binding in human and rat substantia nigra. *Nature*; **309**: 350–2.

Van Hoesen G. W. (1982). The parahippocampal gyrus: new observations regarding its cortical connections in the monkey. *Trends in Neuroscience*; **52**: 345–50.

Waddington J. L. (1986). Behavioural correlates of the action of selective D-1 dopamine receptor antagonists: impact of SCH 23390 and SKF 83566, and functionally interactive D-1:D-2 receptor systems. *Biochemical Pharmacology*; **35**: 3661–7.

Weinberger D. R., Berman K. F., Zec R. F. (1987). Psychologic dysfunction of dorsolateral prefrontal cortex in schizophrenia: I. Regional cerebral blood flow evidence. *Archives of General Psychiatry*; **43**: 114–24.

Wyatt R. J. (1986). The dopamine hypothesis: variations on a theme (11). *Psychopharmacology Bulletin*; **22**(3): 923–7.

7   *The neuropathology of schizophrenia: a critical review of recent work*

P. L. LANTOS

The search to find structural abnormalities which may underlie the development of schizophrenia has been long, controversial and in many respects unrewarding. There is probably no other disease which has put the neuropathologist to a harder task. The view has long been held that schizophrenia is a disease of the mind and not of the brain: genetic, environmental and social factors may all play a role in the aetiology, but structural changes need not necessarily be associated with the development of the disease. Indeed, the neuropathologist has been confronted with an impossible and daunting quest: to find the biological substrate which would explain the symptomatology of an ill defined, enormously complex and heterogeneous mental disease.

The sights of morphological studies have been lowered during the years. The real question—what structural alterations in the brain are responsible for schizophrenia—has often been changed to a more modest one—are there any changes in the schizophrenic brain at all? If no pathognomonic clues can be found, does this profound psychosis leave the brain completely unaffected? Or perhaps the clues are there and have been so all the time, but our methods of investigations were too crude to reveal them?

The search for the structural (neuropathological) basis of schizophrenia has waxed and waned during the last 90 years since Alzheimer, in 1897, described neuronal abnormalities, fibrillary astrocytosis and loss of nerve cells in the cerebral cortex. The early period of initial observation lasted until the 1920s, and was followed by a decade of more critical studies which cast considerable doubts on the validity of previous work. Interest was rekindled only in 1952 when, at the First International Congress of Neuropathology in Rome, the morphological abnormalities of schizophrenia were discussed. However, no consensus was achieved on the significance of often controversial findings. Until very recently, only a few studies were undertaken during the following 30 years.

In many cases, this early work was carried out on small samples of clinically ill-defined, poorly preserved and uncontrolled material. However, several important facts have emerged. The cerebral changes, whether naked eye or histological appearances were slight, inconsistent, and frequently of doubtful validity and controversial interpretation. Some abnormalities resulted from surgical and electroconvulsive treatment or from agonal and post-mortem changes. Neither the site, nor the nature of abnormalities was unequivocally established: argument existed, and still does, about whether the disease process is localized or diffuse, cortical or subcortical, neuronal or glial.

After a long period of relative inactivity, interest in the neuropathology of schizophrenia has been stimulated by two separate developments: one in psychiatry and the other in the neurosciences. First, a more precise clinical definition of schizophrenia has been established: this is an absolute prerequisite for any meaningful neuropathological examination. Moreover, it has been proposed that two biologically distinct syndromes can be distinguished within the nosological entity of schizophrenia. Type I schizophrenia is characterized by positive symptoms, is acute and reversible, responds well to neuroleptics and is not associated with intellectual impairment. In the type II syndrome, the symptomatology is negative, the disease process is chronic and probably irreversible, its response to neuroleptics is poor, and intellectual impairment is sometimes present. The postulated pathology is also different: increased dopamine receptors in type I and cell loss with structural changes in type II (Crow, 1980; 1982). An aetiological classification, with relevance to possible pathology, has also been attempted, distinguishing familial and sporadic cases: in the former group molecular biology might yield the most valuable information, while the sporadic cases should be subjected to neuroimaging and structural investigations; these cases are most likely to have brain damage (Murray *et al.*, 1985).

Second, recent, spectacular progress in the neurosciences has opened up new approaches to the scientific study of schizophrenia: developments in neuroimaging, neurochemistry, neuroanatomy and neuropathology have been particularly relevant to, and instrumental in initiating, new research in a previously barren field.

More than any other single technique, neuroimaging has provided evidence of structural abnormalities in the brain. Although as long ago as 1927 pneumoencephalography revealed dilatation of the cerebral ventricles (Jacobi and Winkler, 1927), it was the invention of the computer tomographic (CT) scan and its application to psychiatric disorders that has created an entirely different atmosphere for morphological research. Johnstone *et al.* (1976) reported, for the first time, cortical atrophy and enlargement of the cerebral ventricles in elderly schizophrenic patients: the cross-sectional area of ventricles was larger than in age-matched controls. This dilatation involved not only the lateral ventricles, but also the third (Dewan *et al.*, 1983) and fourth (Pandurangi *et al.*, 1984) ventricles.

In addition, dilated cortical sulci and fissures (Weinberger *et al.*, 1979b), atrophy of the anterior cerebellar vermis (Weinberger *et al.*, 1979a), reversal of the normal asymmetry of the brain (Luchins *et al.*, 1979), a decrease in density associated with cortical atrophy (Golden *et al.*, 1980), an increased incidence of aqueduct stenosis (Reveley and Reveley, 1983) and occasional cavitation of the septum pellucidum (Lewis and Mezey, 1985) were also observed. There is now a considerable amount of information on the CT scan appearances of schizophrenia and the results have been recently reviewed (Weinberger, 1984; Reveley, 1985; Kovelman and Scheibel, 1986). While the importance of CT scanning is beyond doubt, some of the results are contradictory, and others are not supported by post-mortem evidence. The lack of age and sex-matched controls in many cases has been responsible for the confusing results, but there are many variables which can influence CT scanning, including the type of illness, drug treatment, premorbid state, methodology of scanning and the physiological state of the individual at the time of investigation.

Magnetic resonance imaging (Johnstone *et al.*, 1986; Nasrallah *et al.*, 1986; Buchsbaum and Haier, 1987) and positron emission tomography (Kling *et al.*, 1986; Buchsbaum and Haier, 1987) are newer techniques in neuroimaging which respectively enable more precise localization of finer abnormalities, and an assessment of cerebral metabolism.

The last few decades have also witnessed an unprecedented progress in the methods available to neuropathologists and other neuroscientists in the study of the brain. Electron microscopy, quantitative morphometry, histochemistry and immunocytochemistry have provided a sound, scientific basis for neuropathological examinations. Finer details of brain cells have been revealed, and the precise configuration of synapses established by the electron microscope. Localization of enzymes has clarified the activity of cell organelles, and thus bridged a gap between structure and function. It has been realized that neurotransmitters and neuropeptides are localized in certain areas of the brain, and their overproduction or deficit underlies the development of diseases of hitherto unknown aetiology and pathogenesis. Tracer studies revealed intricate and previously unknown connections between various brain areas. These developments, in turn, prepared the way to new approaches to the neuropathological study of schizophrenia.

The aim of this review is to look critically at more recent work on the neuropathology of schizophrenia without giving a detailed account of earlier research, the results of which have been reviewed in recent years and will not be repeated here (Corsellis, 1976; Stevens, 1982a; Weinberger *et al.*, 1983; Corsellis and Janota, 1985; Kirsch and Weinberger, 1986; Kovelman and Scheibel, 1986; Meltzer, 1987).

NEUROPATHOLOGICAL STUDIES

While CT scanning has opened up entirely new approaches to the study of mental illness, and has become invaluable in the diagnosis of psychiatric disorders, there is little doubt that considerable differences may exist between the appearances observed in living patients on scans and the brain slices examined by neuropathologists after death. Moreover, the ventricular enlargement observed by CT scan in schizophrenia does not necessarily indicate whether it was caused by general atrophy or selective shrinkage of one or more areas.

Since the brain is an immensely complex organ in which cortical areas, nuclear formations, and subcortical centres are intricately interconnected, neuropathological examinations have, for a long time, attempted to identify a particular, defined area as the morphological substrate of schizophrenia. Aided by the newly introduced investigative techniques including quantitative morphometry and immunohistochemistry, it has become possible to assess pathological changes in various parts of the brain, some of which have long been implicated in the pathogenesis of schizophrenia. The evidence emerging from these investigations, sometimes complex and always controversial, will be briefly reviewed.

The temporal lobes

The temporal lobe has been the prime candidate for attempts to find a cerebral structure responsible for schizophrenia and clinical, neurochemical and neuropathological evidence implicating the temporolimbic areas has been recently reviewed (Andreasen, 1986).

In a controlled morphometric study of the limbic system, diencephalon and several parts of the basal ganglia, it was shown that the volumes of the hippocampus, parahippocampal gyrus and amygdala as well as periventricular diencephalic structures and the internal pallidum were reduced in schizophrenic patients (Bogerts, 1984; Bogerts *et al.*, 1985). The authors regarded this shrinkage of the medial part of the temporal lobe as a focal degenerative process of unknown aetiology. Tissue loss from the temporal lobe was convincingly demonstrated in a large post-mortem series, confirming neuroradiological evidence of ventricular enlargement. Of 232 brains, 41 with schizophrenia and 29 with affective disorder were selected; the brains were weighed and coronal slices at the level of the intraventricular foramina assessed. When age, sex and year of birth were taken into account, schizophrenic brains were lighter (by 6%), their lateral ventricles larger, and the parahippocampal cortices significantly thinner (by 11%). The dilatation of the lateral ventricles was particularly severe in the temporal lobe: the cross-section of the inferior horn was larger by 97%, while that of the anterior horn increased only by 19% (Brown *et al.*, 1986).

In a prospective study, 56 schizophrenics were compared with 56 age- and sex-matched controls. In addition, 30 cases of Alzheimer's disease and 30 controls were also evaluated. Brain weight, ventricular size, macroscopical changes and histological alterations were assessed. Data were analysed in the total sample and in a so-called purified group. Cases with focal, diffuse or other 'specific' pathology were excluded from the latter. Brain weight was significantly reduced in both the total and 'purified' samples. Ventricular size, as assessed by the naked eye, was significantly increased in the total sample, but not in the 'purified' group (Bruton *et al.*, 1988). Further attention was paid to the lateral ventricles: the ventricular system was filled with radiopaque medium and x-rayed, and the image of the lateral ventricle was then divided into four compartments in the sagittal plane. The area of the anterior horn and body of the ventricle did not show any significant difference between the schizophrenic and control brains, but the occipital, and particularly the temporal horns, were significantly dilated. These results not only confirm previous findings of larger ventricles in schizophrenia, but also show that the temporal horn is particularly affected (Colter *et al.*, 1988).

In the same series, gliosis, which may be associated with atrophy, has been assessed. While the dementia group had higher ratings for gliosis than controls in the grey matter, the white matter, and in the periventricular regions, the 'purified' schizophrenia group did not show any significant increase in any of these areas (Roberts *et al.*, 1988). This finding is in accordance with earlier observations of the same group. The amount of gliosis was quantitatively measured by computed densitometry of the immunoreactivity of an antibody to glial fibrillary acidic protein (GFAP). No significant differences were found between the schizophrenic and control groups in 20 separate brain areas (Roberts *et al.*, 1985). The conclusion that emerges from these studies is consistent with the hypothesis that the structural changes seen in schizophrenia could result from a developmental anomaly, manifested as hypoplasia of the medial temporal lobe (Roberts *et al.*, 1988).

These gross abnormalities of the temporal lobes have led to further histological and quantitative assessments of this region in order to establish loss of nerve cells and fibre systems. Volumes of the whole hippocampal formation, the entire pyramidal layer and the hippocampal areas CA1/CA2, CA3 and CA4 were reduced, while the alveus, fimbria, prosubiculum and subiculum were not significantly decreased. The absolute number of pyramidal cells was diminished in all four CA areas, but there were no significant changes in the prosubiculum/subiculum, the presubiculum/parasubiculum and in the granular cell layer of the dentate fascia. Pyramidal cell loss was more severe in paranoid patients than in catatonics, but no significant differences were found in any of the subgroups defined by the presence or absence of hereditary factors, duration of illness and age of onset. The mean number of glial cells in the schizophrenic group was not significantly different from controls, thus indicating that nerve cell loss is not necessarily accompanied by an increase of glial cells. This study, although using a relatively small sample (13 schizophrenic patients) without sex-matched controls, has shown significant losses of nerve cells in the hippocampus, a process which is likely to impair its proper functioning (Falkai and Bogerts, 1986).

Another quantitative histological study has revealed a consistently abnormal orientation of pyramidal cells in the brains of 10 chronic schizophrenic patients compared with eight controls. Measurement of over

13 000 cells has indicated significant differences between the two groups: the cellular disarray was most pronounced at the interfaces of CA1/prosubiculum and CA1/CA2. Only smaller degrees of abnormalities were observed in controls, and the authors have stipulated that the severity of histopathological appearances may correspond to a clinical spectrum of symptomatology from normal through borderline state to the severely schizophrenic (Kovelman and Scheibel, 1984).

The abnormal orientations of pyramidal cells in the hippocampus and dendritic irregularities, disrupting the normal synaptic pattern, could represent a congenital, developmental disorder, possibly specific to schizophrenia (Scheibel and Kovelman, 1981). Cytoarchitectural irregularities were also observed in the parahippocampal gyrus and ventral insular cortex, including heterotopic displacement of single groups of nerve cells in the entorhinal region. The disturbed structural arrangement in the second layer of the medial and central fields of entorhinal region may suggest a disturbance of neuronal migration during the later phase of cortical development (Jakob and Beckmann, 1986). That damage to the hippocampus may result in schizophrenia-like symptoms has been known for some time: tumours, infarctions, infections and traumas affecting the medial temporal lobe are frequently associated with symptoms similar to or indistinguishable from those of schizophrenia (Torrey and Peterson, 1974). These studies, however, show for the first time the existence of hippocampal pathology in schizophrenia. The hippocampus is, however, often a target of diverse disease processes from anoxia to Alzheimer's disease, and there is no convincing evidence yet to suggest that the changes observed in the medial temporal lobe are specific for, or indeed could explain the development of schizophrenia.

Frontal lobe

The frontal lobe has long been suspected of being affected in schizophrenia, and decreased metabolic activity (hypofrontality) has been demonstrated by measurements of regional cerebral blood flow (Ingvar and Franzen, 1974). More recent functional investigations implicating the involvement of the frontal lobe, particularly the dorsolateral prefrontal cortex have been reviewed (Morihisa and Weinberger, 1986). In an early quantitative analysis of the cerebral cortex, including frontal areas 10, 4 and 24, a striking loss of neurons was observed, particularly in the deeper cortical layers (Colon, 1972). The author, however, considered this change to be more characteristic of dementia than schizophrenia. In an histological study, using silver impregnation technique to demonstrate neuronal processes, Tatetsu (1964) examined one occipital, one temporal, one parietal and four frontal areas: he observed both axonal and dendritic abnormalities, which could represent the morphological expression of congenital malformation.

Neuronal and glial density, neuron–glia ratios and neuronal size were quantitatively assessed in the prefrontal, anterior cingulate and primary motor cortex of 10 schizophrenics and 10 controls. Neuronal density was significantly lower in layer VI of the prefrontal, layer V of the cingulate and layer III of the motor cortex. The glial density was also lower in most layers of all three cortical areas. However, there were no differences in the neuron–glia ratios and in neuronal size between the schizophrenic and control groups. These findings do not support the presence of neuronal degeneration in the schizophrenic cortex, but suggest that cytoarchitectural variations in the cortex might exist in schizophrenia (Benes *et al.*, 1986).

However, evidence of neuronal abnormalities was observed in the orbitofrontal cortex (area 10 and 11) of eight schizophrenic patients by a combined Golgi and electron microscope study. Golgi's method, which enables an entire neuron with all its processes to be seen, revealed pyramidal cells with abnormal, thickened and sinuous main dendrites, suggesting an increase in the number of spines. In addition there were irregularly arranged, triangular cells with thickened dendrites and increased density of spines in layer VI. Splitting of myelin lamellae and granular, vacuolar and membranous deposits similar to lipofuscin granules were also observed on ultrastructural examination. These appearances were interpreted as possible expressions of altered function (Senitz and Winkelmann, 1981).

Although these findings are undoubtedly interesting, their intepretation requires utmost caution. Increase in the density of dendritic spines should be verified by quantitative assessment and by the use of appropriate controls. Splitting of myelin lamellae is often seen in post-mortem tissue which did not have the benefit of immediate fixation: this change is likely to be an artefact rather than a pathological phenomenon.

Basal ganglia, the diencephalon and mesencephalon

Several structures of the deep grey matter have also been subjected to the scrutiny of quantitative morphometry. In addition to the limbic system, parts of the basal ganglia were measured by planimetry on myelin-stained serial sections from the brains of 13 schizophrenic patients and nine controls. The volume of the internal part of the globus pallidus was significantly reduced and the external part of the pallidum showed only a slight trend towards volume reduction, whereas all the other structures examined, the putamen, caudate, accumbens and the bed nucleus of the stria terminalis did not differ from their control counterparts (Bogerts *et al.*, 1985). These findings were confirmed in a somewhat larger series, using 14 patients and 13 controls (Bogerts, 1984).

Quantitative measurements have also been extended to the diencephalon and mesencephalon. Volume and linear measurements of the entire thalamus, all large thalamic subnuclei and some extrathalamic brain parts (the red nucleus, subthalamic nucleus and internal capsule) were carried out on serial sections. The only significant change was the reduction in the thickness of the periventricular grey matter around the third ventricle (Lesch and Bogerts, 1984). The enlargement of the third ventricle seen on CT scan could thus be caused by the loss of periventricular grey matter in the diencephalon. This plays an important role in the integration of central vegetative functions, and its atrophy may be responsible for some of the vegetative symptoms seen in schizophrenia.

A quantitative study of the melanin-containing dopaminergic neurons of the nigro-striatal system (A9) and the mesolimbic system (A10) was carried out on serial sections from six schizophrenic brains and compared with age-matched controls (nine), Parkinson's disease (five) and post-encephalitic parkinsonism (six). In Parkinson's disease, both cell groups, as expected, displayed considerable neuronal loss, and in the post-encephalitic cases both systems had almost completely disappeared. In schizophrenia, there was a significant decrease in the volume of the nigro-striatal area, with a decrease in the mean volume of glial nuclei. In the mesolimbic region, the mean volume of nerve cells was diminished (Bogerts *et al.*, 1983).

The involvement of the diencephalon and mesencephalon was confirmed in an histological study in which 28 schizophrenic brains were compared with 28 non-schizophrenic patients from the same hospital and with 20 age-matched, non-psychiatric patients from a general hospital. The sections, taken from selected areas, were stained to demonstrate cell bodies, nerve fibres, myelin sheaths, glial fibrils and iron deposits. Although minor changes affecting cellular structures, myelin and axons were observed, the most striking abnormality was the presence of an increased amount of glial fibres (fibrillary gliosis), found chiefly in the periventricular regions of the diencephalon, the periaqueductal structures of the mesencephalon and in the basal forebrain in 17 out of 28 cases. The hypothalamus, midbrain tegmentum and substantia innominata were most often involved. The nature and distribution of this change suggest a previous or low-grade inflammation (Stevens, 1982b). More interestingly, the gliosis is present in those areas which contain major tracts and nuclei of the limbic system. This study confirms and expands earlier findings by Nieto and Escobar (1972), who described gliosis around the third ventricle and cerebral aqueduct in schizophrenic brains. The pathological significance of these observations was not known, and the authors remained cautious in their interpretation.

Interesting and somewhat unexpected lesions were found in the brains of 13 young schizophrenics (average age 38). While the brains appeared to be normal, blocks of tissue taken from the septal nuclei and from the nucleus ansae peduncularis contained swollen, degenerate and fragmented neurons on histological and ultrastructural examination. The abnormal neurons were replete with vacuoles which appeared to contain lipid. The excessive amount of lipid droplets distorted the configuration of the cells, pushed the nuclei to the periphery of the perikaryon, and resulted in occasional fragmentation of cells. In other neurons, lipofuscin granules were abundant, and in yet other cells both lipid droplets and lipofuscin were found. Neurons were affected in both locations in all schizophrenic cases. The author considered these vacuolated cells to be similar to, but not identical with, granulovacuolar degeneration of hippocampal neurons in ageing and Alzheimer's disease, and with the neuronal storage disease of ceroid lipofuscinosis (Averback, 1981). These similarities, however, do not bear close scrutiny, and the possible functional effect of the changes remains a matter of speculation.

The corpus callosum

In a quantitative study of the volume of the thalamus, lentiform nucleus, hippocampus, temporal lobe, brain weight, average corpus callosum width, average cingulate gyrus height and average cortical mantle width of 10 chronic schizophrenic patients, only the corpus callosum was found to be significantly different (i.e. thicker) in the schizophrenic group, compared with psychiatric controls (Rosenthal and Bigelow, 1972). This finding was subsequently considered as a possible expression of interhemispheric dysfunction in schizophrenia, and gave further impetus to the study of the corpus callosum.

The corpus callosum was measured in a blind assessment of 64 brains. The mean corpus callosum midsections of 21 early onset chronic schizophrenic brains were significantly thicker than in eight brains of late onset schizophrenia, in 13 cases of neurological disease, and in 14 patients with other psychiatric diagnoses (Bigelow *et al.*, 1983). An histological analysis of the corpus callosum was then carried out in 18 schizophrenics, 7 manic-depressives, and 11 medical and surgical controls. A quantitative assessment of glial cells and callosal fibres did not reveal any differences between the various groups. Blind ratings of the amount of gliosis (0–4), however, showed more severe gliosis in late onset schizophrenics than in early onset cases or in controls. There was also severe gliosis in the corpus callosum of manic-depressive patients; indeed in the splenium it was more pronounced than in early onset schizophrenics (Nasrallah *et al.*, 1983). More surprisingly, this work also showed that control cases had a thicker corpus callosum than schizophrenic patients, and pathology may thus be associated with thinner rather than thicker callosal connection. This increased gliosis was similar to that found in other parts of the brain (Stevens, 1982b). The shortcomings of this work are obvious; indeed the authors themselves acknowledge two weak points.

First, the brains had been fixed for various lengths of time: diseased brains had been in formalin much longer than controls, and different fixation times could result in subtle structural changes. Second, the average age of the late onset schizophrenic and manic-depressive groups, those with severe gliosis, was much higher (73.3 and 70.4 years, respectively) than the early onset and control groups (65.6 and 64.4 years, respectively).

The increased amount of glial fibrils is more likely to be the consequence of ageing than any disease process.

The corpus callosum has attracted much attention with the realization of asymmetry of function of the cerebral hemispheres in relation to psychopathology. The idea that abnormalities of the corpus callosum may, by causing a deficit of interhemispheric integration, play a central role in producing schizophrenic symptoms is an attractive one, but has not been supported by convincing and unequivocal neuropathological evidence.

Cavity of the septum pellucidum and aqueduct stenosis

Callosal abnormalities, particularly thinning and gliosis, may be associated with ventricular enlargement, frequently found on CT scanning. Another structure, dividing the two lateral ventricles, is the septum pellucidum. While separation of its two leaflets to form a cavity (cavum septi pellucidi) occurs in normal brains, a prevalence of 0.15% of such cavities was found in 22 000 neurological and psychiatric patients. A statistical association between this anomaly and a referral diagnosis of functional psychosis was reported in six cases (Lewis and Mezey, 1985). All were male and had an early history of developmental delay with life-long disturbances of emotion and behaviour before the onset of a schizophrenia-like psychosis in early adulthood. The authors suggested that septal cavities may signal an underlying functional abnormality which could be relevant to the development of psychosis.

Another abnormality of the ventricular system which appears to be associated with psychosis is aqueduct stenosis. Two CT scan studies have demonstrated aqueduct stenosis in four (Reveley and Reveley, 1983) and in five (Roberts *et al.*, 1983) schizophrenic patients. The precise cause of aqueduct stenosis has not been established, since neuropathological examination was not carried out, but the underlying causes are manifold including birth injury, malformations, infections and tumours. It was thought possible that intrinsic brainstem pathology might be responsible both for the aqueduct stenosis and the psychosis, and that aqueduct stenosis in adults carries a significant risk of developing schizophrenia (Roberts *et al.*, 1983).

The brainstem

Histological examination of the brainstem showed that only one of the eight schizophrenic brains had mild perivascular cuffing by mononuclear cells, indicating that brainstem histological abnormalities may not be present in schizophrenia (Hankoff and Peress, 1981). However, an earlier work reported the presence of glial nodules and perivascular infiltration in the trigeminal nuclei in six out of seven schizophrenic brains. The lesions were suggestive of an encephalitic process and a latent and persistent viral infection was thought to affect the function of the adjacent 'integrative' reticular nuclei, leading to schizophreniform psychosis (Fisman, 1975).

The cerebellum

Computed tomographic examinations have revealed cerebellar atrophy, particularly loss of the vermian cortex, in schizophrenic patients (Heath *et al.*, 1979; Weinberger *et al.*, 1979a). This finding has stimulated the neuropathological examination of post-mortem brains. In a morphometric study of the anterior cerebellar vermis of 47 brains from the Yakovlev collection, the area of the vermis was smaller in five out of 12 brains of schizophrenic patients than in control brains (Weinberger *et al.*, 1980). These findings thus confirm the results of previous CT studies. A quantitative analysis of the principal efferent neurons in the cerebellum from the brains of 23 leucotomized schizophrenic patients, 23 leucotomized controls and 37 normal controls did not reveal any significant differences among the three groups in Purkinje cell density in the anterior and posterior vermis and in the hemispheres, in the size of the Purkinje cell or its nucleus in the anterior vermis, and in multipolar cell density in the dentate nucleus (Lohr and Jeste, 1986).

There are various possible reasons for the discrepancy between CT scan and macroscopical findings on one hand and this quantitative histological analysis on the other. The vermis may be grossly atrophied, while Purkinje cell density remains normal; pathological changes may not be apparent on single measurement of density or size; cerebellar atrophy may characterize only a subgroup of schizophrenia; and, finally, the controls may not have been entirely normal.

A stereological light microscope study of eight schizophrenic brains and 12 controls, however, revealed a more complex picture of cerebellar pathology. The number of Purkinje cells per unit line length of the Purkinje cell layer (numerical linear density) was significantly fewer in chronic schizophrenics, although their number per unit area of cortex (numerical areal density) did not differ in the two groups. The difference in numerical densities correlated with the finding that the surface area of Purkinje cell layer per unit volume of cortex (surface density) was greater in schizophrenia. The volume of Purkinje cell layer per unit volume of cortex (volume density) was the same in the two groups. The greater surface density of Purkinje cell layer in schizophrenia is consistent with an 'overdevelopment' of this layer in the vermis. These stereological studies indicate that there are possibly two distinct pathological processes which affect the Purkinje cell layer of the cerebellar vermis in chronic schizophrenia: one is an overdevelopment of this layer and the other a loss of cell bodies of these neurons (Reyes and Gordon, 1981).

Electron microscope studies

From neuropathological studies of schizophrenic brains it was realized that structural changes underlying the development of schizophrenia might be too subtle to be detected by light microscopy. Therefore the search was pursued at ultrastructural level: a few electron microscope investigations have now been carried out. Abnormal, lipid and pigment-laden neurons were commonly found in the septal nuclei and in the nucleus ansae peduncularis (Averback, 1981). Axonal deposits of lipofuscin-like bodies and splitting myelin lamellae were also observed in the orbitofrontal cortex (Senitz and Winkelmann, 1981). The presence of dark, shrunken neurons was thought to be related to the schizophrenic process (Kleshchinov and Oifa, 1986). The metabolic activity of these dark neurons was studied by electron-cytochemistry. Ribonucleoproteins, Mg-activated ATPase and succinate dehydrogenase were all diminished: these findings indicated decreased functional activity of dark, hyperchromatic neurons in schizophrenia (Kleshchinov and Vostrikov, 1985). Synapses in the frontal lobe, supra-optic nucleus, and caudate nucleus displayed a spectrum of changes ranging from mild to severe: from variation in the shape of synaptic vesicles to advanced degeneration of synapses (Anders, 1978).

Area 10 of the frontal lobe was examined ultrastructurally in biopsies obtained from five schizophrenic patients and four controls. The nerve cells contained prominent Golgi complexes, the nerve fibres displayed membranous structures, and many synapses appeared abnormal. Granular and vesicular material was deposited at the axonal–oligodendroglial interface of myelinated fibres; this material was apparently transferred to the inner mesaxon and the outer layers of the myelin sheaths, splitting and destroying them in the process. A large amount of lipofuscin-like material accumulated in oligodendroglial cells. Of these changes, the authors considered the deposition of granular and vesicular material in myelinated nerve fibres as a 'specific' phenomenon, resulting from metabolic disturbances of the neurons, possibly as a consequence of an enzyme defect (Miyakawa *et al.*, 1972).

While electron microscopy could reveal previously hidden details of cells, and thus undoubtedly has an important role in the neuropathological investigation of schizophrenia, the above studies have contributed little to the understanding of this disease. Most studies were carried out on post-mortem brains, and even a short delay after death can cause post-mortem changes which may be, and often are, confused with pathology. Moreover, even biopsy material fixed by immersion into aldehyde will develop fixation artefacts: the dark, shrunken neuron is a well-recognized artefact in biopsy material. It is quite likely that most changes described in these electron microscope studies—split myelin lamellae, abnormal synapses— are post-mortem or fixation artefacts. The only abnormality which could be genuine is the accumulation of granular and vesicular material in nerve cells (Averback, 1981) and nerve fibres (Miyakawa *et al.*, 1972).

CONCLUSIONS

From this brief review of the neuropathology of schizophrenia a rather mixed and somewhat contradictory picture emerges. Clearly, there is no consensus on the constitution of the structural basis of this disease. Are the abnormalities diffuse or localized? Do they affect the cortical ribbon or the deep grey matter? What part of the cortex and which deep grey nuclei are preferentially involved? Are the nerve cells or glial cells the target of the disease process? Are the structural changes cellular at all or, more subtly, subcellular? After so many years, these questions still remain largely unanswered.

What is the reason for this apparent lack of success? The difficulties hindering the neuropathological study of schizophrenia are *nosological*, *methodological* and *conceptual*.

The nosological problems have been largely overcome by the clear definition of disease, but the heterogeneity of this psychosis is still daunting. The proposal of two distinct syndromes, perhaps with different pathologies, has helped to focus the neuropathologist's attention.

The methodological difficulties, although the most numerous, are the easiest to solve. They are both *clinical* and *neuropathological*. Among the former, the lack of proper age and sex-matched controls was a shortcoming which detracted from the value of several studies. Previous treatment, the presence of any other neurological or generalized disease and the agonal state are factors which might all influence the appearance of the brain. These should therefore be recorded, and proper control material should be incorporated. The neuropathological problems relate to the methods by which the brains are examined, and are purely technical. Standardized sampling, fixation, sectioning, staining, stereology, and quantitation are just as important as the use of age- and sex-matched controls. For example, comparison of schizophrenic brains kept for years in fixatives with those fixed for a short time can introduce a variety of errors.

Conceptual difficulties relate to the cause, development and nature of the disease. There is a tendency to study a particular brain area, be this the hippocampus, cerebellar vermis or hypothalamus, as if schizophrenia could be explained as a hippocampal, cerebellar or hypothalamic disease, and not a disease of the brain as a whole. Although it is convenient to assess well-defined areas, this approach may lead to false localization. The nucleus basalis of Meynert, little known until a few years ago, is now blamed for most neurodegenerative disorders, although the assumption of its central role, e.g. in Alzheimer's disease, is quite untenable. Even if there were a true pathogenetic localization, no subcortical nucleus or limbic area can be studied in isolation from its afferent and efferent connections.

Neuronal loss and gliosis are end stage cellular phenomena which indicate previous pathological processes. Neuronal loss in a given area of the brain does not reveal the nature of the disease. The overall pattern of cell loss may be more discriminating, but is unlikely to be pathognomonic. Neuronal loss is an age-related phenomenon, although the possibility exists that the physiological process of neuronal fallout increases abnormally in schizophrenia. It has to be also considered that abnormalities of the surviving neurons may be more instrumental in producing the disease than the neuronal loss itself. In Alzheimer's disease, and particularly in Parkinsons's disease, there is a well recognized pattern of neuronal loss, yet these disorders are diagnosed by other histological hallmarks: plaques and tangles in Alzheimer's, and Lewy bodies in Parkinson's disease.

Gliosis, or more precisely astrocytic fibrillary gliosis, is a response to a variety of local and diffuse disease processes: its presence is not more characteristic of previous infection than of previous hypoxia. A further conceptual pitfall is to view schizophrenia in terms of extremes: a disease without any cerebral damage or one with major, easily recognizable pathology. Since the structural alterations are subtle, immense care should be taken to identify minimal deviation from the normal, to distinguish between artefacts and genuine changes, and to recognize individual variations. Evidence already emerging suggests subtle, yet important changes: abnormal neurons with thickened dendrites and altered pattern of the dendritic tree may result in synaptic abnormalities. This observation would shift the emphasis from histological alterations towards cellular and subcellular changes. It would also explain the lack of spectacular progress in this field, and would open up new avenues of research.

New methods, and their application to the study of psychiatric disorders, have greatly increased our knowledge of Alzheimer's disease and Creutzfeldt-Jakob disease. It is likely that similar progress is going to be made in schizophrenia by the use of electron microscopy, immunocytochemistry, binding studies, and developmental studies.

Recent results give ground for cautious optimism. Schizophrenia is, after all, not the graveyard, merely the scientific battleground of neuropathologists.

REFERENCES

Alzheimer A. (1897). Beitrage zur pathologischen Anatomie der Hirnrinde und zur anatomischen Grundlage einiger Psychosen. *Monatschrift für Psychiatrie und Neurologie*; 2: 82–120.

Anders V. N. (1978). Ultrastructural features of cerebral synapses in schizophrenic patients. *Zhurnal Nevropatologii i Psikhiatrii*; 78: 1065–70.

Andreasen N. C. (1986). (Ed.) Is schizophrenia a limbic disease? In: *Can Schizophrenia Be Localized in the Brain?* pp. 39–52. Washington: American Psychiatric Press.

Averback P. (1981). Structural lesions of the brain in young schizophrenics. *Canadian Journal of Neurological Sciences*; 8: 73–6.

Benes F. M., Davidson J., Bird E. D. (1986). Quantitative cytoarchitectural studies of the cerebral cortex of schizophrenics. *Archives of General Psychiatry*; 43: 31–5.

Bogerts B. (1984). Zur Neuropathologie der Schizophrenien. *Fortschritte der Neurologie und Psychiatrie*; 52: 428–37.

Bogerts B., Hantsch J., Herzer M. (1983). A morphometric study of the dopamine-containing cell groups in the mesencephalon of the normals, Parkinson patients and schizophrenics. *Biological Psychiatry*; 18: 951–69.

Bogerts B., Meertz E., Schonfeldt-Bausch R. (1985). Basal ganglia and limbic system pathology in schizophrenia. A morphometric study of brain volume and shrinkage. *Archives of General Psychiatry*; **42**: 784–91.

Brown R., Colter N., Corsellis J. A. *et al.* (1986). Postmortem evidence of structural brain changes in schizophrenia. Differences in brain weight, temporal horn area, and parahippocampal gyrus compared with affective disorder. *Archives of General Psychiatry*; **43**: 36–42.

Bruton C. J., Colter N., Johnstone E. C., Roberts G. W., Brown R., Crow T. J. (1988). Neuropathology of schizophrenia: I. Global assessment. *Neuropathology and Applied Neurobiology*; (in press).

Buschbaum M. S., Haier R. J. (1987). Functional and anatomical brain imaging: impact on schizophrenia research. *Schizophrenia Bulletin*; **13**: 115–32.

Colon E. J. (1972). Quantitative cytoarchitectonics of the human cerebral cortex in schizophrenic dementia. *Acta Neuropathologica* (Berlin); **20**: 1–10.

Colter N., Bruton C. J., Johnstone E. C., Roberts G. W., Brown R., Crow T. J. (1988). Neuropathology of schizophrenia: II. Lateral ventricle. *Neuropathology and Applied Neurobiology*; (in press).

Corsellis J. A. N. (1976). Psychoses of obscure pathology. In: *Greenfield's Neuropathology* (Blackwood W., Corsellis J. A. N., eds.), pp. 903–15. London: Edward Arnold.

Corsellis J. A. N., Janota I. (1985). Neuropathology in relation to psychiatry. In: *The Scientific Foundations of Psychiatry. Handbook of Psychiatry, vol 5* (Shepherd M., ed.), pp. 206–21. Cambridge: Cambridge University Press.

Crow T. J. (1980). Molecular pathology of schizophrenia: more than one disease process? *British Medical Journal*; **280**: 66–8.

Crow T. J. (1982). The biology of schizophrenia. *Experientia*; **38**: 1275–82.

Dewan M. J., Pandurangi A. K., Lee S. H. *et al.* (1983). Central brain morphology in chronic schizophrenic patients: a controlled CT study. *Biological Psychiatry*; **18**: 1133–40.

Falkai P., Bogerts B. (1986). Cell loss in the hippocampus of schizophrenics. *European Archives of Psychiatry and Neurological Sciences*; **236**: 154–61.

Fisman M. (1975). The brainstem in psychosis. *British Journal of Psychiatry*; **126**: 414–22.

Golden C. J., Graber B., Coffman J., Berg R. A., Newlin D. B., Bloch S. (1980). Brain density deficits in chronic schizophrenia. *Psychiatry Research*; **3**: 179–84.

Hankoff L. D., Peress N. S. (1981). Neuropathology of the brainstem in psychiatric disorders. *Biological Psychiatry*; **16**: 945–52.

Heath R., Franklin D., Shraberg D. (1979). Gross pathology of the cerebellum in patients diagnosed and treated as functional psychiatric disorders. *Journal of Nervous and Mental Disease*; **167**: 585–92.

Ingvar D. H., Franzen G. (1974). Distribution of cerebral activity in chronic schizophrenia. *Lancet*; **ii**: 1484–86.

Jacobi W., Winkler H. (1927). Encephalographische Studien an chronisch Schizophrenen. *Archiv für Pyschiatrie und Nervenkrankheiten*; **81**: 299–332.

Jakob W., Beckmann H. (1986). Prenatal developmental disturbances in the limbic allocortex in schizophrenics. *Journal of Neural Transmission*; **65**: 303–26.

Johnstone E. C., Crow T. J., Frith C. D., Husband J., Kreel L. (1976). Cerebral ventricular size and cognitive impairment in chronic schizophrenia. *Lancet*; **ii**: 924–6.

Johnstone E. C., Crow T. J., Macmillan J. F., Owens D. G., Bydder G. M.,

Steiner R. E. (1986). A magnetic resonance study of early schizophrenia. *Journal of Neurology, Neurosurgery and Psychiatry*; **49**: 136–9.

Kirsch D. G., Weinberger D. R. (1986). Anatomical neuropathology in schizophrenia: post-mortem findings. In: *The Neurology of Schizophrenia* (Nasrallah H. A., Weinberger D. R., eds.), pp. 325–428. Amsterdam: Elsevier.

Kleshchinov V. N., Oifa A. I. (1986). Ultrastructure of neurons with initial signs of ischemization in schizophrenia. *Zhurnal Nevropatologii i Psikhiatrii*; **86**: 1037–41.

Kleshchinov V. N., Vostrikov V. M. (1985). Electron-cytochemical characteristics of hyperchromic neurons in schizophrenia. *Zhurnal Nevropatologii i Psikhiatrii*; **85**: 989–92.

Kling A. S., Metter E. J., Riege W. H., Kuhl D. E. (1986). Comparison of PET measurement of local brain glucose metabolism and CAT measurement of brain atrophy in chronic schizophrenia and depression. *American Journal of Psychiatry*; **143**: 175–80.

Kovelman J. A., Scheibel A. B. (1984). A neurohistological correlate of schizophrenia. *Biological Psychiatry*; **19**: 1601–21.

Kovelman J. A., Scheibel A. B. (1986). Biological substrates of schizophrenia. *Acta Neurologica Scandinavica*; **73**: 1–32.

Lesch A., Bogerts B. (1984). The diencephalon in schizophrenia: evidence for reduced thickness of the periventricular grey matter. *European Archives of Psychiatry and Neurological Sciences*; **234**: 212–19.

Lewis S. W., Mezey G. C. (1985). Clinical correlates of septum pellucidum cavities: an unusual association with psychosis. *Psychological Medicine*; **15**: 43–54.

Lohr J. B., Jeste D. V. (1986). Cerebellar pathology in schizophrenia? A neuronometric study. *Biological Psychiatry*; **21**: 865–75.

Luchins D. J., Weinberger D. R., Wyatt R. J. (1979). Anomalous lateralization associated with a milder form of schizophrenia. *American Journal of Psychiatry*; **136**: 1598–9.

Meltzer H. Y. (1987). Biological studies in schizophrenia. *Schizophrenia Bulletin*; **13**: 77–111.

Miyakawa T., Sumiyoshi S., Deshimaru M. *et al.* (1972). Electron microscopic study on schizophrenia. Mechanism of pathological changes. *Acta Neuropathologica (Berlin)*; **20**: 67–77.

Morihisa J. M., Weinberger D. R. (1986). Is schizophrenia a frontal lobe disease? An organizing theory of relevant anatomy and physiology. In: *Can Schizophrenia Be Localized in the Brain?* (Andreasen N. C., ed.), pp. 19–36. Washington: American Psychiatric Press.

Murray R. M., Lewis S. W., Reveley A. M. (1985). Towards an aetiological classification of schizophrenia. *Lancet*; **i**: 1023–6.

Nasrallah H. A., Andreasen N. C., Coffman J. A. *et al.* (1986). A controlled magnetic resonance imaging study of corpus callosum thickness in schizophrenia. *Biological Psychiatry*; **21**: 274–82.

Nasrallah H. A., McCalley-Whitters M., Bigelow L. B., Rauscher F. P. (1983). A histological study of the corpus callosum in schizophrenia. *Psychiatry Research*; **8**: 251–60.

Nieto D., Escobar A. (1972). Major psychoses. In: *Pathology of the Nervous System, vol 3* (Minckler J., ed.), pp. 2654–5. New York: McGraw-Hill.

Pandurangi A. K., Dewan M. J., Lee S. H. *et al.* (1984). The ventricular system in chronic schizophrenic patients. A controlled computed tomography study. *British Journal of Psychiatry*; 144: 172–6.

Reveley M. A. (1985). CT scans in schizophrenia. *British Journal of Psychiatry*; 146: 367–71.

Reveley A. M., Reveley M. A. (1983). Aqueduct stenosis and schizophrenia. *Journal of Neurology, Neurosurgery and Psychiatry*; 46: 18–22.

Reyes M. G., Gordon A. (1981). Cerebellar vermis in schizophrenia. *Lancet*; i: 700–1.

Roberts G. W., Bruton C. J., Colter N., Johnstone E. C., Brown R., Crow T. J. (1988). Neuropathology of schizophrenia: III. Gliosis. *Neuropathology and Applied Neurobiology*; (in press).

Roberts G. W., Colter N., Lofthouse R., Bogerts B., Zech M., Crow T. J. (1985). Gliosis in schizophrenia: a survey. *Biological Psychiatry*; 21: 1043–50.

Roberts J. K. A., Trimble M. R., Robertson M. (1983). Schizophrenic psychosis associated with aqueduct stenosis in adults. *Journal of Neurology, Neurosurgery and Psychiatry*; 46: 892–8.

Scheibel A. B., Kovelman J. A. (1981). Disorientation of the hippocampal pyramidal cell and its processes in the schizophrenic patients. *Biological Psychiatry*; 16: 101–2.

Senitz D., Winkelmann E. (1981). Über morphologische Befunde in der orbito-frontalen Rinde bei Menschen mit schizophrenen Psychosen. Eine Golgi- und eine elektronenoptische Studie. *Psychiatrie, Neurologie und medizinische Psychologie* (Leipz); 33: 1–9.

Stevens J. R. (1982a). The neuropathology of schizophrenia. *Psychological Medicine*; 12: 695–700.

Stevens J. R. (1982b). Neuropathology of schizophrenia. *Archives of General Psychiatry*; 39: 1131–9.

Tatetsu S. (1964). A contribution to the morphological background of schizophrenia. With special reference to the finding in the telencephalon. *Acta Neuropathologica (Berlin)*; 3: 558–71.

Torrey E. F., Peterson M. R. (1974). Schizophrenia and the limbic system. *Lancet*; ii: 942–6.

Weinberger D. R. (1984). Computed tomography (CT) findings in schizophrenia: speculation on the meaning of it all. *Journal of Psychiatric Research*; 18: 477–90.

Weinberger D. R., Kleinman J. E., Luchins D. J., Bigelow L. B., Wyatt R. J. (1980). Cerebellar pathology in schizophrenia: a controlled post mortem study. *American Journal of Psychiatry*; 137: 359–61.

Weinberger D. R., Torrey E. F., Neophytides A. N., Wyatt R. J. (1979b). Structural abnormalities in the cerebral cortex of chronic schizophrenic patients. *Archives of General Psychiatry*; 36: 935–9.

Weinberger D. R., Torrey E. F., Wyatt R. J. (1979a). Cerebellar atrophy in chronic schizophrenia. *Lancet*; ii: 718–19.

Weinberger D. R., Wagner R. L., Wyatt R. J. (1983). Neuropathological studies of schizophrenia: a selective review. *Schizophrenia Bulletin*; 9: 193–212.

8 The neurodevelopmental origins of dementia praecox

ROBIN M. MURRAY, SHÔN W. LEWIS, MICHAEL J. OWEN
and ALICE FOERSTER

It is one of the dogmas of psychiatry that schizophrenia is a deteriorating condition. Kraepelin distinguished between dementia praecox and manic-depressive psychosis in large part on this basis, and recently several groups have taken deteriorated outcome as the major validating criterion for choosing the most satisfactory operational definition of schizophrenia (Brockington et al., 1978; Stephens et al., 1982).

The last decade has provided increasing testimony to the occurrence of brain disease in schizophrenia, and not unnaturally in view of the above, this has generally been interpreted as evidence of an adult onset neuro-degenerative disorder. For example, Stevens (1982), commenting on evidence of abnormal computed tomographic (CT) brain scans in schizo-phrenics, suggested that such findings could indicate 'that a progressive destructive process occurs in this disease.' Woods and Wolf (1983) went further and postulated 'a progressive, genetically determined, system-specific neuronal degeneration as the underlying disorder (manifest radio-logically as ventricular enlargement and behaviourally as schizophrenia).' Crow (1987) pointed to schizophrenic patients 'who progress to a defect state of intellectual impairment with the hallmarks (e.g. temporal disorien-tation) of a dementing illness.'

But how much support is there for the idea that schizophrenia is a progressive disorder? Noting that until the 1930s about 60% of all patients hospitalized for schizophrenia remained there indefinitely, Wing (1987) stated that it is generally assumed that 'the patients who remained in hospital or who died there were clinically severely impaired and this gave rise to the concept of deterioration (deficit increasing with time)'. His own studies of institutionalized schizophrenics did not support this view (Wing and Brown, 1970); indeed, the most severely impaired patients actually improved slightly over an 8-year period. Manfred Bleuler (1974) who followed patients for over 20 years considered that after 5 years patients tended to improve. He stated: 'The old assumption that schizophrenia is usually a progressive disease which leads to an increasingly severe dementia, is incorrect'. The long-term studies of Ciompi (1980; 1983) also convinced him that when outcome is poor, it depends on adverse psychosocial influences rather than a progressive organic process.

Thus, it seems that in the industrialized West the majority of schizophrenic patients do not follow an inevitable deteriorating course to a 'defect' state. Such an outcome is even more unusual in the Third World (Sartorius *et al.*, 1986).

DO STRUCTURAL AND COGNITIVE ABNORMALITIES ANTEDATE ONSET?

If progressive clinical deterioration is not the rule in schizophrenia, what is the significance and natural history of more quantifiable characteristics, such as structural abnormalities and intellectual impairment? When CT first demonstrated enlarged ventricles and cortical sulcal widening in chronic schizophrenics (Johnstone *et al.*, 1976; Weinberger *et al.*, 1979), these were widely regarded as the end stage of progressive changes. However, these findings have since been shown not to correlate with the length of illness or treatment, and follow-up studies over periods up to 8 years show no significant deterioration in the CT appearances; furthermore, they are present in young patients and at the initial stages of the illness (reviewed by Shelton and Weinberger, 1986; Reveley and Trimble, 1987). Thus, enlargement of cerebral ventricles and cortical sulci must either result from an acute process at the very onset of the illness or else antedate it. The study by Weinberger *et al.* (1980), which evaluated premorbid social adjustment retrospectively in 51 chronic schizophrenics, suggested the latter; those patients with CT scan evidence of brain atrophy had significantly poorer premorbid adjustment. Similar findings were reported by Williams *et al.* (1985) and Pearlson *et al.* (1985).

One of the best replicated clinical correlates of these CT abnormalities is cognitive impairment (Owens *et al.*, 1985; Goldberg and Weinberger, 1986). Again this has generally been assumed to be a consequence of deterioration. Indeed, Johnstone *et al.* (1978) termed it 'the dementia of dementia praecox'. But if the structural abnormalities do not change, one must ask whether the cognitive deficits really are progressive. The evidence is less persuasive than is sometimes assumed. For example Klonoff *et al.* (1970) re-examined 66 chronic patients after a period of 8 years and reported that Wechsler Adult Intelligence Scores (WAIS) scores actually improved. Smith (1964) also found an increase in IQ when schizophrenic patients were retested after an average of 8.4 years. Furthermore, Albee *et al.* (1963) found no deterioration in the IQs of schizophrenics between the highest premorbid test results and those carried out during the illness, and after up to 10 years on chronic wards.

There is considerable evidence that the premorbid IQ scores of schizophrenics obtained during childhood, adolescence, and early adult life are lower than the scores of their siblings and peers (reviewed by Aylward *et al.*, 1984). For example, Lane and Albee (1970) reported that preschizophrenics had lower childhood IQ scores than controls; this was particularly so for those who developed chronic disease. One of the most persuasive studies is that of Offord and Cross (1971), who found that the average results of IQ tests given during elementary and junior high school to 26 schizophrenics, to their siblings and to a control group were 86.6; 94.3; and 98.5 respectively. These authors concluded that the schizophrenics comprised two groups, one with and one without childhood intellectual impairment, and stated 'certain preschizophrenics have childhood symptomatology suggestive of possible minimal brain damage'.

Negative symptoms have also been associated with CT scan abnormalities in some studies (Andreasen *et al.*, 1982; Pearlson *et al.*, 1984), and when prominent at the start of illness these also indicate a poor outcome (Kolakowska *et al.*, 1985). Indeed, Wing (1987) stated 'the negative impairment tends to antedate florid onset and is a better predictor of social outcome than the florid symptoms'.

Thus, it seems that a number of abnormalities particularly associated with chronic schizophrenia, and which Crow (1980) has brought together as type II schizophrenia, do not necessarily occur as part of an ongoing process of deterioration. In many patients they appear to predate the onset of delusions, hallucinations, and thought disorder; when present they tend to be associated with poor outcome. Crow (1985) has recently added abnormal movements to the type II syndrome, and such signs also seem frequently to precede the onset of positive symptoms (O'Neil and Robins, 1958; Ricks and Nameche, 1966; Watt, 1974), and portend a serious outcome (Manschreck, 1986).

OBSTETRIC COMPLICATIONS

We must therefore ask ourselves whether there are factors of possible aetiological significance that occur before the onset of delusions and hallucinations, and which are associated with the characteristics just described. Several American studies showed that schizophrenics had suffered more obstetric complications than their siblings (Lane and Albee, 1966; Pollack *et al.*, 1966; Woerner *et al.*, 1973). As these studies were based on retrospective reports, some doubt persisted because of the possibility of biased recall. However, the issue was settled by a series of Scandinavian studies which relied on records made at the time of birth (McNeil and Kaij, 1978; Jacobsen and Kinney, 1980; Parnas *et al.*, 1982); once again preschizophrenics suffered more obstetric complications than control subjects. Most recently, Lewis and Murray (1987) reported that a history of obstetric complications (defined as any abnormal event in pregnancy and labour known to increase mortality risk) was recorded in 17% of 207 schizophrenic patients versus only 8% of 748 other psychiatric patients.

These findings have been reviewed elsewhere (McNeil and Kaij, 1978; Lewis and Murray, 1987; Lewis *et al.*, 1988). Generally, birth complications have been more frequently implicated than pregnancy complications, but this may be because they are more easily identified—anoxia, long labour and prematurity have attracted most blame.

Several groups have now examined the relationship between obstetric complications and adult ventricular size. These have been reviewed elsewhere (Murray *et al.*, 1985; Lewis *et al.*, 1988), but are summarized in Table 8.1. It can be seen that, with the exception of Nimgaonkar *et al.*

Table 8.1 Obstetric complications and adult CT scan findings

Authors	Sample	Conclusions
Roberts (1980)	341 psychiatric patients	Excess of 'early traumatic events' in those with abnormal scans
Reveley *et al.* (1984)	21 MZ schizophrenics	OCs confined to those with no FH
	18 MZ normals	OCs associated with increased VBR
Pearlson *et al.* (1985)	19 schizophrenics	VBR increased in 4 with early developmental abnormality
Turner *et al.* (1986)	30 schizophrenics	VBR correlated positively with 'early physical trauma'
DeLisi *et al.* (1986)	26 schizophrenics and 10 well siblings	OC or head injury in 7/8 schizophrenics with increased VBR
Schulsinger *et al.* (1984)	35 offspring of schizophrenics	VBR negatively correlated with length and weight at birth and positively with prematurity
Lewis and Murray (1987)	236 psychiatric patients	Scan abnormal in 42% of those with definite OCs, 20% of those with possible OCs, and 13% of those with no OCs
Owens *et al.* (1988)	61 schizophrenics	OCs associated with a combination of increased VBR and widening of cortical sulci and fissures
Nimgaonkar *et al.* (1988)	52 schizophrenics	No relationship between OCs and any CT variables

FH = Family history; MZ = monozygotic; OCs = obstetric complications; VBR = ventricular brain ratio or ventricular size.

(1988), all the studies have found that obstetric complications or early developmental hazards are predictive of increased ventricular size in adult life. This relationship has been reported in normal twins and psychiatric patients in general, but particularly in schizophrenia; among schizophrenics, the relationship has been especially noticeable in those without a family history of serious psychiatric disorder but also holds in those with such a history.

Owen *et al.* (1988) reported that schizophrenics with a history of obstetric complications were more likely to have a combination of increased ventricular size and widening of the cortical sulci and fissures than patients without such a history. In addition, the former had more abnormal premorbid personalities, and presented at a significantly younger age (Lewis *et al.*, 1988). Other studies also report an earlier onset for those patients with a history of obstetric complications (McNeil and Kaij, 1978; Pearlson *et al.*, 1985). This pathoplastic effect of early developmental injury is also suggested by Green *et al.* (1987), who examined the occurrence of minor physical anomalies of the type associated with insults to the fetus (e.g. curved fingers, furrowed tongue, low seated ears). These are found more frequently in schizophrenics (Guy *et al.*, 1983), but Green *et al.* (1987) showed that such anomalies are particularly common in those who present before age 18. These investigators concluded that early onset patients were especially likely to have a central nervous system compromised by injury during pregnancy.

THE NEUROPATHOLOGICAL CONSEQUENCES OF EARLY BRAIN INJURY

Several lines of evidence suggest that a relationship exists between early brain insults, CT scan abnormalities, and schizophrenia. It therefore becomes important to establish the causal mechanisms that are implicated. Immature vascular autoregulation renders the fragile blood vessels in the neonatal brain very sensitive to acute hypoxia and hypercapnia. Haemorrhage from the germinal matrices in the frontal, temporal and occipital horns of the lateral ventricles is the typical pattern in the preterm infant. Recent CT and ultrasound studies have shown that infants born at less than 35 weeks' gestation are particularly susceptible to intra- or periventricular haemorrhage (*Lancet*, 1984; DeVries *et al.*, 1985). The latter can cause periventricular necrosis, followed by the appearance of small cavities which later reabsorb, causing a compensatory enlargement of lateral and third ventricles.

Asphyxia in the full-term infant produces a different, although overlapping, pattern of damage, which is the single most important perinatal cause of neurological morbidity (Kreusser and Volpe, 1984). The most vulnerable regions are the cerebral cortex, especially the hippocampus and subiculum, as well as some diencephalic structures. In the cerebral neocortex, the relative avascular 'border zones' that exist between the anterior and middle, and the middle and posterior, cerebral arteries are especially susceptible to damage; these regions become frontal and parieto-temporal association areas in the adult. The depths of the cortical sulci are also relatively avascular, and ischaemic injury here leads to later sulcal widening.

Hypoxic-ischaemic injury does not necessarily arise during labour. Volpe (1981) noted that more than two-thirds of such cases had a normal delivery; in these cases asphyxia during pregnancy occurred secondary to placental insufficiency, maternal disease or antepartum haemorrhage. In less than one-quarter of cases was the asphyxia confined to the perinatal period. Recent studies (Taylor *et al.*, 1985; Nelson and Ellenberg, 1986) have further emphasized the role of pregnancy, rather than of birth complications, in the development of cerebral palsy, developmental delays and behaviour disorders.

It is clear that a variety of complications in pregnancy and at birth can produce radiological appearances reminiscent of those reported in schizophrenia: enlarged lateral and third ventricles, widening of cortical sulci, and regions of frontal hypodensity (Leichty *et al.*, 1983; DeVries *et al.*, 1985).

What are the cellular consequences of such injury? It is easy to see how obstetric complications might impair neuronal proliferation and migration, as well as the multiplication and ramification of axons. However, in the last decade it has become apparent that the immature brain consists of a large excess of neurons, and that, during development, a large proportion of these neurons die and the axons of the remainder thin out. This process eliminates early errors of connection (Janowsky and Finlay, 1986).

Neurons compete with one another to form terminations on target sites, and if the process of innervation is interrupted, neuronal death occurs. Conversely, the destruction of an area of neurons reduces the fall-out rate of adjacent neurons. A rationalization of axonal connections also occurs. In the early brain, axons project diffusely, forming connections which would be wholly abnormal in the mature brain. In normal early development, axon retraction occurs both simultaneously and subsequently to neuronal fall-out. Like neuronal fall-out, axon retraction can be halted if adjacent areas are injured. The peak period of neuronal fall-out in the midbrain and brainstem is during the second trimester, while in the neocortex it begins in the last month or two of gestation (Finlay and Slattery, 1983). Axon retraction in the neocortex starts at the same time, and continues into early childhood.

Thus, early brain damage can slow or even prevent the disappearance of particular neurons and their axons. In this way, immature patterns of cells and their projections will persist, and early anomalous connections will continue to exist in the otherwise mature nervous system.

NEUROPSYCHOLOGICAL CONSEQUENCES OF EARLY BRAIN DAMAGE

It is well known that spasticity, mental retardation and epilepsy may follow early brain damage. But what of those more subtle signs of brain dysfunction—'soft' neurological signs and neuropsychological deficits—which occur with increased frequency in schizophrenia (Rochford *et al.*, 1970; Tucker *et al.*, 1975; Quitkin *et al.*, 1976; Woods *et al.*, 1986)? Hadders-Algra *et al.* (1986) identified a series of 6-year-old children with minor neurological dysfunctions, and noted an over-representation of infants who had been premature or suffered retardation of intrauterine growth. Astbury *et al.* (1987) found that 18 out of 57 very low birth weight children were neuropsychologically deviant at 5 years. These children had lower IQ scores, increased 'soft' signs with more tremor and poorer balance and coordination, and showed more behavioural disturbance.

Dunn *et al.* (1985) followed up a cohort of low birth weight infants to age 13 years. They had a striking excess over controls of abnormalities in coordination, tone, and reflexes, as well as lower IQs, poorer educational achievement, more abnormal EEGs and more psychiatric disturbance.

Neuroimaging studies have shown that preterm and asphyxiated term infants are not only especially likely to show ventricular enlargement and other sequelae of periventricular haemorrhage, but that the changes persist at follow-up. These radiologically deviant children also have an increased risk of neurodevelopmental and behavioural abnormalities (Leichty *et al.*, 1983; DeVries *et al.*, 1985; Stewart *et al.*, 1987). Because the techniques have only recently been introduced, few such children have been followed after the age of 4–5 years (Stewart, A, personal communication; Weisglas-Kuperus *et al.*, 1987). However, Bergstrom *et al.* (1984) carried out CT scans on 101 children with minor neurodevelopmental disorders, and in whom perinatal damage was the commonest known cause. Twenty-five per cent had abnormal scans, with ventricular enlargement the commonest finding.

NEUROPATHOLOGY

Two planimetric studies of post-mortem schizophrenic brains have shown volume decreases in regions which are known to be susceptible to hypoxic–ischaemic injury. Brown *et al.* (1986) found that, compared with patients with affective disorder, the brains of schizophrenic patients were 6% lighter, with lateral ventricles that were enlarged, especially the temporal horns. The parahippocampal cortex was also significantly thinner. Bogerts *et al.* (1985) reported volume losses in periventricular and limbic structures in schizophrenia, and commented particularly on atrophy of the hippocampus and parahippocampal gyrus. An earlier study by the same group (Lesch and Bogerts, 1984) noted a reduction in the thickness of the periventricular grey matter around the third ventricle; this could be a long-term consequence of periventricular haemorrhage. Indeed, Bogerts (1988) considers it likely that these changes 'reflect dysplasias due to prenatal developmental disturbances, or that they are caused by perinatal pathological influences such as obstetric birth complications'.

Recently, histopathological studies have been reported. Jakob and Beckmann (1986) examined an autopsy series of 64 schizophrenics. Twenty-two had grossly normal brains, while the remaining 42 had abnormal gross configuration or abnormal sulcogyral pattern of the temporal lobe. Twenty of this latter group showed cytoarchitectural abnormalities, with fewer neurons in certain layers throughout the cortex, and misplaced and irregularly arranged cells throughout the parahippocampal gyrus. Abnormalities were found particularly in patients with early onset. These authors suggested that the findings are a consequence of a 'disturbance of neuronal migration in a later phase of cortical development'.

Kovelman and Scheibel (1984) reported neuronal disorganization with disruption particularly in the anterior and middle portions of the hippocampus. They found misplaced (heterotopic) neurons and alterations in the pyramidal cell orientation together with dendrite irregularities. They considered that 'these structural changes originate during a relatively early stage of nervous system development, most probably during the period of cell migration into the hippocampal primordinum.' Falkai and Bogerts (1986) reported that volumes of the hippocampal formation, the whole pyramidal band and the hippocampal segments (CA1, CA2, CA3 and CA4) were decreased in 13 schizophrenics compared with 11 age-matched controls. The absolute number of pyramidal cells was also diminished. Again, these findings are highly suggestive of an early developmental anomaly. Furthermore, none of these quantitative studies found evidence of gliosis in the affected regions, supporting the contention that the abnormalities originate in the immature brain, where only a transient gliosis occurs in response to injury.

GENE-ENVIRONMENT INTERACTION

The hippocampus, and particularly its pyramidal cells, is particularly vulnerable to hypoxic–ischaemic injury (Spector, 1965), and such damage has profound biochemical and behavioural consequences. For example, exposure of newborn rats to 25 minutes of anoxia produces an increase in the concentration of beta-adrenergic receptors in the hippocampus in the mature rat; hyperactivity during early development is succeeded by defects on complex learning tasks and decreased response to amphetamine, possibly through altered modulation of the dopaminergic system (Hershkowitz *et al.*, 1983).

It is evident that the vast majority of individuals who suffer complications in the uterus or at birth do not develop schizophrenia. Obstetric insult does not necessarily equate with cerebral damage; a history of obstetric complications is given by a proportion of perfectly normal individuals. Moreover, Lewis and Murray (1987) noted that such a history was obtained in 8% of non-schizophrenic psychiatric patients. Why should some develop schizophrenia? The answer to this presumably lies in the interaction of at least three variables: the site of the lesion incurred, the timing of the injury, and the presence or otherwise of a genetic predisposition to schizophrenia. Whether the last is a necessary condition for the later emergence of schizophrenia, or whether in many cases the injury itself can be a sufficient cause, is not yet clear. Certainly individuals at increased genetic risk of schizophrenia who suffer obstetric complications are more likely to develop the illness than their siblings who do not, thus showing that the two risk factors can operate in an additive fashion (Parnas *et al.*, 1982; Schulsinger *et al.*, 1984). Those psychiatric geneticists prepared to concede a role to obstetric complications have generally considered them as one of a number of non-specific environmental stressors (e.g. Gottesman and Shields, 1977). This seems most unlikely in view of the neuropathological evidence reviewed above.

As early as 1970, Mednick proposed that 'pregnancy and birth complication factors lead to defective hippocampal functioning which in combination with genetic and environmental factors could conceivably play a vital predispositional role in at least some forms of schizophrenia'. He further suggested that these forms are the early onset, poor prognosis and poor premorbid types. Venables (1973) also thought that schizophrenia might be secondary to hippocampal dysfunction, while Schmajuk (1987), reviewing the consequences of early hippocampal lesions in animals, considered that such animals 'may provide an adequate model for several symptoms of schizophrenia'. It is premature to conclude that the hippocampus is the sole and certain site of pathology, but hippocampal damage may well play a significant role. In addition, it provides a useful model of how genetic and early environmental factors may interact.

In a review of the genetic control of hippocampal development, Nowakowski (1987) described inbred strains of mice with abnormal hippocampal pyramidal cells which either migrate too far (NZB/BINJ strain) or not far enough (H1d, dreher, and reeler strains). As a result of this genetic defect in migration, axons from normal cells either fail to find their target pyramidal cells (because they are not where they ought to be) or have to follow an abnormal pathway to do so. Similarly, outgoing axons from the abnormally positioned cells either terminate on the wrong cells, or have to follow an unusual trajectory to reach their target. Thus the heterotypically positioned neurons become interconnected with other neurons in the developing brain in abnormal ways. The hippocampus becomes substantially 'rewired' with alterations both in neuron number and cytoarchitecture. Furthermore, this modified neuronal circuitry extends elsewhere, with degeneration of cells at other sites on which hippocampal axons normally terminate.

Nowakowski (1987) pointed out that environmental hazards which cause defects in neuronal migration have been implicated in a variety of human neurodevelopmental pathologies, including the effect of mercury poisoning, the fetal alcohol syndrome and mental retardation. Perhaps certain individuals predisposed to schizophrenia might inherit a pattern of neuronal migration in the hippocampus which renders it especially vulnerable to hypoxic–ischaemic and other damage in fetal or neonatal life.

BRAIN MATURATION AND THE ONSET OF SCHIZOPHRENIA

Thus obstetric complications can cause areas of neuronal necrosis, with apparent cerebral atrophy (though in reality dysplasia) and ventricular enlargement, but also substantially altered neuronal circuitry. It is not difficult to see how this could impair intellectual and personality development and cause neurological 'soft' signs, i.e. the negative syndrome which both antedates onset and predicts poor outcome in schizophrenia (Fig. 8.1).

But why should pre- or perinatal hazards produce the positive clinical syndrome of schizophrenia some two decades later? Certainly, a long latent period between early cerebral insults and their sequelae has been noted in neurological disorders such as epilepsy and dyskinesias (Taylor, 1985; Hadders-Algra et al., 1986). The explanation is likely to arise from the fact that brain development continues throughout childhood, and indeed, profound morphological rearrangements take place during adolescence.

As a rule, new neurons are not added postnatally, though even here there is an exception, interestingly enough in the hippocampus—neurogenesis of hippocampal granule cells appears to add substantially to the existing population of cells in the dentate gyrus in adolescent and adult life (Bayer et al., 1982; Janowski and Finlay, 1986). Myelination also continues into adolescence, and there is some evidence that the deleterious effects of damaged neurons may not become apparent until they myelinate. Thus, experimental lesions made before birth in the dorsolateral prefrontal cortex (DPFC) of primates do not cause obvious behavioural disturbances for several years (Goldman-Rakic et al., 1983). It is only when the DPFC myelinates and takes over functions from other frontal areas that behavioural abnormality becomes apparent. Weinberger (1987) has suggested that such a lesion in the DPFC may underlie schizophrenia.

The regressive processes of cell death, retraction of axonal processes and, above all, of synaptic elimination also continue into adult life. Indeed, cognitive and behavioural spurts during development may result from competitive elimination of excess cortico-cortical axons. And, Goldman-Rakic (1987) states 'adult competence may be achieved in part through synapse elimination, which occurs throughout the entire period of adoles-

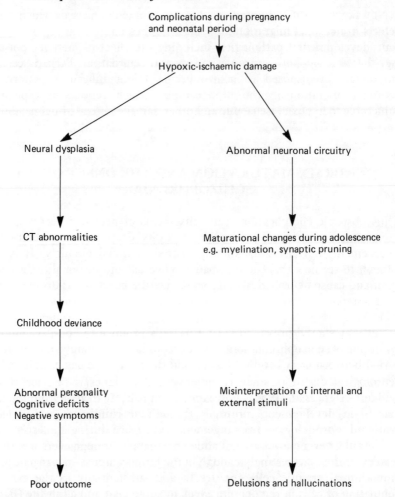

Fig. 8.1   *A model of the neurodevelopmental origins of type I and type II schizophrenia*

cence and young adulthood, and thus mature capacity may depend not on the accretion of synapses but rather on their elimination'.

Feinberg (1982/3) has suggested that synaptic elimination in adolescence may underlie the emergence of psychotic symptoms. He implied that a defective process occurs in a previously normal brain, and indeed this is conceivable. In the present context, it may be that the normal process of adolescent synaptic pruning lays bare a 'faulty wired' system of neuronal interconnections. For example, neurons bordering an early lesion and which would normally degenerate, may be spared, and thus allow the persistence of immature diffuse connections projecting to inappropriate structures or even to the wrong side of the brain.

It is, of course, the interconnecting neuronal circuits which are responsible for the ability of the brain to process the huge variety of stimuli which present to it. Could it be that that aberrant neuronal circuitry underlies the aberrations of information processing seen in schizophrenia, and that the resultant misinterpretation of internal and external stimuli generates positive symptoms such as delusions and hallucinations? Experimental lesions of the hippocampus in animals produce behaviour which has often been described as reflecting the failure of processes such as 'inhibition' and 'gating', and as generating 'interference' (*see* Gray, 1982 for review). Kovelman and Scheibel (1984) claim that the hippocampus may act as a cognitive map modelling internal 'caricatures' of the outside world. If this is so, a synaptically idiosyncratic hippocampus would provide an unreliable basis for interpreting the physical and social environment.

CONCLUSIONS

It is our contention that schizophrenia is a heterogeneous condition with a number of different causes. We suggest that the type which most closely approximates to Kraepelin's original description of dementia praecox is a consequence of abnormal neuronal development during pregnancy and the neonatal period. It is associated with increased ventricular size or cortical atrophy (or more correctly dysplasia), and disordered cytoarchitecture, particularly in the hippocampus and associated cortex. Hypoxic–ischaemic insult is a major known cause of the early damage, but certain individuals may inherit patterns of neuronal migration which make them especially vulnerable to this and other hazards of fetal and neonatal life.

Our model proposes that neural dysplasia results in premorbid cognitive deficits and abnormal personality, as well as negative symptoms and abnormal CT scans, features which augur a poor prognosis (the type II syndrome). Then, brain maturational changes in adolescence, possibly myelination or synaptic pruning, reveal immature neuronal circuitry; this renders individuals susceptible to misinterpretations of stimuli and the consequent early onset of hallucinations and delusions (the type I syndrome). Brain maturation in adolescence and early life is therefore responsible for the development of positive symptoms, but also for the fact that once this phase of maturation ends, schizophrenia is rarely a progressive deteriorating condition.

The neurodevelopmental hypothesis can, of course, account for only a minority of those psychotic cases currently termed schizophrenic. It is, for example, extremely unlikely that neurodevelopmental deviance can help to explain the excess of women over the age of 35 years who present with schizophrenia. We are conscious also that much of the evidence we have quoted in support of the hypothesis is of a circumstantial nature. However, its credibility should soon be evaluated, since many of the predictions of this model are readily testable.

REFERENCES

Albee G., Lane E. A., Corcoran C., Werneke A. (1963). Childhood and intercurrent intellectual performance of adult schizophrenics. *Journal of Consulting Psychology*; 27: 364–6.

Andreasen N. C., Olsen S. A., Dennent J. W., Smith A. R. (1982). Ventricular enlargement in schizophrenia: relationship to positive and negative symptoms. *American Journal of Psychiatry*; 139: 297–302.

Astbury J., Orgill A. Bajuk B. (1987). Relationship between two year behaviour and neurodevelopmental outcome at five years of very low birthweight survivors. *Developmental Medicine and Child Neurology*; 29: 370–9.

Aylward E., Walker E., Bettes B. (1984). Intelligence in schizophrenia: meta-analysis of the research. *Schizophrenia Bulletin*; 10: 430–59.

Bayer S. A., Yackel J. W., Puri P. S. (1982). Neurons in the rat dentate gyrus granular layer substantially increase during juvenile and adult life. *Science*; 216: 890–2.

Bergstrom K., Bille B., Rasmussen F. (1984). Computed tomography of the brain in children with minor neurodevelopmental disorders. *Neuropaedriatica*; 15: 115–19.

Bleuler M. (1974). The longterm course of the schizophrenic psychoses. *Psychological Medicine*; 4: 244–54.

Bogerts, B., Meertz E., Schonfeldt-Bausch, R. (1985). Basal ganglia and limbic system pathology in schizophrenia. *Archives of General Psychiatry*; 42: 784–91

Bogerts B. (1988). Limbic and paralimbic pathology in schizophrenia: interaction with age and stress related factors. *Proceedings of the First International Congress of Schizophrenia Research* (Schulz S. C., Tamminga T. A., eds.) New York: OUP.

Brockington I. F., Kendell R. E., Leff J. P. (1978). Definitions of schizophrenia: concordance and prediction of outcome. *Psychological Medicine*; 8: 387–98.

Brown R., Colter M., Corsellis J. A. N. *et al.* (1986). Postmortem evidence of structural brain changes in schizophrenia. *Archives of General Psychiatry*; 43: 36–42.

Ciompi L. (1980). The natural history of schizophrenia in the long term. *British Journal of Psychiatry*; 136: 413–20.

Ciompi L. (1983). Schizophrenic deterioration. *British Journal of Psychiatry*; 143: 79–80.

Crow T. (1980). Molecular pathology of schizophrenia; more than one disease process? *British Medical Journal*; 280: 66–8.

Crow T. J. (1985). The two-syndrome concept: origins and current status. *Schizophrenia Bulletin*; 11: 471–85.

Crow T. J. (1987). (ed.) Introduction. In: *Recurrent and Chronic Psychoses. British Medical Bulletin*; 43: 479–83.

DeLisi L. E., Goldin L. R., Hamovit V. R. *et al.* (1986) A family study of the association of increased ventricular size with schizophrenia. *Archives of General Psychiatry*: 43: 148–53.

DeVries L. S., Dubowitz L. M. S., Dubowitz V. *et al.* (1985). Predictive value of cranial ultrasound in the newborn baby. *Lancet*; ii: 137–40.

Dunn H. G., Crichton J. W., Robertson A. M., McBurney K., Grussau R. V. E., Penford P. S. (1985). Evolution of minimal brain dysfunctions to the age of 12 to 15 years. In: *The Sequelae of Low Birth Weight; The Vancouver Study* (Dunn H. G., ed.). Oxford: Blackwell Scientific.

Falkai P., Bogerts B. (1986). Cell loss in the hippocampus of schizophrenics. *European Archives of Psychiatry and Neurological Sciences*; **236**: 154–61.

Feinberg I. (1982/3). Schizophrenia: caused by a fault in programmed synaptic elimination during adolescence? *Journal of Psychiatric Research*; **17**: 319–34.

Finlay B. L., Slattery M. (1983). Local differences in the amount of early cell death in neocortex predict adult local specialisations. *Science*; **219**: 1349–51.

Goldberg T. E., Weinberger D. R. (1986). Methodological issues in the neuropsychological approach to schizophrenia. In: *The Neurology of Schizophrenia*. (Nasrallah H. A., Weinberger, D. R., eds.), pp. 141–156. Amsterdam: Elsevier.

Goldman-Rakic P. S. (1987). Development of cortical circuitry and cognitive function. *Child Development*; **58**: 601–22.

Goldman-Rakic P. S., Isseroff A., Schwartz M. L., Bugbee N. M. (1983). The neurobiology of cognitive development. In: *Handbook of Child Psychology vol. II*. (Haith M. M., Campos J. J., eds.), pp. 281–344. New York: John Wiley.

Gottesman I. I., Shields, J. (1977). Obstetric complications and twin studies of schizophrenia. *Schizophrenia Bulletin*; **3**: 351–4.

Gray J. A. (1982). *The Neuropsychology of Anxiety*. Oxford: Oxford University Press.

Green M. F., Satz P., Soper H. V., Kharabi F. (1987). Relationship between physical anomalies and age of onset of schizophrenia. *American Journal of Psychiatry*; **144**: 666–7.

Guy J. D., Majorski L. V., Wallace C. J., Guy M. P. (1983). The incidence of minor physical anomalies in adult male schizophrenics. *Schizophrenia Bulletin*; **9**: 571–82.

Hadders-Algra M., Touwen B. C., Huisjes H. J. (1986). Neurologically deviant newborns: neurological and behavioural development at the age of six years. *Developmental Medicine and Child Neurology*; **28**: 569–78.

Hershkowitz M., Grimm V. E., Speiser Z. (1983). The effects of postnatal anoxia on behaviour and on the muscarinic and beta-adrenergic receptors in the hippocampus of the developing rat. *Developmental Brain Research*; **7**: 147–55.

Jacobsen, B., Kinney D. K. (1980). Perinatal complications in adopted and non-adopted schizophrenics and controls. *Acta Psychiatrica Scandinavica*; **62** (suppl. 285): 338–45.

Janowsky, J. S., Finlay B. L. (1986). The outcome of perinatal brain damage: the role of normal neuron loss and axon retraction. *Developmental Medicine and Child Neurology*; **28**: 375–89.

Jakob H., Beckmann H. (1986). Prenatal developmental disturbances in the limbic allocortex in schizophrenics. *Journal of Neural Transmission*; **65**: 303–26.

Johnstone E. C., Crow T. J., Frith C. D., Husband J., Kreel, L. (1976). Cerebral ventricular size and cognitive impairment in chronic schizophrenia. *Lancet*; **ii**: 924–6.

Johnstone E. C., Crow T. J., Frith C. D., Stevens M., Kreel L., Husband, J. F. (1978). The dementia of dementia praecox. *Acta Psychiatrica Scandinavica*; **57**: 305–24.

Klonoff H., Fibiger C., Hutton G. H. (1970). Neuropsychological patterns in chronic schizophrenia. *Journal of Nervous and Mental Disease*; **150**: 291–300.

Kolakowska T., Williams A. O., Ardern M. *et al.* (1985). Schizophrenia with good and poor outcome. Early clinical features, response to neuroleptics and signs of organic dysfunction. *British Journal of Psychiatry*; **146**: 229–39.

Kovelman J. A., Scheibel A. B. (1984). A neurohistological correlate of schizophrenia. *Biological Psychiatry*; **19**: 1601–21.

Kreusser K. L, Volpe J. L. (1984). The neurological outcome of perinatal asphyxia. In: *Early Brain Damage vol. 1*. (Alueli C. R., Finger S., eds.), pp. 151–187. New York: Academic Press.

Lancet (1984). Ischaemia and haemorrhage in the premature brain ii: 847–8.

Lane E., Albee G. (1966). Comparative birth weights of schizophrenics and their siblings. *Journal of Psychology*; **64**: 227–31.

Lane E., Albee G. (1970). Intellectual antecedents of schizophrenia. In: *Life History Research in Psychopathology* (Roff, M., Ricks, D. F. eds.), pp. 189–207. Minneapolis: University of Minnesota Press.

Leichty E. A., Gilmor R. L., Bryson C. Q., Bull M. J. (1983). Outcome of high-risk neonates with ventriculomegaly. *Developmental Medicine and Child Neurology*; **25**: 162–8.

Lesch A., Bogerts B. (1984). The diencephalon in schizophrenia; evidence for reduced thickness of the periventricular grey matter. *European Archives of Psychiatry and Neurological Sciences*; **234**: 212–19.

Lewis S. W., Murray R. M. (1987). Obstetric complications, neurodevelopmental deviance and risk of schizophrenia. *Journal of Psychiatric Research* (in press).

Lewis S. W., Murray R. M., Owen M. (1988). Obstetric complications in schizophrenia. Methodology amd mechanisms. *Proceedings of the First International Congress of Schizophrenia Research*. Schulz S. C., Tamminga T. A. (eds.) New York: OUP.

McNeil T. F., Kaij L. (1978). Obstetric factors in the development of schizophrenia: complications in the births of preschizophrenics and in reproductions by schizophrenic parents. In: *The Nature of Schizophrenia. New Approaches to Research and Treatment* (Wynne L. C., Cromwell R. L., Matthyssee S., eds.), pp. 401–29. New York: Wiley.

Manschreck T. C. (1986). Motor abnormalities in schizophrenia. In: *The Neurology of Schizophrenia. vol. 1.* (Nasrallah H. A., Weinberger D. R., eds.), pp. 65–96. Amsterdam: Elsevier.

Mednick S. A. (1970). Breakdown in individuals at high risk for schizophrenia. *Mental Hygiene*; **54**: 50–63.

Murray R. M., Lewis S. W., Reveley A. M. (1985). Towards an aetiological classification of schizophrenia. *Lancet*; **i**: 1023–6.

Nelson K. B., Ellenberg J. H. (1986). Antecedents of cerebral palsy: multivariate analysis of risk. *New England Journal of Medicine*; **315**: 81–6.

Nimgaonkar V. L., Wesscly S., Murray R. M. (1988). Prevalence of familiality, obstetric complications and structural brain damage in schizophrenic patients. *Psychological Medicine*; (in press).

Nowakowski R. S. (1987). Basic concepts of CNS development. *Child Development*; **58**: 568–95.

Offord D., Cross L. (1971). Adult schizophrenia with scholastic failure or low I. Q. in childhood. *Archives of General Psychiatry*; **24**: 431–6.

O'Neil P., Robins L. (1958). Childhood patterns predictive of adult schizophrenia. *American Journal of Psychiatry*; **115**: 385–91.

Owen M. J., Lewis S. W., Murray R. M. (1988). Obstetric complications and cerebral abnormalities in schizophrenia. *Psychological Medicine*; (in press).

Owens D. G. C., Johnstone E. C., Crow T. J., Frith C. D., Jagoe J. R., Kreel L.

(1985). Lateral ventricular size in schizophrenia: relationship to the disease process and its clinical manifestations. *Psychological Medicine*; 15: 27–41.

Parnas J., Schulsinger F., Teasdale T. W., Schulsinger H., Feldman P. M., Mednick S. A. (1982). Perinatal complications and clinical outcome within the schizophrenia spectrum. *British Journal of Psychiatry*; 140: 416–20.

Pearlson G. D., Garbacz D. J., Breakey W. R., Ahn H. S., De Paulo, J. R. (1984). Lateral ventricular enlargement associated with persistent unemployment and negative symptoms in both schizophrenia and bipolar disorder. *Psychiatric Research*; 12: 1–9.

Pearlson G. D., Garbacz D. J., Moberg P. J., Ahn, H. S., De Paulo, J. R. (1985). Symptomatic familial, perinatal and social correlates of computerised axial tomography (CAT) changes in schizophrenics and bipolars. *Journal of Nervous and Mental Disease*; 173: 42–50.

Pollack M., Woerner M., Goodman W., Greenberg I. (1966). Childhood development patterns of hospitalised adult schizophrenic and non-schizophrenic patients and their siblings. *American Journal of Orthopsychiatry*; 36: 510–17.

Quitkin F., Rifkin A., Klein D. F. (1976). Neurologic soft signs in schizophrenia and character disorders. *Archives of General Psychiatry*; 33: 845–53.

Reveley A. M., Reveley M. A., Murray R. M. (1964). Cerebral ventricular enlargement in non-genetic schizophrenia. *British Journal of Psychiatry*: 144: 89–93.

Reveley M. A., Trimble M. R. (1987). Application of imaging techniques. In: *Recurrent and Chronic Psychoses* (Crow T. J., ed.). *British Medical Bulletin*; 43: 616–33.

Ricks D., Nameche G. (1966). Symptoms, sacrifice and schizophrenia. *Mental Hygiene*; 50: 541–51.

Roberts J. (1980). *The Use of the CT Scanner in Psychiatry*. MPhil Thesis. University of London.

Rochford J., Detre T., Tucker G. *et al.* (1970). Neuropsychological impairments in functional psychiatric diseases. *Archives of General Psychiatry*; 22: 114–19.

Sartorius N., Jablensky A., Korten A. *et al.* (1986). Early manifestations and first-contact incidence of schizophrenia in different cultures. *Psychological Medicine*; 16: 909–28.

Schmajuk N. A. (1987). Animal models for schizophrenia: the hippocampally lesioned animal. *Schizophrenia Bulletin*; 13: 317–27.

Schulsinger F., Parnas J., Petersen E. T. *et al.* (1984). Cerebral ventricular size in the offspring of schizophrenic mothers. *Archives of General Psychiatry*; 41: 602–6.

Shelton R. C., Weinberger D. R. (1986). X-ray computerised tomography studies in schizophrenia: a review and synthesis. In: *The Neurology of Schizophrenia* (Nasrallah H. A., Weinberger D. R., eds.), pp. 207–50. Amsterdam: Elsevier.

Smith A. (1964). Mental deterioration in chronic schizophrenia. *Nervous and Mental Diseases*; 139: 479–87.

Spector R. G. (1965). Enzyme chemistry of anoxic brain injury. In: *Neurohisto-chemistry* (Adams W. M., ed.) pp. 547–57. New York: Elsevier.

Stephens J. H., Astrup C., Carpenter W. T., Shaffer J. W., Goldberg J. A. (1982). A comparison of nine systems to diagnose schizophrenia. *Psychiatric Research*; 6: 127–43.

Stevens J. R. (1982). Neuropathology of schizophrenia. *Archives of General Psychiatry*; 39: 1131–9.

Stewart A. L., Reynolds E. O. R., Hope P. L. *et al.* (1987). Probability of neurodevelopmental disorders estimated from ultrasound appearance of brains of very preterm infants. *Developmental Medicine and Child Neurology*; 29: 3–11.

Taylor D. C. (1975). Factors influencing the occurrence of schizophrenia-like psychosis in patients with temporal lobe epilepsy. *Psychological Medicine*; 5: 249–54.

Taylor D. J., Howie P. W., Davidson J., Davidson D., Drillien, C. M. (1985). Do pregnancy complications contribute to neurodevelopmental disability? *Lancet*; i: 713–16.

Tucker G. J., Campion E. W., Silberfarb P. M. (1975). Sensorimotor functions and cognitive disturbance in psychiatric patients. *American Journal of Psychiatry*; 132: 17–21.

Turner S. W., Toone B. K., Brett-Jones R. (1986). CT scan changes in early schizophrenia. *Psychiological Medicine*; 16: 219–25.

Venables P. H. (1973). Input regulation and psychopatholgy. In: *Psychopathology* (Hammer M., Salzinger K., Sutton S., eds.), pp. 261–84. New York: Wiley.

Volpé J. J. (1981). *Neurology of the Newborn*. Philadelphia: Saunders.

Watts N. (1974). Childhood and adolescent routes to schizophrenia. In: *Life History Research in Psychopathology*, Vol 3. (Ricks D., Thomas A., Roff M., eds.), pp. 194–211. Minneapolis: University of Minnesota Press.

Weinberger D. R. (1987). Implications of normal brain development for the pathogenesis of schizophrenia. *Archives of General Psychiatry*; 44: 660–9.

Weinberger D. R., Cannon-Spoor E., Potkin S. G., Wyatt R. J. (1980). Poor premorbid adjustment and CT scan abnormalities in chronic schizophrenia. *American Journal of Psychiatry*; 137: 1410–13.

Weinberger D. R., Torrey E. F., Neophytides A. N., Wyatt R. J. (1979). Lateral cerebral ventricular enlargement in chronic schizophrenia. *Archives of General Psychiatry*; 36: 735–9.

Weisglas-Kuperus N., Vleman-Vleeschdragger M., Baerts W. (1987). Ventricular haemorrhages and hypoxic-ischaemic lesions in proteons infants. *Developmental Medicine and Child Neurology*; 29: 623–9.

Williams A. O., Reveley M. A., Kolakowska T., Ardern M., Mandelbrote B. M. (1985). Schizophrenia with good and poor outcome II: Cerebral ventricular size and its clinical significance. *British Journal of Psychiatry*; 146: 239–46.

Wing J. K. (1987). Has the outcome of schizophrenia changed? *Recurrent and Chronic Psychoses* (Crow, T. J., ed.). *British Medical Bulletin*; 43: 741–53.

Wing J. K., Brown G. W. (1970). *Institutionalism and Schizophrenia*. Cambridge: Cambridge University Press.

Woerner M. G., Pollack M., Klein D. F. (1973). Pregnancy and birth complications in psychiatric patients. *Acta Psychiatrica Scandinavica*; 49: 712–21.

Woods B. T., Kinney D. K., Jurgelun-Todd D. (1986). Neurologic abnormalities in schizophrenic patients and their families. *Archives of General Psychiatry*; 43: 657–63.

Woods B. T., Wolf J. (1983). A reconsideration of the relation of ventricular enlargement to duration of illness in schizophrenia. *American Journal of Psychiatry*; 140: 1564–70.

9 *Genetics of schizophrenia*

PETER MCGUFFIN

The existence of a genetic contribution to schizophrenia is one of the best established aetiological facts concerning this puzzling disorder. Seymour Kety has pointed out that even if schizophrenia is a myth (which it was once fashionable to proclaim) then it is surely 'a myth with a genetic basis'. But, sadly, there have been no recent major breakthroughs in the area. Instead, as Gottesman *et al.* (1987) have described it, the past decade has been one of 'modest gains while playing for time'. In part, these modest gains have consisted of a rediscovery and burnishing of older truths.

First among these is the idea put forward more than 60 years ago by Luxenburger (quoted in Jaspers, 1962) that, for the purposes of genetic research, 'schizophrenia' is no more than a working hypothesis. A major modification has been the tightening of the hypothesis by the introduction of operational definitions. Nevertheless, the application of these new definitions in family, twin and adoption strategies, has led to the familiar conclusion that schizophrenia, whatever it may be, is something with a substantially genetic basis. Other old truths concern heterogeneity. Despite the obvious clinical differences in phenomena, course and outcome between patients huddled under the same diagnostic umbrella, we are able to achieve no better insight into aetiology by creating further subgroupings. Furthermore, although the separation is not always clear cut between this population and those under the other Kraepelinian umbrella of manic depressive insanity, the 'two entities' provide the best shelters available.

Elsewhere in genetic research, meanwhile, real and obvious growth has taken place. Advances in quantitative methods have led to the development of an essentially new branch of genetics, genetic epidemiology (Morton, 1982), concerned with the transmission of common diseases. Even more spectacular has been the flourishing of the new genetics of recombinant DNA which, since its beginnings about 15 years ago, has thrown the science of genetics into a sustained phase of 'revolution' (Kuhn, 1962). In this chapter, I will attempt to describe how these new developments can be, and are being, applied to the problems posed by 'schizophrenia', but we should perhaps first start on the more familiar territory of old truths, and consider the ways in which we define the phenotype.

DEFINITION OF THE PHENOTYPE

Many different operational definitions of schizophrenia have now been introduced, with considerable variation in their constituent items, their combinatorial rules and the amount of emphasis placed upon cross-sectional signs and symptoms as against longitudinal aspects (e.g. *see* Berner *et al.*, 1983). There is no doubt that operationalism enhances reliability and improves the repeatability of research findings, but it is difficult to endorse this approach unreservedly as 'the remedy for diagnostic confusion' (Kendell, 1975), since reliability alone does not ensure validity. Thus competing definitions of schizophrenia must be regarded purely as alternative conventions and it is specious to argue that one is 'more correct' than the others. At best we can judge which definition is most useful for some particular purpose. In recognition of this, various authors have produced outcome studies using a number of operational definitions in an attempt to decide which has the greatest predictive utility (e.g. Brockington *et al.*, 1978; Bland and Orne, 1979; Stephens *et al.*, 1982). Similarly, it might be asked which definition best predicts response to treatment (Murray and Murphy, 1978) or best delineates a disorder with high heritability (Robins and Guze, 1970; Gottesman and Shields, 1972).

Surprisingly, some investigators have not taken such a coolly detached view of the new explicit definitions of schizophrenia and their potential shortcomings. They have, in effect, attempted to put the cart before the horse by asking whether schizophrenia is 'really' a familial condition once it has been defined using a new, more explicit, convention. Adopting this stance, Pope *et al.* (1983) reported that none of the total of 199 first degree relatives of schizophrenics had an illness fulfilling the Diagnostic and Statistical Manual of Mental Disorders (DSM-III) criteria for schizophrenia. Shortly afterwards, Abrams and Taylor (1983) applied their own criteria to a sample of 128 first degree relatives of schizophrenics, and claimed that only two were affected, giving a lifetime prevalence of 1.6%. It is noteworthy that neither group had any control sample or independent estimate of the frequency of operationally defined schizophrenia in the general population. It is known from other investigations that applying a restrictive operationally explicit definition of schizophrenia in studies of people who are not relatives of schizophrenics, may yield prevalence figures as low as 0.2% (Kendler *et al.*, 1985). If this is so, the sample size required to reject confidently the hypothesis that schizophrenia is familial would need to be substantially higher than that in either of the two 'negative' studies.

It seems likely that a combination of methods of low sensitivity (e.g. relying upon case records rather than carrying out interviews), insufficient sample size, and restrictive criteria conspired to produce falsely negative results. This is supported by the results of other investigations where more satisfactory methods have been used with larger sample sizes. Thus, studies using a modification of the criteria of Feighner *et al.* (1972); or the

DSM-III definition (American Psychiatric Association, 1980), have amply confirmed that schizophrenia does not cease to be a familial condition once it has been operationally defined (Guze *et al.*, 1983; Baron *et al.*, 1985; Kendler *et al.*, 1985).

Confirmation of familiality is not, of course, equivalent to confirmation of a genetic contribution. For many, the most compelling evidence that schizophrenia has an important genetic component comes from adoption studies. The best known adoption work predated the widespread use of operational research definitions. Although a large study is currently in progress in Finland, this has so far been the subject only of preliminary reports (Tienari *et al.*, 1981) and there are, at present, no published results from studies where the use of operational criteria was built into the original design. Fortunately, an updating of the Danish adoption material collected by Kety *et al.* (1976) provided adequate clinical detail for a 'recycling' exercise (Kendler and Gruenberg, 1984). A DSM-III definition of 'schizophrenia spectrum' was applied, consisting of schizophrenia plus schizotypal personality disorder. This proved to be much more restrictive than the original researchers' concept of 'spectrum disorder', so that only 19 out of 34 original index adoptees retained a spectrum diagnosis, while a further five were diagnosed as having schizophreniform disorder. However, this also had the result of increasing the apparent magnitude of the genetic effect, since 22% of 69 biological relatives of index adoptees now received a diagnosis of spectrum disorder compared with 2% of 137 control relatives, a much more striking difference than had been found earlier in the absence of explicit criteria.

Recent reports based on twin data also suggest that DSM-III and some of its predecessors perform well when judged by the ability to define a highly heritable syndrome (McGuffin *et al.*, 1984; Farmer *et al.*, 1987b). Again there are, as yet, no purpose-built data sets, but one of the larger series from the pre-operational era, that of Gottesman and Shields (1972), has proved sufficiently robust to stand recycling. Using detailed case abstracts, researchers applied a variety of operational diagnostic criteria to a series consisting of 22 monozygotic (MZ) twin pairs (26 probands), and 32 dizygotic (DZ) pairs (34 probands). The investigators worked blind in that abstracts were identified only by a code number so that the zygosity and identity of the co-twin were unknown. Some of the important results are given in Table 9.1. Assuming a multifactorial liability/threshold model, as described below, heritabilities were calculated for each definition. Heritability is the proportion of phenotypic variance contributed by additive gene effects. As we can see, DSM-III and its predecessors, the criteria of Feighner *et al.* (1972) and Spitzer *et al.* (1978), defined highly heritable syndromes. Against expectation, a definition based on Schneider's (1959) first rank symptoms gave a heritability estimate of zero. All the definitions listed in Table 9.1 prove to have very satisfactory inter-rater reliability, and indeed Schneider's definition on this occasion gave perfect agreement between two blind raters.

Table 9.1 Twin concordance and heritabilities of operational criteria for schizophrenia (data from McGuffin *et al.*, 1984; Farmer *et al.*, 1986)

Criteria	MZ twins No. probands	Con-cordance (%)	r	DZ twins No. probands	Con-cordance (%)	r	h^2 (±s.e.)
Spitzer *et al.*(1978)							
Broad	22	45.5	0.86	23	8.7	0.45	0.83±0.4
Narrow	19	52.6	0.90	21	9.5	0.48	0.83±0.4
Feighner *et al.*(1972)							
Probable	21	47.6	0.88	22	9.1	0.46	0.84±0.4
Definite	19	47.4	0.88	18	11.1	0.52	0.72±0.4
DSM-III(APA, 1980)	21	47.6	0.87	21	9.5	0.44	0.85±0.4
Schneider(1959)	9	22.2	0.74	4	50.0	0.91	0±0.49

MZ: monozygotic; DZ: dizygotic
Concordance is expressed probandwise
r = correlation in liability
h^2 = approximate broad heritability

For all this, the study has a number of shortcomings. The original abstracts were not specifically designed for this type of investigation, and this may have affected the Schneider definition most adversely. Although by rating conservatively the blind raters obtained excellent agreement, it is likely that this was at the expense of sensitivity. Also, the sample size was comparatively small, resulting in high standard errors for the heritability estimate, and since the study is in effect a repeated reassessment of the same subjects, the estimates of heritability cannot be assumed to be independent. There is hence no simple way of testing whether they differ significantly. Nevertheless, it is reasonable to suggest that the North American criteria all provide quite satisfactory definitions of the phenotype, whereas Schneider's first rank symptoms, from the point of view of genetic studies, may be less useful.

It has been pointed out (Kendell, 1982) that outcome validity and aetiological validity are not necessarily one and the same. However, it is of interest that the definitions which proved most useful in the genetic study of twins, i.e. DSM-III, Feighner's criteria and Spitzer's research diagnostic criteria, also appear to be among the most effective in predicting outcome (Brockington *et al.*, 1978; Helzer *et al.*, 1981; Stephens *et al.*, 1982).

Despite these encouraging results, it would be a mistake to assume that the work of defining the phenotype at the clinical level is done. To their credit, the authors of DSM-III have not rested, but continue to revise their definitions of psychiatric disorders in the light of new knowledge (American Psychiatric Association, 1987). Farmer *et al.* (1987b) in their twin studies scrutinizing the validity of the DSM-III definition of schizophrenia have adopted an exploratory stance, attempting to find ways in which the criteria can be 'improved' by repositioning the boundaries of the disorder. To do this, they examined the effect of subsuming other disorders within the category of 'schizophrenia'. Here they again followed the precedent of Gottesman and Shields (1972), who showed that an over-strict or an over-generous definition of schizophrenia lowered the MZ/DZ concordance ratio, and that the 'most genetic' definition was found in the middle of the spectrum. The findings of Farmer *et al.* (1987b) were similar (Table 9.2). Broadening the definition of schizophrenia to include not only schizotypal personality disorder and atypical psychosis, but also affective disorder with mood incongruent delusions, produced the highest MZ/DZ concordance ratio. However, further broadening to include any axis 1 diagnosis resulted in a marked lowering of the ratio. Again it is important

Table 9.2 Combinations of DSM-III categories and the effect on MZ/DZ concordance ratio (data from Farmer *et al.*, 1987b)

Diagnoses	MZ twins		DZ twins		MZ/DZ
	No. of probands	*Proband-wise con-cordance (%)*	*No. of probands*	*Proband-wise con-cordance (%)*	*Con-cordance ratio*
Schizophrenia	21	47.6	21	9.5	5.01
Schizophrenia + schizotypal persona-lity + atypical psy-chosis + affective disorder with mood incongruent de-lusions	22	59.1	26	7.7	7.68
Schizophrenia plus any axis 1 diagnosis	27	70.4	34	29.4	2.39

MZ: monozygotic; DZ: dizygotic

to bear in mind the limitations of method, and to point out that the MZ/ DZ concordance ratio is a comparatively crude index. Nevertheless, there is an implication that, from the genetic standpoint, the DSM-III definition of the phenotype could be 'improved' by being slightly broadened.

THE TRANSMISSION OF SCHIZOPHRENIA: MODELS AND MUDDLES

We have by now accumulated an impressive body of evidence to convince all but the most determined sceptic that genes make an important contribution to the aetiology of schizophrenia. We have therefore arrived, painstakingly and with some soul-searching, at a conclusion which, in the first quarter of this century, was simply assumed to be true without much question. But, given that there is a genetic basis for schizophrenia, it becomes important to discover *how* it is transmitted since we are clearly not dealing with a simple Mendelian disorder.

The natural, most straightforward place to start, is with single gene models. These have an intuitive appeal to most clinicians, once they have allowed themselves to accept the notion of incomplete penetrance. Penetrance, the probability of manifesting a trait given a particular genotype, is necessarily either zero or one for Mendelian dominant and recessive traits (Table 9.3). However, it is important to emphasize that dominance and recessivity are properties of the phenotype *and are not intrinsic to the underlying genotype*. For example, it is now possible to detect 'heterozygous carriers' of classical recessive disorders, e.g. phenylketonuria and various haemoglobinopathies. So, if we were to reclassify phenotypes so that both detected carriers and those with overt disease are called 'affected', we could convert a recessive condition to a 'dominant' one. It follows that penetrance is also dependent on the definition of the phenotype. Simple, Mendelian transmission is compared with a general autosomal two-allele single major locus (SML) model in Table 9.3. Here we consider a single locus where A_1 is the normal allele and A_2 the 'disease' allele. The f_1, f_2 and

Table 9.3 Penetrances in simple mendelian and general single major locus (SML) models

	Genotypes		
Model	A_1A_1	A_1A_2	A_2A_2
Recessive	0	0	1
Dominant	0	1	1
General	$0 \leqslant f_1 \leqslant 1$	$0 \leqslant f_2 \leqslant 1$	$0 \leqslant f_3 \leqslant 1$

f_3 are the penetrances of the three genotypes A_1A_1, A_1A_2 and A_2A_2 respectively.

Heston's (1970) solution was to redefine the phenotype to include not just schizophrenia but 'schizoid disease' and to propose a fully penetrant dominant gene. An immediate objection to this interesting proposal is that it would require all non-schizophrenic monozygotic co-twins of schizophrenics to be 'schizoid', and this appears not to be the case. Other workers, (e.g. Slater and Cowie, 1971; Elston and Campbell, 1970) have fitted models to family data, and propose solutions where all A_2A_2 homozygotes are affected (i.e. $f_3 = 1$), where there are no 'sporadics' ($f_1 = 0$), and there is a low penetrance (f_2) of under 20% in heterozygotes. Both groups of workers used 'incidence data', i.e. the lifetime expectancies or the morbid risks of schizophrenia in various classes of relatives of schizophrenics. It has been shown that having estimated the population frequency of a trait (K_p), observations on pairs of relatives can provide estimates of two further parameters, the variance due to additive gene effects (V_A) and the variance due to dominance (V_D). It is possible to derive expressions relating K_p, V_A, and V_D to the four parameters of the general SML model, the gene frequency, q, and the penetrances, f_1, f_2, f_3. We therefore have three known values and four unknowns, and it is impossible to arrive at a unique solution. Hence there is no single 'correct' answer when SML models are applied in this way, and a statistical goodness-of-fit test may be misleading (James, 1971).

One way around the problem was proposed by Suarez *et al.* (1976), who showed that if the SML model parameters are all constrained within the biologically meaningful limits of zero and one, the area of fit of the model can be graphically delineated so that it may be possible to *exclude* SML inheritance. O'Rourke *et al.* (1982) applied this test to all available published data, and reported that the findings were mathematically incompatible with SML inheritance.

A polygenic or multifactorial (MF) liability/threshold model was first suggested for schizophrenia by Gottesman and Shields (1967). They adopted the model of Falconer (1965), who proposed that a variable termed 'liability to develop the disorder' is continuously distributed within the population, but only those individuals whose liability at some time exceeds a certain threshold manifest the disorder. In the MF model, liability is composed of predominantly additive effects of many genes at different loci together with environmental effects.

The MF model has appeal for a number of reasons. First, if severity of illness can be equated with severity on the liability scale, it might explain why concordance in twins or first degree relatives increases with severity of illness of the proband. Second, the risk of schizophrenia for an individual increases with the number of affected relatives, which again might be explained by invoking the notion of liability. Third, the persistence of schizophrenia in the population, despite the selective disadvantage conferred by the condition (i.e. the reduced chance of producing offspring), is more easily explicable in terms of MF than of SML transmission. Subsequent modifications, including multiple thresholds, have been introduced by Reich *et al.* (1972), and it is also possible to incorporate shared family environmental effects (Falconer, 1981). It is a model of this type that we applied earlier to twin data (*see* Table 9.1), but a considerably more complex and arguably more realistic model based on path analysis has been put forward by McGue *et al.* (1983, 1985), using data points from pooled western European family and twin studies. The same data set was also tested for fit to the general SML model, again leading to its rejection and acceptance of the MF model. It was estimated that the genetic heritability was substantial at 63%, with cultural transmission accounting for a further 29% of the variance. Interestingly, McGue *et al.* applied a similar analysis to twin and family data on tuberculosis as a precaution against misleading results of the modelling procedure itself. Here it was found that the overwhelming component was cultural transmission, accounting for 62% of the variance in liability, while the genetic heritability was only 6%.

McGue *et al.* pointed out that although it is possible to exclude a 'pure' SML model where the major locus is the sole source of resemblance between relatives, the findings on schizophrenia could still be explained either by a polygenic multifactorial model or by a major gene operating against a multifactorial background. Their analyses, together with the other attempts at modelling discussed so far, have been concerned purely with incidence data on pairs of relatives. A more satisfactory approach, which is to be preferred to this and to piecemeal attempts to fit 'oligogenic' models (Stewart, 1980), is to carry out a complex segregation analysis in which information from entire pedigrees is utilized, and in which a 'mixed' (Morton, 1982) or 'combined' model (Reich *et al.*, 1982) is adopted. Here the strategy is altogether more comprehensive, and the method makes use of likelihood theory (Edwards, 1972). The procedure is to test a full, 'mixed' model against reduced models which form its subsets. Computer programs use an iterative optimization routine to arrive at a 'best fit' for each model, in which the likelihood that the hypothesis is correct, given the observed data, is maximized. Hypotheses can be compared directly using a likelihood ratio test which depends on the fact that twice the difference in log likelihoods approximates very closely to a chi-square distribution.

So far, the mixed model approach to complex segregation analysis has proved useful in resolving the mode of inheritance of a number of traits and diseases, but has yielded disappointingly inconclusive results in schizophrenia. One of the problems is that, for all its sophistication, the method lacks power to distinguish between models if all we have is dichotomous data on nuclear families (i.e. affected/unaffected) (e.g. Carter and Chung, 1980; Risch and Baron, 1984). One way of increasing the power of segregation analysis is to collect data on extended pedigrees which can now be readily handled by computer programs (Lalouel *et al*, 1983). Ability to resolve models would also be greatly enhanced by the development of some reliable and continuous measure that is strongly correlated with liability. Here measures of 'schizotypia' (*see* Chapter 14) are of particular interest. Unfortunately, defining a measure to capture schizo-typal traits, which at the same time produces high scores in the non-schizophrenic relatives of patients, has proved remarkably difficult (for a recent discussion, *see* Gottesman, 1987).

HETEROGENEITY: IS THERE A GENETIC SPLIT?

It is apparent from our discussion so far that the problem of resolving the mode of inheritance in schizophrenia is complicated, and it is therefore scarcely surprising, in the interests of parsimony and ease of analysis, that modellers have usually begun with the simplifying assumption that schizophrenia is a unitary condition. However, few would argue with the fact that schizophrenia is clinically heterogeneous, and it is reasonable to consider that this might be a reflection of aetiological heterogeneity. Do subforms of schizophrenia therefore 'breed true' in families? Slater (1947) pointed out that there was statistically significant homotypia (i.e. a tendency for like to go with like) with regard to clinical subtype in parent/offspring pairs. Subsequent researchers have also demonstrated a tendency towards homotypia in first degree relatives for Kraepelinian/Bleulerian subtypes such as hebephrenic or paranoid schizophrenia (Tsuang *et al.* 1974; Scharfetter and Nusperli, 1980). More recently, an analysis of twin data (McGuffin *et al.*, 1987) showed a tendency towards homotypia, both for operationally defined hebephrenic and paranoid categories and for more novel subtypes derived by multivariate statistical methods (Farmer *et al.*, 1984). However, the separation of subtypes was not clear-cut: even among identical twins it proved possible to identify probands with one subtype of schizophrenia and co-twins with another. It was also observed that, as with family study material, there was a tendency for probands with the paranoid form of disorder to have a lower frequency of schizophrenia among relatives than probands with non-paranoid or hebephrenic illnesses.

A multiple threshold liability-continuum model offers an explanation of these findings. For example, if we take the material from Kallmann's (1938) family study (still one of the largest data sets available and the one used by Slater to demonstrate homotypia), we could propose that so-called 'nuclear' schizophrenia (hebephrenic and catatonic forms) lies beyond a more extreme threshold of severity than 'peripheral' schizophrenia (simple and paranoid forms). On applying a two-threshold isocorrelational model (Reich *et al.*, 1979) and making such assumptions, an excellent fit was obtained (McGuffin *et al.*, 1987). These findings strongly suggest that subtypes differ from each other quantitatively rather than qualitatively, with those forms of disorder with greater impairment and earlier onset occupying a more extreme position on a liability continuum. Indeed, Gottesman and Shields (1972) previously noted a positive relationship between impairment in the proband (as reflected in duration of hospitalization) and concordance for schizophrenia in MZ twins.

A rather different approach to subtyping has been taken by Crow (1980, 1985). He has proposed that type I schizophrenia is characterized by prominent positive symptoms and a good response to neuroleptics, and is usually associated with a normal computed tomographic (CT) brain scan appearance and the absence of negative features and cognitive impairment. A type II form of schizophrenia is associated with negative symptoms, a poor response to neuroleptics, and a tendency to show enlarged lateral cerebral ventricles on CT brain scan. It is suggested that type I disorder may be associated with underlying abnormalities in brain dopaminergic systems, and that type II disorder has a different pathogenesis which may be infective in origin. It is allowed that these categories overlap to a considerable extent, and that in practice 'mixed forms' will occur. On applying an operationalized version of Crow's (1980) criteria to twin material, it was found again that there was some tendency towards homotypia, but this was incomplete. Thus, for example, four out of 15 MZ pairs presented with different subtypes. Once again it is possible to invoke a quantitative explanation of the differences between the subtypes by using the liability concept. Thus MZ concordance for probands with a type I disorder was 53% with a DZ concordance of 19%. Where the proband had a type II or mixed disorder, the MZ concordance was 64% versus 0% in DZs. This may suggest that type II/mixed schizophrenia is a 'more genetic' or 'more severe' form.

The predominant impression, therefore, is of the existence of 'more severe' and 'less severe' forms of schizophrenia in terms of their relative positions on the continuum of liability. An older and indeed more cut-and-dried view recently reintroduced by Murray *et al.* (1985; Chapter 8) is that schizophrenia can usefully be separated into genetic and non-genetic varieties. The existence of organic phenocopies is well documented (Davison and Bagley, 1969), but it is usually assumed that these are comparatively uncommon in clinical practice. For example, obvious organic states accounted for less than 4% of cases in a recent large series of psychotic patients (Johnstone *et al.* 1986). Murray *et al.* (1985) have suggested that a substantial proportion of schizophrenics who are 'family history negative' have environmental causes, which normally go undetected and will continue to do so until brain neuroimaging and other techniques become sufficiently sensitive.

Earlier twin and family studies do have some bearing on this interesting proposition but, by and large, do not provide support. Only a minority of thoroughly investigated schizophrenics have secondary cases among their near relatives, so that over 60% can be classified as 'family history negative' (Bleuler, 1978). This does not embarrass either SML, MF or 'mixed' models of transmission which can accommodate a high proportion of 'chance isolates', i.e. genetic cases with no affected relatives. Indeed, in most formulations their occurrence is predicted.

Twins and their families can provide particularly useful information, since the high rate of discordance in identical twins might conceivably be explained by an admixture of genetic and non-genetic cases. However, Luxenburger (1928) was the first to show that discordant pairs had other affected family members as often as did concordant pairs, results which were subsequently replicated by other investigators (Kringlen, 1967). On studying the adult offspring of MZ twins discordant for schizophrenia, Fischer (1971) found a similarly high morbid risk for the disorder, both in the children of the schizophrenic probands and in the children of the non-schizophrenic co-twins. This finding has since been confirmed and extended in the offspring of MZ and DZ twins by Gottesman and Bertelsen (personal communication). It therefore seems highly unlikely that hypotheses of a genetic/sporadic admixture can explain discordance of schizophrenia in identical twins, and the data suggest that non-genetic varieties of schizophrenia are uncommon.

Taking a different tack, Reveley *et al.* (1982) found that schizophrenic twins had significantly larger cerebral ventricles measured on CT brain scans than their identical but non-schizophrenic co-twins. Subsequently, a relationship between enlarged ventricles, a history of birth complications and absence of psychiatric disorder among other family members was reported (Reveley *et al.*, 1984). Some studies of singletons have also found an inverse relationship between enlargement of cerebral ventricles and evidence of a familial predisposition (Turner *et al.*, 1986), but others have either failed to find such a relationship (Farmer *et al.*, 1987a; McGuffin *et al.*, 1987) or have found just the opposite, that is enlarged ventricles among patients with one or more first degree relatives also affected by schizophrenia (Nasrallah *et al.*, 1982;, DeLisi *et al.*, 1986).

The relationship of birth injuries to genetic risk also presents problems of interpretation. Pollin and Stabenau (1968) are frequently quoted as finding that the schizophrenic index case in discordant MZ pairs were more likely than the non-affected co-twin to have had a history of birth trauma, low birth weight and a submissive/dependent premorbid personality. Although other studies concur regarding premorbid personality factors, there has been no convincing replication of the specific birth history findings (Gottesman and Shields, 1982). Nevertheless, there is some support for a *general* role of birth trauma in the causation of schizophrenia (McNeill and Kaij, 1978), but even here there are some apparent anomalies. The fact that obstetric complications are more common in twins than in singletons suggests that we might expect a modest increase in the frequency of schizophrenia among twins compared with the general population, but such an increase does not occur.

MARKERS AND THE NEW GENETICS OF
RECOMBINANT DNA

Currently, there is a dramatic rate of progress in the new genetics of recombinant DNA (Weatherall, 1986) and in achieving a comprehensive map of the human genome (White *et al.*, 1985). Studies of linkage and marker association present an enticing and exciting prospect for psychiatric genetics. In particular, genetic marker studies can greatly improve the prospect of detecting major gene effects, and of resolving heterogeneity in conditions such as schizophrenia. A key question is: 'how large an effect must a gene have in order for it to be detectable using marker strategies?' The answer to this is not yet clear, but it is probable that genes playing a comparatively modest role can be detected, and it is possible that several loci affecting a single trait may be identifiable. An example from an earlier era of marker studies is the association between blood group 'O' and duodenal ulcer. Numerous publications attest to the veracity of this association, yet it has been calculated that ABO type accounts only for about 1% of the variance in liability to duodenal ulcer (Edwards, 1965). More recently, the analysis of data on multiple sclerosis and the HLA complex suggests that an affected sibling method can detect linkage with genes of only modest effect, in this case accounting for only about 3% of variance (Suarez *et al.*, 1982).

It is worth noting that the phenomena of *association* and *linkage* differ in a number of ways. Linkage is observed when two loci are in close proximity on the same chromosome, so that *within families*, genes at the two loci do not (as is usually the case) assort independently. Thus, if we are considering a disease inherited at a single locus, we would expect different alleles to 'stick with' the disease in different families. By contrast, association is usually sought in populations, where the frequency of certain alleles or haplotypes (sets of alleles inherited together at closely adjacent loci) are compared for their frequency in patients with the disease and either unaffected controls or members of the general population. The occurrence of an association can indicate either that the allele itself predisposes to the illness (and here it is usual to invoke the notion of pleiotropy where the same gene can have two or more apparently different effects), or else that the marker and the disease locus are so tightly linked that linkage disequilibrium is present.

Unfortunately, the term 'genetic marker' has sometimes been misused in the psychiatric literature to denote almost any type of biological characteristic which may be inherited and which has a putative relationship with a mental disorder. However, the term is more correctly restricted to reliably detectable characters which have a known, simple mode of inheritance and which are *polymorphic* (i.e. there exist two or more alleles with a gene frequency of at least 1%). Prior to the advent of recombinant DNA technology, several types of marker were available. These are sometimes now referred to as 'conventional' or 'classical' markers. These include red cell antigens (e.g. ABO, rhesus, MNS), human leucocyte antigens (HLA), and various red cell enzymes and serum protein polymorphisms. In addition, using high resolution banding methods it may be possible to demonstrate chromosomal banding polymorphisms. Regrettably, even with excellent laboratory facilities, it is usually possible to study only about

30 different loci using classical markers, so that only a small proportion of the human genome, at most 20–30%, can be scanned.

It is perhaps not surprising therefore that the yield of positive results from studies of classical markers in schizophrenia has been quite meagre (McGuffin and Sturt, 1986). The most often replicated finding has been of an association between paranoid schizophrenia and HLA-A9. The results of seven out of nine investigations are consistent for such an association, and an analysis of the combined data makes it extremely unlikely that this has arisen by chance (McGuffin and Sturt, 1986). However, the strength of the association is low so that possessing HLA-A9 appears to increase one's risk of developing a paranoid schizophrenia by less than twofold. Using the method developed by Edwards (1965), it has been calculated that the HLA locus contributes little over 1% of the variance to the liability to paranoid schizophrenia. Thus the existence of an HLA association might require only some slight modification of our earlier discussion of the idea that paranoid schizophrenia differs purely quantitatively from other forms, corresponding to different thresholds on a liability continuum. Instead we might allow that there are overlapping sets of genes, each of which can modify the clinical picture in subtly different ways. Despite a suggestion of a near dominant gene linked to HLA (Turner, 1979) in families multiply affected by schizophrenia, subsequent negative linkage studies effectively rule out such a major locus (McGuffin *et al.*, 1983; Chadda *et al.*, 1986; Andrew *et al.*, 1987).

Negative linkage results are not without value since, when many loci are examined, it is possible to *exclude* those areas of the genome in which there cannot be a major gene for the trait under consideration (Cook *et al.*, 1980). However, there are two major problems about applying exclusion mapping in schizophrenia. First, large samples are required because, except for highly polymorphic loci such as HLA, only a proportion of families will prove informative. Second, a major gene for schizophrenia, if it exists, is likely to show incomplete penetrance and therefore prove more difficult to exclude. One study examined 21 different loci in families containing two or more schizophrenics, but concluded that a dominant gene could be excluded from about only 6% of the genome (McGuffin *et al.*, 1983). Low penetrance would reduce this figure even further.

Fortunately, as we have mentioned, a new generation of markers has now been brought forth by the techniques of the 'new genetics', and provides cause for much greater optimism. So-called restriction fragment length polymorphisms (RFLP) exist because of individual differences in DNA base sequences and consequent variation in the positions of the sites at which bacterial enzymes, called restriction endonucleases, will cleave the DNA molecule. Particular RFLPs can be identified using a probe made from radio-labelled complementary DNA, in conjunction with an electrophoretic technique called the Southern Blot Method. This method means that vastly more markers can be made available in the search for disease genes, and the ultimate aim of the gene mappers (Botstein *et al.*, 1980) is to discover enough markers approximately evenly distributed throughout the genome at fairly close intervals so that they can serve as reference points for the location of all other genes. Recent calculations (Lange and Boehnke, 1982) suggest that well over 200 markers will be needed to span the genome. Although it has been the subject of some controversy, a virtually complete genetic linkage map has now been published (Donis-Keller *et al.* 1987). A further boost has been provided by the finding of hypervariable regions (Jeffreys *et al.*, 1985), which are particularly rich in polymorphisms. These consist of repetitious DNA segments which have become replicated and inserted in numerous points over the genome during the course of evolution. Using a method derived by Jeffreys *et al.* (1985), it is possible to produce a DNA 'fingerprint' which uniquely characterizes every individual and which effectively examines 30 or more loci simultaneously (Jeffreys *et al.*, 1986).

Random marker studies using 'anonymous' probes or known genes, where there is no *a priori* reason for suspecting linkage, have proved successful in Huntington's disease (Gusella *et al.*, 1983; Harper *et al.*, 1985), and there have been interesting early results in manic-depressive illness (Egeland *et al.*, 1987). A different approach is to use gene probes where there is good reason for suspecting a relationship to the disease process. This presupposes that something is known of the pathogenesis of the disorder and where the 'biochemical lesions' are to be found. The new genetics has been highly successful in unravelling the complexities of haemoglobinopathies (Weatherall, 1985) and of some classical inborn errors of metabolism (Emery, 1984; White *et al.*, 1985). The general approach of using 'purpose-built' probes is unlikely to have such immediate application in schizophrenia, where the understanding of the biochemical pathology is less sound and where we cannot, with certainty, identify a lesion or usually obtain access to the relevant tissue.

Broadly speaking, there are two methods which can be attempted. The first is to select 'candidate genes' and clone them to produce probes. For example, abnormalities in catecholamine pathways have been implicated in the functional psychoses, so that suitable genes of interest might include those coding for the enzymes involved in catecholamine metabolism. Abnormalities in dopamine D2 receptor populations have been the subject of repeated reports in schizophrenia (*see* Chapter 6), so that isolation of the gene for the D2 receptor could prove to be a considerable benefit (Tobin, 1987).

A second, and potentially even more powerful, strategy is to attempt to make disease-specific probes. Here the idea is to isolate specific forms of mRNA from post-mortem or biopsy tissue and carry out subsequent studies *in vitro*. A cell-free protein synthesizing system can be set up, and proteins produced in response to added mRNA can be separated and analysed by two-dimensional electrophoresis on gel. It may then be possible to characterize a specific protein or proteins involved in the pathogenesis of the disease, and subsequently to synthesize and clone complementary DNA for use as probes. This general method has been used to identify a specific mRNA species which show altered levels in Down's syndrome (Whatley *et al.*, 1984), and work has already begun in applying this approach in schizophrenia and other 'functional' psychoses.

It is clear that in order to maximize the exciting prospects offered by the 'new genetics' in schizophrenia, a very careful coordination of clinical and laboratory research resources will be required. First, a sufficient number of families needs to be collected, consisting of two or more generations, with at least two offspring and with multiple members affected. Second, there will need to be a marshalling of laboratory resources and a need to ensure that the potentially informative material reaches the laboratories where the relevant techniques can be employed. A logical, but inevitably expensive answer would be to set up a collaborative network of data banks of transformed lymphocytes obtained from well-characterized families which can be made available as a resource to participating laboratories.

REFERENCES

Abrams R., Taylor M. A. (1983). The genetics of schizophrenia: a reassessment using modern criteria. *American Journal of Psychiatry*; 140: 171–5.

American Psychiatric Association (1980). *DSM-III: Diagnostic and Statistical Manual of Mental Disorders*. Washington, DC: American Psychiatric Association.

American Psychiatric Association (1987). *DSM-III R: Diagnostic and Statistical Manual of Mental Disorders. Revised.* Washington DC: APA.

Andrew B., Watt D. C., Gillespie C., Chapel, H. (1987). A study of genetic linkage in schizophrenia. *Psychological Medicine*; 17: 363–73.

Baron M., Gruen R., Kane J., Asnis L. (1985). Modern research criteria and the genetics of schizophrenia. *American Journal of Psychiatry*; 142: 697–701.

Berner P., Gabriel E., Katschnig H. et al. (1983). *Diagnostic Criteria for Schizophrenia and Affective Psychoses*. World Psychiatric Association. American Psychiatric Press Inc.

Bland R. C., Orn H. (1979). Diagnostic criteria and outcome. *British Journal of Psychiatry*; 134: 34.

Bleuler M. (1978). *The Schizophrenia Disorders* (translated by S. Clemens). New Haven: Yale University Press.

Botstein D., White R. L., Skocnick M., Davis R. W. (1980). Construction of a genetic linkage map in man using restrictive fragment length polymorphisms. *American Journal of Human Genetics*; 32: 312–31.

Brockington I. F., Kendell R. E., Leff J. P. (1978). Definitions of schizophrenia: concordance and prediction of outcome. *Psychological Medicine*; 8: 387–98.

Carter C. L., Chung C. S. (1980). Segregation analysis of schizophrenia under a mixed model. *Human Heredity*; 30: 350–6.

Chadda R., Kulhara P., Singh T., Sehgal P. S. (1986). HLA antigens in schizophrenia: a family study. *British Journal of Psychiatry*; 149: 612–15.

Cook P. J. L., Noades J. E., Lomas C. G., Buckton K. E., Robson E. B. (1980). Exclusion mapping illustrated by the MNSs blood group. *Annals of Human Genetics*; 44: 61–73.

Crow T. J. (1980). Molecular pathology of schizophrenia: more than one disease process? *British Medical Journal*; 280: 66–8.

Crow T. J. (1985). The two syndrome concept: origins and current states. *Schizophrenia Bulletin*; 11: 471–86.

Davison K., Bagley C. R. (1969). Schizophrenia-like psychosis associated with organic disorders of the central nervous system: a review of the literature. In: *Current Problems in Neuropsychiatry* (R. N. Herrington, ed.), pp. 113–84. Ashford, Kent: Headley Brothers.

DeLisi L. E., Goldin L. R., Hamovit V. R. *et al.* (1986). A family study of the association of ventricular size with schizophrenia. *Archives of General Psychiatry*; 43: 148–53.

Doris-Keller H., Green P., Helms P. *et al.* (1987). A genetic linkage map of the human genome. *Cell*; 51: 319–37.

Edwards A. W. F. (1972). *Likelihood*. Cambridge: Cambridge University Press.

Edwards J. H. (1965). Associations between blood groups and disease. *Annals of Human Genetics*; 29: 77–83.

Egeland J. A., Gerhard D. S., Pauls D. L. *et al.* (1987). Bipolar affective disorder linked to DNA markers on chromosome 11. *Nature*; 325: 783–7.

Elston R. C., Campbell A. A. (1970). Schizophrenia, evidence for a major gene hypothesis. *Behaviour Genetics*; 1: 101–6.

Emery A. E. H. (1984). *An Introduction to Recombinant DNA*. Chichester: John Wiley and Sons.

Falconer D. S. (1965). The inheritance of liability to certain disease, estimated from the incidence among relatives. *Annals of Human Genetics*; 29: 51–76.

Falconer D. S. (1981). *Introduction to Quantitative Genetics* (2nd edn.). London: Longman.

Farmer A. E., Jackson R., McGuffin P., Storey P. (1987a). Cerebral ventricular enlargement in schizophrenia: consistencies and contradictions. *British Journal of Psychiatry*; 150: 324–30.

Farmer A. E., McGuffin P., Gottesman I. I. (1984). Searching for the split in schizophrenia: a twin study perspective. *Psychiatry Research*; 13: 109–18.

Farmer A. E., McGuffin P., Gottesman I. I. (1987b). Twin concordance for DSM-III schizophrenia: scrutinising the validity of the definition. *Archives of General Psychiatry*; 44: 634–41.

Feighner J. P., Robins E., Guze S. B., Woodruffe R. A., Winokur G., Munoz R. (1972). Diagnostic criteria for use in psychiatric research. *Archives of General Psychiatry*; 26: 57–63.

Fischer M. (1971). Psychoses in the offspring of schizophrenic monozygotic twins and their normal co-twins. *British Journal of Psychiatry*, 115: 981–90.

Gottesman I. I. (1987). The borderlands of psychosis or the fringes of lunacy. *British Medical Bulletin*; 43: 557–69.

Gottesman I. I., McGuffin P., Farmer A. E. (1987). Clinical genetics as clues to the 'real' genetics of schizophrenia. (A decade of modest gains while playing for time.) *Schizophrenia Bulletin*; 13: 23–48.

Gottesman I. I., Shields, J. (1967). A polygenic theory of schizophrenia. *Proceedings of the National Academy of Sciences*; 58: 199–205.

Gottesman I. I., Shields J. (1972). *Schizophrenia and Genetics: A Twin Study Vantage Point*. London: Academic Press.

Gottesman I. I., Shields J. (1982). *Schizophrenia, the Epigenetic Puzzle*. Cambridge: Cambridge University Press.

Gusella J. F., Wexler N. S., Connerlly P. M. *et al.* (1983). A polymorphic marker genetically linked to Huntington's disease. *Nature*; **306**: 234–8.

Guze S. B., Cloninger C. R., Martin R. L., Clayton, P. J. (1983). A follow-up and family study of schizophrenia. *Archives of General Psychiatry*; **40**: 1273–6.

Harper P. S., Youngman S., Anderson M. A. (1985). Genetic linkage between Huntington's disease and the DNA polymorphism G8 in South Wales. *Journal of Medical Genetics*; **22**: 44–50.

Helzer J. E., Brockington I. F., Kendell R. E. (1981). Predictive validity of DSM-III and Feighner definitions of schizophrenia: a comparison with research Diagnostic Criteria and CATEGO. *Archives of General Psychiatry*; **38**: 791–7.

Heston L. L. (1970). The genetics of schizophrenia and schizoid disease. *Science*; **167**: 249–56.

James, J. (1971). Frequency in relatives for an all-or-none trait. *Annals of Human Genetics*; **35**: 47–9.

Jaspers K. (1962). *General Psychopathology* (translated by Hamilton M. W., Hoeing, J.). Manchester: Manchester University Press.

Jeffreys A. J., Wilson, V., Thein S. L. (1985). Hypervariable 'minisatellite' regions in human DNA. *Nature*; **314**: 67–73.

Jeffreys A. J., Wilson V., Weatherall D. J., Ponder B. A. J. (1986). DNA 'fingerprints' and segregation analysis of multiple markers in human pedigrees. *American Journal of Human Genetics*; **39**: 11–24.

Johnstone E. C., Crow T. J., Johnson A. L., McMillan J. F. (1986). The Northwick Park study of first episodes of schizophrenia: presentation of the illness and problems relating to admission. *British Journal of Psychiatry*; **148**: 115–20.

Kallmann F. J. (1938). *The Genetics of Schizophrenia*. New York: J. J. Augustus.

Kendell R. E. (1975). Schizophrenia: the remedy for diagnostic comparison. In: *Contemporary Psychiatry. British Journal of Psychiatry Special Publication no. 9* (Silverstone T., Barraclough B., eds.) pp. 11–17. Ashford, Kent: Headley Brothers.

Kendell R. E. (1982). The choice of diagnostic criteria for biological research. *Archives of General Psychiatry*; **39**: 1334–9.

Kendler K. S., Gruenberg A. M. (1984). An independent antigen of the Danish adoption study of schizophrenia VI. The pattern of psychiatric illness as defined by DSM III in adoptees and relatives. *Archives of General Psychiatry*; **41**: 555–64.

Kendler K. S., Gruenberg A. M., Tsuang M. T. (1985). Psychiatric illness in first degree relatives of schizophrenics and surgical control patients. *Archives of General Psychiatry*; **42**: 770–9.

Kety S. S., Rosenthal D., Wender P. H., Schulsinger F., Jacobsen B. (1976). Mental illness in the biological and adoptive families of individuals who have become schizophrenic. *Behaviour Genetics*; **6**: 219–25.

Kringlen E. (1967). *Heredity and Environment in the Functional Psychoses*. London: Heinemann.

Kuhn T. S. (1962). *The Structure of Scientific Revolutions*. Chicago: University of Chicago Press.

Laloulel J. M., Rao D. C., Morton M. E., Elston, R. L. (1983). A unified model for complex segregation analysis. *Journal of Human Genetics*; **35**: 816–26.

Lange K., Boehnke M. (1982). How many polymorphic marker genes will it take to span the human genome. *American Journal of Human Genetics*; **34**: 842–5.

Luxenburger H. (1928). Vorlaufizer Bericht uber Psychiatrische Serien Untersu-

124 *Schizophrenia: The major issues*

chungen an Zwillinger. *Zeitschift für gesamte Neurologie und Psychiatrie*; 116: 297–326.

McGue M., Gottesman, I. I., Rao, D. C. (1983). The transmission of schizophrenia under a multifactorial threshold model. *American Journal of Human Genetics*; 35: 1161–78.

McGue, M., Gottesman I. I., Rao D. C. (1985). Resolving genetic models for the transmission of schizophrenia. *Genetic Epidemiology*; 2: 99–110.

McGuffin P., Farmer A. E., Gottesman I. I. (1987). Is there really a split in schizophrenia? The genetic evidence. *British Journal of Psychiatry*; 150: 581–92.

McGuffin P., Farmer A. E., Gottesman I. I., Murray R. M., Reveley A. (1984). Twin concordance for operationally defined schizophrenia. Confirmation of familiality and heritability. *Archives of General Psychiatry*; 41: 541–5.

McGuffin P., Festenstein N., Murray R. M. (1983). A family study of HLA antigens and other genetic markers in schizophrenia. *Psychological Medicine*; 13: 31–43.

McGuffin P., Sturt E. (1986). Genetic markers in schizophrenia. *Human Heredity*; 36: 65–88.

McNeill R. F., Kaij L. (1978). Obstetric factors in the development of schizophrenia: complications in the birth of pre-schizophrenia and in the reproduction of schizophrenic parents. In: *The Nature of Schizophrenia* (Wynn L. C., Chomarsen R. L., Matthews S., eds.), pp. 401–429. Chichester: Wiley.

Morton N. E. (1982). *Outline of Genetic Epidemiology*. Basel: Karger.

Murray R. M., Lewis S., Reveley A. M. (1985). Towards an aetiological classification of schizophrenia. *Lancet*; i: 1023–6.

Murray R. M., Murphy D. L. (1978). Drug response and psychiatric nosology. *Psychological Medicine*; 7: 667–81.

Nasrallah H. A., Charles G. J., McCauley-Whitters M., Kuperman S. (1982). Cerebral ventricular enlargement in subtypes of chronic schizophrenia. *Archives of General Psychiatry*; 39: 774–7.

O'Rourke D. H., Gottesman I. I., Suarez B. K., Rice J., Reich T. (1982). Refutation of the single locus model in the aetiology of schizophrenia. *American Journal of Human Genetics*; 33: 630–49.

Pollin W., Stabenhau J. R. (1968). Biological, psychological and historical differences in a series of monozygotic twins discordant for schizophrenia. In: *The Transmission of Schizophrenia* (Rosenthal D., Kety S. S., eds.). Oxford: Pergamon.

Pope H. G., Jonas J., Cohen B. A., Lipinski J. F. (1983). Heritability of schizophrenia. *American Journal of Psychiatry*, 140. 132–3.

Reich T., Cloniger C. R., Wette R., James J. (1979). The use of multiple thresholds and segregation analysis in analysing the phenotypic heterogeneity of multifactorial traits. *Annals of Human Genetics*; 42: 371.

Reich T., James J. W., Morris C. A. (1972). The use of multiple thresholds in determining the mode of transmission of semi-continuous traits. *Annals of Human Genetics*; 36: 163–84.

Reich T., Rice J., Cloninger C. R. (1982). The detection of a major locus in the presence of multifactorial variation. In: *Genetic Research Strategies in Psychobiology and Psychiatry* (Gershon E. S., Matthysse S., Breakfield A. O., Ciaranello, R. D., eds.). pp. 353–68. Pacific Grove: Boxwood Press.

Reveley A. M., Reveley M. A., Clifford C. A., Murray R. M. (1982). Cerebral ventricular size in twins discordant for schizophrenia. *Lancet*; i: 540–1.

Reveley A. M., Reveley M. A., Murray R. M. (1984). Cerebral ventricular enlargement in non-genetic schizophrenia: a controlled twin study. *British Journal of Psychiatry*; **144**: 89–93.

Risch N., Baron M. (1984). Segregation analysis of schizophrenia and related disorders. *American Journal of Human Genetics*; **36**: 1039–59.

Robins E., Guze S. B. (1970). Establishment of diagnostic validity in psychiatric illness: its application to schizophrenia. *American Journal of Psychiatry*; **126**: 983–7.

Scharfetter C., Nusperli M. (1980). The group of schizophrenias, schizo-affective psychoses and affective disorders. *Schizophrenia Bulletin*; **6**: 586–91.

Schneider K. (1959). *Clinical Psychopathology* (translated by Hamilton M. W.). London and New York: Grune and Stratton.

Slater E. (1947). Genetical causes of schizophrenia symptoms. *Monatsschrift für Psychiatrie und Neurologie*; **113**: 50–8. (Reprinted in *Man, Mind and Heredity*) Shields, J., Gottesman I. I., eds.).

Slater E., Cowie V. (1971). *The Genetics of Mental Disorder*. Oxford: Oxford University Press.

Spitzer R. L., Endicott J., Robins E. (1978). *Research Diagnostic Criteria. Instrument No. 58*. New York: New York State Psychiatric Institute.

Stephens J. H., Astrup C., Carpenter W. T., Schaffer J. W., Goldberg J. (1982). A comparison of nine systems to diagnose schizophrenia. *Psychiatry Research*; **6**: 127–43.

Stewart J. (1980). Schizophrenia: the systematic construction of genetic models. *American Journal of Human Genetics*; **32**: 47–54.

Suarez B. K., Reich T., Trost J. (1976). Limits of the genetic two allele single major locus model with incomplete penetrance. *Annals of Human Genetics*; **40**: 231–44.

Suarez B. K., O'Rourke, D., Van Eerdwegh P. (1982). Power of the affected sib pair method to detect disease susceptibility loci of small effect: an application to multiple sclerosis. *American Journal of Medical Genetics*; **12**: 309–26.

Tienari P., Sorri, A., Lahti, J. *et al.* (1987). Interaction of genetic and psychosocial factors in schizophrenia. *Schizophrenia Bulletin*; **13**: 477–84.

Tobin A. J. (1987). Molecular biology and schizophrenia: lessons from Huntington's disease. *Schizophrenia Bulletin*; **13**: 199–204.

Tsuang M. T., Fowler R. C., Cadoret R. J., Monnelly E. (1974). Schizophrenia among first degree relatives of paranoid and non paranoid schizophrenics. *Comprehensive Psychiatry*; **15**: 295–302.

Turner S., Toone B., Brett-Jones A. (1986). Computerised tomography scan changes in early schizophrenia - preliminary findings. *Psychological Medicine*; **16**: 219–26.

Turner W. J. (1979). Genetic markers for schizophrenia. *Biological Psychiatry*; **14**: 177–205.

Weatherall D. J. (1985). *The New Genetics and Clinical Practice* 2nd edn. Oxford: Oxford University Press.

Whateley S. A., Hall C., Davison A. N., Lim, L. (1984). Alterations in the relative amounts of specific mRNA species in the developing human brain in Down's syndrome. *Biochemistry Journal*; **220**: 179–87.

White R., Leppert M., Bishop T. *et al.* (1985). Construction of linkage maps with DNA markers for human chromosomes. *Nature*; **313**: 101–5.

10 *Aetiology of psychosis: the way ahead*

T. J. CROW

The premise of this chapter is that the aetiology of schizophrenia is basically genetic and that, with the exception of a small number of anomalous cases, there is no significant environmental contribution. It is argued that a molecular approach to the aetiology of psychosis can be devised that makes logical use of current information about the disease and will lead to identification of the causative agent. This agent is assumed to reside at a specific locus within the genome; certain predictions are made concerning the nature of the gene sequence.

OCKHAM'S RAZOR AND MULTIFACTORIAL/POLYGENIC THEORIES

To embark on this strategy it is necessary to consider various alternative concepts: that the aetiology of the disease is multifactorial, and that diverse genetic influences ('polygenes') are involved. Murray *et al.* (1985), for example, have suggested that: 'Up to one third of schizophrenics have enlarged cerebral ventricles, and this appears to be a consequence of environmental damage ... a simple division into familial and sporadic cases would facilitate research'.

There are a number of problems with this view. The figure of one-third is entirely arbitrary. The distribution of ventricular size in schizophrenia has not been demonstrated to be bimodal, therefore the population of patients with schizophrenia cannot rationally be divided into those with and those without structural changes in the brain. There is also considerable doubt about whether the presence of a degree of ventricular enlargement which is detectable on computed tomographic (CT) scanning is associated with absence of a family history (Owens *et al.*, 1985; McGuffin *et al.*, 1987).

On the question of environmental 'phenocopies' Slater and Cowie (1971) commented: 'Most of the organically and psychogenically determined psychoses pass off after a relatively short interval into a state which has an understandable relation to the basic pathogenesis ... All these symptomatic schizophrenia-like states, even when taken together, represent only a small part of the number of cases which are diagnosed as schizophrenic'.

This observation is borne out by the finding in the Northwick Park study of first episodes of schizophrenia that, in less than 6% of 268 cases was an organic illness identified which might have contributed to the psychiatric state (Johnstone *et al.*, 1987).

The notion that the genetics of schizophrenia will be difficult to investigate on account of its complexity has been expressed by Sturt and McGuffin (1985): 'We must therefore consider the implications of transmission due to several "susceptibility" loci for the disorder, each of which could be located anywhere on the human genome and could exhibit any form of interaction in their effects on manifest disease'. These authors go on to say: 'We hold out little hope for finding linkages between random polymorphisms and disorders like schizophrenia ... the complexity of the causal pathway from DNA to disorder will not yield to simple solutions ...'.

These opinions take no cognisance of the arguments against a polygenic theory mounted by Karlsson (1974), who pointed out that it is difficult to reconcile such a mode of transmission of psychosis with the apparently dominant pattern that he observed in his extended Icelandic pedigrees. The case that more than one locus (or at most two) is involved is not compelling.

Approximately 650 years ago William of Ockham wrote: 'It is vain to do with more what can be done with fewer' (Russell, 1961).

Science can hardly advance without some such principle of conceptual economy. This is perhaps the most important reason for excluding multifactorial and polygenic theories of psychosis at the present time. It is not that one or other of these theories (or even both) may not be right. Rather, it is that a simpler theory has not been ruled out. There is a case (Crow, 1986b) that the Kraepelinian dichotomy of the psychoses into manic-depressive illness and dementia praecox may have been premature in relation to aetiology, although justified with respect to symptomatology and outcome. It may be that progress will depend upon the spectrum of psychoses being considered as a whole.

The question of whether significant non-genetic contributions to aetiology remain to be identified is addressed by some studies. Karlsson (1970) analysed the findings of adoption studies, and concluded that adoption away from a family in which schizophrenia was present did not reduce risk. This suggests that the role of the genetic factor is *not* that it predisposes the individual to some pathogenic influence in the postnatal environment. Similarly, Crow and Done (1986) found in pairs of siblings with the disease that there was no interaction with respect to age of onset, i.e. that onset was related to age of the individual and unrelated to onset of illness in the sibling. This appears to rule out an environmental factor which is common to the siblings and occurs at a defined point in time.

The strongest argument for an environmental factor is the fact of discordance in twins. Thus Murray *et al.* (1986; Chapter 8) wrote that twin studies in addition to confirming the role of heredity 'also emphasise the role of the environment, as only about half of MZ [monozygotic] pairs are concordant for schizophrenia in spite of sharing the same genes.' While this conclusion has an appealing simplicity, one should note that it may not be justified. If somatic mutation plays a role as it does in the genetics of the immune system, and perhaps in the pathogenesis of autoimmune disease, this could account for discordance for psychosis in MZ pairs of twins in the absence of a significant environmental contribution. Interest in this possibility is perhaps increased if there is a high rate of mutation in the psychosis gene itself (*see below*). A related possibility is found in the work of Boklage (1977), who demonstrated in a series of twins collected at the Maudsley Hospital that concordance for schizophrenia was a function of concordance for handedness. Boklage attributes discordance for psychosis to discrepancies between the two sides of the body in early development, i.e. in symmetry determination. The genetic mechanisms of such determination are of considerable interest.

A STRATEGY FOR IDENTIFYING THE PSYCHOSIS GENE

The potential importance of the conclusion that the aetiology of psychosis is primarily genetic is that it enables us to define more precisely the size of the problem. Specifically, the haystack in which the needle of causation is to be found is the human genome. Somewhere among these 50 000 genes is one which in individuals with psychosis assumes a different form.

Two approaches, which may be complementary, can be envisaged:

1. a systematic search for linkage, using for example the hypervariable minisatellites described by Jeffreys *et al.* (1985)
2. an attempt to identify the gene and its molecular characteristics from what we know about the disease.

Both may be required. While the former may be successful in locating a chromosomal region for the gene, a quite different strategy may be necessary to identify the pathogen itself.

What is proposed here is a strategy of successive approximations which makes use of plausible and testable assumptions. For example, it seems reasonable to suppose that the gene is a brain gene. If there were a marker for genes which are expressed in the brain this could then be utilized. Sutcliffe *et al.* (1984) suggested that a genetic element (the ID sequence) which they had found to be expressed in a small cytoplasmic species occurred exclusively in the brain. They suggested the ID sequence was an identifier involved in regulating brain specific transcription. It is as yet unclear whether the ID sequence has any specific relation to the brain (Chickaraishi, 1986). However, even if it does, use of this information may not be of great help in identifying the psychosis gene, as it has been estimated that approximately 30 000 genes are expressed exclusively in the brain (Sutcliffe *et al.*, 1984).

PSYCHOSIS AND THE EVOLUTION OF THE HUMAN BRAIN

A more promising strategy is to make use of the hypothesis that psychosis is specific to man. This concept seems first to have been considered by Crichton-Browne (1879), and later by Southard (1915) and Parfitt (1956). The concept is consistent with the notion that psychosis is a disturbance of genetic mechanisms which have been subject to recent evolutionary change (*see below*). It has been estimated that the amino acid differences between man and his nearest primate relative, the chimpanzee, amount to no more than 1% (King and Wilson, 1975). Thus, if we were able to identify those regions of DNA which distinguish man from the chimpanzee and gorilla, we might assume that it is in this segment of the genome that the psychosis gene is to be found. We might further adopt a sequential approach, and assume that it is in the part of this segment which is expressed in the brain.

An even more specific hypothesis is that psychosis is a disorder of the mechanisms of cerebral development. This theory might explain the distribution of age of onset, and also perhaps why age of onset appears to be genetically determined. It derives support from a recent analysis of a CT scan study conducted at Northwick Park. This study included 127 patients with schizophrenia, among whom were over 100 chronically institutionalized individuals, and a comparison group of 45 patients with non-schizophrenic disorders. Among the institutionalized patients, age of onset was found to be a powerful predictor of outcome (Johnstone *et al.*, 1988). When age and duration of illness were taken into account, patients with an age of onset below the median (25 years for males, and 28 years for females) were found to have more negative symptoms and greater impairment on tests of cognitive function, including the Withers and Hinton tests of the sensorium, the Boston naming test, age disorientation, and the Peabody test. On the CT scans, in addition to the well established finding of a degree of ventricular enlargement, brain area in the patients with schizophrenia was reduced. This seems more likely to be the result of a failure of development than a process of atrophy.

In this study, age of onset was also relevant to the question of structural change and to the relationship between such change and cognitive impairment. Although apparently unrelated to either ventricular size or brain area, age of onset was relevant to asymmetries in the posterior half of the brain: patients with early onset had significantly smaller asymmetries by comparison both with schizophrenic patients of later onset and patients with non-schizophrenic disorders (Colter *et al.*, 1988). Moreover, in the early onset group, significant relationships between cognitive and structural variablоо wоrо оооn that wоrо abооnt in tho group aо a wholо: thооо relationships were with brain area rather than with ventricular size. Thus it seems that early onset of illness arrests the development of cerebral asymmetries and leads to cognitive impairment, and that there is some relationship between cognitive deficits and structural change, although the precise sequence of such changes (i.e. the relationship between brain area and asymmetry) remains unclear.

These findings are consistent with the concept that psychosis is a disorder of some component of the mechanisms of cerebral development. A number of growth factors (proto- or cellular oncogenes) have been identified, and some of these (e.g. N-*myc*, *erb* B, *ras*, *sis*, *neu* and *c-fos*) (*see* Breakefield and Stern, 1986; Hunt *et al.*, 1987) are expressed in the brain. Since the number of oncogenes to be identified may be quite limited (e.g. of the order of 20) (Weinberg, 1982) and most seem to be represented as a single copy in the genome, the oncogene theory is relatively precise; it is certainly investigable.

An even more specific form of the hypothesis is that psychosis relates particularly to those genetic mechanisms which determine cerebral laterality (Crow, 1984, 1986a). Luys (1881), Crichton-Browne (1879) and Southard (1915) each considered the possibility that psychosis has a selectivity for the left hemisphere. Each investigated the hypothesis in post-mortem material; Luys and Southard considered it supported, although the results of their studies are not easy to interpret. Recent investigations provide further support. Thus Reynolds (1983) found the content of dopamine in the left, but not in the right, amygdala to be increased in patients with schizophrenia by comparison with controls, and Brown *et al.* (1986) found the parahippocampal gyrus to be reduced in width in schizophrenic patients by comparison with those with affective disorders, the difference between the groups being significantly greater on the left side. Most convincing are the findings of a study in which the ventricle has been assessed in post-mortem material by a radiological technique (Crow *et al.*, unpublished observations). In this way, in contrast with CT, it is possible to examine its structure from the lateral aspect. Brains of patients with significant Alzheimer-type or vascular change were excluded from the schizophrenic sample. The findings demonstrate enlargement of the ventricle which is selective to the temporal and posterior horns; by contrast, in Alzheimer's cases, enlargement was relatively uniform throughout the extent of the ventricle. Of particular interest is the finding of a significant ($P < 0.001$) group by diagnosis interaction, the increase being greater on the left side in the schizophrenic patients.

It seems therefore that schizophrenia may indeed be a disorder of the mechanisms which control the development of cerebral lateralization. Although the question is controversial, there is reason to suppose that asymmetry of function and structure in the brain is a relatively late evolutionary development, and may either have been a specifically human departure or have developed greatly in man (e.g. *see* Hamilton, 1977;

Warren, 1977). According to Levy (1977): 'bilateralisation of function arose in response to specifically human pressures, occurring in a socially organised species, the members of which were mutually interdependent . . .'.

If this is the case, the genetics of this evolutionary development may be the key to understanding the aetiology of psychosis.

Some other characteristics of the psychosis gene can be predicted. From the above discussion, it might appear that a failure or anomaly of cerebral development is sufficient to account for the phenomena. This is far from the case—one must also explain the acute episodes of illness which disrupt function and are sometimes of abrupt onset. One explanation is that they are due to expression of an integrated virus or 'virogene' (Crow, 1984, 1986b). An attraction of this hypothesis is that such sequences have an apparent affinity for proto-oncogene sequences. A number of retroviral sequences have been identified in the human genome, and some have been acquired relatively late in man's evolution (Benveniste and Todaro, 1976). Other types of sequence such as LINE elements and the THE-1 human transposon have some similar characteristics, and might be considered as possible candidates for the psychosis virogene. A further feature which may be predicted to characterize the sequence is a high degree of variation between individuals. There are two reasons why this may be the case: first to account for apparent variations in form of psychosis between generations as described in the 'continuum' concept (Crow, 1986b), and second because it appears that the persistence of psychosis in the face of a fertility disadvantage requires a high rate of mutation (Crow, 1987). Thus it is predicted that the psychosis gene represents a 'hot-spot' in the genome and that this variability influences gene expression. Such a high rate of variation might arise by unequal recombination at meiosis. It is suggested that this could occur in transmission through the male, and might be related to the seasonality of birth (Crow, 1987).

Strategies to test the virogene hypothesis are as follows:

1. a search for linkage in families with psychosis, making use of virogene elements and proto-oncogenes as candidates
2. recovery of nucleic acids from post-mortem brain for assessment, using *in situ* and dot-blot hybridization with the candidate sequences
3. selective (or 'subtraction') hybridization to attempt to identify the genomic regions of interest. Thus one can envisage comparisons of human versus non-human primate DNA, brain versus non-brain mRNA, and of left versus right brain mRNA at particular stages of development as approaches to the problem.

CONCLUSIONS

A strategy to investigate the aetiology of psychosis has been developed from the virogene hypothesis—the concept that psychosis is due to a viral sequence which is integrated in the human genome and is expressed to cause episodes of illness. The major clue to the location of the virogene is that, according to the evidence of a recent post-mortem study (Brown *et al.*, 1986), the disease is directly related to the mechanisms of cerebral lateralization. This also provides a possible explanation of the persistence of the disease—that it is an anomaly of the genetic mechanisms which have been of particular importance in the evolution of cerebral function in man, and which perhaps are associated with a high degree of variation, i.e. a genomic 'hot-spot'. According to this concept the psychosis gene is located at the site of the cerebral dominance gene (a growth factor), has characteristics (e.g. direct terminal repeats) of a viral sequence, and includes a variable sequence which determines its expression and perhaps timing.

REFERENCES

Benveniste R. E., Todaro G. J. (1976). Evolution of C-type viral genes evidence for an Asian origin of man. *Nature*; 261: 101–8.

Boklage C. E. (1977). Schizophrenia, brain asymmetry development and twinning: a cellular relationship with etiologic and possibly prognostic implications. *Biological Psychiatry*; 12: 19–35.

Breakefield X. O., Stern D. F. (1986) Oncogenes in neural tumours. *Trends in Neurosciences*; 9: 150–5.

Brown R., Colter N., Colsellis J. A. N. *et al.* (1986). Post-mortem evidence of structural brain changes in schizophrenia. *Archives of General Psychiatry*; 43: 36–42.

Chickaraishi D. M. (1986). The ID, brain identifier, model of neuronal expression: a re-evaluation. *Trends in Neurosciences*; 9: 543–6.

Colter N., Crow T. J., Johnstone E. C., Owens D. G. C. (1988). Developmental arrest of cerebral asymmetries in early onset schizophrenia (in press).

Crichton-Browne J. (1879). On the weight of the brain and its component parts in the insane. *Brain*; 2: 42–67.

Crow T. J. (1984). A re-evaluation of the viral hypothesis: is psychosis due to retroviral integration at the site of the cerebral dominance gene? *British Journal of Psychiatry*; 145: 243–53.

Crow T. J. (1986a). Left brain, retrotransposons and schizophrenia. *British Medical Journal*; 193: 3–4.

Crow T. J. (1986b). The continuum of psychosis and its implication for the structure of the gene. *British Journal of Psychiatry*; 149: 419–29.

Crow T. J. (1987). Mutation and psychosis; a possible explanation for seasonality of birth. *Psychological Medicine*; 17: 821–8.

Crow T. J., Done D. J. (1986). Age of onset of schizophrenia in siblings: a test of the contagion hypothesis. *Psychiatry Research*; 18: 107–17.

Hamilton C. R. (1977). An assessment of hemispheric specialisation in monkeys. *Annals of the New York Academy of Sciences*; 299: 222–32.

Hunt S. P., Pini A., Evan G. (1987). Induction of c-fos-like protein in spinal cord neurons following sensory stimulation. *Nature*; 328: 632–4.

Jeffreys A. J., Wilson V., Thein S. L. (1985). Hypervariable 'minisatellite' regions in human DNA. *Nature*; 314: 67–73.

Johnstone E. C., Bydder G. M., Colter N., Crow T. J., Frith C. D., Owens D. G. C. (1988). The spectrum of structural brain changes in schizophrenia: age of onset as a predictor of cognitive and clinical impairments and their cerebral correlates (in press).

Johnstone E. C., Macmillan J. F., Crow T. J. (1987). The occurrence of organic disease of possible or probable aetiological significance in a population of 268 cases of first episode schizophrenia. *Psychological Medicine*; 17: 371–9.

Karlsson J. L. (1970). The rate of schizophrenia in foster-reared close relatives of schizophrenic index cases. *Biological Psychiatry*; 2: 285–90.

Karlsson J. L. (1974). Inheritance of schizophrenia. *Acta Psychiatrica Scandinavica Supplementum* 247.

King M. C., Wilson A. C. (1975) Evolution at two levels in humans and chimpanzees. *Science*; 188: 107–16.

Levy J. (1977) The mammalian brain and the adaptive advantage of cerebral asymmetry. *Annals of the New York Academy of Sciences*; 299: 264–72.

Luys M. J. (1881). Contribution a l'étude d'une statistique sur le poids des hemispheres cerebraux à l'état normal et à l'état pathologique. *L'Encephale*; 1: 644–6.

McGuffin P., Farmer A., Gottesman, I. I. (1987). Is there really a split in schizophrenia? The genetic evidence. *British Journal of Psychiatry*; 150: 581–92.

Murray R. M., Lewis S. M., Reveley, A. M. (1985). Towards an aetiological classification of schizophrenia. *Lancet*; i: 1023–6.

Murray R. M., Reveley A. M., McGuffin P. (1986). Genetic vulnerability to schizophrenia. In: *Schizophrenia* (Roy A., ed.) pp. 13–16. W. B. Saunders, Philadelphia: Psychiatric Clinics of North America.

Owens D. G. C., Johnstone E. C., Crow T. J., Frith C. D., Jagoe J. R., Kreel L. (1985). Lateral ventricular size in schizophrenia: relationship to the disease process and its clinical manifestations. *Psychological Medicine*; 15: 27–41.

Parfitt D. N. (1956). The neurology of schizophrenia. *Journal of Mental Science*; 102: 671–718.

Reynolds G. P. (1983). Increased concentrations and lateral asymmetry of amygdala dopamine in schizophrenia. *Nature*; 305: 527–9.

Russell B. (1961). *History of Western Philosophy*. London: George Allen & Unwin.

Slater E., Cowie V. (1971). *The Genetics of Mental Disorders*. Oxford: Oxford University Press.

Southard E. E. (1915). On the topographic distribution of cortex lesions and anomalies in dementia praecox, with some account of their functional significance. *American Journal of Insanity*; 71: 603–71.

Sturt E., McGuffin P. (1985). Can linkage and marker association resolve the genetic aetiology of psychiatric disorders? Review and argument. *Psychological Medicine*; 15: 455–62.

Sutcliffe J. G., Milner R. J., Gottesfeld J. M., Reynolds W. (1984). Control of neuronal gene expression. *Science*; 225: 1308–15.

Warren J. M. (1977). Functional lateralisation in the brain. *Annals of the New York Academy of Sciences*; 299: 273–80.

Weinberg R. A. (1982). Fewer and fewer oncogenes. *Cell*; 30: 3–4.

11 Clinical pharmacology of schizophrenia

STEPHEN M. STAHL and KATHLEEN M. WETS

'Antipsychotic' is a term widely used to denote the effectiveness of a drug to combat psychoses in schizophrenic patiènts, as well as several other types of psychoses. 'Neuroleptic', on the other hand, refers to drugs that affect several integrating systems of the brain, as well as having the potential for eliciting a parkinsonian-like syndrome. These terms are now used interchangeably. Delay and Deniker (1952) coined the term 'neuroleptic syndrome' to refer to the psychological profile caused by neuroleptics characterized in humans by emotional quieting, affective indifference, and psychomotor slowing.

The discovery of the antipsychotic effect of chlorpromazine in the early 1950s marked the beginning of modern psychopharmacology. Its clinical application profoundly changed the lives of thousands of hospitalized schizophrenic patients, allowing many of them to leave hospital and to function effectively in the community. Antipsychotic drugs not only increased the rate of remission, but also shortened the length of psychotic episode for many with schizophrenia. Recent research on neuroleptic/antipsychotic drugs, however, has pointed out their limitations. For example, neuroleptic agents are primarily effective against the positive symptoms of schizophrenia, such as delusions and hallucinations, and are much less effective for the negative symptoms of schizophrenia, such as alogia, apathy and affective flattening. Furthermore, there are some patients with positive symptoms refractory to treatment, and these patients derive little or no benefit from the currently available antipsychotic drugs. However, the most troubling and limiting use of neuroleptic drugs is the production of unwanted movement disorders. Acute dose-limiting side-effects known as the extrapyramidal reactions of pseudoparkinsonism, akathisia, and dystonia, are coupled with the chronic disfiguring and often permanent movement disorder known as tardive dyskinesia. Intensive preclinical and clinical research during the last decades on the aetiology of schizophrenia and the mechanisms of action of antipsychotic drugs has increased the possibilities of developing new drugs with more potent antipsychotic effect and without the many undesirable side-effects of today's therapies.

The dopamine hypothesis of schizophrenia came into existence primarily as a result of increased understanding about the mechanism of action of the neuroleptic drugs. The dopamine hypothesis of schizophrenia postulates overactive dopamine (DA) neurotransmission as an underlying cause in schizophrenic symptomatology. This hypothesis has as its foundation two lines of pharmacological evidence: (1) dopamine receptor antagonists (e.g. haloperidol) are often effective antipsychotics and (2) drugs that increase DA activity (e.g. amphetamines) induce psychosis in non-psychotic subjects, and can exacerbate psychosis in schizophrenic patients with active symptoms of psychopathology (*see* Meltzer and Stahl, 1976).

Results from various investigators have led to the conclusion that a mechanism of action common to effective antipsychotic agents is an inhibition of dopamine action, usually blockade of post-synaptic dopamine receptors. Further experiments suggest that at least two classes of dopamine receptors exist which have different affinities for receptor-active agents (Cools and Van Rossum, 1976, 1980; Kebabian *et al.*, 1977; Setler *et al.*, 1978; Titeler *et al.*, 1978; Kebabian and Calne, 1979; Spano *et al.*, 1979; Richelson, 1980; Sokoloff *et al.*, 1980a; 1980b; Costall and Naylor, 1981; Snyder, 1981). Current nomenclature distinguishes the two receptors as D1 and D2 dopamine receptors (Table 11.1). The D1 receptors are coupled to adenylate cyclase and, in binding assays, are selectively labelled by drugs such as the agonist SKF-38393 (Setler *et al.*, 1978; Munemura *et al.*, 1980; Mackenzie and Zigmond, 1985; Scatton and Dubois, 1985) and the antagonist SCH-23390 (Hyttel, 1983). The other DA receptors, the D2 receptors, do not enhance adenylate cyclase and are preferentially labelled by receptor agonists such as (+)-4-propyl-9-hydroxynaphthoxazine (PHNO) (Martin *et al.*, 1984) or antagonists such as sulpiride (*see* Martres *et al.*, 1985).

It is still unclear whether there is any correlation between synaptic locations (pre- versus post-synaptic) or DA anatomical locations (nigro-striatal versus mesolimbic) and the D1/D2 receptor classification. It has been proposed that the antipsychotic effect of neuroleptic drugs is mediated primarily by blockade of D2 dopamine receptors. This assumption is based on the occurrence of a linear correlation between drug affinity for central D2 dopamine receptors in animals and antipsychotic potency in man (Peroutka and Snyder, 1980). Several new compounds have been synthesized in an attempt to exploit this principle and are discussed below. It is hoped that this subcategorization of receptors will make it possible to

Table 11.1 Classification of dopamine D1/D2 receptors

	D1	*D2*
Adenylate cyclase stimulation	Yes	No
Selective agonists	SKF-38393	(+)-PHNO
Selective antagonists	SCH 23390	Sulpiride

design drugs which will selectively activate or inhibit either the D1 or D2 receptors. These new selective drugs will, in turn, help to clarify the importance of these two DA receptors in schizophrenia, as their respective roles are currently obscure.

To understand better the mechanisms of action of antipsychotics and their neuroleptic effect, it helps to examine their influence on the various dopamine pathways in the brain, specifically the nigrostriatal and mesolimbic pathways. The nigrostriatal system originates from the substantia nigra, termed A-9, and the mesolimbic systems originate from the ventral tegmentum, termed A-10. Nigrostriatal activity (A-9 innervated) is thought to relate to the motor effects of drugs, whereas mesolimbic activity (A-10 innervated) is associated with emotional and cognitive activity (Creese, 1983).

Much research is, and has been, done on dopamine and schizophrenia. However, since schizophrenia is a disorder primarily characterized by bizarre and fragmented thoughts, it is impossible to replicate 'true-to-life' animal models. Nonetheless, animal behavioural analogues of human psychosis and of motor side-effects have been developed, based on observations of administration of antipsychotics and of various other dopaminergic agents to animals. Behavioural correlates in rats associated with DA receptor activity include antagonism of apomorphine- and amphetamine-induced stereotypies, hyperactivity, induction of catalepsy, and activity in conditioned avoidance escape paradigms (*see* Iversen and Iversen, 1975).

Neuroleptic actions in animals are linked to human responses based on the effect they have on the two dopamine pathways of interest, namely the mesolimbic and nigrostriatal pathways. As mentioned above, it is generally believed that in humans the 'antipsychotic' action of neuroleptics is mediated via DA blockade in the mesolimbic pathways. In rats, neuroleptic effects in this pathway are associated with suppression of the conditioned avoidance response and hyperactivity (Davidson *et al.*, 1983; White and Wang, 1983; Martres *et al.*, 1984; Vasse *et al.*, 1985). The various extrapyramidal side-effects seen in neuroleptic-treated schizophrenic patients are thought to result from actions on the nigrostriatal system. In the rat, neuroleptics have a direct effect on turning behaviour, acute stereotypy and catalepsy, behaviours believed to be mediated by nigrostriatal pathways (Davidson *et al.*, 1983; White and Wang, 1983; Martres *et al.*, 1984; Vasse *et al.*, 1985). All this suggests that the effect of neuroleptics on animal behaviours associated with nigrostriatal pathways (e.g. turning behaviour) can be used as a predictor of extrapyramidal symptoms in humans, and that their effect on behaviours associated with mesolimbic pathways in animals (e.g. conditioned avoidance response) can be used to predict antipsychotic activity (*see* Table 11.2).

Most of the current neuroleptics have comparable actions on both sets of animal behaviours (i.e. turning behaviour and conditioned avoidance response), and are categorized as conventional or 'typical' neuroleptics.

Table 11.2 Properties of nigrostriatal and mesolimbic dopamine systems

	Nigrostriatal A-9	Mesolimbic A-10
Man	Extra-pyramidal side-effects	Psychosis
Rats	Turning behaviour Stereotypy Catalepsy	Conditioned avoidance response Hyperactivity

However, certain compounds, such as clozapine, benzamide derivatives, and piquindone, have preferential action on mesolimbic mediated behaviours (conditioned avoidance and hyperactivity), and have, on this basis, been categorized as 'atypical' neuroleptics. This classification of certain neuroleptics as atypical is thus based strictly on animal behaviour studies. This distinction is important for, if true, it predicts that 'atypical' neuroleptics should have more antipsychotic efficacy and fewer extrapyramidal effects, at a given dose, than do the 'typical' neuroleptics.

NEUROLEPTICS

Effective antipsychotic agents have been available for over 30 years, but all produce varying degrees of side-effects, either autonomic effects, such as hypotension, or extrapyramidal effects, such as parkinsonism and tardive dyskinesia (*see* Davis, 1980). Haloperidol and the phenothiazine drugs ('typical') are examples of antipsychotic agents with relatively low hypotensive liability but marked extrapyramidal effects (Baldessarini, 1980), whereas clozapine ('atypical') is an antipsychotic agent with few or no extrapyramidal effects but marked hypotensive activity (Simpson and Lee, 1978).

Although all neuroleptics interact with the DA system, most neuroleptics are also capable of blocking various other neurotransmitter systems, such as the adrenergic, cholinergic, histaminergic or serotonergic receptors in the brain. These properties may explain many of the (sometimes undesirable) side-effects of neuroleptic administration such as sedation, dry mouth, constipation, and various cardiovascular disturbances. These autonomic symptoms can be avoided, in some cases, by selecting neuroleptics that have less anticholinergic or adrenergic blocking activities.

The most troublesome side-effects associated with neuroleptic therapy, however, are those related to neurological impairment, and are generally referred to as the extrapyramidal side-effects (EPRS). A variety of these neurological syndromes follow the use of almost all typical antipsychotic drugs. These reactions are particularly prominent during treatment with the piperazine group of phenothiazine drugs and with haloperidol. In general, there is a positive correlation between the incidence and severity of these disorders and the age of the patient. Four types of extrapyramidal syndromes are associated with the use of antipsychotic drugs, the most common being a rigid akinetic parkinsonian syndrome usually accompanied by tremor and occurring in approximately 40% of neuroleptic-treated schizophrenics (Enna and Coyle, 1983). Akathisia, described as a compelling need to be in constant motion and restless agitation, is seen in approximately 20% of patients. A few patients, about 5% of those treated, develop acute dystonia. Among the features common to this syndrome are dystonic posturing, tongue protrusion, facial grimacing and torticollis.

The fourth group of extrapyramidal syndromes associated with neuroleptic administration is collectively termed the dyskinesias, and is observed in about 30% of patients. The severity of the symptoms is dose related, and recovery can occur following termination of neuroleptic treatment.

The most intractable neurological side-effect is tardive dyskinesia (TD). Tardive dyskinesia is characterized by stereotyped involuntary and choreiform movements. This disorder usually becomes apparent after several years of treatment, may worsen when the drug is withdrawn, and can be irreversible.

The growing concern over the risk of tardive dyskinesia has pushed researchers to look for antipsychotics with fewer extrapyramidal effects, i.e. with less nigrostriatal activity, such as the new atypical neuroleptics. The hypothesis, yet unproven, is that drugs which are devoid of acute EPRS would also be less likely to cause tardive dyskinesia (Stahl, 1986). Thus current research is focused on developing new drugs with a preferential action on mesolimbic and extrastriatal dopamine D2-containing neurons without affecting the nigrostriatal dopamine system of the brain. This selectivity could result in a maintained antipsychotic efficacy with few or, at best, no EPRS.

Another objective of research in schizophrenia is to find drugs with a high selectivity for the dopamine systems without effects on other neurotransmitter systems, so as to minimize the well known, predominantly autonomic, side-effects of neuroleptic compounds. It may therefore be possible, by increasing the specificity of the dopamine receptor blockade, to eliminate adverse effects while optimizing therapeutic effects in this class of drugs.

Typical neuroleptics

The contrasts among the various typical neuroleptic agents are not impressive, in that they do not differ appreciably or significantly among themselves with respect to their overall clinical effectiveness, even though patients will often respond to one drug and not to another. The aliphatic phenothiazines (e.g. chlorpromazine) are supposedly more effective against the 'positive' symptoms of schizophrenia (Johnstone *et al.*, 1978) than the piperazine compounds (e.g. trifluoperazine and the butyrophenones), which are said to be more useful in combating the 'negative' symptoms such as social withdrawal and blunting of affect, but this has yet to be proved beyond doubt. Neuroleptics, in general, are not impressively effective in treating negative symptoms over the long course of chronic schizophrenic illness. The most significant difference among the various typical neuroleptics is in their side-effects. Chlorpromazine and thioridazine are soporific, whereas haloperidol is much less so, and chlorpromazine has a moderate incidence of EPRS, lower than that of the phenothiazines and butyrophenones.

Phenothiazines and thioxanthenes

The phenothiazines as a class, and especially chlorpromazine, the prototype, are among the most widely used drugs in the practice of medicine today. Phenothiazine and thioxanthene derivatives have many pharmacological and therapeutic applications in common. They have similar three-ringed structures, with substitutions usually at positions 2 and 10. Substitutions of a chlorine in position 2 (e.g. chlorpromazine and chlorprothixene) increase potency for depressing both motor activity and conditioned avoidance response in animals (the so-called 'typical' profile), and for improving psychotic behaviour as well as increasing EPRS in humans. Substitution at position 10 also influences pharmacological activity, and the phenothiazines and thioxanthenes are divided into three groups based on substitution at this site: aliphatic/piperidine/piperazine.

The group with an aliphatic side chain includes chlorpromazine and chlorprothixene. The group with piperidine side chains have approximately the same order of clinical potency, but appear to have a lower incidence of extrapyramidal side-effects. Thioridazine is an example of a piperidine phenothiazine, but is considered by some investigators to be an atypical neuroleptic due to its stronger antagonism of the D2 receptor in mesolimbic regions than in nigrostriatal regions (White and Wang, 1983; *see* Maidment and Marsden, 1987a, b). The most potent phenothiazine antipsychotic compounds are of the third group, which have a piperazine group in position 10, such as prochlorperazine, thioxanthene, and thiothixene. In addition, these derivatives apparently do not cause as much drowsiness as others.

Chlorpromazine, the most extensively studied congener in this class, may be taken as the prototype drug. Chlorpromazine has the behavioural profile common to the typical neuroleptics, in particular its ability to induce catalepsy in rats at doses effective for depressing locomotor activity (Fielding and Lal, 1978).

Catalepsy is an akinetic state of hypomobility accompanied by muscular weakness and hypotonia. Catalepsy resembles, but is not the same as, the catatonia seen in some schizophrenic patients. In man, catatonic symptoms are relieved by phenothiazines rather than being exacerbated by them. It appears that this cataleptogenic action in animals is in fact more closely linked to the induction in man of EPRS effects, such as dystonia and pseudoparkinsonism (Jenner and Marsden, 1979).

Neuroleptic induction of catalepsy in animals was originally thought to be part of the 'effective' action of neuroleptic drugs. However, as newer neuroleptics were developed, it became evident that induction of catalepsy was greatly variable, and could even be absent in compounds that showed incontestable antipsychotic activity (*see* Worms *et al.*, 1983).

Butyrophenones

Haloperidol, a butyrophenone, was synthesized by Janssen and introduced for the treatment of psychoses in Europe in 1958. It is an extremely potent antipsychotic agent, but its pharmacology differs only in degree, not in kind, from the piperazine phenothiazines. Haloperidol, like most typical neuroleptics, calms and induces sleep in excited patients, but this sedative effect is less prominent than that of chlorpromazine. Haloperidol also has less prominent autonomic effects than most of the other antipsychotic drugs. However, haloperidol does produce a high incidence of extrapyramidal reactions. This is not surprising in view of the fact that haloperidol antagonizes apomorphine-induced hyperactivity at doses close to those which induce catalepsy in rats (Puech *et al.*, 1976; Worms, 1982) (*see* Fig. 11.1), which implies that haloperidol has high nigrostriatal activity. Overall, haloperidol treatment increases striatal D2 receptors without altering D1 receptors (Rupniak *et al.*, 1985).

Atypical neuroleptics

Catalepsy, as defined earlier, is induced in rats by neuroleptics, and is a behavioural effect believed to be broadly analogous to some of the Parkinson-like side-effects seen in patients treated with these drugs. The ability of neuroleptics to induce catalepsy probably reflects an action within the nigrostriatal and extrapyramidal DA systems. What differentiates the typical neuroleptics from the atypical neuroleptics is not the specific behavioural effects they have, but rather the difference between the doses blocking hyperactivity in rats and the doses which induce catalepsy. Although the benzamides and other atypical neuroleptics can induce catalepsy, in general, the doses required are of a much higher magnitude in comparison to the dose required to inhibit apomorphine- or amphetamine-induced hyperactivity.

Extrapolating from the animal behaviour model, the hypothesis for atypical neuroleptic action in man states that the dose of an atypical agent required to be effective for combating psychosis (hyperactivity) is lower than the dose which will induce EPRS (catalepsy). This is not always true for the typical neuroleptics, where the 'window' between these two doses is

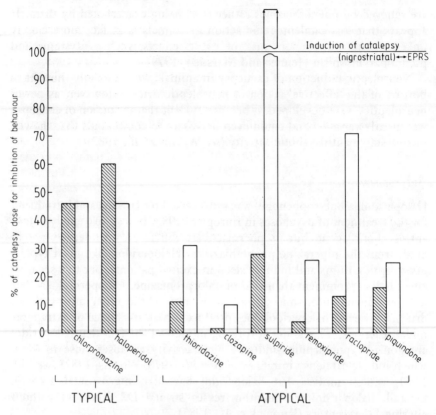

Fig. 11.1 Behavioural profile of typical and atypical neuroleptics. Typical neuroleptic profile shows how nigrostriatal and mesolimbic effects are fairly closely intermeshed; whereas the atypical profile displays a discernible differentiation between the doses affecting activity at these two pathways. Data presented in this histogram are approximations based on the results of various investigators: Ogren et al., 1984, 1986; Davidson et al., 1983; Creese et al., 1976; Worms et al., 1983. ▨ Hyperactivity (mesolimbic) ↔ psychosis; ☐ stereotypies (nigrostriatal) ↔ EPRS

not large and, as a consequence, the effective antipsychotic dose does invariably cause various extrapyramidal reactions (*see* Fig. 11.1).

Dibenzodiazepines

Clozapine, an atypical neuroleptic, was synthesized in 1960. Early studies showed clozapine to be a unique antipsychotic which did not induce extrapyramidal effects (Stille *et al.*, 1971; Schmutz, 1975). Pharmacologically, clozapine is strongly sedative and a muscle relaxant. In rats, clozapine is relatively inactive in producing catalepsy, does not antagonize apomorphine- or amphetamine-induced stereotyped behaviour, and has low potency in blocking conditioned avoidance responses in animals. Clozapine does block dopamine receptors; however, unlike haloperidol, it may not chronically alter striatal D2 receptor function, but does appear to have some effect on the striatal D1 receptors (Rupniak *et al.*, 1985).

Clozapine has provided a tool for the examination of the properties of antipsychotic agents. It shows a spectrum of action on dopaminergic systems that differs from that of haloperidol, producing greater dopamine turnover changes in the limbic system than in the corpus striatum. However, it is as potent as chlorpromazine in its ability to inhibit the D1-receptor-mediated activation of adenylate cyclase from both the caudate nucleus and limbic system (Clement-Cormier *et al.*, 1974; Karobath and Leitich, 1974; Miller *et al.*, 1974). Clozapine, like chlorpromazine, has a central sedative action and strong antagonistic effects against adrenaline, noradrenaline, acetylcholine and histamine. It also has a strong analgesic action. Except for its inability to induce catalepsy, the pharmacological profile of clozapine resembles that of chlorpromazine, but it clearly differs from haloperidol.

In man, clozapine has few EPRS in patients successfully treated with this drug (Gerlach *et al.*, 1974; 1975; Matz *et al.*, 1974; Simpson and Varga, 1974; Chiu *et al.*, 1976; Battegay *et al.*, 1977; Thorup and Fog, 1977; Gelenberg and Doller, 1979; Leon, 1979; Juul Povlsen *et al.*, 1985). It is also claimed not to induce tardive dyskinesia (Gerlach *et al.*, 1974; Matz *et al.*, 1974; Simpson and Varga, 1974; Juul Povlsen *et al.*, 1985). This category of drug, however, is characterized clinically and pharmacologically by induction of a wide range of unwanted motor effects, some acute, disfiguring and occasionally life-threatening, others chronically disabling. Clozapine administration can lead to the metabolic type bone marrow suppression, which may lead to reduced white blood cell counts and granulocytopenia. Agranulocytosis risk, projected at 2.5 cases/1000 patients treated, is comparable to some estimates for chlorpromazine, but clozapine is still considered by most authors to have more risk of agranulocytosis than the other neuroleptic drugs. At therapeutic doses, clozapine has more pronounced cardiovascular effects, such as hypotension and tachycardia, than standard drugs. These responses are dose-dependent, and can be particularly troublesome with high starting doses. Clozapine may also lower the seizure threshold, particularly in patients with histories of convulsions or brain trauma. This problem, also encountered with standard neuroleptics, is generally manageable by dose reduction.

Due to clozapine's troublesome side-effects, it has received a bad reputation; however clozapine's promise as an antipsychotic is that it represents an alternative therapy for treatment of refractory psychotic patients who have responded suboptimally to other standard treatments. Additionally, clozapine's low profile of EPRS effects, has led patients in a multicentre trial to report their satisfaction with clozapine over other medications they have taken (Kane, 1987). Currently, US multicentre trials are in progress looking at clozapine's effectiveness with refractory patients. The initial results from these trials look promising and, in the 125 patients treated, no agranulocytosis developed.

Benzamides

The antipsychotic substituted benzamides were first developed during the 1960s by Justin-Besancon *et al.* (1964), as centrally active pharmacological tools. As a group, they include sulpiride, remoxipride and raclopride, all of which possess, to a greater or lesser degree, some antiemetic, antipsychotic and antidyskinetic activity in man. Sulpiride, the most tested drug in this series, is claimed to exert an antipsychotic action in the virtual absence of extrapyramidal effects. With respect to the mechanism of action, sulpiride possesses a neurochemical spectrum compatible with blockade of DA receptors in the limbic and extrapyramidal areas, thus resembling the typical neuroleptics, the major difference between the benzamides and the typical neuroleptics being that these benzamide derivatives do not block D1 receptors, and are weak in competing with $[^3H]$-butyrophenones for binding to striatal membrane preparations. Kebabian *et al.* (Kebabian *et al.* 1977; Kebabian and Calne 1979) have suggested that benzamides may behave as selective D2 receptor antagonists. Although this classification is consistent with their inactivity in the cyclase system, it cannot account for their low potencies in neuroleptic binding assays since labelled butyrophenones are believed mainly to label D2 sites (Lin and Wilk, 1982).

Looking at the animal models which identify cerebral dopamine antagonists and define atypical neuroleptics, substituted benzamide drugs show the so-called atypical profile. For example, in animal experiments sulpiride is able to inhibit apomorphine-induced hyperactivity in rats without causing pronounced catalepsy, and is a weak antagonist for apomorphine or amphetamine-induced stereotyped behaviour in rats (Worms, 1982) (*see* Fig. 11.1).

Sulpiride

Sulpiride's preclinical pharmacological profile was characterized by very potent blockade of apomorphine emesis in the dog, weak antagonism of apomorphine and amphetamine-induced stereotyped behaviour, weak induction of catalepsy, and weak suppression of spontaneous motility in mice (Jenner *et al.*, 1982). Sulpiride is essentially inactive as an antagonist of the D1-receptor, but is an effective antagonist of the D2 receptor. Sulpiride appears to have little interaction with other neurotransmitters. In particular, sulpiride does not affect the levels of metabolites for 5-hydroxytryptamine (5HT) or noradrenaline.

Peselow and Stanley (1982) reviewed the clinical trials of sulpiride in schizophrenic patients and found that, although the methodological designs varied and the studies had numerous flaws (lack of standardized objective rating scales), there was a global improvement in approximately 75% of patients treated with sulpiride. Several open studies have remarked on the low incidence of anticholinergic and sedative side-effects, in addition to the low incidence of extrapyramidal symptoms (Mielke *et al.*, 1977). From the various trials conducted it seems clear that sulpiride is an effective antipsychotic agent (*see* review in Peselow and Stanley, 1982), but further tests are warranted to assess whether chronic administration of sulpiride does indeed fail to induce tardive dyskinesia.

Remoxipride

Remoxipride is another substituted benzamide, and a new potential atypical neuroleptic. It has been shown to be a potent dopamine receptor antagonist, with preferential activity in mesolimbic brain areas of the rat, and acting predominantly on the D2 receptors (Ogren *et al.*, 1984). Additionally, remoxipride has been found not to have other potent pharmacological activities, and appears to cause only small effects in the cardiovascular system.

It is well established that classical neuroleptics such as haloperidol and chlorpromazine cause catalepsy in the rat by blocking DA receptors in the striatum. The potency of these agents, in this respect, is positively correlated to their propensity to induce extrapyramidal side-effects in man. Remoxipride causes a weak and atypical form of catalepsy (animals move when stimulated) at doses markedly higher than those required for blockade of mesolimbic DA receptors (*see* Fig. 11.1). It is a potent antagonist of apomorphine-induced hyperactivity in the rat, markedly more potent than sulpiride and thioridazine. Stereotypies are affected by remoxipride only at a much higher dose level. As with sulpiride, there is a wide separation between the doses of remoxipride that cause catalepsy and those required to block apomorphine-induced hyperactivity (for review *see* Ogren *et al.*, 1984) (*see* Fig. 11.1).

Clinical trials have begun, using remoxipride in schizophrenic patients (McCreadie *et al.*, 1985; Lindstrom *et al.*, 1985; Lund Laursen and Gerlach, 1986; Chouinard, 1987), and early results suggest that the atypical profile in animal behavioural models may indeed predict fewer extrapyramidal side-effects at doses which are effective in reducing psychosis. The investigators also report no significant cardiovascular side-effects caused by administration of remoxipride in these subjects.

Raclopride

Raclopride is another potential atypical neuroleptic of the benzamide type, with a similar pharmacological and behavioural profile to remoxipride. In rats, a marked separation exists between the dose of raclopride required to block apomorphine-induced hyperactivity and the dose causing catalepsy (*see* Fig. 11.1).

In vitro, raclopride binds selectively to striatal D2 receptors (Farde *et al.*, 1985). *In vivo*, [^{11}C]-raclopride's high specificity for striatal D2 receptors has uniquely been confirmed in the living human brain through use of positron emission tomography (PET), since [^{11}C]-raclopride passes rapidly through the blood–brain barrier (Farde *et al.*, 1986).

Raclopride has no known potent pharmacological effects with other receptor systems, and has been found to have no direct interaction with receptors such as the adrenergic, serotoninergic, histaminergic or muscarinic systems. Even at high doses, it causes only minor effects on the cardiovascular system (Kohler *et al.*, 1985; Hall *et al.*, 1986; Ogren *et al.*, 1986; *see* Raclopride, Drugs of the Future, 1987).

Clinical trials with raclopride have just started; Wahlen *et al.* (1987) reported that in the 10 schizophrenic patients they tested, the mean total EPRS was reduced by 55%. More studies are needed to assess raclopride's antipsychotic activity further and to determine whether it has any significant extrapyramidal effects after chronic administration.

Piquindone

Recently, a non-benzamide neuroleptic, piquindone (Ro 22-1319), has been discovered which is a member of a novel class of chemical compounds, the pyrroloisoquinolines. These compounds have been designed by computer to conform to a three-dimensional molecular model of the dopamine receptor (Olson *et al.*, 1981), and it is a D2 receptor antagonist (Davidson *et al.*, 1983). Its pharmacological profile suggests potent antipsychotic activity, with lower liability for extrapyramidal effects or tardive dyskinesia than drugs such as haloperidol.

In rats, piquindone blocks the conditioned avoidance response at doses corresponding to a relatively potent antipsychotic agent, while it is less potent in producing acute stereotypy and catalepsy (approximately one-sixth to one-tenth that of haloperidol) (Davidson *et al.*, 1983). This implies that, in man, the dose at which piquindone is an effective antipsychotic is much lower than the dose required to induce EPRS (*see* Fig. 11.1). Piquindone may therefore preferentially block dopamine receptors in the mesolimbic system rather than the nigrostriatal system.

Piquindone appears to be no more sedative than the other antipsychotic agents, is essentially free of other peripheral autonomic activity, and does not produce significant hypotensive or cardiotoxic effects in the dog (Davidson *et al.*, 1983).

Cohen *et al.* (1988a, b) conducted a two-week study in two centres on male schizophrenic veterans; 26 patients received active treatment. The data from this study suggest that piquindone has a beneficial short-term effect on the positive symptoms and, to a lesser degree, on the negative symptoms of schizophrenia. Since this study was only 2 weeks in duration, it is difficult to conclude whether piquindone does in fact cause less EPRS as is predicted by its animal behaviour profile. However, Cohen *et al.*

Table 11.3 Summary of pharmacological properties of typical and atypical neuroleptics

Pharmacological action	Typical neuroleptics	Atypical neuroleptics
Extrapyramidal actions turning behaviour stereotypy catalepsy pseudoparkinsonism	+ + +	+
Antipsychotic actions conditioned avoidance response hyperactivity antipsychotic effects	+ + +	+ + +

(1988a,b) felt that piquindone did in fact induce lower incidences of pseudoparkinsonism in comparison with conventional neuroleptic therapy. Furthermore, in an earlier study conducted by Uhr *et al.* (1986) using piquindone in patients with Gilles de la Tourette syndrome, it was found that therapeutic efficacy was achieved without the occurrence of any extrapyramidal symptoms. More clinical trials are currently being conducted on piquindone to assess its profile in chronic administration. If the results continue to be favourable, not only will there be a novel treatment for schizophrenic patients but they will also support the current animal model being used to discriminate psychotic activity from extrapyramidal activity.

NEW TREATMENTS

Much research and energy is currently being invested in these new atypical neuroleptics. However, other new and very different treatments are also being studied. Dopamine is still the main target for both typical and atypical neuroleptic treatment, since this neurotransmitter is hypothesized to play the major role in this disorder. There are, however, some researchers who believe that dysfunction in other neurochemical systems, such as the neuropeptides, sigma opiates and serotonin receptors, may actually be the primary cause of schizophrenia. The hypothesis is that these defective systems would in some manner affect dopamine transmission, making dopamine dysfunction a secondary or peripheral cause of schizophrenia. Already some promising results are being generated from research in these areas.

Cholecystokinin

In the past decade there has been increasing interest in the role of peptides as neurotransmitters or neuromodulators in the central nervous system. Cholecystokinin (CCK), a peptide with a central nervous system concentration greater than that found in the gut (Boza and Rotondo, 1985), is found predominantly in the form of CCK-8, an octapeptide, in the brain (Dockray, 1977; Rehfeld, 1978; Schneider *et al.*, 1979). CCK-8's probable role as a neurotransmitter or neuromodulator (Pinget *et al.*, 1978, 1979; Rehfeld *et al.*, 1979; Ishibashi *et al.*, 1979), and its coexistence with dopamine in neurons of the mesencephalon (Hokfelt *et al.*, 1980; Skirboll *et al.*, 1981), suggest that it may play a role in the pathogenesis or treatment of schizophrenia (*see* Nair *et al.*, 1985). Preliminary biochemical studies suggest that CCK has an antagonistic effect on DA-mediated neurotransmission (Fuxe *et al.*, 1980; Markstein and Hokfelt, 1984), and for this reason it is currently believed that administration of CCK-8 may prove to be an effective therapy for schizophrenic patients.

In laboratory animals, CCK has been shown to have effects on catalepsy and antagonism of amphetamine-induced stereotyped gnawing and other neuroleptic-like effects (Zetler, 1980, 1981, 1982, 1983). Initial clinical trials with CCK-8 and -33 in neuroleptic-resistant chronic schizophrenic patients found an improvement in clinical symptoms (Moroji *et al.*, 1982; Nair *et al.*, 1982; 1984; Bloom *et al.*, 1983; Verhoeven *et al.*, 1986). However, further investigations were not so encouraging (Hommer *et al.*, 1984; Lotstra *et al.*, 1984; Mattes *et al.*, 1985a; 1985b; Boza and Rotondo, 1985; Tamminga *et al.*, 1986; Albus *et al.*, 1986; Peselow *et al.*, 1987). Although these latter results are largely negative, great interest still remains in the potential of agonists (or even antagonists) of CCK receptors as novel antipsychotic agents.

Neurotensin

Neurotensin (NT) is another neuropeptide which has been linked to modulation of dopaminergic activity (*see* Nemeroff, 1986). Neurotensin appears to have preferential influence on mesolimbic, as opposed to mesostriatal, DA neuronal function (Nemeroff *et al.*, 1983). Already considerable data support the hypothesis that NT possesses a pharmacological profile resembling that of the neuroleptic drugs (Quirion, 1983; Nemeroff *et al.*, 1984; Nemeroff and Cain, 1985). Clinical trials involving NT in schizophrenic patients have yet to be initiated, although some preliminary work by Nemeroff (1986) shows that NT may be reduced in a subpopulation of schizophrenics.

Sigma opiates (rimcazole)

An 'ideal' neuroleptic would selectively antagonize apomorphine-elicited mesolimbic behaviours, without altering the intensity of stereotypic behaviours in the animal model. In man, this 'ideal' drug would theoretically combat psychosis without inducing any EPRS. In view of these limitations, a new potential antipsychotic agent has been identified: rimcazole, a sigma opiate site inhibitor.

The behavioural profile of rimcazole in animal models is similar to most neuroleptics: it blocks responses associated with apomorphine- or dopamine-stimulation of post-synaptic dopaminergic receptors in mesolimbic areas, i.e. hyperactivity (Ferris *et al.*, 1982). However, unlike neuroleptics, rimcazole elicited these effects without blocking responses associated with DA agonist-stimulation of post-synaptic dopaminergic receptors in striatal areas, i.e. stereotypy and catalepsy. Rimcazole also failed to block conditioned avoidance responses in rats (Ferris *et al.*, 1982).

Biochemical studies have shown that, unlike the typical neuroleptics, rimcazole has a specific but indirect effect on dopaminergic activity in the limbic area, and is entirely free of direct or indirect effect on dopaminergic activity in the striatal areas (Ferris *et al.*, 1982). Rimcazole is also unlike the atypical antipsychotics in that it has no D2 antagonistic properties. Ferris *et al.* (1986) found, however, that rimcazole is a good competitive inhibitor of sigma receptor sites in the brain.

Several independent open-label trials of rimcazole in schizophrenic patients have been reported (Davidson *et al.*, 1982; Guy *et al.*, 1983; Chouinard and Annable, 1984; Schwarcz *et al.*, 1985), and suggest that it is indeed an effective antipsychotic agent. The drug appears to be relatively free from neurological, cardiovascular, anticholinergic and CNS-depressant side-effects, except that it does possibly lower seizure threshold, which may limit its use in man.

Schwarcz *et al.* (1985) reported that rimcazole is slow in achieving full therapeutic efficacy, and is therefore a poor choice of drug for patients needing immediate behavioural control. However, the impressive absence of side-effects, and the presumed low or absent risk for tardive dyskinesia may make it an ideal drug for maintenance therapy of responsive patients.

A number of neuroleptics, such as haloperidol and piquindone, apparently block sigma receptors as well as D2 receptors. New chemical entities such as BMY 14802 (a buspirone analogue), and HR 375, may have only sigma antagonist properties. These agents are especially interesting as prospective novel antipsychotic drugs.

5-Hydroxytryptamine antagonists

Recent studies in rats and marmosets show that 5-hydroxytryptamine (5HT3) antagonists are as effective as other neuroleptic agents at antagonizing behaviours thought to be mediated by dopamine systems (Brittain *et al.*, 1987; Costall *et al.*, 1987). However, these agents are not direct D2 receptor antagonists. Some investigators have concluded that agents such as GR38032F, a potent selective antagonist at 5HT3 receptors, may represent a new class of psychoactive agents with the ability to exert antischizophrenic activity in the absence of the side-effects normally associated with neuroleptic treatment.

Three potent 5HT3 antagonists are receiving special attention with regard to their possible antipsychotic properties: ICS 205-930, which has proved to be an effective antiemetic treatment (Leibundgut and Lancranjan, 1987), and is also undergoing evaluation by Sandoz as an antimigraine agent (Pharmaprojects, May 1987); MDL 72222, also undergoing evaluation for its antimigraine activity by Merrell Dow (Pharmaprojects, May 1987); and GR38032F, which can reduce behavioural consequences of chronic infusion of dopamine into the mesolimbic nucleus accumbens of the rat and marmoset (Costall *et al.*, 1987; *see also* Hagan *et al.*, 1987).

CONCLUSION

In conclusion, the clinical pharmacology of schizophrenia today comprises the use of typical neuroleptic drugs. These drugs produce extrapyramidal side-effects at the doses required to control psychosis. Dawning on the horizon is a new era of so-called atypical neuroleptic drugs. These drugs, now in early clinical trials, may reduce psychotic symptoms at doses which do not produce extrapyramidal side-effects. In the more distant future, several new treatments based upon novel pharmacological mechanisms are being developed: CCK antagonists and agonists, neurotensin agonists and antagonists, sigma opiate antagonists, and 5HT3 receptor antagonists.

Although the introduction of the typical neuroleptics in the early 1950s revolutionized the treatment of schizophrenia, only slight improvements have occurred over the subsequent 30 years, resulting in a plethora of 'me too' drugs. It is hoped the atypical neuroleptics will come to represent a new chapter in the treatment of schizophrenia, characterized by substantial improvement in the side-effect profile of the typical drugs. However, an actual breakthrough in the treatment of schizophrenia will probably be derived from exploring novel pharmacological mechanisms, such as those represented by the neuropeptides, sigma opiates, or serotonin receptors.

REFERENCES

Albus M., Von Gellhorn K., Munch U., Naber D., Ackenheil M. (1986). A double-blind study with ceruletide in chronic schizophrenic patients: biochemical and clinical results. *Psychiatry Research*; **19**: 1–7.

Baldessarini R. J. (1980). Drugs and the treatment of psychiatric disorders. In: *The Pharmacological Basis of Therapeutics* (Gilman A. E., Goodman L. S., Gilman A., eds.), pp. 391–447. New York: Macmillan.

Battegay R., Cotar B., Fleischhauer J., Rauchfleisch U. (1977). Results and side effects of treatment with clozapine (Leoponex R). *Comprehensive Psychiatry*; **18**: 423–8.

Bloom D. M., Nair N. P. V., Schwartz G. (1983). CCK-8 in the treatment of chronic schizophrenia. *Psychopharmacology Bulletin*; **19**: 361–3.

Boza R., Rotondo D. J. (1985). Is cholecystokinin therapeutic in chronic schizophrenia. *Journal of Clinical Psychiatry*; 46: 485–6.

Brittain R. T., Butler A., Coates I. H. *et al.* (1987). GR38032F, a novel selective 5HT3 receptor antagonist. *British Journal of Pharmacology*; 90: 87P.

Chiu E., Borrows G., Stevenson J. (1976). Double-blind comparison of clozapine with chlorpromazine in acute schizophrenia in acute schizophrenic illness. *Australian and New Zealand Journal of Psychiatry*; 10: 343–7.

Chouinard G. (1987). Early phase II clinical trial of remoxipride in treatment of schizophrenia with measurements of prolactin and neuroleptic activity. *Journal of Clinical Psychopharmacology*; 7: 159–64.

Chouinard G., Annable L. (1984). An early phase II clinical trial of BW 234U in the treatment of acute schizophrenia in newly admitted patients. *Psychopharmacology*; 84: 282–4.

Clement-Cormier Y. C., Kebabian J. W., Petzold G. L., Greengard P. (1974). Dopamine sensitive adenylate cyclase in mammalian brain: a possible site of action of antipsychotic drugs. *Proceedings of the National Academy of Sciences (USA)*; 71: 1113–17.

Cohen J. D., Van Putten T., Marder S., Berger P. A., Stahl S. M. (1988a). The efficacy of piquindone, a new atypical neuroleptic, in the treatment of the positive and negative symptoms of schizophrenia. *Journal of Clinical Psychopharmacology*; (in press).

Cohen J. D., Van Putten T., Marder S., Berger P. A., Stahl S. M. (1988b). Treatment of the symptoms of schizophrenia with piquindone, a new atypical neuroleptic. *Psychopharmacology Bulletin*; (in press).

Cools A., Van Rossum J. M. (1976). Excitation-mediating and inhibition-mediating dopamine-receptors: a new concept towards a better understanding of electrophysiological, biochemical, pharmacological, functional and clinical data. *Psychopharmacologia*; 45: 243–54.

Cools A., Van Rossum J. M. (1980). Minireview: multiple receptors for brain dopamine in behavior regulation: concept of dopamine-E and dopamine-I receptors. *Life Sciences*; 27: 1237–53.

Costall B., Domeney A. M., Kelly M. E., Naylor R. J., Tyers M. B. (1987). The antipsychotic potential of GR38032F, a selective antagonist of $5HT_3$ receptors in the central nervous system. *British Journal of Pharmacology*; 90: 89P.

Costall B., Naylor R. J. (1981). Minireview: the hypothesis of different dopamine receptor mechanisms. *Life Sciences*; 28: 215–29.

Creese I. (1983). Classical and atypical antipsychotic drugs: new insights. *Trends in Neurosciences*; 6: 479–81.

Creese I., Burt D. R., Snyder S. (1976). Dopamine receptor binding predicts clinical and pharmacological potencies of antischizophrenic drugs. *Science*; 192: 481–3.

Davidson A. B., Boff E., MacNeil D. A., Wenger J., Cook L. (1983). Pharmacological effects of Ro 22-1319: a new antipsychotic agent. *Psychopharmacology*; 79: 32–9.

Davidson J., Miller R., Wingfield M., Zung W., Dren A. T. (1982). The first clinical study of BW 234U in schizophrenia. *Psychopharmacology Bulletin*; 18: 173–6.

Davis J. M. (1980). Antipsychotic drugs. In: *Comprehensive Textbook of Psychiatry* (Kaplan H. I., Freedman A. M., Sadock B. J., eds.). Baltimore: Williams and Wilkins.

Delay J., Deniker P. (1952). Trente-huit cas de psychoses traitées par la cure prolongée et continué de 4560RP. Le Congres des Al et Neurol de Langue Fr. *Comptes Rendus du Congrés* Paris: Masson et Cie.

Dockray G. J. (1977). Isolation, structure and biological activity of two cholecystokinin octapeptides from sheep brain. *Nature*; 270: 359–61.

Enna S. J., Coyle J. T. (1983). Neuroleptics. In: *Neuroleptics, Neurochemical, Behavioral and Clinical Perspectives* (Coyle J. T., Enna S. J., eds.), pp. 1–14. New York: Raven Press.

Farde L., Ehrin E., Erikson L. *et al.* (1985). Substituted benzamides as ligands for visualization of dopamine receptor binding in the human brain by positron emission tomography. *Proceedings of the National Academy of Sciences (USA)*; 82: 3863–7.

Farde L., Hall H., Ehrin E., Sedvall G. (1986). Quantitative analysis of D_2 dopamine receptor binding in the living human brain by PET. *Science*; 231: 258–61.

Ferris R. M., Harfenist M., McKenzie G., Cooper B., Soroko F. E., Maxwell R. A. (1982). BW 234U (*cis*-9-[3-(3,5-dimethyl-1-piperazinyl) propyl] carbazole dihydrochloride): a novel antipsychotic agent. *Journal of Pharmacy and Pharmacology*; 34: 388–90.

Ferris R. M., Tang F. L. M., Chang K. J., Russell A. (1986). Evidence that the potential antipsychotic agent rimcazole (BW234U) is a specific, competitive antagonist of sigma sites in brain. *Life Sciences*; 38: 2329–37.

Fielding S., Lal H. (1978). Behavioral actions of neuroleptics. In: *Neuroleptics and Schizophrenia*, Vol 10 of Handbook of Psychopharmacology (Iversen L. L., Iversen S. D., Snyder S. H., eds.), pp. 91–125. New York: Plenum Press.

Fuxe K., Andersson V., Locutelli V. *et al.* (1980). Cholecystokinin peptides produce marked reduction of dopamine turnover in discrete areas in the rat brain following intraventricular injection. *European Journal of Pharmacology*; 67: 329–31.

Gelenberg A., Doller J. (1979). Clozapine versus chlorpromazine for the treatment of schizophrenia: preliminary results from a double-blind study. *Journal of Clinical Psychiatry*; 40: 238.

Gerlach J., Koppelhus P., Helweg E., Monrad A. (1974). Clozapine and haloperidol in a single-blind crossover trial. Therapeutic and biochemical aspects in the treatment of schizophrenia. *Acta Psychiatrica Scandinavica*; 50: 410–24.

Gerlach J., Thorsen K., Fog R. (1975). Extrapyramidal reactions and amine metabolites in cerebrospinal fluid during haloperidol and clozapine treatment with schizophrenic patients. *Psychopharmacologia*; 40: 341–50.

Guy W., Manov G., Wilson W. H. *et al.* (1983). Psychotropic actions of BW 234U in the treatment of inpatient schizophrenics: a dose-range study. *Drug Development Research*; 3: 245–52.

Hagan R. M., Butler A., Hill J. M., Jordan C. C., Ireland S. J., Tyers M. B. (1987). Effect of the $5HT_3$ receptor antagonist, GR38032F, on responses to injection of a neurokinin agonist into the ventral tegmental area of the rat brain. *European Journal of Pharmacology*; 138: 303–5.

Hall H., Wedel I. (1986). Comparisons between the *invitro* binding of two substituted benzamides and two butyrophenones to dopamine D_2 receptors in the rat striatum. *Acta phasmacologica Toxicologica;* 58: 368–73.

Hokfelt T., Rehfeld J. F., Skirboll L., Ivenmark B., Goldstein M., Markey K. (1980). Evidence for coexistence of dopamine and CCK in mesolimbic neurons. *Nature*; 285: 476–8.

Hommer D. W., Picker D., Roy A., Ninan P., Boronow J., Paul S. M. (1984). The effects of ceruletide in schizophrenia. *Archives of General Psychiatry*; **41**: 617–19.

Hyttel J. (1983). SCH-23390—the first selective dopamine D-1 antagonist. *European Journal of Pharmacology*; **91**: 153–4.

Ishibashi S., Oomura Y., Okajima T., Shibata S. (1979). Cholecystokinin, motilin and secretion effects on the central nervous system. *Physiology and Behavior*; **23**: 401–3.

Iversen S. D., Iversen L. L. (1975). (eds.) *Behavioral Pharmacology*. Oxford: Oxford University Press.

Jenner P., Marsden C. O. (1979). The mechanism of action of substituted benzamides drugs. In: *Sulpiride and Other Benzamides* (Spano P. F., Trabucchi M., Corsin G. U., Gessa G. L., eds.). New York: Raven Press.

Jenner P., Theodorou A., Marsden C. D. (1982). Specific receptors for substituted benzamide drugs in brain. In: *The Benzamides: Pharmacology, Neurobiology and Clinical Aspects* (Rotrosen J., Stanley M., eds.), pp. 109–141. New York: Raven Press.

Johnstone E. C., Crow T. J., Frith C. D., Carney M. W., Price J. C. (1978). Mechanism of the antipsychotic effect in the treatment of acute schizophrenia. *Lancet*; **i**: 848–51.

Justin-Besancon L., Laville C., Thominet M. (1964). Le metoclopramide et son homologues. Introduction a leur etude biologique. *Compte Rendue de l'Academie des Sciences (Paris)*; **258**: 4384–6.

Juul Povlsen U., Noring U., Fog R., Gerlach J. (1985). Tolerability and therapeutic effect of clozapine. *Acta Psychiatrica Scandinavica*; **71**: 176–85.

Kane J. (1987). Clozapine found effective for schizophrenia, awaits FDA review. *Psychiatric News*; 5 June.

Karobath M., Leitich H. (1974). Antipsychotic drugs and dopamine-stimulated adenylate cyclase prepared from corpus striatum of rat brain. *Proceedings of the National Academy of Sciences (USA)*; **71**: 2915–8.

Kebabian J. W., Calne D. B. (1979). Multiple receptors for dopamine. *Nature*; **277**: 93–6.

Kebabian J. W., Calne D. B., Kebabian P. R. (1977). Lergotrile mesylate: an *in vivo* dopamine agonist which blocks dopamine receptors *in vitro*. *Communications in Psychopharmacology*; **1**: 311–18.

Kohler C., Hall H., Ogren S-O., Gawell L. (1985). Specific *in vitro* and *in vivo* binding of ^{3}H-raclopride: a potent substituted benzamide drug with high affinity for dopamine D_2 receptors in the rat brain. *Biochemical Pharmacology*; **34**: 2251–9.

Leibundgut U., Lancranjan I. (1987). First results with ICS 205-930 (5HT$_3$ receptor antagonist) in prevention of chemotherapy-induced emesis. *Lancet*; **i**: 1198.

Leon C. A. (1979). Therapeutic effects of clozapine. *Acta Psychiatrica Scandinavica*; **59**: 471–80.

Lin C. W., Wilk S. (1982). A comparison of the effect of substituted benzamides in radioceptor binding assays with their effects on brain dopaminergic systems *in vivo*. In: *The Benzamides: Pharmacology, Neurobiology, and Clinical Aspects* (Rotrosen J., Stanley M., eds.), pp. 51–60. New York: Raven Press.

Lindstrom L., Besey G., Stening G., Widerlov E. (1985). An open study of remoxipride, a benzamide derivative, in schizophrenia. *Psychopharmacology*; **86**: 241–3.

Lotstra F., Verbanck P., Mendlewicz J., Vanderhaeghen J. J. (1984). No evidence of antipsychotic effect of caerulein in schizophrenic patients free of neuroleptics: a double-blind cross-over study. *Biological Psychiatry*; 19: 877–82.

Lund Laursen A., Gerlach J. (1986). Antipsychotic effect of remoxipride, a new substituted benzamide with selective antidopaminergic activity. *Acta Psychiatrica Scandinavica*; 73: 17–21.

McCreadie R. G., Morrison D., Eccleston D., Gall R., Loudon J., Mitchell M. (1985). An open multicentre study of the treatment of florid schizophrenia with remoxipride. *Acta Psychiatrica Scandinavica*; 72: 139–43.

Mackenzie R. G., Zigmond M. J. (1985). Chronic neuroleptic treatment increases D_2 but not D_1 receptors in rat striatum. *European Journal of Pharmacology*; 113: 159–65.

Maidment N. T., Marsden C. A. (1987a). Repeated atypical neuroleptic administration effects on central dopamine metabolism monitored by *in vivo* voltammetry. *European Journal of Pharmacology*; 136: 141–9.

Maidment N. T., Marsden C. A. (1987b). Acute administration of clozapine, thioridazine and metoclopramide increases extracellular DOPAC and decreases extracellular 5HIAA, measured in the nucleus accumbens and striatum of the rat using *in vivo* voltammetry. *Neuropharmacology*; 26: 187–93.

Markstein R., Hokfelt T. (1984). Effect of cholecystokinin-octapeptide on dopamine release from slices of cat caudate nucleus. *Journal of Neuroscience*; 4: 570–5.

Martin G. E., Williams M., Pettibone D. J., Yarbrough G. G., Clineschmidt B. V., Jones J. H. (1984). Pharmacologic profile of a novel potent direct-acting dopamine agonist (+)-4-propyl-9-hydroxynaphthoxazine [(+)PHNO]. *Journal of Pharmacology and Experimental Therapeutics*; 230: 569–76.

Martres M.-P., Sales N., Bouthenet M.-L., Schwartz J.-C. (1985). Localization and pharmacological characterization of D-2 dopamine receptors in rat cerebral neocortex and cerebellum using [^{125}I]iodosulpiride. *European Journal of Pharmacology*; 118: 211–19.

Martres M.-P., Sokoloff P., Delandre M., Schwartz J., Protais P., Costentin J. (1984). Selection of dopamine antagonists discriminating various behavioral responses and radioligand binding sites. *Naunyn-Schmiedeberg's Archives of Pharmacology*; 325: 102–15.

Mattes J. A., Hom W., Rochford J. M., Orlosky M. (1985a). Ceruletide for schizophrenia: a double-blind study. *Biological Psychiatry*; 20: 533–8.

Mattes J. A., Hom W., Rochford J. M. (1985b). A high-dose, double-blind study of ceruletide in the treatment of schizophrenia. *American Journal of Psychiatry*; 142: 1482–4.

Matz R., Rick W., Oh D., Thompson H., Gershon S. (1974). Clozapine a potential antipsychotic agent without extrapyramidal manifestations. *Current Therapeutic Research*; 16: 687–95.

Meltzer H. Y., Stahl S. M. (1976). The dopamine hypothesis of schizophrenia: a review. *Schizophrenia Bulletin*; 2: 19–76.

Mielke D. H., Gallant D. M., Roniger J., Kessler C., Kessler L. R. (1977). Sulpiride: evaluation of antipsychotic activity in chronic schizophrenic patients. *Psychopharmacology Bulletin*; 13: 40–1.

Miller R. J., Horn A. S., Iversen L. L. (1974). The action of neuroleptic drugs on dopamine-stimulated adenosine cyclic 3,5-monophosphate production in rat neostriatum and limbic forebrain. *Molecular Pharmacology*; 10: 759–66.

Moroji T., Watanabe N., Aoki N., Itoh S. (1982). Antipsychotic effects of ceruletide (caerulein) on chronic schizophrenia. *Archives of General Psychiatry*; **39**: 485–6.

Munemura M., Cote T. E., Tsuruta K., Eskay R. L., Kebabian J. W. (1980). The dopamine receptor 1n the intermediate lobe of the rat pituitary gland: pharmacological characterization. *Endocrinology*; **107**: 1676–83.

Nair N. P. V., Bloom D. M., Debonnel G., Schwartz G., Mosticyan S. (1984). Cholecystokinin-octapeptide in chronic schizophrenia: a double-blind placebo-controlled study. *Progress in Neuropsychopharmacology and Biological Psychiatry*; **8**: 711–14.

Nair N. P. V., Bloom D. M., Nesforos J. N. (1982). Cholecystokinin appears to have antipsychotic properties. *Progress in Neuropsychopharmacology and Biological Psychiatry*; **6**: 509–12.

Nair N. P. V., Lal S., Bloom D. M. (1985). Cholecystokinin peptides, dopamine and schizophrenia—a review. *Progress in Neuropsychopharmacology and Biological Psychiatry*; **9**: 515–24.

Nemeroff C. B. (1986). The interaction of neurotensin with dopaminergic pathways in the central nervous system: basic neurobiology and implications for the pathogenesis and treatment of schizophrenia. *Psychoneuroendocrinology*; **11**: 15–37.

Nemeroff C. B., Cain S. T. (1985). Neurotensin—dopamine interactions in the central nervous system. *Trends in Pharmacological Sciences*; **6**: 201–5.

Nemeroff C. B., Kalivas P. W., Prange A. J. (1984). Interaction of neurotensin and dopamine in limbic structures. In: *Catecholamines: Neuropharmacology and Central Nervous System—Theoretical Aspects* (Usdin E., Carlsson A., Dahlstromm A., Engel J., eds.), pp. 199–206. New York: Alan R. Liss.

Nemeroff C. B., Luttinger D., Hernandez D. E. *et al.* (1983). Interactions of neurotensin with brain dopamine systems: biochemical and behavioral studies. *Journal of Pharmacology and Experimental Therapeutics*; **225**: 337–45.

Ogren S. O., Hall H., Kohler C., Magnusson O., Sjostrand S-E. (1986). The selective dopamine D_2 receptor antagonist raclopride discriminates between dopamine mediated motor functions. *Psychopharmacology*; **90**: 287–94.

Ogren S. O., Hall H., Kohler C. *et al.* (1984). Remoxipride, a new potential antipsychotic compound with selective anti-dopaminergic in the rat brain. *European Journal of Pharmacology*; **102**: 459–74.

Olson G. L., Cheung H.-C., Morgan K. D., Blount J. F., Todaro L., Berger L. (1981). A dopamine receptor model and its application in the design of a new class of rigid pyrrolo-[2,3-g] isoquinoline antipsychotics. *Journal of Medicinal Chemistry*; **24**: 1026–34.

Peroutka S. J., Snyder S. H. (1980). Relationship of neuroleptic drug effects on brain dopamine, serotonin, alpha-adreneric and histamine receptors to clinical potency. *American Journal of Psychiatry*; **137**: 1518–19.

Peselow E., Angrist B., Sudilovsky A. *et al.* (1987). Double-blind controlled trials of cholecystokinin octapeptide in neuroleptic-refractory schizophrenia. *Psychopharmacology*; **91**: 80–4.

Peselow E. D., Stanley M. (1982). Clinical trials of benzamides in psychiatry. In: *The Benzamides: Pharmacology, Neurobiology, and Clinical Aspects* (Rotrosen J., Stanley M., eds.), pp. 163–194. New York: Raven Press.

Pinget M., Straus E., Yalow R. S. (1978). Localization of cholecystokinin like immunoreactivity in isolated nerve terminals. *Proceedings of the National Academy of Sciences (USA)*; **75**: 6324–6.

Pinget M., Straus E., Yalow R. S. (1979). Release of cholecystokinin peptides from synaptosome-enriched fraction of rat cerebral cortex. *Life Sciences*; **25**: 339–42.

Puech A. J., Simon P., Boissier J. R. (1976). Antagonism by sulpiride of three apomorphine-induced effects in rodents. *European Journal of Pharmacology*; 36: 439–41.

Quirion R. (1983). Interactions between neurotensin and dopamine in the brain: an overview. *Peptides*; 4: 609–15.

Raclopride (1987). *Drugs of the Future*; 12: 506–7.

Rehfeld J. F. (1978). Immunochemical studies on cholecystokinin II. distribution and molecular heterogeneity in the central nervous system and small intestine of man and dog. *Journal of Biological Chemistry*; 253: 4022 30.

Rehfeld J. F., Golterman N., Larsson L-I., Emson P. M., Lee C. M. (1979). Gastrin and cholecystokinin central and peripheral neurons. *Federal Proceedings*; 38: 2325–29.

Richelson E. (1980). Neuroleptics and neurotransmitter receptors. *Psychiatric Annals*; 10: 21–40.

Rupniak N. J., Hall M. D., Mann S. *et al.* (1985). Chronic treatment with clozapine, unlike haloperidol, does not induce changes in striatal D-2 receptor function in the rat. *Biochemical Pharmacology*; 34: 2755–63.

Scatton B., Dubois A. (1985). Autoradiographic localization of D_1 dopamine receptors in the rat brain with [^{3}H] SKF 38393. *European Journal of Pharmacology*; 111: 145–6.

Schmutz J. (1975). Neuroleptic piperazinyl-dibenzo-azepines. Chemistry and structure-activity relationships. *Arzneimittel Forschung*; 25: 712–20.

Schneider B. S., Monahan J. W., Hirsch J. (1979). Brain cholecystokinin and nutritional status in rats and mice. *Journal of Clinical Investigations*; 64: 1348–56.

Schwarcz G., Halaris A., Dren A., Manberg P. (1985). Open label evaluation of the novel antipsychotic compound BW 234U in chronic schizophrenics. *Drug Development Research*; 5: 387–93.

Setler P. E., Sarau H. M., Zerkle C. L., Saunders H. L. (1978). The central effects of a novel dopamine agonist. *European Journal of Pharmacology*; 50: 419–30.

Simpson G. M., Lee J. H. (1978). A ten year review of antipsychotics. In: *Psychopharmacology: A Generation in Progress* (Lipton M. A., DiMascio A., Killan K. F., eds.), pp. 1131–1137. New York: Raven Press.

Simpson G. M., Varga E. (1974). Clozapine—a new antipsychotic agent. *Current Therapeutic Research*; 16: 679–86.

Skirboll L. R., Grace A. A., Hommer D. W. *et al.* (1981). Peptide-monoamine coexistence; studies of actions of cholecystokinin like peptide on the electrical activity of midbrain dopamine neurons. *Neuroscience*; 6: 2111–24.

Snyder S. H. (1981). Dopamine receptors, neuroleptics and schizophrenia. *American Journal of Psychiatry*; 138: 460–4.

Sokoloff P., Martres M. P., Schwartz J. C. (1980a). Three classes of dopamine receptor (D-2 D-3, D-4) identified by binding studies with ^{3}H-apomorphine and ^{3}H-domperidone. *Naunyn Schmiedeberg's Archives of Pharmacology*; 315: 89–102.

Sokoloff P., Martres M. P., Schwartz J. C. (1980b) ^{3}H-Apomorphine labels both dopamine postsynaptic receptors and autoreceptors. *Nature*; 288: 293–6.

Spano P. F., Frattola L., Govoni S., Tonon G. C., Trabucchi M. (1979). In: *Dopaminergic Ergot Derivatives and Motor Function*. Wenner-Gren Center International Symposium Series. Vol 31. (Fuxe K., Calne D. B., eds.), pp. 159–171. Oxford: Pergamon Press.

Stahl S. M. (1986). Tardive dyskinesia: natural history studies assist the pursuit of preventative therapies. *Psychological Medicine*; 16: 491–4.

Stille G., Lauener H., Eichenberger E. (1971). The pharmacology of 8-chloro-11-(4-methyl-1-piperazinyl)-5H-dibenzo[b,e] [1,4] diazepine (clozapine). *Farmaco edizione pratica*; 26: 603–25.

Tamminga C., Littman R., Alphs L., Chase T., Thaker G., Wagman A. (1986). Neuronal cholecystokinin and schizophrenia: pathogenic and therapeutic studies. *Psychopharmacology*; 88: 387–91.

Thorup M., Fog R. (1977). Clozapine treatment of schizophrenic patients, plasma concentration and coagulation factors. *Acta Psychiatrica Scandinavica*; 55: 123–6.

Titeler M., Weinreich P., Sinclair D., Seeman P. (1978). Multiple receptors for brain dopamine. *Proceedings of the National Academy of Sciences (USA)*; 75: 1153–6.

Uhr S. B., Pruitt B., Berger P. A., Stahl S. M. (1986). Case report of four patients with Tourette syndrome treated with piquindone, a D_2 receptor antagonist. *Journal of Clinical Psychopharmacology*; 6: 128–30.

Vasse M., Protais P., Costentin J., Schwartz J. C. (1985). Unexpected potentiation by discriminant benzamide derivatives of stereotyped behaviours elicited by dopamine agonists in mice. *Naunyn-Schmiedeberg's Archives of Pharmacology*; 329: 108–16.

Verhoeven W. M., Westenberg H. G., Van Ree J. M. (1986). A comparative study on the antipsychotic properties of desenkephalin-gamma-endorphin and ceruletide in schizophrenic patients. *Acta Psychiatrica Scandinavica*; 73: 372–82.

Wahlen A., Farde L., Wiesel F., Jansson P., Uppfeldt G. (1987). Biochemical effects of the potential antipsychotic drug raclopride in schizophrenic patients. IUPHAR Sydney (meeting) 1987.

White F. J., Wang R. Y. (1983). Differential effects of classical and typical antipsychotic drugs on A9 and A10 dopamine neurons. *Science*; 221: 1054–57.

Worms P. (1982). Behavioral pharmacology of the benzamides as compared to standard neuroleptics. In: *The Benzamides: Pharmacology, Neurobiology, and Clinical Aspects* (Rotrosen J., Stanley M., eds.), pp. 7–16. New York: Raven Press.

Worms P., Broekkamp C. L. E., Lloyd K. G. (1983). Behavioral effects of neuroleptics. In: *Neuroleptics: Neurochemical, Behavioral and Clinical Perspectives* (Coyle J. T., Enna S. J., eds.). New York: Raven Press.

Zetler G. (1980). Anticonvulsant effects of coerulein and cholecystokinin octapeptide, compared with those of diazepam. *European Journal of Pharmacology*; 65: 297–300.

Zetler G. (1981). Central depressant effects of coerulein and cholecystokinin octapeptide (CCK-8) differ from those of diazepam and haloperidol. *Neuropharmacologia*; 20: 277–83.

Zetler G. (1982). Ceruletide, ceruletide analogues, and cholecystokinin octapeptide (CCK-8): effects on motor behaviour, hexobarbital-induced sleep and harman-induced convulsions. *Peptides*; 3: 701–4.

Zetler G. (1983). Neuroleptic-like effects of ceruletide and cholecystokinin octapeptide: interactions with apomorphine, methylphenidate and picrotoxin. *European Journal of Pharmacology*; 94: 261–70.

12 *Drug treatment of schizophrenia*

D. A. W. JOHNSON

Drugs form an essential part of all treatments for schizophrenia, but it is only by taking advantage of all possible therapies—social, psychological and pharmacological—that the individual patient may minimize the handicaps of schizophrenia, and reach the best possible level of function.

The decision to prescribe long-term maintenance neuroleptic therapy must be based on a careful evaluation of all known facts, and the true risk–benefit ratio must be fully explored. It is essential that this should be an ongoing evaluation, continuously revised in the light of the changing state of our knowledge.

THE ROUTE OF ADMINISTRATION

The best method of drug administration has been a matter for debate. The depot injection has several advantages. It overcomes the problems of oral administration, giving a more predictable and consistent blood level, and bypasses the initial biotransformation process of the gut and liver. It is likely that these two factors are responsible for the lower total dose required to maintain therapeutic control. However, the most important clinical advantage is the control it gives over medication compliance. It has been repeatedly demonstrated that non-compliance is high, with over one-third of day patients and 40–65% of outpatients discontinuing regular medication within 6 weeks. Urinalysis has shown the presence of drugs never prescribed in 10% of inpatients. Drug compliance is a complex matter. The only possible way to discuss the treatment of symptoms or side-effects sensibly is to have an exact knowledge of the drugs actually taken by the patient. This can only be achieved with the use of depot injections.

The principal potential advantage of oral medication is the flexibility of prescription provided by the short duration of action. It is likely that because of the solubility of neuroleptics in the body lipids, and the presence of metabolites over long periods, this flexibility is grossly reduced in maintenance therapy. After some months of treatment with either oral medication or depot injections the clinical response to dose reduction will be delayed, sometimes for many weeks, with a consequent reduction in the advantage of oral medication in this respect.

It is true that a number of double-blind studies have demonstrated that, under research conditions, a spectrum of schizophrenic patients can be equally well maintained on oral or depot medication. All these studies have involved either highly selected patient samples or service conditions unlike the normal clinical setting, particularly because the research strategy produced an enormous increase in the level of staff–patient contact. Because of this, the expectation of a better level of compliance resulting in an improved outcome on depot injections remains unchallenged by these studies.

MAINTENANCE MEDICATION

The need for long-term maintenance therapy in first illness schizophrenia remains unclear. Only one double-blind placebo controlled trial has evaluated this need (Kane *et al.*, 1982). At 12 months, patients with a final diagnosis of schizophrenia had fewer relapses on drugs (0 versus 41%, $P < 0.01$), while a subgroup who met research diagnostic criteria (RDC) requirements also had fewer relapses on drugs (0 versus 46%). A drug discontinuation trial by Johnson (1979) found that patients with a first illness of Schneider-positive schizophrenia had a better prognosis over 2 years if they received medication for at least 12 months. Both these studies support the need for maintenance medication to be continued for at least one year following a first illness. A further relevant consideration is the recent work by the Northwick Park Group, which suggested that the earlier drug therapy is commenced in a first illness the better the long-term prognosis.

The importance of maintenance neuroleptic treatment in the prevention of acute psychiatric relapse and rehospitalization has been repeatedly demonstrated, and is now generally accepted (*see* reviews by Dencker, 1984; Glazer, 1984; Hogarty, 1984; Johnson, 1984; Kane, 1984; Leff *et al.*, 1984). However, it is clear that not all patients benefit equally. There is a general consensus that approximately one-third of all schizophrenics will relapse over a 2-year period despite regular medication in an appropriate dose. It must be remembered that for many patients who ultimately relapse the event has been delayed or modified by the use of drugs. It is not an all or none phenomenon. Hogarty (1984) reviewed the principal studies and concluded that the prophylactic efficacy of maintenance medication is probably greatest among patients who have been able to survive in the community for one year, or had achieved a full remission prior to maintenance therapy.

Research suggests that approximately 20% of chronic schizophrenics can survive free of relapse and with an equal level of function without medication. Unfortunately, at the present time it is not possible to identify either good prognosis patients, or good drug responders with accuracy.

The duration of maintenance therapy remains uncertain, but all discontinuation studies after varying periods of survival on regular medication give similar results (Hogarty *et al.*, 1976; Johnson, 1976b; 1979; Capstick, 1980; Dencker and Elgen, 1980; Wistedt, 1981; Johnson *et al.*, 1983). Even after 5 years, 80% of patients will relapse when drugs are stopped. Long-term medication appears to control symptoms, but has little or no effect on the natural history as measured by the risk of a further acute relapse. Two studies (Johnson, 1976a; Johnson *et al.*, 1983) also suggest that psychiatrists are no better at selecting the good prognosis patient no longer requiring medication than patients who stop medication for a range of dissimilar reasons.

If long-term medication is required for periods in excess of 5 years, it is reasonable to explore the possibility of adopting a strategy of drug holidays to reduce the total dosage and the risk of side-effects. However, an analysis of the reported studies shows that after only 3 months free of drugs, calculated from the date of the first missed injection, patients are clinically disadvantaged, with no overall reduction in the risk of side-effects. Indeed, it has been suggested that intermittent medication may increase the risk of tardive dyskinesia (Friedhoff and Alport, 1978).

THE IMPLICATIONS OF RELAPSE

So far only the presence or absence of a relapse has been reported. If we are to understand the full significance of drug therapy for patients and evaluate the true risk-benefit ratio, we must examine the full consequences of a relapse in terms of patient function, duration of changes and implications for the long-term prognosis. It is also important to examine any differences between patients who relapse on routine medication, and those who relapse having discontinued drugs.

Research in Manchester suggests that a relapse is more than a relatively brief episode with acute positive symptoms which may result in a relatively short period of inpatient or day patient admission. Even 12–18 months after the resolution of their acute symptoms, less than half the patients had returned to their pre-relapse level of work or social function. These longer-term effects were confirmed by the independent assessment of the families' views (Johnson, 1981; Johnson *et al.*, 1983). These results agree with those of other authors (Hogarty *et al.*, 1975) that many months are required to regain pre-relapse levels of function, and some patients may never do so. The discontinuation study of Johnson *et al.* (1983) also suggested that a relapse without the benefit of continuing medication was likely to be both more acute in onset and more severe in symptoms, with greater disruption to both patient and community.

More recent research suggests that the onset of even apparently quite acute episodes in fact start some months before positive symptoms are identified. Changes in work and social function have been recorded 3 or more months before new acute symptoms in ongoing prospective research. In addition, a change of mood or affect is noted in almost half the patient population. In this patient group, social and work function remains reduced, albeit improving, 18 months after resolution of acute symptoms. During this interval, the life styles of both patients and their families remained altered and less rewarding. Further, it has been suggested that for some patients each acute relapse may be a downward step towards the development of permanent, often negative, handicaps. The true meaning of a schizophrenic relapse and its consequences is an area that requires further careful evaluation.

An additional problem that is seldom recognized is the effect of relapse on the total amount of medication prescribed. At the time of relapse, patients may be prescribed three times their maintenance dose. It has been found that, 18 months after a relapse, patients had received 20% more medication, and their current prescription was on average one-third higher than controls, which means the disparity in drugs received is likely to increase further. A relapse also results in additional polypharmacy, with more anticholinergic drugs, more antidepressants and more benzodiazepines in particular being prescribed. These drug differences may have important long-term effects, both on side-effects and function.

Maintenance drug therapy is likely to have a buffer effect against stress and life events, either preventing a relapse or modifying the consequences (Hogarty, 1984; Leff *et al.*, 1984). In addition, Hogarty *et al.* (1974) have demonstrated that patients undergoing rehabilitation or social therapy require this protection by drugs. Psychotherapy, behaviour therapy, occupational therapy and all forms of rehabilitation are stressful to some degree. Patients undergoing these therapies without the continuation of regular maintenance may actually do worse than patients receiving no treatment at all. A combination of drug therapy and social therapy offers the best prognosis to the patient.

THE DOSAGE FOR MAINTENANCE

The issue of the correct dose for maintenance therapy is complex and unclear. Perhaps this is not surprising, since the illness itself is subject to many influences, and prescribed drugs are only one factor influencing progress.

The relationship between plasma levels, drug dose and clinical response gives no clear guidelines for clinical practice. It has been suggested that there is a therapeutic window for treatment response, with a critical lower dose below which there is no therapeutic response, and a higher level above which the therapeutic response diminishes. Two recent studies (Johnstone *et al.*, 1983; Smith *et al.*, 1984) demonstrated a curvilinear response, with an increase beyond a critical threshold reversing the therapeutic gain of the lower dose. Unfortunately, for different reasons these studies did not establish the dose at which this reversal may take place. This concept is not new since previous papers have also reported exacerbations of psychotic symptoms on high doses of neuroleptics, which improve on dose reduction (Curry *et al.* 1970; Van Putten, 1974; Simpson *et al.*, 1976). This apparent upper limit could be due to one of several reasons: a pharmacodynamic effect due to a paradoxical reversal of receptor response; a global clinical effect caused by an intensification of side-effects cancelling out the previous therapeutic gain; or an artefact of the habit of prescribing higher doses to patients with a poor prognosis or to drug non-responders.

The possibility that very high doses may increase the therapeutic effect, particularly among patients resistant to standard neuroleptic doses, has been investigated by a number of authors (Rifkin *et al.*, 1971; Quitkin *et al.*, 1975; McClelland *et al.*, 1976; Dencker *et al.*, 1978; McCreadie *et al.*, 1979). The consensus is that very high doses have not proved beneficial in improving either the overall level or the speed or response in acute psychosis. McCreadie *et al.* (1979) suggested that high doses may be useful if used only for patients who fail to achieve reasonable plasma levels with standard doses, but so far this hypothesis has not been fully explored.

The need to explore the minimum dose that will maintain the majority of patients free from relapse is, perhaps, the most important issue concerning dose at the present time. Baldessarini and Davis (1980) reviewed controlled studies that permitted estimates of the equivalent dose of chlorpromazine to be plotted against reduction of relapse. They found no significant dose effect between 100 mg and 2000 mg/day, and no mean difference in outcome at doses above and below 310 mg. Kane (1984) suggested that these findings may indicate that patients can generally be maintained on doses lower than 300 mg/day of chlorpromazine equivalent. At least one study (Capstick, 1980) has demonstrated that some chronic patients can be successfully maintained on very small doses, relapsing when the drug is discontinued.

In a trial of only 10% of the existing dose prescription of fluphenazine decanoate, Kane *et al.* (1983) compared a low dose group (1.25–5.0 mg every 2 weeks) with a standard dose group (12.5–50.0 mg every 2 weeks) over 12 months in outpatients. The relapse rate was significantly higher in the low dose group (56% versus 7%). Kane (1984) subsequently studied a group of patients on 20% of the standard dose and reported a reduced relapse rate of 20% over 12 months. Marder *et al.* (1984) reported a double-blind comparison of a low dose group of 20% of the previous dose with a standard group in outpatients (5 mg versus 25 mg fluphenazine decanoate every 2 weeks). At the end of 12 months the two doses appear to be having an equal effect. However, during the second year, the low dose group became significantly disadvantaged with a wide separation of the survival curves after 15 months.

The standard dose group had a negligible relapse rate the second year, while the low dose group had a fairly constant relapse rate throughout both years (31% versus 64% at 24 months). The apparent equal outcome at 12 months may have been an artefact of the entry procedure into the trial, since most relapses in the standard dose group occurred within the first 3 months. It is likely that some early relapses occurred before stabilization on the standard dose had been established. This study also raises the question of caution when looking at outcome after 12 months. Continuing on a low dose may postpone a relapse, but for a moderate term only, and studies of 24–36 months are probably required to confirm a trend.

A study of a reduction to 20% of the standard dose in recently discharged patients in Birmingham had to be abandoned because the high relapse rate in the low dose group raised ethical problems. A recent study of a reduction to only 50% (Johnson *et al.*, 1987) again showed a significantly higher relapse rate in the low dose group at 12 months (7% versus 32%). After an interval of 24–36 months from dose reduction, 56–76% of patients had experienced a relapse, while an even higher proportion (76–79%) had resumed their former standard dose because of a deteriorated mental state.

The low dose studies all suggest that if relapse is the sole criterion of assessment, standard dose therapy is superior. However, the authors of the earlier papers suggested that the risks of side-effects may be less, and the comfort and function of the patient improved by the use of very low doses. It was further suggested that any relapse as a consequence of a reduced dose may have a less dramatic onset than relapse following complete withdrawal of medication, so early remedial therapy may be offered. These practical advantages have not been established. In the study by Johnson *et al.* (1987), the social and work function changes were carefully monitored, and the side-effects independently evaluated. No clear advantages were shown for the lower dose in either reduction of extrapyramidal side-effects, or improved social function, but a reduced prevalence or lower rate of symptom emergence for tardive dyskinesia was suggested. No correlations were found between absolute dose, absolute scores or changes in scores for mental state, social function or extrapyramidal side-effects. The reduction in the risk of tardive dyskinesia was greatest among those patients originally on the highest doses.

It is recognized that individual patients can occasionally survive on very low dose prescriptions. However, in general, it is the patient who has early tardive dyskinesia or has been identified as being particularly at risk who has most to gain from a very low dose regimen, providing they fully understand the increased risks of an acute relapse with its potential to cause longer-term changes.

POLYPHARMACY

In considering the total dose of drugs received by a patient, it is not enough to consider the neuroleptic drugs alone. It is necessary to evaluate the full range of drugs prescribed as part of maintenance therapy. Michel and Kolakowska (1981) and Edwards and Kumar (1984) highlighted the problems of polypharmacy in reviews of prescriptions given to inpatients and daypatients at two hospitals. In these studies at least 10% of patients were prescribed two neuroleptics simultaneously, and depot and oral medication were mixed in 20% of patients. Anticholinergics were prescribed to 50%, antidepressants to 14%, and benzodiazepines to 25–33%. Similar results were found by Johnson (1983), who monitored prescriptions to both inpatients and outpatients over the years 1970–83. Despite a trend to rationalize prescribing habits over the years, 28% of patients maintained in the community in 1983 were still receiving three or more different categories of drugs at the same time. This figure represents an underestimation of the true polypharmacy, since 23% were prescribed two different types of neuroleptic. Anticholinergic drugs were prescribed to 61% of the patients taking maintenance drugs, antidepressants to 12%, and benzodiazepines to 13%. Again these values are likely to be an underestimation, since these are point prevalence figures.

EXTRAPYRAMIDAL SIDE-EFFECTS

Neuroleptic drugs all produce extrapyramidal symptoms but their exact prevalence and the need for treatment remains controversial. The reported prevalence rates vary from 4% to 88%, although most cluster around 40%. These results are difficult to interpret since most studies were carried out on long-term patients of uncertain diagnosis, possibly with secondary complications. Further, essential dependent variables, such as the duration of observation, dose of drugs, category of neuroleptic, and even whether drugs were used singly have been omitted. It is doubtful if many of these studies allow any meaningful interpretation.

Until recently, all surveys reported the presence of extrapyramidal signs or symptoms, either following repeated detailed physical examinations, or using procedures that involved the motivation and cooperation of the patient. Under these conditions, the presence of a measurable change does not necessarily indicate that the patient is either disabled or uncomfortable. Consequently, such reported prevalence rates may be quite different from the frequency of morbidity requiring treatment at any particular time. Indeed, they may give a very false impression of the true problem in clinical practice.

A prospective study of morbidity from extrapyramidal symptoms in chronic schizophrenic patients receiving a single neuroleptic drug for maintenance therapy, was carried out over 15 months (Johnson, 1978). The 15-month prevalence rate was among the highest ever reported (81%). However, the importance of this study is the demonstration of the variability of morbidity, and therefore the need for treatment over time (Table 12.1). A high initial rate falls to a fairly stable monthly prevalence of 15–24% after 5 months. The reason for the continuing difference found between one-monthly and 3-monthly rates is that the population experiencing morbidity is not constant. There is an ongoing exchange between patients with or without symptoms.

Although many clinicians previously prescribed anticholinergic drugs

Table 12.1 Morbidity from extrapyramidal symptoms in patients on depot injections

| Month | Prevalence (%) | |
	Monthly	*3-Monthly*
1	68	
2	62	
3	62	74
4	48	
5	30	
6	15	59
7	24	
8	20	
9	22	29
10	16	
11	19	
12	20	24
13	17	
14	24	
15	21	28

almost routinely when extrapyramidal symptoms appeared, and sometimes even on a prophylactic basis, this practice is no longer common. With neuroleptic agents, as with any drug, the drug should be stopped if at all possible when a patient develops toxic effects. When this is not advisable, the drugs should be reduced to as low a dose as possible without losing their therapeutic effect. Only when neither strategy is possible nor effective, should a second drug be prescribed to neutralize the unwanted effects. Discontinuation of the neuroleptic is seldom advisable, so the usual appropriate strategy is dose reduction, extrapyramidal effects being dose dependent. In at least one-half of patients, the symptoms can be abolished by dose changes, generally without loss of therapeutic effect (Johnson, 1973; 1977). With the depot injection form of drug administration, it is probably best to omit the next injection and then increase the interval between injections, retaining the same injection dose. A minority of patients are more comfortable on smaller injection doses given at more frequent intervals. It must be remembered that, with the long-acting depot injection form of drug administration, the interval between dose change and reduction of side-effects may be considerable, often as long as 12 weeks. Even with oral medication, patients are likely to have developed their own secondary drug depots, since neuroleptic drugs are soluble in body lipids, and the interval between dose reduction and symptom resolution may also be considerable.

ANTICHOLINERGIC MEDICATION

The regular use of anticholinergic drugs should be reserved for the first 3–5 months of maintenance treatment, when the dose of neuroleptics is frequently relatively high. Anticholinergic drugs should also be prescribed for a reasonable period after any dose reduction in response to side-effects, perhaps one month for patients on oral medication and 3 months for those on depot injections. Fewer than one-half of patients are likely to require longer periods of continued anticholinergic medication.

McClelland *et al.* (1974) reviewed the literature on the discontinuation of anticholinergic drugs in schizophrenic patients receiving regular neuroleptic medication. They found only a small minority (4–27%) developed extrapyramidal symptoms on stopping anticholinergic drugs. In the morbidity study reported above (Johnson, 1978), the associated reappearance of extrapyramidal symptoms on stopping anticholinergic drugs was 10%.

Rifkin *et al.* (1978) carried out a different literature search and reported the reappearance of symptoms in 9–43% of patients. Jellinek *et al.* (1981) reported the highest reappearance of extrapyramidal symptoms on discontinuation of drugs (62%). Although the emphasis of these results may vary, the conclusion is the same: probably only a minority of patients prescribed anticholinergic drugs need to continue taking them. Prescribing figures suggest that currently approximately 60% of patients on maintenance therapy receive anticholinergic drugs whereas the research data suggest that only 30% of patients need these drugs at any one time.

It must be remembered that extrapyramidal symptoms are not the only indication for the use of anticholinergic drugs. The akinetic syndrome (akinetic depression) responds rapidly to these drugs. Johnson (1981) estimated that 10–15% of all depressive symptoms in schizophrenic patients may be due to this syndrome.

Additional facts must be considered when prescribing anticholinergic drugs. The scientific evidence is sparse and conflicting. These drugs may not have all the clinical effects frequently attributed to them. It is clear that not all drug-induced extrapyramidal symptoms are relieved by anticholinergic medication, nor is each type of symptom relieved equally. The main therapeutic effect is probably seen in the reduction of tremor or rigidity. Anticholinergic drugs are also very effective in relieving the acute dystonic syndrome, particularly when given by injection. It is likely these agents have very little effect in reducing akathisia and may actually make this syndrome worse.

The anticholinergic drugs have their own range of important side-effects. A review of the literature (Johnson, 1982, 1984) shows that some of their unwanted effects are very similar to the neuroleptic effects they are prescribed to relieve. They can produce tremor and dyskinesia, and may precipitate tardive dyskinesia, although they are not thought to be a primary cause. The dry mouth syndrome, together with blurred vision, is also produced by anticholinergic drugs. Toxic psychoses have been reported.

The use of these drugs in therapeutic doses has been shown to reduce the plasma level of maintenance neuroleptic drugs. Some of the studies suggest that the therapeutic action of neuroleptic medication can be reduced regardless of whether the drug plasma level is changed. Simpson *et al.* (1980) have been critical of the methodology of some of these studies, and their own research has failed to show a reduction of plasma levels when anticholinergic drugs were added to neuroleptic therapy. Johnstone *et al.* (1983) also confirmed that the addition of anticholinergic drugs may not alter the low plasma levels produced by depot injection therapy, nor were prolactin levels changed. Their study did demonstrate, however, that the addition of anticholinergic drugs can produce a worsening of positive symptoms, together with a disturbance of sleep patterns. The implications of these studies are important not only for clinical practice, but also for research methodology.

It should also be remembered that anticholinergic drugs reduce the absorption of many drugs when taken by mouth. This may have implications for the treatment of other conditions in schizophrenic patients.

TARDIVE DYSKINESIA

At the present time, the greatest limitation on the use of the antipsychotic drugs may be the suggested long-term risks of tardive dyskinesia. The first important fact to recognize clearly is that the risks from oral medication and depot injections are identical. This must be the case, since the mode of central action is identical.

The cause of tardive dyskinesia remains a matter for speculation. An important factor seems to be the action of dopamine as a neurotransmitter. Some features of the syndrome might be explained by the development of supersensitivity of dopamine receptors. The problems of aetiology have been reviewed in several recent studies (Baldessarini, 1974; Casey, 1978; Gerlach, 1979; Jeste *et al.*, 1979; APA Task Force, 1980; Jeste and Wyatt, 1981; Barnes *et al.*, 1983). The usual form is persistent, but transient forms occur, and it is likely that the earliest signs are reversible in some patients (Quitkin *et al.*, 1977).

Tardive dyskinesia may, on rare occasions, appear after a few months of medication, but it becomes increasingly common after 2 years, and may appear for the first time after dose reduction or drug withdrawal. Anticholinergic drugs can uncover latent or accentuate existing tardive dyskinesia. The relationship between dosage, total drug prescribed and duration of medication is uncertain. It is important to recognize that neuroleptic drugs are not the only cause for abnormal movements in chronic schizophrenic patients. The natural history of schizophrenic illness associated brain changes of different aetiologies may also produce abnormal movements that are identical or very similar to drug-related dyskinesia (Owens and Johnstone, 1980). Older patients and women may have a higher risk and a poor prognosis for remission. The prevalence of tardive dyskinesia has been estimated to range from 5 to 56% of patients treated with long-term neuroleptics. The highly varied outcome of tardive dyskinesia following the discontinuation of neuroleptic drugs, and the studies of prevalence have been reviewed in detail by the APA Task Force (1980). Another review cautions that 'even the basic descriptive facts concerning the epidemiology and natural history of the illness remain tentative and impressionistic' (Smith and Baldessarini, 1980).

DEPRESSIVE SYMPTOMS IN SCHIZOPHRENIA

The importance of depression in the life of a schizophrenic patient has only recently been investigated in depth. Random interviews have suggested that affective symptoms are the most common symptoms experienced by schizophrenic patients in the community (Cheadle *et al.*, 1978). Prospective monitoring has not only revealed the frequency of true clinical depression at all stages of the illness, whether or not the patient is receiving drugs, but suggested that the overall morbidity from depression lasted more than twice as long as morbidity from positive schizophrenic symptoms, although was not so severe (Johnson, 1981). More recent work (Johnson, 1988) also suggested that the aetiology of post-psychotic depression and depressions occurring after one year's freedom from acute or positive symptoms are likely to be different. The second type is likely to be more closely related to schizophrenic activity. The issue of aetiology is complex, and it is unlikely that a single cause is responsible for all depression, even in an individual patient (Johnson, 1986). Collectively, the known facts increasingly suggest true pharmacogenic depression is uncommon, although the akinetic syndrome may be present in 10–15% of treated patients.

The place of tricyclic antidepressants in the treatment of depression occurring in the course of a schizophrenic illness is unclear and controversial. The weight of evidence suggests these drugs have little beneficial effect on the depressed mood and may worsen the schizophrenic symptoms. Siris *et al.* (1987) suggested that their main effect may be in a subgroup of patients with 'negative' type symptoms. It is clear that there is no justification for their routine use in depressed schizophrenic patients, and they should only be used cautiously on a trial basis in resistant syndromes after careful evaluation.

REFERENCES

American Psychiatric Association (APA) Task Force (1980). Task Force on late neurological effects of antipsychotic drugs: tardive dyskinesia. *American Journal of Psychiatry*; **137**: 1163–72.

Baldessarini R. J. (1974). Tardive dyskinesia: an evaluation of the aetiological association with neuroleptic therapy. *Canadian Psychiatric Association Journal*; **19**: 551–4.

Baldessarini R. J., Davis J. M. (1980). What is the best maintenance dose of neuroleptics in schizophrenia? *Psychiatric Research*; **3**: 115–22.

Barnes T. R. E., Kidger T., Gore S. M. (1983). Tardive dyskinesia: a 3 year follow-up study. *Psychological Medicine*; **13**: 71–81.

Capstick N. (1980). Long term fluphenazine decanoate maintenance dosage requirements of chronic schizophrenic patients. *Acta Psychiatrica Scandinavica*; **61**: 256–62.

Casey D. E. (1978). Managing tardive dyskinesia. *Journal of Clinical Psychiatry*; **39**: 748–53.

Cheadle A. J., Freeman H. L., Korrer J. (1978). Chronic schizophrenic patients in the community. *British Journal of Psychiatry*; **132**: 211–27.

Curry S. H., Marshall J. H. L., Davis J. M., Janowsky D. S. (1970). Chlorpromazine levels and effects. *Archives of General Psychiatry*; **22**: 289–95.

Dencker S. J. (1984). The risk-benefit ratio of depot neuroleptics. A Scandinavian perspective. *Journal of Clinical Psychiatry*; **45**: 22 7.

Dencker S. J., Elgen K. (1980). Depot neuroleptic treatment in schizophrenia. *Acta Psychiatrica Scandinavica Supplementum*; **279**: 5–103.

Dencker S. J., Johansson R., Ludin L. (1978). High doses of fluphenazine enanthate in schizophrenia: a controlled study. *Acta Psychiatrica Scandinavica*; **57**: 405–14.

Edwards S., Kumar V. (1984). A survey of prescribing psychotropic drugs in a Birmingham psychiatric hospital. *British Journal of Psychiatry*; **145**: 502–7.

Friedhoff A. J., Alport M. (1978). Receptor sensitivity modification as a patient treatment. In: *Psychopharmacology: A Generation of Progress* (Lipton M. A., Dimascio M., Killam K., eds.), pp. 797–801. New York: New Raven Press.

Gerlach J. (1979). Tardive dyskinesia. *Danish Medical Bulletin*; **46**: 209–45.

Glazer A. C. (1984). Depot fluphenazine: risk-benefit ratio. *Journal of Clinical Psychiatry*; **45**: 28–35.

Hogarty G. E. (1984). Depot neuroleptics: the relevance of psychosocial factors. *Journal of Clinical Psychiatry*; **45**: 36–42.

Hogarty G. E., Goldberg S. C., Schooler N. R. (1974). Drug and sociotherapy in the after care of schizophrenic patients. Two year relapse rates. *Archives of General Psychiatry*; **31**: 603–8.

Hogarty G. E., Goldberg S. C., Schooler N. R. (1975). Drug and sociotherapy in the aftercare of schizophrenic patients. In: *Drugs in Combination with Other Therapies* (Greenblatt M., ed.). New York: Grune & Stratton.

Hogarty G. E., Ulrich R., Goldberg S. C. (1976). Sociotherapy and the prevention of relapse among schizophrenic patients. In: *Evaluation of Psychological Therapies* (Spitzer R. L., Klein D. F., eds.), pp. 285–93. Baltimore: The Johns Hopkins Press.

Jellinek T., Gardos G., Cole J. O. (1981). Adverse effects of antiparkinson drug withdrawal. *American Journal of Psychiatry*; **138**: 1567–71.

Jeste D. V., Potkin S. G., Sinha S. (1979). Tardive dyskinesia—reversible and persistent. *Archives of General Psychiatry*; 36: 585–90.

Jeste D. V., Wyatt J. R. (1981). Changing epidemiology of tardive dyskinesia: an overview. *American Journal of Psychiatry*; 138: 297–309.

Johnson D. A. W. (1973). The side-effects of fluphenazine decanoate. *British Journal of Psychiatry*; 123: 519–22.

Johnson D. A. W. (1976a). The expectations of outcome for maintenance therapy in schizophrenia. *British Journal of Psychiatry*; 128: 246–50.

Johnson D. A. W. (1976b). The duration of maintenance therapy in chronic schizophrenia. *Acta Psychiatrica Scandinavica*; 53: 298–301.

Johnson D. A. W. (1977). Practical considerations in the use of depot neuroleptics for the treatment of schizophrenia. *British Journal of Hospital Medicine*; 17: 546–68.

Johnson D. A. W. (1978). Prevalence and treatment of drug-induced extrapyramidal symptoms. *British Journal of Psychiatry*; 132: 27–30.

Johnson D. A. W. (1979). Further observations on the duration of depot neuroleptic maintenance therapy in schizophrenia. *British Journal of Psychiatry*; 135: 524–30.

Johnson D. A. W. (1981). Studies of depressive symptoms in schizophrenia. *British Journal of Psychiatry*; 139: 89–101.

Johnson D. A. W. (1982). (ed.) Depot injectable antipsychotic drugs. In: *Therapeutics Today (2) Haloperidol Decanoate and the Treatment of Chronic Schizophrenia* pp. 12–31. Auckland and New York: ADIS Press.

Johnson D. A. W. (1983). Chronic schizophrenia: is additional medication necessary? In: *Modern Trends in the Chemotherapy of Schizophrenia*. Proceedings of a Special Symposium, VIIth World Congress of Psychiatry (Hall, P. ed.), pp. 36–43. Denmark: Lundbeck.

Johnson D. A. W. (1984). Observations on the use of long-acting depot neuroleptic injections in the maintenance treatment of schizophrenia. *Journal of Clinical Psychiatry*; 45: 13–21.

Johnson D. A. W. (1986). Depressive symptoms in schizophrenia: some observations on the frequency, morbidity and possible causes. In: *Contemporary Issues in Schizophrenia* (Kerr A., Snaith P., eds.). London: Gaskell.

Johnson D. A. W. (1988). The significance of depression in the prediction of relapse in chronic schizophrenia. *British Journal of Psychiatry*; 152: 320–3.

Johnson D. A. W., Ludlow J. M., Street K., Taylor R. D. W. (1987). Double blind comparison of half dose and standard dose flupenthixol decanoate in the maintenance treatment of stabilised outpatients with schizophrenia. *British Journal of Psychiatry*; 151· 634–8.

Johnson D. A. W., Pasterski G., Ludlow J. M., Street K., Taylor R. D. W. (1983). The discontinuation of maintenance neuroleptic therapy in chronic schizophrenic patients: drug and social consequences. *Acta Psychiatrica Scandinavica*; 67: 339–52.

Johnstone E. C., Crow T. J., Ferrier I. N. *et al.* (1983). Adverse effects of anticholinergic medication on positive schizophrenic symptoms. *Psychological Medicine*; 13: 513–27.

Kane J. M. (1984). The use of depot neuroleptics. Clinical experience in the United States. *Journal of Clinical Psychiatry*; 45: 5–12.

Kane J., Rifkin A., Quitkin F., Nayak D., Ramoz-Lorenzi J. (1982). Fluphenazine vs placebo in patients with remitted acute first episode schizophrenia. *Archives of General Psychiatry*; 39: 70–3.

Kane J. M., Rifkin A., Woerner M. (1983). Low dose neuroleptic treatment of outpatient schizophrenics. *Archives of General Psychiatry*; **40**: 893–6.

Leff J., Kuipers L., Berkowitz R., Eberlein-Fries R., Sturgeon R. (1984). Psychological relevance and benefit of neuroleptic maintenance. *Journal of Clinical Psychiatry*; **45**: 43–9.

Marder S. R., van Putten T., Mintz J. *et al.* (1984). Costs and benefits of two doses of fluphenazine. *Archives of General Psychiatry*; **41**: 1025–9.

McClelland H. A., Blessed G., Bhater S. (1974). The abrupt withdrawal of antiparkinsonian drugs in schizophrenic patients. *British Journal of Psychiatry*; **124**: 151–9.

McClelland H. A., Farquharson R. G., Leyburn P. (1976). Very high dose fluphenazine decanoate. *Archives of General Psychiatry*; **33**: 1435–9.

McCreadie R. G., Flanagan W. L., McNight J., Jorgensen A. (1979). High dose flupenthixol decanoate in chronic schizophrenia. *British Journal of Psychiatry*; **135**: 75–9.

Michel K., Kolakowska, T. (1981). A survey of prescribing psychotropic drugs in two psychiatric hospitals. *British Journal of Psychiatry*; **138**: 217–21.

Owens D. G. C., Johnstone E. C. (1980). The disabilities of chronic schizophrenia—their nature and factors contributing to their development. *British Journal of Psychiatry*; **135**: 384–5.

Quitkin F., Rifkin A., Gochfeld L. (1977). Tardive dyskinesia: are the first signs reversible? *American Journal of Psychiatry*; **134**: 84–7.

Quitkin F., Rifkin A., Kaplan J. H. (1975). Treatment of acute schizophrenia with ultra-high dose fluphenazine. *Comprehensive Psychiatry*; **16**: 279–83.

Rifkin A., Quitkin F., Carillo C. (1971). Very high dosage fluphenazine for non chronic treatment refractory patients. *Archives of General Psychiatry*; **25**: 398–403.

Rifkin A., Quitkin F., Kane J. (1978). Are prophylactic antiparkinson drugs necessary? A controlled study of procyclidine withdrawal. *Archives of General Psychiatry*; **35**: 483–9.

Simpson G. M., Cooper T. B., Bark N. (1980). Effect of antiparkinsonian medication on plasma levels of chlorpromazine. *Archives of General Psychiatry*; **37**: 205–8.

Simpson G. M., Varga E., Haher G. J. (1976). Psychotic exacerbations produced by neuroleptics. *Diseases of the Nervous System*; **37**: 367–9.

Siris S. G., Adan F., Cohen M., Mandeli J., Aronson A., Fasano–Dube B. (1987). Targeted treatment of depression like symptoms in schizophrenia. *Psychopharmacology Bulletin*; **23**: 85–9.

Smith J. M., Baldessarini R. J. (1980). Changes in the prevalence, severity, and recovery in tardive dyskinesia with age. *Archives of General Psychiatry*; **37**: 1368–73.

Smith R. C., Baumgartner R., Misra C. H. (1984). Haloperidol: plasma levels and prolactin response as predictors of clinical improvement in schizophrenia: chemical v radioreceptor plasma level assays. *Archives of General Psychiatry*; **41**: 1044–9.

Van Putten T. (1974). Why do schizophrenic patients refuse to take their drugs? *Archives of General Psychiatry*; **31**: 67–72.

Wistedt B. (1981). A depot withdrawal study. A controlled study of the clinical effects of withdrawal of depot fluphenazine decanoate and flupenthixol decanoate in chronic schizophrenic patients. *Acta Psychiatrica Scandinavica*; **65**: 65–84.

13 *Language disorders in schizophrenia and their implications for neuropsychology*

CHRISTOPHER D. FRITH and HEIDELINDE A. ALLEN

Neuropsychology has a long tradition in the study of schizophrenia, which is marked by phases concerned with establishing schizophrenia either as a 'functional' or as an 'organic' disorder (Rogers, 1987). Earlier research tended to focus on differences between schizophrenic and 'organic' patients (Goldstein, 1939, 1944, 1959). Recent research, however, has focused on the similarities between these groups (e.g. Liddle, 1987). Both lines of research have been based on the use of psychological tests. There now exists an enormous armamentarium of neuropsychological tests; e.g. Mohr and Sidman (1975) required a whole page simply to cite tests of aphasia. However, the utility of this research tradition, in which batteries of neuropsychological tasks are administered to schizophrenic patients, is seriously undermined by conceptual and methodological problems.

Conceptually, the approach is problematic because it is assumed that cognitive processes are unitary functions which can be localized by the use of psychological tests. However, both Luria (1973, 1980), writing from the viewpoint of neuropsychology, and Shallice (1981), writing from that of cognitive psychology, consider this assumption unjustified.

Methodologically, the approach suffers from many problems. In particular, Miller (1986) has argued that psychiatric neuropsychology violates the usual rules for demonstrating a relationship between structure and function by omitting one of three requirements. Two requirements are usually adhered to:

1. subjects are classified according to differences in performance on neuropsychological tests
2. conclusions are drawn as to the locus of function and dysfunction on the basis of task performance.

However, the crucial additional condition is missing, that is the actual demonstration of the 'right lesion in the right location' (Miller, 1986). Instead, localized or lateralized brain dysfunction is inferred from 'phenotypic similarities in task performance between psychiatric subjects and individuals with known brain damage' (Miller, 1986). This practice is based on the notion that, if damage to brain system X is known to produce poor performance on task T, then any new subject or class of subjects having poor performance on T must have a lesion in X. This argument is logically fallacious, and in any case inconsistent with empirical evidence showing there is no necessary relationship between lesion site and performance (Shallice, 1981; Howard, 1985). This is not, of course, surprising if we remember Luria's principle, that performance of a single task may be carried out by various mechanisms so that poor performance on T may relate to factors other than having a lesion at X.

In spite of these obvious and difficult problems, neuropsychological testing is still used in the search for brain abnormalities in schizophrenia with reasoning by analogy from the test results of brain-damaged subjects (e.g. Seidman, 1983; Flor-Henry, 1986; Liddle, 1987). Since Miller (1986) provides an excellent and detailed analysis of the problems associated with this approach we shall not go into any further detail here, but merely conclude that localization of the 'lesion' in schizophrenia will not be established by test and analogy studies. Instead, we recommend the use of 'cognitive' neuropsychology. In this approach, we first infer the psychological processes that underlie test performance and then relate these processes, rather than test performance, to underlying brain systems. Such an approach is not, of course, restricted to the cognitive domain. Cognitive neuropsychology has at least three advantages over the traditional approach:

1. the assumption that cognitive processes are complex functional systems is consistent with empirical evidence (Luria, 1980; Shallice, 1981)
2. the methodology of cognitive psychology does not rely on reasoning by analogy and group studies. By not assuming homogeneity, we avoid losing valuable information by lumping together different functional deficits
3. the cognitive approach has demonstrated its utility in advances in the understanding of acquired dyslexia (Coltheart *et al.*, 1980) and jargon aphasia (Butterworth, 1985).

TOWARDS A COGNITIVE NEUROPSYCHOLOGY OF SCHIZOPHRENIA

Conceptual considerations

In developing such an approach to schizophrenia, we adopt Marr's (1982) distinction between a computational level and a level of implementation; i.e. we distinguish between the operations that the nervous system carries out, and the nervous machinery that carries out these operations. Broadbent (1986), among others, argued that we must first 'establish the correct computational (symbolic) model in order to verify models of implementation'. The utility of this approach has been demonstrated by research on the working of the visual system (Marr, 1982) and the auditory system (Moore, 1973). In other words, we need a computational model of the psychological processes produced by the abnormal nervous system in schizophrenia before we can relate these processes to brain systems.

In this chapter we shall develop a model of the psychological processes associated with schizophrenia at a computational level, and then examine how this fits with possible implementations in the central nervous system. The model is not very detailed as yet, but is a necessary first step towards a cognitive neuropsychology of schizophrenia.

Explaining symptoms

Our starting point for inferring the psychological processes underlying schizophrenia must be symptoms, since these are virtually all the data we have about this disorder. Performance on psychological tests, although providing valuable information, must be treated as a secondary source of information, i.e. having inferred psychological processes underlying symptoms we can then test predictions derived from these processes by examining performance on suitable psychological tests. We follow Crow (1980) in believing that there is a fundamental distinction between positive symptoms (hallucinations and delusions) and negative symptoms (flattening of affect, poverty of speech, lack of volition).

In addition to the distinctions pointed out by Crow, we note that positive symptoms concern abnormalities in the patient's experience, while negative symptoms concern abnormalities in the patient's behaviour and should more properly be called signs. (At this stage we shall not consider abnormalities of language and speech, since these symptoms will be considered in detail in the second half of the chapter.) We also note that neither type of symptom involves failure of cognition. Thus patients do not complain of problems with memory or of difficulties in finding words, rather, those with positive symptoms complain that their thoughts are being observed or their actions controlled or commented upon. Likewise patients with negative symptoms do not act incompetently, they fail to act at all. Thus we might argue that the primary disorder is not cognitive (a disorder of knowledge), but conative (a disorder of will).

Frith (1987) has described in some detail how certain disorders in relations between will and action might lead to the positive and negative symptoms of schizophrenia. The essence of this argument is that there are two distinct routes to action in normal behaviour. At one extreme, actions occur solely as responses to changes in the environment, and may thus be called stimulus driven. At the other extreme, actions occur solely due to internal plans or goals, and may thus be called spontaneous or willed. Negative symptoms reflect an impairment in the mechanism by which will is turned into action. At the same time there is no impairment in actions occurring in response to external stimuli.

Obviously the consequences of actions, whatever their source, are monitored. This is essentially a feedback loop. We do something and then we see what happens. In addition, however, there is an internal monitoring system. This system is largely conscious, and may probably be identified with working memory. In relation to action, however, it is 'memory for the future' that needs to be monitored. In other words we need to monitor all those actions that we *could* perform in the current circumstances and, in particular, we need to know which actions we have just initiated. This system for the internal monitoring of action therefore involves feedforward, rather than feedback. This monitoring system has information, not only about which actions are available, but also about the source of these actions, i.e. whether they are stimulus generated or intentions of will.

The positive symptoms of schizophrenia occur when there is a failure of this internal monitoring system, such that the patient is no longer aware of his intentions of will. As a consequence, when he performs such actions his experiences will be abnormal. He may come to believe that alien forces are determining his thoughts or actions (delusions of control, thought insertion) or he may believe that his actions have been elicited by irrelevant stimuli (delusions of reference). We have described in detail elsewhere (Frith, 1987; Frith and Done, 1988) the ways in which various positive symptoms can arise from this abnormality of internal monitoring.

The two critical components of this model for the control of action are the route to willed action and the internal monitor. How do these relate to the brain?

Goldberg (1985) has suggested that the two routes to action are mediated via different systems in the brain and can be impaired independently of one another. In Parkinson's disease, for example, willed actions are relatively more impaired than stimulus generated ones. It seems likely that willed intentions originate in the prefrontal cortex and are converted into actions in the basal ganglia. Following Gray (1982), we have suggested that the internal monitoring may be carried out in the hippocampus (Frith and Done, 1988).

We have presented very briefly a neuropsychological model which attempts to account for most schizophrenic symptoms. In the remainder of this chapter we shall consider in more detail how this model might relate to one feature of schizophrenia, namely language disorder. This feature is of considerable interest, since it can readily be observed, and has been studied extensively. In addition, computational models have been developed for other types of language disorder (the aphasias), and there is some knowledge of the brain systems involved in these disorders. Clearly, it would be useful to relate schizophrenic language disorders to the aphasias.

LANGUAGE DISORDER IN SCHIZOPHRENIA AS A NEGATIVE SIGN

Our starting point is the hypothesis that all schizophrenic language disorders are a manifestation of restricted cognitive processes due to a defect in the mechanism of *willed intention* (Frith, 1987). This is a radical thesis in that it implies, contrary to extant views:

1. that the primary cause of speech disorder in schizophrenia is *not* a loss of processing control due to a defect in some inhibitory mechanism
2. that positive and negative speech disorders are *not* dichotomous and therefore are *not* distinct entities
3. that both linguistic and cognitive knowledge structures are *intact* and hence that, in Chomsky's terms, performance, rather than competence, is impaired.

With regard to (1), the hypothesis of a loss of processing control has dominated research over the past few decades, but has yielded slender dividends in terms of providing insights into disordered language processes in schizophrenia. Much of this research is conceptually and methodologically problematic (Allen, 1983a) and has not supported the hypothesis (Allen, 1982, 1983b; Allen and Allen, 1985; Allen and Frith, 1983).

(2) The view that positive and negative speech disorders are dichotomous has also been prominent and presumes that these speech disorders represent the consequence of different antecedents, namely loss of control in the case of the former and processing restriction in the case of the latter. However, detailed analysis suggests that the two kinds of language disorder are not qualitatively different (Allen, 1983b, 1984, 1987), both being associated with restricted processing. This leads to the problem of how we can consider positive features such as neologisms to be signs of restricted processing, as our model suggests. Andreasen (1979) has observed that negative speech disorder is more common and characteristic of schizophrenia than positive speech disorder, but these latter features still have to be explained.

We would like to describe schizophrenic speech in terms of positive and negative errors, but seek to explain both types of error as consequences of one common antecedent, namely a restriction in the production of willed intentions. This is consistent with Hughlings-Jackson's notion that destructive lesions induce a negative condition which allows positive errors to occur largely by means of reducing voluntary control over lower functions (cited by Head, 1926).

(3) There is a long-standing debate as to whether schizophrenic language disorder is a linguistic (Chaika, 1977, 1982) or a cognitive (Fromkin, 1975; Lecours and Vernier-Clement, 1976) problem. Thus, for example, Chaika (1982) draws parallels between aphasics and schizophrenics, suggesting that the latter also have some damage in the mechanisms responsible for the storage and application of language rules. Lecours and Vernier-Clement (1976) dispute this and suggest that while 'ordinary speakers think and talk standard, ... jargon aphasics think standard, but talk deviant ... schizophrenic speakers think quaint and talk accordingly'. Unfortunately this research is based on a dichotomy between

language and cognition which is neither useful (Bransford and McCarrell, 1974) nor warranted (Allen, 1983a) and is, moreover, obscured by conflicting results (Faber and Bierenbaum Reichstein, 1981). There is no convincing evidence that knowledge structures (linguistic or otherwise) are impaired in schizophrenia. We propose that the knowledge structures are intact and that utterances emerge at a reduced level or are ill-formed because of a defect at the performance as opposed to the competence level. Below we list some of the empirical criteria that could be used to test this hypothesis.

1. Language elements implicated in an error can and will be used correctly on other occasions. Consistent with this, clinical observation suggests that speech disorder in schizophrenia is often intermittent.
2. The same kind of errors will be found in normal and schizophrenic subjects. While there is much evidence suggesting quantitative rather than qualitative differences, there is a lack of detailed study on this topic.

We conclude that there are good conceptual grounds for proposing that schizophrenic speech disorders are the consequence of a deficit in performance rather than in competence and that this performance deficit reflects a problem in the generation of willed intentions. In the next section we shall consider the empirical evidence relevant to this hypothesis in relation to both microlevel and macrolevel language organization, concerned with within-sentence and discourse processes respectively.

Microlevel language organization

We shall use Butterworth's (1985) model to distinguish between more or less independent language processing systems. He proposed six such systems: semantic, lexical, syntactic, prosodic, phonological and phonetic. So far as research into schizophrenia is concerned, we can at present examine the lexical, syntactic and semantic systems. However, this distinction is somewhat arbitrary, since much of the research was not conducted within this framework.

Lexical system

This system selects words from an inventory (lexicon) of word forms, and proceeds in two stages. The first stage is the selection of an item from a 'semantic lexicon', guided by the semantic specification for the utterance. This item contains the 'address' of the phonological form of the word. The second stage uses this address for accessing the phonological form. An important aspect of this system is that word selection is not an isolated event, but is crucially bound up with the processing of a total idea and therefore with its context. An extensive and diverse range of studies have investigated the production and perception of words by schizophrenic patients. The main approaches may be grouped as follows:

Word association tests represent a long line of research (e.g. Murphy, 1923: Mefferd, 1979). It has been concluded that word production is comparable to normal subjects (Schwartz, 1978). However, a recent study (Allen, 1988) throws doubt on this. This study used a format with a compound stimulus (e.g. palm-hand), and hence required contextual processing. It was found that schizophrenic patients with incoherence, and those with poverty of speech, produced more unrelated word responses than those without speech disorders. Taken together, this suggests that speech disordered schizophrenics have normal lexical structures, but fail to process context.

Referential speaking studies are typically formulated as discrete word sampling tasks to determine whether schizophrenic performance is a reflection of deviant internal associative structures or of inappropriate editing (Smith, 1970; Cohen *et al.*, 1974; Kagan and Oltmanns, 1981). These studies consistently showed that schizophrenics produce: (1) responses that inadequately discriminate display items; (2) poorer performance with increased task complexity; (3) increased response latency and response length with increased task complexity.

These results again indicate restricted processing capacity, but cannot rule out general poor performance due to non-specific factors.

Memory studies. Traupman (1975) and Koh and Peterson (1978), among others, reported that, relative to normal subjects, schizophrenics showed recall, but not recognition, deficits. Since recall, in contrast to recognition, relies crucially on inter-item processing (e.g. chunking on the basis of semantic inter-relationships), subsequent research has addressed the question of whether schizophrenics are unable to use semantic word attributes. This research (e.g. Koh *et al.*, 1974) found that schizophrenics recognize and readily organize semantic information, provided this is explicitly suggested to them. Their difficulty lies in actively initiating the organization of such information themselves. This again suggests intact lexical structures, but a defect in self-initiated performance.

Pause studies. Maher *et al.* (1983) studied pause patterns in four speech disordered and four non-speech disordered schizophrenics, and found that the former showed an exaggerated increase in pause length before words of low contextual probability *within* clauses. Rochester *et al.* (1977), in contrast, reported that speech disordered schizophrenics produced significantly longer pauses at the *initiation* of clauses. They also reported, as did Cohen *et al.* (1974), that longer pauses in speech disordered schizophrenics were positively associated with increased production of abnormal utterances. These observations may be understood in terms of the demonstration by Goldman-Eisler (1958) and Beattie and Butterworth (1979) that many speech pauses reflect points where lexical choice is difficult. For instance, this happens at points within a clause where there is a range of possible continuations. On the other hand, pauses at the initiation of clauses reflect higher level speech planning (Goldman-Eisler, 1972). Taken together with the findings of the word association and memory studies, this again suggests intact lexical structure, but increasing delays and errors when it is necessary to select items from the lexicon or generate ideas spontaneously, without the help of external stimuli.

Type-token ratio studies. These measure the number of different words as a ratio of the total number of words produced. A low type-token ratio implies repetition, and thus may indicate the stereotyped behaviour that has long been associated with schizophrenia (Frith and Done, 1988). Manschrek *et al.* (1981) showed that speech disordered schizophrenics produced lower type-token ratios than non-speech disordered patients. Allen (1983b) found low type-token ratios associated with both positive and negative speech disorder. Again these findings suggest an impoverishment of spontaneous production. They are also consistent with the finding of reduced word output in a verbal fluency task requiring subjects to generate examples of categories such as 'animals' (Allan and Frith, 1983).

Syntactic system

On the basis of semantic and pragmatic information, the syntactic system produces a syntactic frame, with labelled slots for lexical items. In this way, it provides the grammatical order of lexical items.

Perception of syntactic organization. Rochester *et al.* (1973) used Fodor and Bever's (1965) click paradigm and found that schizophrenics, like normal subjects, perceptually displaced clicks towards the nearest syntactic boundary. This suggests that they were normally influenced by syntactic rules. The same pattern of results was found by Carpenter (1976) who, in addition, carried out a sentence comprehension task which also showed that schizophrenics were able to use syntactic rules normally in speech perception.

Production of syntactic organization. Rausch *et al.* (1980) compared schizophrenics, normal subjects and aphasics, and found that schizophrenic patients constructed semantically and grammatically correct sentences from jumbled words with the same speed and accuracy as normal subjects. Consistent with this, Andreasen (1982) and Allen and Allen (1985) also found no evidence of disturbed syntax. However, Morice and Ingram (1982, 1983) found that the speech of schizophrenics, compared to manic and normal speakers, was marked by reduced syntactic complexity. More specifically, Morice and McNicol (1986) found that schizophrenic speakers produced fewer relative clauses and less clausal embedding. These observations suggest that many schizophrenics are able to use syntax correctly in both speech perception and production, but they are less likely to use complex syntactical devices. The consequence of this is speech relatively impoverished in both form and content, since syntax is a device for expressing relationships between semantic concepts and ideas.

Semantic system

This system encodes a 'thought' or intention, and then generates a semantic specification which provides a blueprint for parallel analyses in the lexical, syntactic and prosodic systems.

While there are many studies which have measured the meaningfulness of schizophrenic speech (e.g. Andreasen, 1979; Ragin and Oltmanns, 1987), there are few specifically concerned with identifiable semantic features within the sentence. Among these are those of Morice and Ingram (1982) and of Morice and McNicol (1986) who reported a correspondence between increased syntactic complexity and semantic deviance, i.e. exaggerated sentence length, more unfinished sentences and words, more pause fillers, repeated words and retraced false starts. In a similar study, Allen (1983b) measured speech disruptions in terms of word whiskers (uhs, etc.), aborted words, nonsense words, within-word hesitations, and the repetition of syllables, words and phrases. However, she, in contrast, found no significant differences between speech disordered schizophrenics, non-speech disordered schizophrenics and normal subjects. Similarly, Allen and Allen (1985) analysed ideas produced in a picture description task and found no significant differences between the same three groups in the production of incomplete ideas and semantically abnormal ideas.

The differences in findings between the studies of Morice and of Allen are striking. We suggest that they can be explained by a crucial difference in task requirements. In the Morice studies, the speech had to be generated spontaneously, whereas in Allen's studies speech was elicited by asking subjects to describe pictures. These results are predicted from the hypothesis that semantic errors are more likely when speech generation depends on a spontaneous act of will (willed intention) rather then being elicited by a stimulus.

Macrolevel language organization

Schemas

A wide range of research has shown that abstract knowledge structures or schemas play a crucial role in discourse processing. The important point about schemas is that they embody expectations guiding the lower order processing of information (Schank and Abelson, 1977). Schemas act as global constraints, establishing a meaningful whole, characterized in terms of a discourse topic or theme.

Hoffman (1986) argued that schizophrenic speech disorder and hallucinations are the consequences of a primary defect in discourse planning. This argument is based on analyses showing thematically disjointed discourse, e.g. thematic intrusions inconsistent with the intended discourse plan. Hoffman proposed that these intrusions are involuntary, and therefore that there is a lack of concordance between the intended message and that actually produced.

In contrast, Harrow *et al.* (1986) argued that disjointed speech reflects cognitions that deviate from consensual norms. More specifically, Harrow and Quinlan (1985) proposed that schizophrenics do not share conventional social norms, and that their discourse is thus guided by qualitatively different schemas. They claimed that this hypothesis is supported by the finding that schizophrenics rated their own disorganized speech as adequate (Harrow and Miller, 1980). Thus, in contrast to Hoffman, they believed that there is no discrepancy between what the schizophrenic speaker intends to say and what he actually says.

In contrast to all these observations, Allen (1984) found no evidence of thematically inappropiate discourse intrusions, but instead found that speech disordered schizophrenics (both positive and negative) produced fewer inferential ideas than non-speech disordered schizophrenics. In addition, she found that speech disordered schizophrenics produced fewer and less elaborated ideas (Allen, 1983b). Here again, differences between Allen's studies and the others may be due to the greater involvement of willed intentions in free speech than in picture description.

Taken together, all these observations suggest that schizophrenic speech is characterized by:

1. a restricted ability to produce thematically coherent discourse (a problem that is greater in free speech than in picture description)
2. restricted production of inferences and ideas.

Cohesion devices

While thematic structure is necessary for the global organization of discourse into coherent texts, cohesion devices are necessary for organization at a more local level. They do so by connecting elements within ideas to elements in the previous or immediately following part of the discourse. In this way, one can distinguish meaningfully integrated ideas from collections of unrelated and therefore incoherent ideas. Rochester and Martin (1979) were the first to examine the use of cohesion devices in schizophrenia, and they found that schizophrenics were less effective than normal subjects at connecting discourse elements. Wykes and Leff (1982) and Harvey *et al.* (1986) found that schizophrenic speakers used fewer competent cohesion devices than manic speakers. Allen and Allen (1985) found that positive speech disordered schizophrenics tended to omit certain cohesive links. Harvey and Brault (1986) found that, in mania, there was a positive relationship between incompetent cohesion and increased pressure of speech, whereas in schizophrenia there was a positive relationship between incompetent cohesion, and poverty of content and derailment.

Overall, these observations suggest that both positive and negative speech disorder in schizophrenia are associated with a reduced ability to generate cohesion devices. Presumably these devices cannot be elicited by external stimuli (except possibly by using cliches), but depend upon spontaneous willed intentions.

Conclusions

We have summarized the research relating to language production in schizophrenia, both within sentences (lexical, syntactic and semantic processes) and between sentences (schemas and cohesion devices). The observations confirm:

1. that lexical and syntactic knowledge structures are intact
2. that errors of performance (rather than competence) occur at all levels of production
3. that both positive and negative errors tend to occur at a point in language production (or in situations such as free speech) where responses have to be generated spontaneously (i.e. self-willed), rather than being elicited by current stimuli or by previous responses. This leads to *poverty* in the production of ideas and inferences, and a reduction of syntactic complexity. In addition, there is a failure to structure discourse at higher levels leading to *incoherence*.

LANGUAGE DISORDER IN SCHIZOPHRENIA AND THE BRAIN

Does this analysis of language disorder in schizophrenia lead us any nearer to a specification of the disordered brain systems associated with it? We might have a clue if schizophrenic speech disorder resembled any of the aphasias, but it does not. Incoherent schizophrenic speech superficially resembles jargon aphasia. However, Butterworth (1985) has shown that jargon aphasia essentially reflects a word finding difficulty, in that the patient knows the word he wants to produce but cannot generate the appropriate phonology. As a result, he tries again (repetitions), produces other words, or even other strings of phonemes (neologisms). In addition, he is unable to monitor his own errors.

Schizophrenics (at least those with negative symptoms) also have word finding difficulties (poor verbal fluency, poverty of speech), but this is not to do with phonology. Rather, it is with the spontaneous generation of the word at a much earlier stage of speech production, before phonology becomes relevant. Apart from this crucial difference, it may well be that schizophrenic incoherence does resemble jargon aphasia, in that both are manifestations of a strategy for coping with production failure at certain stages in the speech generation process. The incoherent schizophrenic fails to generate a new idea or an appropriate discourse structure. He therefore starts again (repetitions, stereotypies), produces old ideas (poverty of content), or generates ideas or structures at random (incoherence). Like the jargon aphasic, he is also unable to monitor his idea or an appropriate discourse structure; he is also unable to monitor his own output. However, although both kinds of patient may be using similar strategies for coping with their problems, the problems themselves are very different: turning a word into phonology is the main problem for the jargon aphasic, whereas spontaneously generating an idea is that of the schizophrenic. It is therefore very likely that the associated brain damage is also different.

Working only on the basis of language disorder, it would be difficult to specify a disordered brain system. Elsewhere (Frith, 1987), it has been suggested that the negative symptoms of schizophrenia result from a failure to produce self-generated actions. Similar problems may be observed in patients with frontal lobe lesions and patients with Parkinson's disease. This would implicate the dopamine system of the brain and, in particular, a loop involving the prefrontal cortex and the basal ganglia. Hence, an attractively parsimonious explanation would be that the language disorder associated with schizophrenia is simply one of many problems caused by a failure in this system. On the other hand, the possibility cannot yet be ruled out that the language disorder arises from a specific failure in the speech generating system.

REFERENCES

Allen H. A. (1982). Dichotic monitoring and focused versus divided attention in schizophrenia. *British Journal of Clinical Psychology*; 21: 205–12.

Allen H. A. (1983a). An investigation of cognitive processes in positive and negative symptom schizophrenia. Unpublished PhD Thesis. Uxbridge: Brunel University.

Allen H. A. (1983b). Do positive and negative symptom subtypes of schizophrenia show qualitative differences in language production? *Psychological Medicine*; 13: 787–97.

Allen H. A. (1984). Positive and negative symptoms and the thematic organisation of schizophrenic speech. *British Journal of Psychiatry*; 144: 611–17.

Allen H. A. (1988). The status of and relation between cognitive, symptom and social variables in schizophrenia. (in press).

Allen H. A., Allan D. S. (1985). Positive symptoms and the organisation within and between ideas in schizophrenic speech. *Psychological Medicine*; 15: 71–80.

Allen H. A., Frith C. D. (1983). Selective retrieval and free emission of category exemplars in schizophrenia. *British Journal of Psychology*; 74: 481–90.

Andreasen N. C. (1978). Thought, language and communication disorders. II. Diagnostic significance. *Archives of General Psychiatry*; 36: 1325–30.

Andreasen N. C. (1982). There may be a schizophrenic language. *The Behavioural and Brain Sciences*; 5: 588–9.

Beattie G. W., Butterworth B. (1979). Contextual probability and word frequency as determinants of pauses and errors in spontaneous speech. *Language and Speech*; 22: 201–11.

Bransford J. D., McCarrell N. S. (1974). A sketch of a cognitive approach to comprehension: some thoughts about what it means to comprehend. In: *Cognition and Symbolic Processes* (Weimer W. B., Palermo D. S., eds.), pp. 189–229. New York: Erlbaum.

Broadbent D. E. (1986). The computation of control. *The Behavioural and Brain Sciences*; 9: 553–4.

Butterworth B. (1985). Jargon aphasia: processes and strategies. In: *Current Perspectives in Dysphasia* (Newman S., Epstein R., eds.) pp. 61–97. New York: Churchill Livingstone.

Carpenter M. D. (1976). Sensitivity to syntactic structure: good versus poor premorbid schizophrenics. *Journal of Abnormal Psychology*; 85: 41–50.

Chaika E. (1977). Thought disorder or speech disorder in schizophrenia? *Schizophrenia Bulletin*; 8: 587–91.

Chaika E. (1982). Thought disorder or speech disorder in schizophrenia? *Schizophrenia Bulletin*; 8: 587–91.

Cohen B. D., Nachmani G., Rosenberg S. (1974). Referent communication disturbances in acute schizophrenia. *Journal of Abnormal Psychology*; 83: 1–13.

Coltheart M., Patterson K. E., Marshall J. C. (eds.) (1980). *Deep Dyslexia*. London: Routledge.

Crow T. J. (1980). Molecular pathology of schizophrenia. More than one dimension of pathology? *British Medical Journal*; 280: 66–8.

Faber R., Bierenbaum Reichstein M. (1981). Language dysfunction in schizophrenia. *British Journal of Psychiatry*; 139: 519–22.

Flor-Henry P. (1986). Auditory hallucinations, inner speech, and the dominant hemisphere. *The Behavioural and Brain Sciences*; 9: 523–4.

Fodor J. A., Bever T. G. (1965) The psychological reality of linguistic segments. *Journal of Verbal Learning and Verbal Behaviour*; 4: 414–20.

Frith C. D. (1987). The positive and negative symptoms of schizophrenia reflect abnormalities in the perception and initiation of action. *Psychological Medicine*; 17: 631–48.

Frith C. D., Done D. J. (1988). Towards a neuropsychology of schizophrenia. *British Journal of Psychiatry*; in press.

Fromkin V. A. (1975). A linguist looks at 'schizophrenic' language. *Brain and Language*; 2: 498–503.

Goldberg G. (1985). Supplementary motor area structure and function: review and hypotheses. *The Behavioural and Brain Sciences*; 8: 567–616.

Goldman-Eisler F. (1958). Speech production and the predictability of words in context. *Quarterly Journal of Experimental Psychology*; 10: 96–106.

Goldman-Eisler F. (1972). Pauses, clauses and speech. *Language and Speech*; 15: 103–13.

Goldstein K. (1939). *The Organism*. New York: American Book Company.

Goldstein H. (1944) Methodological approach to the study of schizophrenic thought disorder. In: *Language and Thought in Schizophrenia* (Kasanin J. S., ed.), pp. 17–40. Berkeley: University of California.

Goldstein K. (1959). Concerning the concreteness in schizophrenia. *Journal of Abnormal and Social Psychology*; 59: 146–8.

Gray J. A. (1982). *The Neuropsychology of Anxiety*. Oxford: Oxford University Press.

Harrow M., Marengo J. T., Ragin A. (1986). Verbal hallucinations and speech disorganisation in schizophrenia: a further look at the evidence. *The Behavioural and Brain Sciences*; **9**: 526.

Harrow M., Miller J. (1980). Schizophrenic thought disorder and impaired perspective. *Journal of Abnormal Psychology*; **89**: 717–27.

Harrow M., Quinlan D. (1985). *Disordered Thinking and Schizophrenic Psychopathology*. New York: Gardner Press.

Harvey P. D., Brault J. (1986). Speech performance in mania and schizophrenia: the association of positive and negative thought disorders and reference failure. *Journal of Communication Disorders*; **19**: 161–73.

Harvey P. D., Earle-Boyer E. A., Levinson J. C. (1986). Distractibility and discourse failure: their association in mania and schizophrenia. *Journal of Nervous and Mental Diseases*; **14**: 274–9.

Head H. (1926). *Aphasia and Kindred Disorders of Speech, Vol. 1*. Cambridge: Cambridge University Press.

Hoffman R. E. (1986). Verbal hallucinations and language production processes in schizophrenia. *The Behavioural and Brain Sciences*; **9**: 503–48.

Howard D. (1985). Aggrammatism. In: *Current Perspectives in Dysphasia* (Newman S., Epstein R., eds.), pp. 1–31. New York: Churchill Livingstone.

Kagan D. L., Oltmanns T. F. (1981). Matched tasks for measuring single-word, referent communication: the performance of patients with schizophrenia and affective disorders. *Journal of Abnormal Psychology*; **90**: 204–12.

Koh S. D., Kayton L., Schwartz C. (1974). The structure of word-storage in the permanent memory of nonpsychotic schizophrenics. *Journal of Consulting and Clinical Psychology*; **42**: 879–87.

Koh S. D., Peterson E. A. (1978). Encoding orientation and the remembering of schizophrenic young adults. *Journal of Abnormal Psychology*; **87**: 303.

Lecours A. H., Vernier-Clement M. (1976). Schizophasia and jargon aphasia; a comparative description with comments on Chaika and Fromkin's respective looks at 'schizophrenic' language. *Brain and Language*; **3**: 516–65.

Liddle P. F. (1987). Schizophrenic syndromes, cognitive performance and neurological dysfunction. *Psychological Medicine*; **17**: 49–57.

Luria A. R. (1973). *The Working Brain*. New York: Basic Books.

Luria A. R. (1980). *Higher Cortical Functions in Man*, 2nd edn. New York: Basic Books.

Maher B. A., Manschreck T. C., Molino M. A. C. (1983). Redundancy, pause distributions and thought disorder in schizophrenia. *Language and Speech*; **26**: 191–9.

Manschreck T. C., Maher B. A., Ader D. N. (1981). Formal thought disorder, the type-token ratio, and disturbed motor movement in schizophrenia. *British Journal of Psychiatry*; **139**: 1–15.

Marr D. (1982). *Vision*. San Francisco: Freeman.

Mefferd R. B. (1979). Word association: capacity of chronic schizophrenics to follow formal semantic, syntactic and instrumental rules. *Psychological Reports*; **45**: 431–42.

Miller L. (1986). Narrow localisation in psychiatric neuropsychology. *Psychological Medicine*; **16**: 729–34.

Mohr J. P., Sidman M. (1975). Aphasia: behavioural aspects. In: *American Handbook of Psychiatry, Vol. 4* (Reiser M. F., ed.), pp. 279–97. New York: Basic Books.

Moore B. J. (1973). Some experiments relating to the perception of complex tones. *Quarterly Journal of Experimental Psychology*; **25**: 451–75.

Morice R. D., Ingram J. C. L. (1982). Language analysis in schizophrenia: diagnostic implications. *Australia and New Zealand Journal of Psychiatry*; **16**: 11–21.

Morice R. D., Ingram J. C. L. (1983). Language complexity and age of onset in schizophrenia. *Psychiatry Research*; **9**: 233–42.

Morice R. D., McNicol D. (1986). Language change in schizophrenia: a limited replication. *Schizophrenia Bulletin*; **12**: 239–51.

Murphy G. (1923). Types of word association in dementia-praecox, manic-depressives, and normal persons. *American Journal of Psychiatry*; **2**: 539–71.

Ragin B., Oltmanns T. F. (1987). Communicability and thought disorder in schizophrenics and other diagnostic groups: a follow up study. *British Journal of Psychiatry*; **150**: 494–500.

Rausch M. A., Prescott T. E., DeWolfe A. S. (1980). Schizophrenic and aphasic language: discriminable or not? *Journal of Consulting and Clinical Psychology*; **48**: 63–70.

Rochester S. R., Harris J., Seeman M. V. (1973). Sentence processing in schizophrenic listeners. *Journal of Abnormal Psychology*; **82**: 350–6.

Rochester S. R., Martin J. R. (1979). *Crazy Talk: A Study of the Discourse of Schizophrenic Speakers*. New York: Plenum.

Rochester S. R., Thurston S., Rupp, J. (1977). Hesitation as clues to failures in coherence: a study of the thought disordered speaker. In: *Sentence Production: Developments in Research and Theory* (Rosenberg S., ed.). Hillsdale, NJ: Erlbaum.

Rogers D. (1987). Neuropsychiatry. *British Journal of Psychiatry*; **150**: 425–7.

Schank R. C., Abelson R. P. (1977). *Scripts, Plans, Goals and Understanding*. Hillsdale, NJ: Erlbaum.

Schwartz S. (1978). Language and cognition in schizophrenia: a review and synthesis. In: *Language and Cognition in Schizophrenia* (Schwartz S., ed.), pp. 237–76. Hillsdale, NJ: Erlbaum.

Shallice T. (1981). Neurological impairment of cognitive processes. *British Medical Bulletin*; **37**: 186–92.

Seidman L. J. (1983). Schizophrenia and brain dysfunction: an integration of recent neurodiagnostic findings. *Psychological Bulletin*; **94**: 195–238.

Smith E. E. (1970). Associative and editing processes in schizophrenic communication. *Journal of Abnormal Psychology*; **75**: 182–6.

Traupman K. L. (1975). Effects of categorizaton and imagery on recognition and recall by process and reactive schizophrenics. *Journal of Abnormal Psychology*; **84**: 307–14.

Wykes T., Leff J. (1982). Disordered speech: differences between manics and schizophrenics. *Brain and Language*; **15**: 117–24.

14 *Schizotypy and schizophrenia*

GORDON CLARIDGE

HISTORICAL BACKGROUND

Although the perspective on schizophrenia offered in this chapter rests on relatively recent experimental work, the ideas behind it are by no means new. From the very beginning of the use of the term 'schizophrenia', and inextricably connected with its description, there was a view that some of its fundamental features could be found in individuals who did not show manifest signs of the illness. Articulated as the concept of 'schizoid personality', such observations, according to Manfred Bleuler (1978), were being made as early as 1910 among the doctors at his father's Burgholzli Clinic. As Bleuler himself notes, the significance of this view of schizophrenia as having 'dimensional' elements was subsequently obscured. Nevertheless, several current themes in schizophrenia research can be traced to it, directly or indirectly, in whole or in part.

One theme concerns the question of defining the exact boundaries of schizophrenia. Although attempts have been made to resolve this by the adoption of narrow overexclusive criteria, the existence of mild, border-line conditions continues to pose a problem for diagnosticians, and are recognized as such in the Diagnostic and Statistical Manual of Mental Disorders (DSM-III) (1980). Admittedly, the concept of 'borderline' is due as much to psychoanalytic thought as to traditional psychiatry (Stone, 1980), but one of its forms—schizotypal personality disorder—certainly owes a substantial part of its origins to the early Bleulerian concept of schizoid personality.

Another influence has been on the formulation of genetic theories of schizophrenia. The present lack of precise genetic markers leaves the form of inheritance an open question. However, a strong contender is the polygenic, diathesis/stress model, for which Gottesman and Shields (1982) have so cogently argued, and which readily incorporates the idea of a graded continuum of liability to schizophrenia that may manifest itself as schizophrenic-like traits existing without signs of overt illness.

An area of enquiry where such genetic theorizing has become especially relevant is high-risk research, which in its most complete form involves the longitudinal follow-up of children considered at increased risk for the disorder, by virtue of their having a schizophrenic parent (Watt *et al.*, 1984). Investigators in these studies have necessarily proceeded in ignorance of the exact mode of inheritance of schizophrenia. Consequently, their aims have varied, some looking for highly specific (organic) predictors in the fashion of a 'classic' disease entity model. However, others, notably Mednick, himself a pioneer in the area, have adopted a different focus. Thus, Watt (1984), summarizing Mednick's views, noted that '... he concludes that there may be no monolithic schizophrenic disorder that follows predictable rules of genetic transmission, as phenylketonuria and Huntington's chorea do. Consequently he recommends that we look for "degrees of schizophrenicity" or schizophrenic vulnerability ...'.

Sharply converging with this view, and the most direct conceptual descendant of the early observations on schizoid personality, is research to which the remainder of this chapter is devoted. This research attempts to define in more detail the nature of 'schizophrenicity' or, as the present author prefers to call it, 'schizotypy', through questionnaire measurement and related experimental investigations of psychologically healthy individuals. Much of the work to which the present author refers, has been carried out in the borderlands between experimental, clinical, and personality psychology; in consequence it has had little impact on mainstream psychiatry (Claridge, 1985). However, an early link with its origins that should be mentioned is the study by Kretschmer (1925) whose proposal for a temperamental dimension of 'schizothymia-cyclothymia', connecting normal personality variations to the major psychoses, was directly in the Bleulerian tradition and was, in turn, the inspiration for at least one of the approaches to the measurement of psychotic traits considered below.

PSYCHOLOGICAL STUDIES OF SCHIZOTYPY

Over the past decade or so there has been a rapidly growing body of research concerned with the measurement of psychotic characteristics among otherwise psychologically healthy people. This work partly reflects attempts by personality psychologists to expand their domain of study to previously rather neglected traits of individual variation and partly stems from an interest among some clinical psychologists in questions about risk for schizophrenia. In both cases, however, the research has proceeded in two phases. The first has involved the construction of questionnaire scales for measuring psychotic traits; the second investigates the correlates of the scales with objective (e.g. biological) characteristics thought relevant to schizophrenia. The evidence pertaining to both of these aspects has been reviewed elsewhere (Claridge, 1987) and the discussion here will be confined to a brief summary, together with an account of some of the more recent work from the present author's laboratory.

Questionnaire measurement of schizotypy

The more prominent of the scales currently in use in this area are summarized in Table 14.1, two features of which require comment.

Table 14.1 Psychotic trait scales

Scales	Reference(s)	Remarks
Schizotypy	Golden and Meehl (1979)	Items drawn from MMPI
Chapman scales		
Perceptual aberration	Chapman *et al.* (1978)	Derived from
Magical ideation	Eckblad and Chapman (1983)	symptomatology of psychosis, mainly schizophrenia
Social and physical anhedonia	Chapman *et al.* (1976)	
Hypomanic personality	Eckblad and Chapman (1986)	
STQ	Claridge and Broks (1984)	
Schizotypal personality (STA)		Modelled on DSM-III criteria for 'schizotypal
Borderline personality (STB)		personality disorder' and 'borderline personality disorder'
Predisposition to hallucination	Launay and Slade (1981) Bentall and Slade (1985b)	Perceptual item content
Schizophrenism	Nielsen and Petersen (1976)	Attention/thought process items
Schizoid cognitions	Rust (1987)	Derived from multiscale inventory of psychotic cognition
Psychoticism (P-scale)	Eysenck and Eysenck (1975)	Part of Eysenck Personality Questionnaire (EPQ)

MMPI: Minnesota multiphasic personality inventory

First, the label attached to a particular scale has varied, depending on the author's predilection, aims, theoretical standpoint and the item content of the questionnaire. In this respect, it should be noted that the term 'schizotypy' was used early on by Meehl (1962) who deserves credit for having been the first modern writer in the clinical field to develop the idea of schizoid personality as a genetic theory of risk for schizophrenia.

Second, the scales differ considerably in their focus, some attempting to sample a range of schizophrenic-like traits, others (e.g. the Launay-Slade Scale) a very specific feature. Particularly notable here is the Eysenck P-scale, which is exceptional for two reasons: (a) because it purports to measure traits relating to psychosis *in general*, rather than to schizophrenia in particular; and (b) because it originated in personality, rather than clinical, psychology, stemming from Eysenck's early adaptation of Kretschmer's ideas to fit his own theory (Eysenck, 1952).

Given the varied item content of the scales shown in Table 14.1, their relationship to one another is naturally of interest, since this bears crucially on such important issues as the possible multidimensional nature of schizotypy and how this might map on to the heterogeneity of schizophrenia itself. Surprisingly, it was not until recently that workers in the field began to conduct proper factor analytical studies and those that have been carried out are as yet unpublished. However, it is possible to report here on what, to date, is the most comprehensive analysis, conducted as a joint exercise between the present author's laboratory and colleagues at Liverpool University (Bentall *et al.*, 1988). Our study included almost all of the scales listed earlier in Table 14.1, together with the remaining two scales—extraversion (E) and neuroticism (N)—from the Eysenck Personality Questionnaire (Eysenck and Eysenck, 1975).

The results of a preliminary analysis of these data are shown in Table 14.2, where it can be seen that three separable components of 'schizotypy' were identified. The first consists mainly of scales having items that refer to perceptual and other cognitive aberrations; although, interestingly, two other rather different scales also loaded highly on this factor—the Eysenck

Table 14.2 Principal components analysis of 'psychoticism' scales*. Factor loadings for Varimax rotation

	I *(Perceptual/* *cognitive)*	*II* *(Social* *anxiety)*	*III* *(Introverted* *anhedonia)*
Scale			
Schizotypal personality (STA)	**0.66**	**0.58**	−0.08
Borderline personality (STB)	**0.65**	**0.50**	−0.04
Perceptual aberration	**0.65**	0.35	0.01
Magical ideation	**0.77**	0.26	−0.09
Social anhedonia	0.21	0.13	**0.80**
Physical anhedonia	−0.16	0.00	**0.79**
Hypomanic personality	**0.83**	0.04	−0.17
Hallucinatory predisposition	**0.68**	0.27	−0.10
Schizophrenism	0.25	**0.75**	0.27
Schizotypy (MMPI)	0.11	**0.65**	0.19
Psychoticism (P)	**0.72**	−0.33	0.22
Neuroticism (N)	0.21	**0.85**	−0.03
Extraversion (E)	0.22	−0.47	**−0.61**

*Details and sources of scales shown in Table 14.1.

P-scale and the new Chapman hypomania scale. The second factor appears to refer to social anxiety aspects of schizotypy, evident in the high loading on the Eysenck neuroticism scale, and by the fact that several of the other scales have items referring to that aspect. The third factor is clearly one of 'anhedonia', the *negative* loading on the Eysenck E-scale suggesting that it represents a blunting of affect associated with introverted personality traits: as such, it appears to capture quite accurately some core features traditionally emphasized in descriptions of the schizoid personality.

It is noteworthy that the results of the study just described agree, in some important respects, with those of other similar analyses that have sampled much smaller sets of the same scales (Muntaner and Garcia-Sevilla, 1985; Raine and Allbutt, 1988). Both of these also identified separate components referring, on the one hand, to perceptual/cognitive and, on the other, to feeling—specifically anhedonic—aspects of schizotypy. The main difference in each case concerned the Eysenck psychoticism scale, which in the Muntaner analysis defined a separate factor and in the Raine analysis was actually correlated with anhedonia. (However, in the latter study, only a measure of *social* anhedonia was included.) Apart from these discrepancies, the findings are therefore highly consistent in pointing to two, cognitive and affective, dimensions of schizotypy that logically coincide with two major clinical features of schizophrenia itself.

Objective correlates of schizotypy

As noted earlier, the scales just described have almost all been included in additional experimental studies of high scoring individuals, using measures that are considered to have some relevance to an understanding of schizophrenia; either because they have theoretical significance in that respect, or because they have actually been shown to differentiate diagnosed schizophrenics from other groups. The experimental paradigm and particular measure chosen for investigation have varied considerably but, as summarized in Table 14.3, have sampled three broad domains: psychophysiological, neuropsychological (hemisphere differences), and cognitive. To date, these studies have had considerable success in demonstrating that normal schizotypal individuals do have underlying biological and psychological features in common with schizophrenia.

Work from the present author's laboratory has, over the years, spanned all three of the approaches shown in Table 14.3; but discussion is confined to the most recent set of experiments, conducted by Beech *et al.* (1988). These studies, which are concentrating on a cognitive approach to the problem, make use of so-called 'negative priming', a paradigm drawn from recent research in general cognitive psychology and designed to investigate inhibitory effects in selective attention (Tipper, 1985). The general form of negative priming is as follows. If a distractor object, forming part of a priming display and which the subject is instructed to ignore, is then re-presented as a probe stimulus requiring a response, the subject's reaction

Table 14.3 Research approaches to experimental study of schizotypy*

A. *Psychophysiological*		
Anhedonia	Electrodermal hyporesponsiveness	Simons (1981, 1982)
Schizophrenism	Electrodermal hyperresponsiveness	Nielsen and Petersen (1976)
Psychoticism	Electrodermal hyporesponsiveness	Robinson and Zahn (1985)
Psychoticism	Physiological 'disassociation'	Claridge and Birchall (1978)
B. *Neuropsychological*		
Schizotypal personality	Hemisphere asymmetry differences	Broks (1984), Broks *et al.* (1984), Rawlings and Claridge (1984)
Schizoid personality	Hemispheric asymmetry differences	Raine and Manders (1988)
C. *Cognitive*		
Perceptual aberration	Idiosyncratic word association	Miller and Chapman (1983)
Psychoticism	Divergent thinking	Woody and Claridge (1977)
Hallucinatory predisposition	Altered reality testing ('signal detection')	Bentall and Slade (1985a)
Schizotypy	Slow processing ('backward masking')	Steronko and Woods (1978)
		Nakano and Saccuzzo (1985)
Psychoticism	Weak cognitive inhibition ('semantic priming')	Bullen and Hemsley (1984)
Schizotypal personality	Weak cognitive inhibition ('negative priming')	Beech and Claridge (1987) Beech *et al.* (1988)

*Questionnaire measures are those referred to in Tables 14.1 and 14.2

to it is delayed, due, it is argued, to a carry-over of the active inhibition required to suppress it during the first (priming) stage.

The negative priming phenomenon has been of particular interest because of its suitability for testing some current theories about selective attention in schizophrenia; notably that proposed by Frith (1979). He has argued that schizophrenia involves a failure to 'limit the contents of consciousness', due to a weakening of inhibitory mechanisms at an early stage of information processing. By extrapolation normal schizotypal subjects could be predicted to show a similar characteristic, manifested as a *reduced* degree of negative priming. Before describing the experiments that bear on this prediction, however, it is necessary to insert a few comments on the questionnaire measure of schizotypy used in our research.

The questionnaire is the STQ, referred to briefly in Table 14.1, and consisting of two scales: 'schizotypal personality' (STA) and 'borderline personality' (STB). As their names imply, the items for each of the scales were closely modelled on the diagnostic criteria for the two corresponding borderline syndromes contained in DSM-III. The use of these criteria as a guideline was deliberate, in that it was felt they provided the best available set of statements from which to extrapolate into normal personality known features related to psychosis. The STQ has been, and is currently being, used in a number of studies other than those referred to here, including a large twin study showing significant genetic effects (Claridge and Hewitt, 1987). On the whole, the STA (schizotypal personality) scale has proved more informative than the STB scale. For example, in the factor analyses discussed in the previous section, it has emerged as the more consistent general measure of schizotypal traits: indeed, Raine and Allbutt (1988) concluded from their study that '. . . if only one scale were to be selected to assess schizoid personality, then this scale would be STA.' Although simultaneously collecting data in our subjects on other scales, for these reasons we have so far tended to concentrate our efforts on STA in our experimental studies, including those on negative priming.

Several experiments using the negative priming paradigm have now been completed, full details being found in the original reports. The first study (Beech and Claridge, 1987) used a procedure which was, briefly, as follows. The subject was required to respond verbally to a series of computer generated displays, making up a sequence of trials. Each trial was in two parts: a prime display followed immediately by a probe target stimulus. This probe consisted of a Stroop colour word, the hue of which the subject had to name. The preceding priming display consisted of a colour bar (to be named) and a surrounding distractor (to be ignored). In half the trials the distractor was neutral (a row of crosses) and in the other half the name of a colour which always predicted the hue of the subsequent probe target word. Negative priming is indicated by a relative slowing of response to the probe under the latter condition, when compared with the neutral condition.

As shown in Fig. 14.1, this effect was substantially confirmed in those normal subjects with low scores on our STA scale. It was, on the other hand, entirely absent in high scorers, supporting the prediction from our hypothesis that such individuals show weakened inhibition in selective attention. A correlation between schizotypy score and negative priming was highly significant ($r = -0.53$; $n = 32$; $P < 0.01$).

Subsequent negative priming experiments have used a different (list-reading) task (Beech *et al.*, 1988). Here the subject is presented with sequences of Stroop colour words and asked to state the *hue* of each word as it appears, but to ignore the *name* of the colour it signifies. Lists are so arranged that the relationship between successive items is varied with respect to information content. In the critical negative priming lists the name of the colour (to be ignored) predicts the hue of the following item to

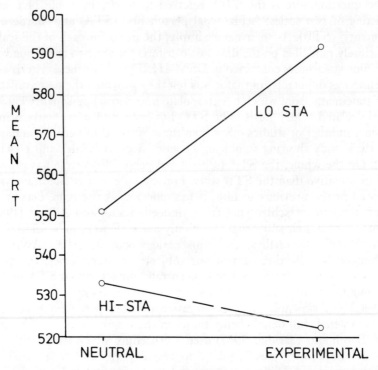

Fig. 14.1   *Diagram showing mean reaction times to probe stimuli for high and low schizotypal subjects, comparing experimental and neutral priming conditions. Note increased reaction time (strong negative priming) in low schizotypes under experimental conditions, but increased reaction time (facilitation) in high schizotypes*

which a response is required. In other lists no such relationship obtains. Negative priming is indicated by a relative slowing of response time to items of the former type.

Using this method, we have confirmed our earlier finding that normal schizotypal subjects fail to show negative priming, significant correlations with STA in two experiments being -0.48 and -0.47 respectively. However, we have also discovered that this relationship does not obtain under all testing conditions. On the contrary, it is confined to situations where the stimuli are displayed for a very short period (100 ms): at longer exposure times negative priming reappears and no association with schizotypy is observed. This finding is of interest in its own right, in pointing to a quite subtle basis for schizotypy. Thus, it suggests that it is in the *early*, automatic phases of information processing that the presumed weakening of cognitive inhibition lies, rather than in the later stages where conscious mechanisms can intervene to influence performance.

Another feature of the above data worth noting is that the significant relationships observed between STA and negative priming do not necessarily indicate merely an *absence* of the effect. In some extreme scorers, the opposite of negative priming occurs, the response to the target stimulus actually being *facilitated* by prior exposure to the 'distractor' information. This suggests that the latter is not merely suppressed, but actively processed to a high level. It also suggests that some highly schizotypal individuals are capable, albeit preconsciously, of deriving benefit to their cognitive processing from the presumed weakening of inhibition that normally helps to filter out non-salient detail.

Compared with other studies on the experimental correlates of schizotypy, the above studies were unusual in being initiated solely as a result of theoretical considerations and being undertaken in advance of comparable investigations of appropriate clinical samples. However, Beech, in our laboratory at Fair Mile Hospital, has just completed a pilot study of negative priming in schizophrenic patients. Using the list-reading task described above (with an item display time of 100 ms), he compared 18 schizophrenics with 18 psychiatric controls. As predicted, the latter showed a significant negative priming effect which was, however, absent in the schizophrenics.

Two differences between schizophrenic patients and normal schizotypal subjects should be noted, however. First, the absolute reaction times in schizophrenics, indeed, in both clinical groups, were much slower. Secondly, schizophrenic patients did not show evidence of the facilitation effect we have observed in some of our normal subjects. Both of these results may have been due to the fact that all of the patients were receiving medication at the time of testing. Another possible explanation, referring back to an earlier point, is that the weakening of inhibition presumed to underlie such variations in cognitive processing may have some optimum value; imparting a benefit on the normal schizotype, but disrupting the performance of the schizophrenic. However, it should be emphasized that, even in the latter case, the schizophrenics in our study performed better (i.e. showed faster reaction times) than the psychiatric controls under the negative priming condition. This, incidentally, illustrates a particular advantage of the negative priming paradigm in the context of cognitive research on schizophrenia. Predicting, as it does, a relative *benefit* to performance it avoids the difficulty, inherent in other methodologies, that the differences observed in schizophrenic patients might merely reflect deficits of an entirely non-specific kind.

SCHIZOTYPY AND SCHIZOPHRENIA

With a few past exceptions (e.g. Meehl, 1962; Eysenck and Eysenck, 1975), the theory that psychotic traits in normal personality have a degree of continuity with psychotic states has rarely been seriously explored. Yet now the idea seems beyond reasonable doubt. The research discussed here, of which the example chosen was merely an illustration, quite clearly demonstrates that logically related descriptive, cognitive, neuropsychological, and psychophysiological characteristics found in schizophrenic patients can also be observed in some psychologically healthy individuals. It seems not unlikely that such features are connected with the risk for schizophrenia.

Against the background of this and other evidence, we have recently made suggestions about how these dimensional—and therefore apparently 'normal'—features of schizophrenia might be incorporated into a model of the latter as illness or disease (Claridge, 1987). Briefly, we have proposed that a close analogy can be drawn between schizophrenia and such physical systemic disorders as hypertensive-related diseases (Fig. 14.2). The argument is that in both cases the state of illness proceeds, in part, from an underlying characteristic which is not itself pathological: on the contrary, it serves a normal organismic function, though having natural variation it can also act as a predisposing factor to and mediator of possible malfunction.

It will be seen that, in the case of schizophrenia, this dimensional feature is referred to as the 'schizotypal nervous system': to denote an assumption that the relevant variations would ultimately prove to have a biological (and probably substantial genetic) origin. This does not, of course, preclude their investigation at other levels of enquiry; as, for example, in the cognitive experiments described here. Indeed, studies of the latter type may be conceptually well-placed to bridge what is still a difficult gap in research on schizophrenia and schizotypy: that between their self-evident psychological features and their presumed, though as yet largely unknown, physiological basis.

Even so, the concept of schizotypy itself is already beginning to raise a number of new questions. It is already clear, for example, that 'schizotypy' is too blunt a term, although it is satisfying that the different components discernible in it do seem to map roughly on to well-recognized features of schizophrenia itself. Further research might help to determine whether each separately describes a dimension of risk for a different form of the illness; or, alternatively, whether maximum risk for a unitary disorder is defined by simultaneously high levels on its various components.

An extension to this question concerns the possible relatedness of schizophrenia to the affective psychoses. Although traditionally regarded as separable disease entities, doubt is increasingly being thrown on that view (Brockington et al., 1979). Indeed, there are some signs of a return to the notion of *Einheitpsychose* as a generalized functional psychosis manifesting itself in different forms or degrees of severity (Crow, 1986; *see also* Claridge, 1985, for a discussion of this point). Here it should be noted that Eysenck has always adopted that position and, as we saw earlier, has been alone, even among psychologists, in preferring to measure 'psychoticism' rather than specifically schizophrenic-like traits. It is therefore of some interest that the recent factor analysis of 'schizotypy' reported here

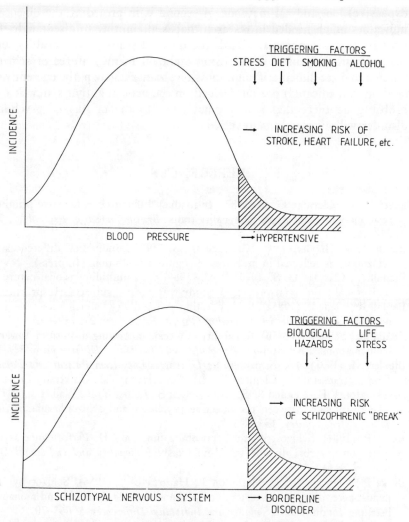

Fig. 14.2 *Hypothetical model for schizophrenia, drawing parallels with hypertensive-related disease. Features to be noted in both cases include: continuum of normal functioning describing dimension of vulnerability; arbitrarily definable borderline state of malfunction; and full-blown disease as interaction between exogenous and endogenous factors*

identified a first major component made up, not only of unambiguous schizophrenic features, but also of scales measuring hypomania and general psychoticism.

Finally, it can be concluded that, as a base for a 'new initiative in schizophrenia research' the line of enquiry discussed here offers several possibilities. One is as a strategy for identifying high-risk predictors for schizophrenia, complementing more traditional (and incidentally more

198   *Schizophrenia: The major issues*

expensive) longitudinal methods. A second is in providing the objective indicators much needed in research that is attempting to disentangle the genetics of schizophrenia. Third, the detailed study of the healthy, but 'schizotypal', individual could throw light on many features of schizophrenia that are difficult, if not impossible, to investigate in the currently ill (and often medicated) person. Indeed, in the present author's view it will probably be there that several vital clues to the origins of psychotic disorder will ultimately be revealed.

REFERENCES

Beech A. R., Claridge G. S. (1987). Individual differences in negative priming: relations with schizotypal personality traits. *British Journal of Psychology*; **78**: 349–56.

Beech A. R., Baylis G. C., Claridge G. S. (1988). Individual differences in schizotypy as reflected in measures of cognitive inhibition. (In press).

Bentall R., Claridge G. S., Slade P. D. (1988). The multidimensional nature of schizotypal traits: a factor analytic study with normal subjects. (In press).

Bentall R., Slade P. (1985a). Reality testing and auditory hallucinations: a signal detection analysis. *British Journal of Clinical Psychology*; **24**: 159–69.

Bentall R., Slade P. (1985b). Reliability of a scale measuring disposition towards hallucinations: a brief report. *Personality and Individual Differences*; **6**: 527–9.

Bleuler M. (1978). *The Schizophrenic Disorders. Long-term Patient and Family Studies* (translated by Clemens S. M.). New Haven: Yale University Press.

Brockington I. F., Kendell R. E., Wainwright S., Hillier V. F., Walker J. (1979). The distinction between the affective psychoses and schizophrenia. *British Journal of Psychiatry*; **135**: 243–8.

Broks P. (1984). Schizotypy and hemisphere function—II. Performance asymmetry on a verbal divided visual-field task. *Personality and Individual Differences*; **5**: 649–56.

Broks P., Claridge G. S., Matheson J., Hargreaves J. (1984). Schizotypy and hemisphere function—IV. Story comprehension under binaural and monaural listening conditions. *Personality and Individual Differences*; **5**: 665–70.

Bullen J. G., Hemsley D. R. (1984). Psychoticism and visual recognition thresholds. *Personality and Individual Differences*; **5**: 735–9.

Chapman L. J., Chapman J. P., Raulin M. L. (1976). Scales for physical and social anhedonia. *Journal of Abnormal Psychology*; **85**: 374–82.

Chapman L. J., Chapman J. P., Raulin M. L. (1978). Body-image aberration in schizophrenia. *Journal of Abnormal Psychology*; **87**: 399–407.

Claridge G. S. (1985). *Origins of Mental Illness*. Oxford: Blackwell.

Claridge G. S. (1987). 'The schizophrenias as nervous types' revisited. *British Journal of Psychiatry*; **151**: 735–43.

Claridge G. S., Birchall P. M. A. (1978). Bishop, Eysenck, Block, and psychoticism. *Journal of Abnormal Psychology*; **87**: 664–8.

Claridge G. S., Broks P. (1984). Schizotypy and hemisphere function—I. Theoretical considerations and the measurement of schizotypy. *Personality and Individual Differences*; **5**: 633–48.

Claridge G. S., Hewitt J. K. (1987). A biometrical study of schizotypy in a normal population. *Personality and Individual Differences*; 8: 303–12.

Crow T. J. (1986). The continuum of psychosis and its implication for the structure of the gene. *British Journal of Psychiatry*; 149: 419–29.

DSM-III (1980). *Diagnostic and Statistical Manual of Mental Disorders*, 3rd edn. Washington, DC: American Psychiatric Association.

Eckblad M., Chapman L. J. (1983). Magical ideation as an indicator of schizotypy. *Journal of Consulting and Clinical Psychology*; 51: 215–25.

Eckblad M., Chapman L. J. (1986). Development and validation of a scale for hypomanic personality. *Journal of Abnormal Psychology*; 95: 214–22.

Eysenck H. J. (1952). Schizothymia-cyclothymia as a dimension of personality. II. Experimantal. *Journal of Personality*; 20: 345–840.

Eysenck H. J., Eysenck S. B. G. (1975). *Manual of the Eysenck Personality Questionnaire*. London: Hodder and Stoughton.

Frith C. D. (1979). Consciousness, information processing and schizophrenia. *British Journal of Psychiatry*; 134: 225–35.

Golden R. R., Meehl P. E. (1979). Detection of the schizoid taxon with MMPI indicators. *Journal of Abnormal Psychology*; 88: 217–33.

Gottesman I. I., Shields J. (1982). *Schizophrenia: the Epigenetic Puzzle*. Cambridge: Cambridge University Press.

Kretschmer E. (1925). *Physique and Character* (translated by Sprott W. J. H.). London: Kegan, Trench and Trubner.

Launay G., Slade P. (1981). The measurement of hallucinatory predisposition in male and female prisoners. *Personality and Individual Differences*; 2: 221–34.

Meehl P. E. (1962). Schizotaxia, schizotypy, schizophrenia. *American Psychologist*; 17: 827–38.

Miller, E. N., Chapman L. J. (1983). Continued word association in hypothetically psychosis-prone college students. *Journal of Abnormal Psychology*; 92: 468–78.

Muntaner, C., Garcia-Sevilla L. (1985). Factorial structure of the Eysenck Personality Questionnaire in relation to other psychosis proneness scales. *Paper presented at the 2nd Conference of the International Society for the Study of Individual Differences, St. Feliu, Spain, June 1985*.

Nakano K., Saccuzzo D. P. (1985). Schizotaxia, information processing and the MMPI 2-7-8 code type. *British Journal of Clinical Psychology*; 24: 217–18.

Nielsen T. C., Petersen N. E. (1976). Electrodermal correlates of extraversion, trait anxiety, and schizophrenism. *Scandinavian Journal of Psychology*; 17: 73–80.

Raine A., Allbutt J. (1988). Factors of schizoid personality. *British Journal of Clinical Psychology*; (in press).

Raine A., Manders D. (1988). Schizoid personality, interhemispheric transfer and left hemisphere overactivation. *British Journal of Clinical Psychology*; (in press).

Rawlings D., Claridge G. S. (1984). Schizotypy and hemisphere function—III. Performance asymmetries on tasks of letter recognition and local-global processing. *Personality and Individual Differences*; 6: 657–63.

Robinson T. N. Jr, Zahn T. P. (1985). Psychoticism and arousal: possible evidence for a linkage of P and psychopathy. *Personality and Individual Differences*; 6: 47–66.

Rust J. (1987). The Rust Inventory of Schizoid Cognitions (RISC): a psychometric measure of psychoticism in the normal population. *British Journal of Clinical Psychology*; **26**: 151–2.

Simons R. F. (1981). Electrodermal and cardiac orienting in psychometrically defined high-risk subjects. *Psychiatry Research*; **4**: 347–56.

Simons R. F. (1982). Physical anhedonia and future psychopathology: an electrodermal continuity? *Psychophysiology*; **19**: 433–41.

Steronko R. J., Woods D. J. (1978). Impairment in early stages of visual information processing in nonpsychotic schizotypic individuals. *Journal of Abnormal Psychology*; **87**: 481–90.

Stone M. H. (1980). *The Borderline Syndromes*. New York: McGraw-Hill.

Tipper S. P. (1985). The negative priming effect: inhibitory priming by ignored objects. *Quarterly Journal of Experimental Psychology*; **37A**: 571–90.

Watt N. F. (1984). In a nutshell: the first two decades of high-risk research in schizophrenia. In: *Children at Risk for Schizophrenia. A Longitudinal Perspective* (Watt N. F., Anthony J., Wynne L. C., Rolf J. E., eds.). Cambridge: Cambridge University Press.

Watt N. F., Anthony J., Wynne L. C., Rolf J. E. (1984). (eds). *Children at Risk for Schizophrenia. A Longitudinal Perspective*. Cambridge: Cambridge University Press.

Woody E. Z., Claridge G. S. (1977). Psychoticism and thinking. *British Journal of Social and Clinical Psychology*; **16**: 241–8.

15 *Social influences on schizophrenia*

PAUL BEBBINGTON and LIZ KUIPERS

Social theories concerning schizophrenia can be divided into two categories. The first, and more audacious, of these are *'grand'* *theories*, aiming to provide a virtually complete explanation of the emergence of the disease. They stand in contrast to a second group of more limited *arousal theories* in which the immediate social world provides stressors that are potentially arousing, but have no specific effects in instigating the schizophrenic reactions. Instead, it is assumed that schizophrenia results from the activation of a pre-existing, probably biological tendency. Finally, the supposed tendency of stressful circumstances to provoke the emergence of florid symptoms of schizophrenia leads to the idea that negative symptoms may be an adaptive withdrawal from overstimulation.

GRAND THEORIES

For good reasons, not least of which is a general lack of supporting evidence, these have become unfashionable and will be reviewed only briefly. Bateson *et al.* (1956) proposed that schizophrenia was the result of the family's 'double bind' communication. Wynne and Singer (1963, 1965) also focused on communication difficulties and found that parents of schizophrenics had a 'fragmented' or 'amorphous' style. Lidz *et al.* (1957) identified parents of schizophrenics as showing both 'schism' and 'skew' in their marriages, together with a narcissistic egocentricity. Laing and Esterson (1964) considered schizophrenia to be a valid and understandable response to particular family and societal pressures. Hirsch and Leff (1975), in an extensive review, looked closely at the experimental evidence on which these early ideas were based, and concluded that the following statements were reasonably supported by the experimental evidence:

1. more parents of schizophrenics are psychiatrically disturbed than parents of normal children, and more of the mothers are 'schizoid'
2. there is a link between allusive thinking in schizophrenics and their parents, but this is also true in normal people, in whom it occurs less frequently
3. the parents of schizophrenics show more conflict and disharmony than parents of other psychiatric patients

4. the pre-schizophrenic child more frequently manifests physical ill health or mild disability early in life than the normal child
5. mothers of schizophrenics show more concern and protectiveness than do mothers of normal subjects, both before and after their offspring fall ill.

Clearly, these findings could be accounted for in terms other than a simple social origin for the disease. For example, points 1–3 could have a genetic basis, whereas points 4 and 5 might merely be reactions to abnormalities in the child that preceded the development of overt schizophrenia but were nevertheless part of the same process.

Finally, although the work of Wynne and Singer (1963, 1965) strongly suggested that parents of schizophrenics communicate abnormally, Hirsch and Leff (1975) were themselves unable to replicate their most definite findings in the only independent attempt to test out these 'grand' social theories of the origins of schizophrenia, although they did find that the parents of their schizophrenic patients had a tendency to talk more. The Finnish adoption study places the grand theories in what might be their proper perspective (Tienari et al., 1987). As might be expected under a genetic model, these workers found an excessive rate of schizophrenia in the adopted offspring of schizophrenic mothers. However, these cases all occurred in the 47% of adoptive families who were rated as severely disturbed, suggesting the possibility of genetic–environmental interactions.

A major problem of these early investigations is that they depend on retrospective inferences about causal direction. One feasible prospective approach is to perform longitudinal studies of families with children who may be at 'high risk' of developing schizophrenia (e.g. Venables, 1977; Goldstein, 1985; 1987a). These, however, have their own problems, such as the length of time required to complete the study, the ethics of intervention, and high drop-out rates (Shakow, 1973).

Most prospective studies of this type have been concerned to identify characteristics, usually in the areas of neuropsychological and social functioning, of the offspring of schizophrenic parents who are at the greatest risk of developing the disorder themselves. Only one study has examined the effect of family interaction prospectively (Goldstein et al., 1968; Doane et al., 1981; Goldstein et al., 1985, 1987b). These workers chose to examine adolescents they regarded as being at increased risk of developing schizophrenia because they were attending a psychiatric outpatient department for 'disturbed behaviour'. Data on 54 cases were available at 5- or 15-year follow-up, mostly at both. Only four adolescents developed definite schizophrenia, but parental abnormalities of communication and affective style, rated at induction, were each clearly associated with the later emergence of schizophrenic spectrum disorders. However, the relevance of the findings to schizophrenia narrowly defined, or to the development of disorder outside this select population is not established.

Indeed, it is possible that the parents were merely reacting to an initial disturbance that was the prodrome of later spectrum disorder: further follow-up studies are clearly required, and the results of the prospective part of the Finnish adoption study are awaited with particular interest (Tienari *et al.*, 1987).

AROUSAL THEORIES OF THE ONSET AND COURSE OF SCHIZOPHRENIA

As Jablensky argues in Chapter 3, the epidemiological evidence makes a purely social cause for schizophrenia unlikely. However, a more circum-scribed role for social factors remains possible. Broadly speaking, arousal theories correspond to the widely held clinical opinion that people with schizophrenia, despite their frequent social withdrawal, are very responsive to their social environment. In one version of this view, schizophrenics are upset by the sorts of experience that would affect anybody, i.e. they are normally sensitive to stress, but they then respond abnormally by develop-ing psychotic symptoms. In another version, not only is the response abnormal, but the sufferer is also abnormally sensitive. According to these arousal theories, social influences act together with factors at other levels to determine at least the timing, and possibly the fact, of schizophrenic breakdown. They fall easily within modern attempts at integrated aetiolo-gical models of psychiatric illness (e.g. Zubin and Spring, 1977; Liberman, 1986; Nuechterlein, 1987). They are underpinned by the concept of psychosocial stress, a concept that only becomes scientifically valuable when it is measured in a circumscribed and specific manner. In schizo-phrenia, such measures have included life events and 'expressed emotion'.

Life events

Apart from direct studies of life events, there are two sources of evidence suggesting that changes in the social milieu may provoke the emergence of schizophrenic symptoms in susceptible individuals. First, it has long been known that acute florid symptoms may recrudesce in patients subjected to too much pressure in rehabilitation programmes, or discharged prema-turely (Wing *et al.*, 1964: Stevens, 1973: Goldberg *et al.*, 1977). Second, the aftermath of certain specific transitions is associated with an increased incidence of schizophrenia. For instance, Steinberg and Durell (1968), in a study of recruits entering military service, showed very high rates of admissions for schizophrenia in the first year after enlistment in compari-son with the second, and this excess of admissions was even more notable in the first month. The finding did not appear to arise because of a greater likelihood of enlistment among people already showing signs of schizo-phrenia, nor because of an increased chance of recognition. The soldiers who developed schizophrenia might have done so in any case, but the timing is suggestive at least of a precipitating effect of enlistment.

The most direct approach to examining the possible causal role of psychosocial events in schizophrenia is to record the occurrence of a whole range of events before onset. The problems inherent in this procedure are considerable and will not be reviewed here in full (*see* Bebbington, 1987). Moreover, schizophrenia creates particular difficulties for this type of research, which must be restricted to those cases where onset is relatively recent, clear-cut, and capable of accurate dating. In particular, this means that cases fulfilling the duration criteria of the Diagnostic and Statistical Manual of Mental Disorders (DSM-III) for schizophrenia cannot be studied in this way. The definition of onset is in any case problematic (Cranach *et al.*, 1981). The safest definition involves a transition from a symptom-free state to a psychotic one. However, most authors also include cases where 'onset' represents a move from neurotic or residual symptoms to florid psychotic ones. Such cases are of interest in themselves, but do reduce the likelihood that the causal relationship operates in the hypothesized direction, since events may be recorded that have actually occurred after onset and perhaps as a result of it. In view of the importance of neurotic symptoms in heralding schizophrenic relapse, this caveat also applies to onset defined as a move from a neurotic to a psychotic state.

The requirements that should be met before concluding that life events have a definite role in engendering episodes of schizophrenia are summarized in Table 15.1. No study so far published meets all of them. Our conclusions about the role of life events in triggering episodes of schizophrenia must therefore depend upon an integrated evaluation of several imperfect studies. Useful evidence comes both from studies showing differences between cases and controls in the frequencies of events, and from those which do not necessarily incorporate controls, but give a good breakdown of the timing of events before onset. The second type of study is less powerful, but derives its value from using cases as their own

Table 15.1 Requirements for life event studies in schizophrenia

---

Standardized method of symptomatic assessment
Standardized method of case definition
Limitation to cases where it is possible to date onset accurately
Onset defined as move from effectively symptom free state to a psychotic one
Structured collection of events from a defined period before onset
Precise dating of events to identifying the salient period of effect
Objective ratings of the impact of events
Objective rating of the degree to which events are independent of actions of the
    subject that might have been due to emergency illness
An appropriate control group

---

controls. This may be the only way of demonstrating an effect if schizophrenic subjects are disturbed by life events with no measurable influence on normals.

The study by Brown and Birley (1968) used fairly sophisticated methods for its day, and suggested that there was an increase in events of various degrees of impact, limited to the 3-week period before onset. Even so, only 45 of their 50 cases had received clinical diagnoses of schizophrenia, and in only 29 cases was onset from a state of normality to the emergence of schizophrenic symptoms. Jacobs and Myers (1976) also used sophisticated methods, but their inconclusive findings are further vitiated by the fact that they chose to examine events in the 6-month antecedent interval, possibly thereby obscuring a real increase in frequency limited to the weeks immediately before onset. This might also have accounted for the negative results in the study of Malzacher *et al.* (1981), although they did give results for the 3-month period before onset. Al Khani *et al.* (1986) used reasonably adequate methods in a Saudi Arabian study, but their results were complicated, showing a credible effect of life events, but only in females who were married or in a first episode. Canton and Fraccon (1985) failed to use onset to define the end of the period of event collection, so the events they recorded could have occurred after onset, thus disqualifying them from consideration as causal agents. Those studies attempting to link events to onset are so few in number they can be readily summarized in tabular form (Table 15.2). Some authors have not been included in this table because they studied schizophrenic patients as part of larger projects and little can be inferred specifically about schizophrenia, either because of small numbers or the way results are presented (Adamson and Schmale, 1965; Hudgens *et al.*, 1970; Eisler and Pollak, 1971; Leff *et al.*, 1973; Harder *et al.*, 1980).

The literature has recently been considerably expanded by the publication of a large WHO collaborative study (Day *et al.*, 1987). Although limited by the lack of control groups, it is important and worth describing in some detail. It was conducted in nine catchment areas from around the world. Five (Aarhus, Honolulu, Nagasaki, Prague and Rochester, NY) were in developed countries, the remainder (Agra, Chandigarh, Cali and Ibadan) in developing countries.

The selection of cases was deliberately broad, and included an appreciable minority of doubtful diagnosis. All told, the study included 386 cases out of the 435 screened and in scope. Numbers in individual centres ranged from 13 to 84, with the smallest numbers coming from Honolulu and Rochester. 'Onset' was considered to have occurred when psychosis was preceded by a state without symptoms, or from one with only minor neurotic or psychotic symptoms. Onset from a symptom free state was commoner in the centres in developing countries, and this may be associated with the relatively benign course of schizophrenia in such locations (Chapter 3; WHO, 1979). Only those cases were included where onset had occurred within 6 months of screening and was capable of being

Table 15.2 Life event studies in schizophrenia

Author	Location	No. subjects	Case selection	Definition of onset	Life event measure	Period of analysis	Control group
Brown and Birley (1968)	S. London	50	Kraepelinian criteria based on PSE. First admissions and readmissions	Normal-psychotic, neurotic-psychotic, or minor major psychotic Onset within 3 weeks of admission, datable to within 1 week	Semistructured interview (early version of LEDS—Brown and Harris 1978)	3 months prior to onset in 3 week subdivisions	325 selected from local firms (i.e. imperfectly random)
Jacobs and Myers (1976)	New Haven	62	Schizophrenia 'broadly defined': first admissions	Onset dated to within days based on emergence or exacerbation of symptoms and changes in social functioning	Modified version of Holmes and Rahe (1967) inventory given at interview	1 year prior to onset in 6 month subdivisions	62 matched for age, sex, social class, ethnicity, from random population sample
Malzacher et al. (1981)	Zurich	33	Clinical definition, cf Brown and Birley 1968: first admissions	Emergence of psychotic symptoms	Life event inventory based on Tennant and Andrews (1976)	6 months prior to onset in 3 month subdivisions	33 matched for age, sex, marital status from random population sample
Canton and Fraccon (1985)	Venice	54	DSM-III criteria: not all first admissions	Not defined	Life event inventory based on Paykel (1971) given at interview	6 months before admission or interview	54 normal normotensive subjects from hypertensive screening clinic matched for age, sex, social class, marital status

Al Khani et al. (1986)	Riyadh	48	Narrow operational definition: 92% CATEGO S+; not all first admissions	Exactly as Brown and Birley (1968)	WHO life events schedule given at interview	6 months prior to onset in 3 month subdivisions; 3 months in 3 week subdivisions	62 members of local community: imperfectly random sample
Chung et al. (1986)	Sydney	15	DSM-III criteria: not all first admissions	Onset within 12 months: 'accurately' datable, normal-psychotic, normal-prodromal, minor-major psychotic	LEDS (Brown and Harris, 1978)	6 months, 13 weeks, 4 weeks prior to onset	Matched for age, sex, partly from local population, partly surgical patients
Day et al. (1987)	Multicentre	386 from 9 centres	Broad range of psychotic cases, classified by local clinical diagnosis and CATEGO. Discrepant classifications in up to 28% of cases	Onset within 6 months, datable to within 1 week. Normal-psychotic; minor neurotic-psychotic; minor-major psychotic	WHO life events schedule given at interview	3 months prior to onset in 3 week subdivisions	No controls

PSE: present state examination

dated to within a one-week period. Events were recorded for the 3-month period preceding onset.

Life events were elicited using the specially developed WHO semi-structured life events interview covering 70 categories with operationally defined threshold criteria. The interviewers themselves rated the impact of the event on the patient, i.e. the rating was not made blind. 'Independence' ratings were also made after the manner of Brown and Harris (1978). Events were reviewed separately by staff from WHO headquarters.

In six of the nine centres, event rates per person were very similar, both to each other and to the rates recorded in London by Brown and Harris (1978). In the Indian and Nigerian centres, which relied on informants for the life event history, rates were lower.

As it was not possible to establish control groups, the value of the findings comes from the patterning of life events before onset. Although this could be artefactual, e.g. due to recall effects, or the 'search after meaning' (Brown, 1974), the results are suggestive. In all the centres, events tended to cluster in the 3 weeks before onset, and to a lesser extent, in the 3-week period before that. When all events were considered together, the rise in events in the three weeks before onset was significant in six of the nine centres. Numbers in Rochester and Honolulu were too small to analyse, and the overall event rate in Ibadan was probably too low to show a significant effect, although the trend was clear. When independent events were considered on their own, the results from Nagasaki became non-significant $(P = 0.1)$. Agra and Chandigarh provided large numbers of patients, and in those centres it was possible to repeat the analyses for moderate and severe events on their own; a significant clustering before onset was again apparent.

Ideally, the analysis should have included separate assessment of independent moderate and severe events, although this might require pooling results from different centres. It would also be of value to have analyses for the different types of onset and for schizophrenia narrowly defined. The centres with fewest onsets from a symptom free state appear to be those with the most marked clustering of life events, which raises the possibility of reverse causality, particularly where results are not given separately for independent events. On the face of it, the Indian and Nigerian centres report more very acute conditions, and yet many of these do not appear to be related to life events. Clearly, this particular study leaves us still lacking an adequate explanation for the differences in the course of schizophrenia in the developed and the developing world. From this evidence at any rate, the acute benign psychoses seen in the latter do not appear to be psychogenic. However, as we will see below, the expressed emotion literature sheds a different light on this issue.

Partly on the basis of the data from their schizophrenia study described above, Brown et al. (Brown et al., 1973; Brown and Harris, 1978) have argued that life events are related in different ways to the onset of schizophrenia and of depression. They distinguish between two types of causal role: a 'formative' role, where events are of fundamental aetiological significance, being more important in the causation of the condition than dispositional factors; and a 'triggering' role, where dispositional factors play the larger part, and life events merely aggravate a strong pre-existing tendency. As triggers, events are seen as precipitating something that would have occurred before long for other reasons: they simply bring onset forward by a short period, and perhaps make it more abrupt. As formative factors, events either substantially advance the time of onset or bring it about altogether. Brown and his colleagues did consider that 'triggering' and 'formative' effects are opposite ends of a continuum rather than entirely different processes. They were of the opinion that their data indicated more of a triggering effect of events in schizophrenia, whereas they might well be formative in depression. Others have suggested (e.g. Tennant *et al.*, 1981) that the findings merely indicate a stronger association between life events and depression than between life events and schizophrenia.

Paykel (1979) has used the index 'relative odds' to express this. He reckoned that in the 6 months following the occurrence of a major event, the risk of developing schizophrenia is increased three- or fourfold over the general population rate, while the risk of developing depression is increased sixfold. However, in view of the inconclusive findings, attempts at the precise quantification of risk must be regarded as premature, and it is plain that the definitive study of life events in schizophrenia is long overdue. Nevertheless, there may be some substance to the triggering role of life events, and to the proposition that schizophrenia is a condition significantly affected by social circumstances. In our view, this proposition receives considerably more support from the literature on expressed emotion.

Expressed emotion

The ideas behind our current concept of expressed emotion (EE) are now quite old, and have been previously reviewed (Kuipers, 1979; Hooley, 1985; Leff and Vaughn, 1985; Koenigsberg and Handley, 1986). The original findings have been replicated a number of times, as indicated in Table 15.3. Relatives are interviewed with the Camberwell Family Interview (CFI), (Brown and Rutter, 1966; Rutter and Brown, 1966). This is recorded, and relatives are assessed according to how many *critical comments* they make, and their overall *hostility* and *emotional over-involvement*. These measures are used to construct a composite score of *expressed emotion*. An estimate of the amount of face-to-face contact between relative and patient is usually made. Vaughn and Leff (1976) combined the results of two similar studies to explore the relationship between EE, contact and medication in a total sample of 128 schizophrenics. These results are shown in Fig. 15.1 and their implications can be summarized: first, relapse in schizophrenia was indeed associated with social circumstances; second,

Table 15.3 Results of prospective studies of EE

Author	Location	No. subjects	Episode	Follow-up	Relapse rate (%) High EE	Low EE
Brown et al.[1] (1962)	S. London	97 (male)	All	1 year	56	21
Brown et al. (1972)	S. London	101	All	9 months	58	16
Vaughn and Leff (1976)	S. London	37	All	9 months	50	12
Leff and Vaughn[2] (1981)	S. London	36	All	2 years	62	20
Vaughn et al. (1984)	Los Angeles	54	All	9 months	56	17
Moline et al.[3] (1985)	Chicago	24	All	1 year	91	31
Dulz and Hand[4] (1986)	Hamburg	46	All	9 months	58	65
MacMillan et al. (1986a)	N. London	67	First	2 years	63	39
Nuechterlein et al.[5] (1986)	Los Angeles	26	All	1 year	37	0
Karno et al. (1987)	S. California	44	All	9 months	59	26
Leff et al. (1987)	Chandigarh, India	76	First	1 year	33	14
Tarrier et al.[6] (1988b)	Salford, England	48	All	9 months	48	21
Vaughan (personal communication)	Sydney, Australia	87	All	9 months	52	23

EE: expressed emotion
NB   Although McCreadie and Robinson (1987) showed some support for an effect of EE, their study was retrospective.
[1] Their measure of 'emotional overinvolvement' was the prototype of EE.
[2] Follow-up of same patients as Vaughn and Leff (1976).
[3] Non-standard criteria for high EE.
[4] An unknown number of subjects were not living with their EE-rated relatives.
[5] All patients on fixed dose fluphenazine.
[6] Patients receiving standard care with or without education in the authors' intervention programme.

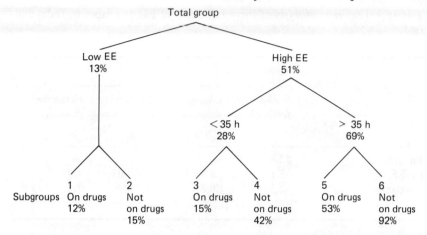

Fig. 15.1   *Relapse rates at 9 months (taken from Vaughn and Leff, 1976). Low EE = 71 patients; high EE = 57 patients*

it was possible to identify those schizophrenics with a high risk of relapse; and third, since factors associated with relapse had been pinpointed, so also had the targets of a possible intervention programme, namely, the effective provision of medication, a reduction of face-to-face contact and a lowering of EE in the family.

Originally developed in Britain, the EE measure has now been used in a number of countries, both in the developed and in the developing world (Table 15.3). With some exceptions, the results of these studies corroborate the predictive value of EE in a range of populations, although not all support the interactions with contact time, or even with medication.

It has been suggested that the better course and outcome of schizophrenia in developing countries (Chapter 3; WHO, 1979) may result from differences in family characteristics reflected by the EE measure, and it has proved feasible to test this in India. Expressed emotion ratings were completed in 93 relatives of both rural and city dwellers near Chandigarh (Wig *et al.*, 1987a). As expected, relapse rates in these samples were low, particularly in the rural areas. However, there was an association between hostility expressed by relatives and relapse within a year, suggesting that the good outcome of schizophrenia might be the result of beneficial family structures and traditions (Leff *et al.*, 1987).

We have looked at these results in more detail. Although related to EE in both Chandigarh and London, relapse is less common in India. Could this lower Indian relapse rate have been due to lower levels of EE. It is possible to test this hypothesis by loglinear analysis. In Table 15.4, we have analysed results from India given by Leff *et al.* (1987), together with data from the London studies published by Vaughn and Leff (1976). The most parsimonious model with acceptable goodness of fit only requires relationships between EE and site, and between EE and relapse. In other words,

Table 15.4 Loglinear analysis of the relationship of EE to relapse in India and London

| | Model of best fit | | | |
	Scaled deviance	Change in deviance (d.f. = 1)	Probability	Parameter estimate
Main effects	42.6	—	—	—
Site-EE	33.1	9.5	<0.005	1.0
EE-relapse	2.3	30.8	<0.0001	1.9

EE: expressed emotion

these data are certainly compatible with the assertion that the better outcome in India is the result of lower levels of EE. Moreover, the parameter estimates suggest that the effect of EE is of considerable strength. So, not only does EE have predictive value across very different cultures, it may also serve to explain the differences in outcome of schizophrenia between those cultures.

However, despite the growing number of corroborative studies, several authors have expressed doubts about the value and validity of the measure. The study by MacMillan *et al.* (1986a) particularly merits description, as the authors concluded from their results that EE is of less use than generally supposed. They studied 77 patients discharged following a first episode of schizophrenia. These patients were also taking part in a controlled double-blind trial of prophylactic medication. Over a 2-year follow-up period, the relapse rate in patients from low EE homes was 38.9% and in patients from high EE homes 63.4%. This difference was significant at the 5% level. However, when the results were reanalysed, controlling for the length of episode before admission and the receipt of placebo rather than active medication, both of which were negatively correlated with outcome, the effect of EE became non-significant. The authors also used relatively sophisticated actuarial analyses, with the interval before relapse as the dependent variable. Although these are not reported in detail, they apparently corroborated the cruder categorical analysis.

The results, which appear to cast doubt on the significance of EE in these first episode patients have provoked debate (MacMillan *et al.*, 1986b; Leff and Vaughn, 1986). The most significant criticisms concern the assumptions that underlie the analyses performed and the conclusions arrived at. First, there is the issue of duration of illness before admission. The implicit assumption here is that the association of EE with relapse is spurious because long-standing illness indicates poor prognosis and also engenders high EE (Fig. 15.2; possibility i). However, there are other interpretations, also summarized in Fig. 15.2. In view of what is known of the characteristics of high EE, it seems equally likely that relatives of this type have difficulty in identifying behaviour as illness related, and referral might consequently be delayed. The association between duration and relapse might then be spurious (Fig. 15.2; possibility ii). Further possibilities include mediating relationships, in which the effect of EE on relapse is mediated by duration, or that of duration by EE (possibilities iii and iv). The clinical importance of EE for relapse would be maintained under possibilities iii and iv.

Second, MacMillan *et al.* (1986a) assumed that the association between medication and continued clinical well-being is necessarily pharmacological. Relatively more of the low EE group were receiving active medication, but it is equally possible that more of this group remained well because they happened to be in low EE homes.

Criticisms similar to these have recently been published by Mintz *et al.* (1987). They have also used the raw data presented by the Northwick Park group to conduct loglinear analyses controlling for drug treatment effects. Under virtually all assumptions, EE emerged as a significant predictor of relapse. MacMillan *et al.* (1987) gave alternative analyses suggesting that the effect of EE remains a non-significant trend. It looks as if it is possible to choose modes of analysis to support either view. MacMillan *et al.* (1987) also took the opportunity to present some of their data anew, free from the numerical errors pointed out by the Los Angeles group.

Nuechterlein *et al.* (1986) have demonstrated an effect of EE on relapse in patients wholly maintained on fixed dose intramuscular fluphenazine.

The findings of the Northwick Park study are roughly in line with those

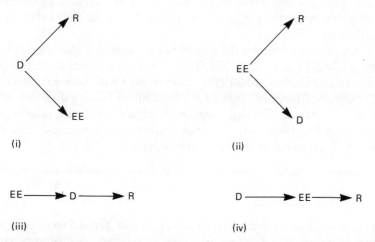

Fig. 15.2 *Possible relationships between duration of illness before referral (D), expressed emotion (EE) and relapse (R)*

of the other studies of EE (*see* Table 15.3) and the issue is of the interpretations that can be placed on them. The Hamburg study, in contrast, does seem to have produced a contrary result (Köttgen *et al.*, 1984; Dulz and Hand, 1986), with a high rate of relapse in patients from low EE families, higher indeed than in those from high EE ones. Vaughn (1986) has argued that defects in method may reduce the credence given to these findings. Not all the patients were living at home with their relative, and there were idiosyncrasies in the allocation of families to EE categories and in the criteria for relapse. In particular, an unknown number of patients counted as relapsing had not recovered in the first place.

In general, the results summarized in Table 15.3 add up to an impressive consensus in favour of the predictive value of EE. Moreover work using measures other than EE provides further support. Buchkrämer *et al.* (1986) have developed ratings based on an interview with whole families, the Munster Family Interview. These ratings have some parallels with constituents of EE, and their assessment of criticism, rather different from that involved in the EE rating, nevertheless appeared highly predictive of relapse. Angermeyer (1982) assessed families in a setting contrived to encourage talk about their differences and at follow-up 2 years later identified features associated with relapse that again had similarities with high EE. The relationship between affective style and EE (Miklowitz *et al.*, 1984; Strachan *et al.*, 1986), discussed below, also suggests that the EE findings are robust.

Among other criticisms of the EE research, those of Seywert (1984) seem unsupported by data, but Hogarty (1985) has recently reviewed the EE studies and argues that EE is only predictive of relapse in men, not women: this point has not previously been made explicit, and seems to have some support from the available evidence (e.g. Vaughn *et al.*, 1984). Brown *et al.* (1972) claimed that EE was equally predictive for male and female sufferers but, even so, EE may be of less clinical significance in women because the prognosis is relatively better for other reasons (Salokangas, 1983).

A lack of enthusiasm for the results of EE research is also apparent in the work of Birchwood *et al.* (1987). Their objections appear to be theoretical (Kuipers and Bebbington, 1988). They argued that high EE develops as the response of some relatives to the burdens of living with someone who has schizophrenia. The argument is therefore about the origins of EE rather than its effects, and does not detract from the overall impression from the literature that the latter are important.

The nature of EE

The expressed emotion measure is an empirically derived composite which covers two distinctly different attributes of relatives, that of criticism and hostility (i.e. intolerance), and that of emotional over-involvement (i.e.

overprotection). The former is a response characterizing both parents and spouses of those with schizophrenia, whereas over-involvement and difficulties in separating are more likely to be found in parents.

Some authors (e.g. Koenigsberg and Handley, 1986) have argued that criticism and over-involvement may be inherently different. It is possible that emotional over-involvement may be particularly associated with poor premorbid social functioning (Brown *et al.*, 1972; Miklowitz *et al.*, 1984). Hooley (1985), however, argued that both criticism and over-involvement are strategies reflecting a need to control situations. Tarrier *et al.* (1988a) failed to distinguish between the two patterns of behaviour from the patient's psychophysiological response to the presence of the relative. Although the attitudes may be distinguishable in terms of their origins and appearance, it is therefore possible that they are indistinguishable in terms of their effects.

Where studies have presented results separately for criticism and emotional over-involvement, they show a similar ability to predict relapse, although it is relatively rare for emotional over-involvement to be present alone (Brown *et al.*, 1972; Vaughn *et al.*, 1984; Leff *et al.*, 1987).

Until recently, for all the utility of the measure, evidence was scarce concerning the construct validity of EE. It may seem far-fetched to use an individual relative's behaviour at a single time to predict the likelihood of a subsequent relapse in the schizophrenic patient with whom that relative lives. It has always been presumed the measure is predictive either because it indicates some continuing feature of the interaction between the relatives or because it reflects their capacity to deal with crises. In the early days of its use, this presumption was supported by little evidence (Kuipers, 1979). However, this situation has now improved (Kuipers *et al.*, 1983; Miklowitz *et al.*, 1984; Strachan *et al.*, 1986; MacCarthy *et al.*, 1986).

In this Chapter, we have assumed, like others before us, that the home environment characterized by high EE represents a form of psychosocial stress. How then is relapse mediated?

It is possible that it operates via physiological arousal. There is some evidence from psychophysiological studies, in line with this suggestion. Tarrier *et al.* (1979) looked at the skin conductance (SC) recordings of schizophrenic patients in the presence and absence of their relatives. They showed that patients had high levels of arousal when high EE relatives entered the room, but not when low EE relatives did so. This difference was only apparent on the first occasion of testing. Sturgeon *et al.* (1984) also showed significantly higher levels of skin conductance response frequencies when parents were interviewed with a high, rather than with a low, EE relative. Tarrier and Barrowclough (1987) demonstrated a differential psychophysiological effect in a man living with one high and one low EE parent, depending on which was present. The arousal provoked by critical relatives seems to be non-specific, and has been observed in disturbed (non-schizophrenic) adolescents (Valone *et al.*, 1984).

This work has now been extended. Tarrier *et al.* (1988a) have shown that when a low EE relative entered the room, the patient's non-specific skin conductance response level decreased. This did not happen when the relative was high EE. This finding replicates the earlier study of Tarrier *et al.* (1979) with much larger numbers ($n = 70$), and emerged despite the fact that in the later study the assessments were carried out in a video studio, not in the patient's home. Patients also completed self-rating scales describing their levels of tension. A lack of correlation with the physiological measures might suggest that each is a distinct, incomplete and only partly overlapping measure of anxiety. Nevertheless, both the higher tension levels in patients with high EE relatives, and the ability of low EE relatives to relax patients were confirmed by self-report.

There was also a significantly higher tonic level of. skin conductance in patients with high EE relatives, whether the relative was present or not, which would support the findings of Sturgeon *et al.* (1984). This probably reflects physiological status at the time of relapse.

Interestingly, physiological arousal failed to distinguish between the two components of EE, i.e. criticism and over-involvement. Moreover, physiological arousal was predicted by levels of EE, but did not correlate with the number of critical comments, suggesting that the difference between high and low EE might indeed be genuinely categorical.

However, despite changes in EE due to a successful social intervention programme (Leff *et al.*, 1982), there were no concomitant changes in the skin conductance recordings of patients which turned out to be related to relapse independently. In other words, the beneficial effects of changes in EE do not appear to be mediated via an arousal system. Turpin *et al.* (1988) have reviewed this research in more detail. It should probably be pursued, but the resources required may be considerable.

Leff and Vaughn (1980) looked at the issue of arousal in an indirect way. They examined the interaction between the experience of life events in the 3 months before the onset of the patient's index admission and the level of EE in the key relative during the patient's recovery from the episode. They were therefore using EE in an unusual manner—it is usually employed to predict future relapse. Moreover, they were not establishing causal relationships between each factor and the onset of illness—they were assuming this, and examining only the proposition that, if causal, the factors operated as mutual substitutes. All the patients were off medication before onset. Leff and Vaughn did find that patients who came from low EE families were more likely to have experienced a life event before the onset of the index illness. It should be said that this finding is at variance with that of Brown and Birley (1968), who found in contrast that life events and 'chronic emotional tension' in the home were additive in their effects on onset, albeit in patients who were not all free of medication.

Showing that EE and life events can operate as mutual substitutes does not necessarily mean they involve similar mechanisms. However, Leff *et al.* (1983) have used material from their intervention study to strengthen their argument. They concluded that in patients unprotected by medication, relapse might be occasioned either by a life event or by living with a high EE relative. In patients taking medication, however, relapse required the experience of *both* a high EE relative *and* a recent life event. In this model, medication operates to raise the threshold for the psychosocial provocation of relapse, suggesting at least the possibility that life events and EE might have a common mechanism. Once more, this interactive model receives some support, albeit tentative, from psychophysiological studies. Tarrier *et al.* (1979) found that after a recent life event, the level of arousal in a patient (as measured by spontaneous fluctuations in skin conductance) was increased by the entry of a relative, whether rated high or low on EE. This response was not seen in patients who had not recently experienced a life event. We may therefore be approaching the position of being able to substantiate the validity of EE from a knowledge of *how* it engenders relapse.

Intervention studies

Once it became apparent that particular attributes of family interaction might have a deleterious effect on the course of schizophrenia, intervening to change these attributes became a logical next step. Four reports of social intervention with the relatives of patients with schizophrenia have now been published, and others are under way (Kuipers and Bebbington, 1988).

Such intervention studies add to the evidence in favour of the predictive value of EE if they can be shown to operate by reducing EE: successful interventions should be successful insofar as they reduce EE, and unsuccessful ones should fail to reduce both EE and relapse rate.

Of four successful interventions, three (Leff *et al.*, 1982, 1985; Falloon *et al.*, 1982, 1985; Barrowclough and Tarrier, 1988; Tarrier *et al.*, 1988b) strongly suggested that lowering EE was the mechanism through which they operated. The fourth intervention, that of Hogarty *et al.* (1986), differed in its results. Its aim was to reduce EE, albeit indirectly. It is therefore of interest that, although good outcome in this study was related to intervention, cases in which intervention was successful were not all associated with a reduction in EE.

A further study (Köttgen *et al.*, 1984) differs from those described above on a number of counts: younger patients, an absence of an educational input, and a more psychodynamically oriented approach. It is possible that the last mentioned could have occasioned a deleterious overstimulation (Strachan, 1986). The intervention was not successful in reducing either EE or relapse rate. The overall evidence from these studies therefore strongly favours a causal role for EE in exacerbating the florid symptoms of schizophrenia.

SOCIAL INFLUENCES ON NEGATIVE SYMPTOMS

Although described long ago (Wing, 1961), 'negative symptoms' have only recently become fashionable as a focus of research (Andreasen, 1985; Crow, 1985). This reflects an increased appreciation of the usefulness of the term, although it clearly means different things to different people, and covers a range of phenomena. Some negative symptoms are actually impairments in social performance—loss of self-care skills, loss of social graces. These may themselves arise from other features, more intrinsic to the process of schizophrenia, such as loss of drive or emotional expression. The definition of a negative symptom is affected by the theoretical standpoint of the investigator. For Crow (1985), the existence of negative symptoms potentially denotes a type of schizophrenia with a particular aetiopathological basis, and it becomes difficult for symptoms which are not immutable to be regarded as negative. On the other hand, clinicians and researchers with an interest in rehabilitation have always seen negative symptoms as prime targets for modification. As Wing (1983) puts it: 'the problem of the severity of negative impairments cannot be separated from the problem of reactivity to environmental factors'.

That some negative symptoms are very responsive to the social environment has been established for a number of years. Wing and Brown (1970), in the Three Hospitals study, showed that the social poverty of the hospital environment was associated with the salience of negative symptoms in the patients. Moreover, these phenomena showed concomitant variation: as the environment changed for the better, so did the patients. Brown *et al.* (1966) showed that this relationship between the degree of environmental stimulation and the patient's condition was also apparent when they were living at home.

There is evidence for believing that negative symptoms may represent an adaptive response to the upsetting consequences of social overstimulation for those with a tendency to develop florid schizophrenic symptoms. Rehabilitation programmes designed to reduce withdrawal and apathy may reactivate delusions and hallucinations (Stone and Eldred, 1959; Wing *et al.*, 1964; Stevens, 1973).

However, the relationship between arousal and negative symptoms in schizophrenia seems complex. This is shown even when the only psychophysiological measures considered are electrodermal. About half of all schizophrenic patients fail to show the normal changes in skin conductance when a novel but innocuous stimulus is presented (Gruzelier and Venables, 1972). Of those that do respond, some show abnormally fast and others abnormally slow habituation to repeated presentations (Gruzelier and Venables, 1972; Patterson and Venables, 1978). There are behavioural differences between responsive and non-responsive patients with schizophrenia. While the latter correspond to chronic sufferers with negative symptoms, the former appear generally overaroused. In this group, slow habituation appears to be associated with slow recovery from recent acute episodes (Frith *et al.*, 1979; Zahn *et al.*, 1981). The electrodermal abnormalities seem to be trait rather than state measures (Dawson *et al.*, 1988).

CONCLUSION

In our view, the studies we have reviewed in this paper taken together provide almost incontrovertible evidence for an important influence of the social environment on the course of schizophrenia. Day (1986) has argued that it is possible to identify at least four types of persistently 'toxic environment': the cognitively confusing; the emotionally intrusive; the overly demanding; and threatening or demoralizing physical environments. This categorization is designed to clarify in order to measure, and is a response to Day's own dissatisfaction with the evidence for the social reactivity of schizophrenia obtained from specific life event studies.

Day's approach is deliberately pragmatic rather than theoretical. However, his environmental types emphasize not only that stress is cognitively mediated, but that the demands of the environment on the cognitive processing capacity of people with schizophrenia may be inherently stressful. In this context, it is of interest that MacCarthy *et al.* (1986) have provided preliminary evidence that the emotionally intrusive environment created by living with a high EE relative may be stressful because it is cognitively confusing.

The social reactivity of schizophrenia is important because it permits and encourages a constructive approach to the management of this disabling condition (Bebbington and Kuipers, 1982; Kuipers and Bebbington, 1985, 1988). A clearer specification of the mechanisms that underlie this reactivity seems likely to have a considerable impact on the process of social management.

REFERENCES

Adamson J. D., Schmale A. (1965). Object loss, giving up and the onset of psychiatric disease. *Psychosomatic Medicine*; **27**: 557–77.

Al Khani M. A. F., Bebbington P. E., Watson J. P., House F. (1986). Life events and schizophrenia: a Saudi Arabian study. *British Journal of Psychiatry*; **148**: 12–22.

Andreasen N. (1985). Positive vs. negative schizophrenia: a critical evaluation. *Schizophrenia Bulletin*; **11**: 380–9.

Angermeyer M. C. (1982). The association between family atmosphere and hospital career of schizophrenic patients. *British Journal of Psychiatry*; **141**: 1–12.

Barrowclough C., Tarrier N. (1988). A behavioural intervention with a schizophrenic patient. *Behavioural Psychotherapy*; (in press).

Bateson G., Jackson D. D., Hally J., Weakland J. H. (1956). Towards a theory of schizophrenia. *Behavioural Science*; 1: 251–64.

Bebbington P. E. (1987). Psychosocial etiology of schizophrenia and affective disorders. In: *Psychiatry* revised edn (Michels R., ed.). Philadelphia: Lippincott.

Bebbington P. E., Kuipers L. (1982). The social management of schizophrenia. *British Journal of Hospital Medicine*; 28: 396–403.

Birchwood M., Cochrane R., Moore, B. (1988). Family coping behaviour and the course of schizophrenia: a follow up study. *Psychological Medicine*; (in press).

Brown G., Bone M., Dalison B., Wing J. (1966). *Schizophrenia and Social Care.* London: Oxford University Press.

Brown G. W. (1974). Meaning, measurement and stress of life events. In *Stressful Life Events: Their Nature and Effects* (Dohrenwend B. S., Dohrenwend B. P., eds.), pp. 217–43. New York: John Wiley.

Brown G. W., Birley J. L. T. (1968). Crises and life changes and the onset of schizophrenia. *Journal of Health and Social Behaviour*; 9: 203–14.

Brown G. W., Birley J. L. T., Wing J. K. (1972). Influence of family life on the course of schizophrenic disorders: a replication. *British Journal of Psychiatry*; 121: 241–58.

Brown G. W., Harris T. O. (1978). *Social Origins of Depression.* London: Tavistock.

Brown G. W., Harris T. O., Peto J. (1973). Life events and psychiatric disorders. Part 2: Nature of causal link. *Psychological Medicine*; 3: 159–76.

Brown G. W., Monck E. M., Carstairs G. M., Wing J. K. (1962). Influence of family life on the course of schizophrenic illness. *British Journal of Preventive and Social Medicine*; 16: 55–68.

Brown G. W., Rutter M. L. (1966). The measurement of family activities and relationships. *Human Relations*; 19: 241–63.

Buchkrämer G., Schulze-Monking H., Lewandowski L., Wittgen C. (1986). Emotional atmosphere in families of schizophrenic outpatients: relevance of a practice-orientated assessment instrument. In: *Treatment of Schizophrenia: Family Assessment and Intervention* (Goldstein M. J., Hand I., Hahlweg K., eds.), pp. 79–84. Berlin: Springer.

Canton G., Fraccon I. G. (1985). Life events and schizophrenia: a replication. *Acta Psychiatrica Scandinavica*; 71: 211–16.

Chung R. K., Langeluddecke, P., Tennant C. (1986). Threatening life events in the onset of schizophrenia, schizophreniform psychosis and hypomania. *British Journal of Psychiatry*; 148: 680–6.

Cranach M. von, Eberlein R., Holl B. (1981). The concept of onset in psychiatry. In: *What is a Case? The Problem of Definition in Psychiatric Community Surveys* (Wing J. K., Bebbington P. E., Robins L. N., eds.). London: Grant MacIntyre.

Crow T. J. (1985). The two-syndrome concept: origins and current status. *Schizophrenia Bulletin*; 11: 471–84.

Dawson M. E., Nuechterlein, K. H., Adams R. M. (1988). Psychophysiology of schizophrenic disorders. In: *Handbook of Clinical Psychophysiology* (Turpin G., ed.), pp. 265–86. Chichester: Wiley.

Day R. (1986). Social stress and schizophrenia: from the concept of recent life events to the notion of toxic environments. In: *Handbook of Studies on Schizophrenia* (Burrows G. D., Norman T. R., eds.), pp. 71–82. Amsterdam: Elsevier.

Day R., Neilsen, J. A., Korten A. *et al.* (1987). Stressful life events preceding the acute onset of schizophrenia: a cross-national study from the World Health Organization. *Culture, Medicine and Psychiatry*; **11**: 123–205.

Doane J. A., West K. L., Goldstein M. J., Rodnick E. H., Jones J. E. (1981). Parental communication deviance and affective style: predictors of subsequent schizophrenia spectrum disorders in vulnerable adolescents. *Archives of General Psychiatry*; **38**: 679–85.

Dulz B., Hand I. (1986). Short term relapse in young schizophrenics: can it be predicted and affected by family (CFI), patient, and treatment variables? An experimental study. In: *Treatment of Schizophrenia: Family Assessment and Intervention* (Goldstein M. J., Hand I., Hahlweg K., eds.), pp. 59–75. Berlin: Springer.

Eisler R. M., Pollak P. (1971). Social stress and psychiatric disorder. *Journal of Nervous and Mental Disease*; **153**: 227–33.

Falloon I. R. H., Boyd J. L., McGill C. W., Razani J., Moss H. B., Gilderman A. M. (1982). Family management in the prevention of exacerbations of schizophrenia. A controlled study. *New England Journal of Medicine*; **306**: 1437–40.

Falloon I. R. H., Boyd J. L., McGill C. W. *et al.* (1985). Family management in the prevention of morbidity of schizophrenia. Clinical outcome of a two year longitudinal study. *Archives of General Psychiatry*; **42**: 887–96.

Frith C. D., Stevens M., Johnstone E. C., Crow T. J. (1979). Skin conductance responsivity during acute episodes of schizophrenia as a predictor of symptomatic improvement. *Psychological Medicine*; **9**: 101–6.

Goldberg S. C., Schooler N. R., Hogarty G. E., Roper M. (1977). Prediction of relapse in schizophrenic outpatients treated by drug and sociotherapy. *Archives of General Psychiatry*; **34**: 171–84.

Goldstein, M. (1985). Family factors that antedate the onset of schizophrenia and related disorders: the results of a 15 year prospective longitudinal study. *Acta Psychiatrica Scandinavica*; **71** (suppl. 319): 7–18.

Goldstein M. (1987a). Psychosocial issues. *Schizophrenia Bulletin*; **13**: 157–71.

Goldstein M. (1987b). The UCLA high-risk project. *Schizophrenia Bulletin*; **13**: 505–14.

Goldstein M., Judd L. L., Rodnick E. H., Alkire A., Gould E. (1968). A method for studying social influence and coping patterns within families of disturbed adolescents. *Journal of Nervous and Mental Disease*; **147**: 233–51.

Gruzelier J., Venables P. H. (1972). Skin conductance orientating activity in a heterogeneous sample of schizophrenics. *Journal of Nervous and Mental Disease*; **155**: 277–87.

Harder D. W., Strauss J. S., Kokes R. F., Ritzler B. A., Gift T. E. (1980). Life events and psychopathology severity among first psychiatric admissions. *Journal of Abnormal Psychology*; **89**: 165–80.

Hirsch S. R., Leff J. P. (1975). *Abnormalities in the Parents of Schizophrenics.* Maudsley Monograph no. 22. Oxford: Oxford University Press.

Hogarty G. E. (1985). Expressed emotion and schizophrenic relapse: implications from the Pittsburg study. In: *Controversies in Schizophrenia* (Alpert M., ed.), pp. 354–65. New York: Guilford Press.

Hogarty G. E., Anderson C. M., Reiss D. J. *et al.* (1986). Family psycho-education, social skills training and maintenance chemotherapy in the aftercare treatment of schizophrenia. I. One year effects of a controlled study on relapse and expressed emotion. *Archives of General Psychiatry*; **43**: 633–42.

Hooley J. M. (1985). Expressed emotion: a review of the critical literature. *Clinical Psychology Review*; 5: 119–39.

Hudgens R. W., Robins E., Delong W. B. (1970). The reporting of recent stress in the lives of psychiatric patients. *British Journal of Psychiatry*; 117: 635–43.

Jacobs S., Myers J. (1976). Recent life events and acute schizophrenic psychosis: a controlled study. *Journal of Nervous and Mental Disease*; 162: 75–87.

Karno M., Jenkins J. H., de la Selva A. *et al.* (1987). Expressed emotion and schizophrenic outcome among Mexican-American families. *Journal of Nervous and Mental Disease*; 175: 143–51.

Koenigsberg H. W., Handley R. (1986). Expressed emotion: from predictive index to clinical construct. *American Journal of Psychiatry*; 143: 1361–73.

Köttgen C., Sonnichsen I., Mollenhauer K., Jurth R. (1984). Group therapy with the families of schizophrenic patients: results of the Hamburg Camberwell family interview study III. *International Journal of Family Psychiatry*; 5: 84–94.

Kuipers L. (1979). Expressed emotion: a review. *British Journal of Social and Clinical Psychology*; 18: 237–43.

Kuipers L., Bebbington P. E. (1985). Relatives as a resource in the management of functional illness. *British Journal of Psychiatry*; 147: 465–71.

Kuipers L., Bebbington P. E. (1988). Expressed emotion research in schizophrenia: theoretical and clinical implications. *Psychological Medicine*; (in press).

Kuipers L., Sturgeon D., Berkowitz R., Leff J. P. (1983). Characteristics of expressed emotion: its relationship to speech and looking in schizophrenic patients and their relatives. *British Journal of Clinical Psychology*; 22: 257–64.

Laing R. D., Esterson A. (1964). *Sanity, Madness and the Family*. Harmondsworth: Penguin.

Leff J. P., Hirsch S. Gaind R., Rohde P., Stevens B. (1973). Life events and maintenance therapy in schizophrenic relapse. *British Journal of Psychiatry*; 123: 659–60.

Leff J. P., Kuipers L., Berkowitz R., Eberlein-Fries R., Sturgeon D. (1982). A controlled trial of social intervention in schizophrenic families. *British Journal of Psychiatry*; 141: 121–34.

Leff J. P., Kuipers L., Berkowitz R., Sturgeon D. (1985). A controlled trial of social intervention in the families of schizophrenic patients: two year follow up. *British Journal of Psychiatry*; 146: 594–600.

Leff J. P., Kuipers L., Berkowitz R., Vaughn C. E., Sturgeon D. (1983). Life events, relatives' expressed emotion and maintenance neuroleptics in schizophrenic relapse. *Psychological Medicine*; 13: 799–806.

Leff J. P., Vaughn C. E. (1980). The interaction of life events and relatives' expressed emotion in schizophrenia and depressive neurosis. *British Journal of Psychiatry*; 136: 146–53.

Leff J. P., Vaughn C. E. (1981). The role of maintenance therapy and relatives' expressed emotion in relapse of schizophrenia: a two year follow up. *British Journal of Psychiatry*; 139: 102–4.

Leff J. P., Vaughn C. (1985). *Expressed Emotion in Families*. New York: The Guilford Press.

Leff J. P., Vaughn C. (1986). First episodes of schizophrenia. *British Journal of Psychiatry*; 148: 215–16.

Leff J. P., Wig N., Ghosh A. *et al.* (1987). Influence of relatives' expressed emotion on the course of schizophrenia in Chandigarh. *British Journal of Psychiatry*; 151: 166–73.

Liberman R. P. (1986). Coping and competence as protective factors in the vulnerability-stress model of schizophrenia. In: *Treatment of Schizophrenia: Family Assessment and Intervention* (Goldstein M. J., Hand I., Hahlweg K., eds.), pp. 201–16. Berlin: Springer.

Lidz T., Cornelison A. R., Fleck S., Terry D. (1957). The intrafamilial environment of the schizophrenic patient. I. *Psychiatry*; 20: 329–42.

MacCarthy B., Hemsley D., Schrank-Fernandez C., Kuipers L., Katz R. (1986). Unpredictability as a correlate of expressed emotion in the relatives of schizophrenics. *British Journal of Psychiatry*; 148: 727–30.

McCreadie R. G., Robinson A. T. D. (1987). The Nithsdale schizophrenia survey: VI. Relatives' expressed emotion: prevalence, patterns and clinical assessment. *British Journal of Psychiatry*; 150: 640–4.

MacMillan J. F., Gold A., Crow T. J., Johnson A. L., Johnstone E. C. (1986a). The Northwick Park study of first episodes of schizophrenia. IV. Expressed emotion and relapse. *British Journal of Psychiatry*; 148: 133–43.

MacMillan J. F., Gold A., Crow T. J., Johnson A. L., Johnstone E. C. (1986b). Expressed emotion and relapse in schizophrenia. *British Journal of Psychiatry*; 148: 741–44.

MacMillan J. F., Crow T. J., Johnson A. L., Johnstone E. C. (1987). Expressed emotion and relapse in first episodes of schizophrenia. *British Journal of Psychiatry*; 151: 320–3.

Malzacher M., Merz J., Ebnother D. (1981). Einschneidende Lebensereignisse im Vorfeld akuter schizophrener Episoden: Erstmals erkrankte Patienten im Vergleich mit einer Normalstichprobe. *Archiv für Psychiatrie und Nervenkrankheiten*; 230: 227–42.

Miklowitz D. J., Goldstein M. J., Falloon R. H., Doane J. A. (1984). Interactional correlates of expressed emotion in the families of schizophrenics. *British Journal of Psychiatry*; 144: 482–7.

Mintz J., Mintz L., Goldstein M. J. (1987). Expressed emotion and relapse in first episodes of schizophrenia: a rejoinder to MacMillan *et al.* (1986). *British Journal of Psychiatry*; 151: 314–19.

Moline R. A., Singh S., Morris A., Meltzer H. Y. (1985). Family expressed emotion and relapse in schizophrenia in 24 urban American patients. *American Journal of Psychiatry*; 142: 1078–81.

Nuechterlein K. H. (1987). Vulnerability models for schizophrenia: state of the art. In: *Search for the Causes of Schizophrenia* (Häfner H., Gattaz W. F., Janzarik W., eds.), pp. 297–316. Berlin: Springer.

Nuechterlein K. H., Snyder K. S., Dawson M. E., Rappe S., Gitlin M., Fogelson D. (1986). Expressed emotion, fixed-dose fluphenazine decanoate maintenance, and relapse in recent onset schizophrenia. *Psychopharmacology Bulletin*; 22: 633–9.

Patterson T., Venables P. H. (1978). Bilateral skin conductance and skin potential in schizophrenic and normal subjects: the identification of the fast habituator group of schizophrenics. *Psychophysiology*; 15: 556–60.

Paykel E. S. (1979). Recent life events in the developments of the depressive disorders. In: *The Psychobiology of the Depressive Disorders: Implications for the Effects of Stress* (Depue R. A., ed.). New York: Academic Press.

Rutter M. L., Brown G. W. (1966). The reliability and validity of measures of family life and relationships in families containing a psychiatric patient. *Social Psychiatry*; 1: 38–53.

Salokangas R. K. R. (1983). Prognostic implications of the sex of schizophrenic patients. *British Journal of Psychiatry*; 142: 145–51.

Seywert F. (1984). Some critical thoughts on expressed emotion. *Psychopathology*; 17: 233–43.

Shakow D. (1973). Some thoughts about schizophrenic research in the context of high risk studies. *Psychiatry*; 36: 353–65.

Steinberg H., Durell J. (1968). A stressful situation as a precipitant of schizophrenic symptoms: an epidemiological study. *British Journal of Psychiatry*; 114: 1097–105.

Stevens B. C. (1973). Evaluation of rehabilitation for psychotic patients in the community. *Acta Psychiatrica Scandinavica*; 46: 136–40.

Stone A. A., Eldred S. H. (1959). Delusion formation during the activation of chronic psychiatric patients. *Archives of General Psychiatry*; 1: 177–9.

Strachan A. M. (1986). Family intervention for the rehabilitation of schizophrenia. *Schizophrenia Bulletin*; 12: 678–98.

Strachan A. M., Leff J. P., Goldstein M. J., Doane A., Burrt C. (1986). Emotional attitudes and direct communication in the families of schizophrenics: a cross-national replication. *British Journal of Psychiatry*; 149: 279–87.

Sturgeon D., Turpin D., Kuipers L., Berkowitz R., Leff J. (1984). Psychophysiological responses of schizophrenic patients to high and low expressed emotion relatives: a follow-up study. *British Journal of Psychiatry*; 145: 62–9.

Tarrier N., Barrowclough C. (1987). A longitudinal psychophysiological assessment of a schizophrenic patient in relation to the expressed emotion of his relatives. *Behavioural Psychotherapy*; 15: 45–57.

Tarrier N., Barrowclough C., Porceddu K., Watts S. (1988a). The assessment of psychophysiological reactivity to the expressed emotion of the relatives of schizophrenic patients. *British Journal of Psychiatry*; 152: 618–24.

Tarrier N., Barrowclough C., Vaughn C. et al. (1988b). The community management of schizophrenia: a controlled trial of a behavioural intervention with families to reduce relapse. *British Journal of Psychiatry*; (in press).

Tarrier N., Vaughn C. E., Lader M. H., Leff J. P. (1979). Bodily reactions to people and events in schizophrenics. *Archives of General Psychiatry*; 36: 311–15.

Tennant C., Bebbington P. E., Hurry J. (1981). The role of life events in depressive illness: is there a substantial causal relation? *Psychological Medicine*; 11: 379–89.

Tienari P., Sorri A., Lahti I. et al. (1987). Genetic and psychosocial factors in schizophrenia: the Finnish adoptive family study. *Schizophrenia Bulletin*; 13: 477–84.

Turpin G., Tarrier N., Sturgeon D. (1988). Social psychophysiology and the study of biopsychosocial models of schizophrenia. In: *Social Psychophysiology: Theory and Clinical Applications* (Wagner H., ed.). Chichester: Wiley.

Valone K., Goldstein M. G., Morton J. P. (1984). Parental expressed emotion and psychophysiological reactivity in an adolescent sample at risk for schizophrenic spectrum disorders. *Journal of Abnormal Psychology*; 93: 448–57.

Vaughn C. (1986). Patterns of emotional response in the families of schizophrenic patients. In: *Treatment of Schizophrenia: Family Assessment and Intervention* (Goldstein M. J., Hand I., Hahlweg K., eds.). Berlin: Springer.

Vaughn C., Leff J. P. (1976). The influence of family and social factors on the course of psychiatric illness: a comparison of schizophrenic and depressed neurotic patients. *British Journal of Psychiatry*; 129: 125–37.

Vaughn C. E., Snyder K. S., Jones S., Freeman W. B., Falloon I. R. H. (1984). Family factors in schizophrenic relapse: replication in California of British research in expressed emotion. *Archives of General Psychiatry*; **41**: 1169–77.

Venables P. (1977). Psychophysiological high risk strategy with Mauritian children: methodological issues. Paper read at the Psychophysiological Conference, London.

Wig N. N., Menon D. K., Bedi H. *et al.* (1987a). The cross-cultural transfer of ratings of relatives' expressed emotion. *British Journal of Psychiatry*; **151**: 156–60.

Wig N. N., Menon D. K., Bedi H. *et al.* (1987b). The distribution of expressed emotion components among relatives of schizophrenic patients in Aarhus and Chandigarh. *British Journal of Psychiatry*; **151**: 160–5.

Wing J. K. (1961). A simple and reliable subclassification of chronic schizophrenia. *Journal of Mental Science*; **107**: 862.

Wing J. K. (1983). Schizophrenia. In: *Theory and Practice of Psychiatric Rehabilitation* (Watts F. N., Bennett D. H., eds.), pp. 45–63. London: Wiley.

Wing J. K., Brown G. W. (1970). *Institutionalism and Schizophrenia*. Cambridge. Cambridge University Press.

Wing J. K., Monck E., Brown G. W., Carstairs G. M. (1964). Morbidity in the community of schizophrenic patients discharged from London mental hospitals in 1959. *British Journal of Psychiatry*; **110**: 10–21.

World Health Organisation (1979). *Schizophrenia: An International Follow-up Study.* Chichester: John Wiley and Sons.

Wynne L. C., Singer M. (1963). Thought disorder and family relations of schizophrenics. *I. Archives of General Psychiatry*; **9**: 191–206.

Wynne L. C., Singer M. (1965). Thought disorder and family relations of schizophrenics. *II. Archives of General Psychiatry*; **12**: 187–212.

Zahn T. P., Carpenter W. T., McGlashan T. H. (1981). Autonomic nervous system activity in acute schizophrenia: II: relationships to short term prognosis and clinical state. *Archives of General Psychiatry*; **38**: 260–6.

Zubin J., Spring B. (1977). Vulnerability: a new view of schizophrenia. *Journal of Abnormal Psychology*; **86**: 103–26.

16 *The contribution of psychological interventions to the treatment and management of schizophrenia*

GEOFF SHEPHERD

This chapter is concerned with the contribution of skills training and other psychological approaches to the treatment and management of schizophrenia. I take as my starting point that schizophrenia is a 'biopsychosocial' condition (Engel, 1977; 1980). Thus, whatever the biological substrate to the disorder, personal and social factors play an important part in determining its course and outcome. Outcome may be partly predicted from measures of previous social functioning (Strauss and Carpenter, 1972; 1974; 1977; Strauss *et al.*, 1977) and the course of the disorder has been shown to be responsive to the impact of life events (Brown and Birley, 1968; Jacobs and Myers, 1976; Chapter 15) and interpersonal stresses within the family (Brown *et al.*, 1962; 1972; Vaughn and Leff, 1976; Chapter 15). However, the causal relationships between these complex sets of variables are not well understood. For example, does poor premorbid social functioning *cause* poor outcome, or is it simply an indication of those individuals who are worst affected? This is unclear and, undoubtedly, the causal connections are not unidirectional. Nevertheless, Strauss and Carpenter (1981) have used these data to build an 'interactive/ developmental' model. Using this they describe how various genetic and perinatal factors may combine to define those individuals who are most predisposed to later development of the disorder, and how various family and other early learning experiences then confer greater or lesser subsequent vulnerability. In those with higher vulnerability, an acute episode may be precipitated by life stresses, the course and outcome of the episode (and any subsequent episodes) being influenced by personal, social and cultural factors.

This type of model provides a framework for integrating the wide range of variables implicated in the aetiology and prognosis of schizophrenia and, by placing events within a developmental context, it goes some way to explaining the most common time of onset of acute symptoms and the mechanism whereby premorbid social functioning may exert its influence. For example, if the individual has a prior history of poor social and occupational functioning, this is likely to be most critical in the early years of adulthood and, if disrupted by illness, it most clearly bodes ill for future reintegration. The model may also help explain some of the cross-cultural differences in outcome of schizophrenia (WHO, 1979; Chapter 3) and the observations of superior functioning in the community on the part of women with the disorder compared to men (Gibbons, 1983).

It is therefore important to examine carefully the extent to which psychological interventions might significantly improve various aspects of patients' social adjustment since, while not necessarily offering a panacea, significantly improving social functioning might make a considerable difference to the course and outcome of the disorder. In considering psychological interventions, I will restrict myself mainly to skills training and other learning-based approaches and some of the service implications that follow from them. I will not consider in detail the experimental work on language and information processing in schizophrenia (Chapter 13) nor the research on interventions with families (Chapter 15).

The use of social treatments in the care of schizophrenic patients has a long history. The early founders of the asylum movement were convinced of the importance of the 'active engagement of the mind' in order to divert it from 'painful and injurious associations' and of the dangers of 'a state of entire indolence and mental inertness' (Appendix to the Parliamentary Select Committee Report of 1827, quoted in Jones, 1972). They believed that this could be best avoided through the application of the principles of moral treatment. These included a strong emphasis on the provision of suitable activities (work, leisure, recreation); the use of praise and encouragement, rather than punishment and physical restraints: and the attempt to offer patients an approximation to 'normal' family life insofar as their disturbances would allow (Bockoven, 1963; Digby, 1985).

Unfortunately, these fine principles were soon to become submerged in the large, impersonal institutions that came to characterize the Victorian era, but by the inter-war period the importance of providing industrial work and other forms of social stimulation in mental hospitals was again recognized. In 1939, Myerson in Boston formulated his 'total push' therapy, which consisted of an effort to remotivate chronic patients through the provision of exercise, diet, games and other forms of recreational and social activities. He also emphasized the importance of praise and reward, rather than blame and punishment (*see* Bennett, 1983). After the Second World War the foundations of modern social psychiatry were laid with the work of people such as T. P. Rees, Maxwell Jones, Carstairs, O'Connor, Tizard and others. This work was most closely associated with the Medical Research Council's Social Psychiatry Research Unit at the Maudsley Hospital, and in 1970 Wing and Brown produced their classic study of three hospitals under the title 'Institutionalism and Schizophrenia'.

This study appeared to demonstrate conclusively that there was an association between a socially impoverished environment and a clinical picture of social withdrawal. Where a stimulating social environment was provided, offering opportunities for personal possessions, contacts with the outside world, flexible routines and high levels of structured activity, the patients showed the lowest levels of negative symptoms such as poverty of speech and mutism. The most important single factor correlating with the severity of negative symptoms was time spent doing nothing. Because of the longitudinal nature of this study it was possible to show that the association between social impoverishment and clinical impoverishment held over time. Thus, as the social environment improved, so did the ratings of the patients' clinical condition, strongly suggesting some causal relationship between them. Although the provision of a socially rich environment tended to minimize the development of negative symptoms, they did not in many cases disappear, even when active rehabilitation programmes were maintained for several years. This suggests the presence of a hard 'core' of untreatable disability in some patients. Wing and Brown also noted the dangers of 'over-stimulation' as well as 'under-stimulation', although it is probably the latter that is common in most hospitals. This study stands out as one of the first convincing demonstrations that psychological and social interventions might be able to affect the course and outcome of schizophrenia.

TOKEN ECONOMIES

With the advent of psychological interventions based on the application of learning-theory principles, the treatment and care of schizophrenia entered a new phase. Starting from the work of Lindsley (1956) and Ayllon and Azrin (1965), the 'token economy' was born. This is essentially a ward-based incentive programme which uses small plastic discs (tokens) dispensed to patients contingent upon the performance of certain social, self-care or instrumental tasks on or off the ward. Targets are usually individualized and subject to regular reviews, so that the 'exchange rate' is continually kept up to date according to the patient's progress.

Probably the best controlled study of the effectiveness of token economy programmes with chronic patients was that reported by Paul and Lentz (1977). This compared a 'social learning' approach (a comprehensive behavioural programme which employed tokens, prompting, modelling, shaping, etc.) with 'milieu therapy' (a type of therapeutic community) and with standard hospital treatment. Outcome was assessed by independent ratings of instrumental role performance, self-care and interpersonal skills at 6-monthly intervals throughout the 4.5-year active treatment period and the 1.5-year follow-up. The patients ($n = 84$) were chronically institutionalized psychotics resident in state hospitals (average length of stay 17 years) and aged between 18 and 55 years. They were randomly assigned to the three experimental conditions. The study is exemplary both for its methodological rigour and attention to detail.

The results were fairly clear-cut. Patients in both experimental groups showed substantial improvements across all aspects of functioning in the first 6 months compared with standard hospital care, and this was maintained throughout the whole of the study period. Patients in the social learning programme generally showed greater gains than those receiving the milieu therapy, particularly in the areas of instrumental role perform-ance and self-care skills. They also showed a greater tendency towards continuing improvement, rather than reaching a plateau and then levelling off. These differences were not so marked regarding interpersonal skills. At the end of the study, 98% of the patients in the social learning programme had achieved a 'significant release' (i.e. a minimum continuous stay in the community of at least 90 days) compared with 71% of the milieu therapy group and 45% of the standard hospital care controls. Once in the community, all patients showed a marked deterioration in functioning, and after 6 months 'psychosocial aftercare' was instituted. This succeeded in reversing the deterioration, and even producing a slight improvement during the remaining one year of follow-up.

Paul and Lentz concluded that a comprehensive social learning ap-proach is the treatment of choice for improving and maintaining functional skills in chronic, institutionalized patients. However, these improvements do not necessarily carry over into post-hospital functioning, and attention must be paid to the generalization (i.e. transfer) of treatment effects. Other reviewers of this literature have come to essentially similar conclusions (*see* Matson, 1980; Shepherd, 1980; Hall, 1983).

Token economies therefore do seem to be effective, but they have their limitations. On a theoretical level, the mechanism by which they work is still not clear. Is it simply a matter of setting up a system whereby expectations about behaviour are conveyed to patients in a clear and consistent manner, where behavioural targets are carefully graded accord-ing to individual levels of functioning, and where attempts to achieve these targets are met with clear and consistent feedback? Or are the *tokens* (i.e. tangible reinforcement) really important? Hall and Baker's work, also of a high methodological standard, suggests that tokens may not be necessary, providing that all the other conditions are met (Baker *et al.*, 1974; 1977; Hall *et al.*, 1977). Elliot *et al.* (1979) suggested that tokens may be important during the acquisition phase, i.e. when new skills are being learned, but that once established, behaviour may be maintained by social reinforcement alone.

It seems likely that the effectiveness of tokens depends upon individual differences within each sample; they are helpful for some people but not for others. In general terms, the more deteriorated and cognitively impaired the individual, the more likely they are to benefit from very clear, tangible reinforcement. This may explain the apparent superiority of the social learning approach in the Paul and Lentz study, where all the subjects were extremely institutionalized and severely impaired. In any event, as services for schizophrenic patients have moved increasingly towards a community base, highly controlled, artificial systems like token economies have fallen out of favour. In recent years, attention has focused on the application of behavioural techniques to teach social and other skills using mainly verbal or informational feedback and it is to these social skills training (SST) approaches that we will turn next.

SOCIAL SKILLS TRAINING

This has a slightly different provenance in the UK compared with the USA. In the UK, an interest in the psychological treatment of people with social difficulties stemmed originally from attempts to provide an experimental analysis of the nature of social interaction (Argyle, 1967). In the USA, the antecedents were more in mainstream behaviour therapy and there has been a preoccupation with certain specific social demands, e.g. assertiveness and heterosexual dating (Wolpe, 1969; Curran, 1977). In the US, skills training has also formed the core of a general 'rehabilitation approach' with an emphasis on improving skills and abilities, rather than just on reducing symptoms; on achieving vocational success where possible; and on involving the client fully in his own care (Anthony *et al.*, 1984; Anthony and Liberman, 1986). Despite the enthusiasm expressed for the skills training approach, the results, particularly with chronic patients, have however been rather modest.

In the last 10 years, there have been several reviews of this field. Hersen and Bellack (1976) concluded that SST seemed 'useful', but they noted the limited evidence for generalization, and the lack of demonstrable durability of behaviour change. Marzillier (1978) concluded there was strong evidence that SST could improve behavioural skills in both inpatient and outpatient samples. However, evidence was lacking for an effectiveness over and above that of plausible alternatives. He also noted the failure to demonstrate generalized or durable effects, particularly with regard to inpatients. Hersen (1979) noted a number of methodological problems in the outcome studies and, although there was clear evidence of significant treatment effects, the maintenance of gains and generalization to extrahospital settings was 'another question'. Wallace *et al.* (1980) found clear evidence for changes in the topographical features of social skills and self-report measures of anxiety and confidence. However, when the effects of training were evaluated in situations dissimilar from the training sessions, the results were 'not particularly promising'. Shepherd (1983; 1986) after reviewing over 50 studies concluded that while there was clear evidence for the effectiveness of SST compared with no treatment or a placebo control, evidence for its relative effectiveness against other plausible treatments (e.g. psychotherapy, drama, etc.) was still weak. He suggested that where generalization had been assessed in terms of transfer within the experimental setting, it had usually been confirmed; however, there had been little attempt to measure 'real-life' gains. Follow-up data were provided in about half the studies and, although the results did indicate some maintenance of treatment effects, there was a strong tendency for any differences between treatments to attenuate. Even Liberman, who has been one of the strongest advocates of SST, acknowledged that generalization remains 'the most challenging obstacle' (Liberman *et al.*, 1986). In one of his most recent articles he concluded that: 'While it has been amply demonstrated that behavioural training produces incremental improvements in social competence, the data are far less convincing that such interpersonal strengthening actually reduces the probability of relapse or symptom exacerbation and increases community tenure and quality of life' (Liberman *et al.*, 1987).

Why should this be so? What can be done about it?

In fact, there is very little reason why SST should generalize. From a behavioural viewpoint, it might be predicted that any new skills that are learned will be strongly associated with the particular stimulus setting in which the learning takes place (the same applies to token economies). Indeed, in other contexts, 'stimulus control' is used to demonstrate the effect of an experimental intervention on a particular response. So, for example, the so-called 'A-B-A' single-case design depends upon this relationship for its logic. Thus, if stimulus-bound learning is *not* to occur, we must take steps to avoid it. Likewise, an analysis of SST based on social psychological theory would also predict that generalization was likely to be a problem. 'Generalization' in social psychological terms refers to the extent to which changes in discrete 'microlevel' skills are translated into improvements in carrying out higher order social roles. 'Role' is a descriptive concept: it describes the relationship between two people whereby their social position is defined (e.g. employer/employee, husband/wife, friend/friend, and so on). By definition, roles cannot be used to prescribe specific behavioural acts, since it is the essence of effective role performance that each person selects which skills are relevant to a particular social situation and which he or she should deploy so as to mesh their interaction with the other most effectively.

One would therefore expect that simple training in specific skills would make little difference to role performance, except where it depends very little on interactive skills and can be specified fairly easily *a priori*. This may account for why it is generally easier to train instrumental than social skills (*see* Baker *et al.*, 1977; Paul and Lentz, 1977). It also explains why the social situations where a simple training approach seems to work best are those where it is relatively easy to be prescriptive about the skills involved, e.g. job interviewing (Kelly *et al.*, 1979). Where the social situation is more fluid, successful performance will depend not only on the possession of certain relevant skills, but also on knowing when to use them and having the confidence to do so. People with schizophrenia are likely to have significant difficulties in both respects.

So, if generalization and maintenance of treatment gains are to occur, they must be 'programmed' in, and not left to chance. This problem (which, of course, is not unique to skills training) has been recognized for some time, and various strategies have been put forward to provide a solution (Liberman *et al.*, 1976; Marholin and Touchette, 1979; Scott *et al.*, 1983). Most of these consist of attempts to blur the distinctions between the artificiality of the treatment setting and the normal contingencies of everyday life. Thus, generalization should be greatest when treatments can be made to contain many of the stimulus elements of everyday life. The suggestions that have been put forward include:

1. varying the time and place of treatment, so that improvements do not become bound up with a particular day and location (avoiding the 'it's-Tuesday-so-it-must-be-social-skills' syndrome)
2. varying the staff involved (for the same reason), without disrupting therapeutic relationships
3. using 'stooges' as *real* strangers and personnel managers as *real* job interviewers, rather than having psychiatric professionals or group members trying to pretend
4. conducting entire sessions *in vivo*, e.g. in shops and restaurants
5. making a conscious effort to fade conspicuous prompting and reinforcement and shifting the emphasis instead towards self-monitoring and self-reinforcement
6. stressing the importance of 'homework' assignments—treatment is only a preparation for homework, which is the *real* treatment.

These ideas seem simple and plausible, yet surprisingly little effort has been directed towards evaluating their effectiveness. At a clinical level, they have already been incorporated into many of the existing treatment packages, but it is not clear to what extent they have contributed to outcome. From the reviews cited above, it would seem that many of the problems still remain. Further research in this area would therefore seem warranted.

An alternative approach to the problem is not to aim to change *behaviour* in the hope that this will transfer and be maintained across settings, but to try to affect the underlying cognitive structures to provide a bridge for transferring behaviour. In recent years, SST like many other psychological treatments has become 'cognitive' (Mahoney, 1977; Trower, 1984), and there has been considerable interest in interventions which aim specifically to change attitudes or cognitions.

An early attempt was reported by Watts *et al.* (1973), where they encouraged psychotic patients to consider the factual basis for their delusional beliefs and the arguments for and against them. This procedure was very similar to the techniques employed in 'Cognitive Therapy of Depression' (Beck *et al.*, 1979), but without the emphasis on behavioural testing. Significant reductions in the strength of delusional beliefs were obtained, but the beliefs were not completely abandoned.

A similar single case study was reported by Shepherd (1984a) where he attempted to modify a patient's paranoid ideas through a mixture of cognitive re-evaluation and behavioural reality testing; e.g. was it true that when the patient entered a pub people turned to look at him? Was this any more or less true than of anyone else entering the pub? The data indicated a reduction in the patient's fear of going out and his feelings of being weak and inadequate, but no change in his estimated likelihood of being attacked or his perceived ability to cope. Behavioural self-reports indicated a marked increase in actual time spent outside the home. Hemsley (1985) and Spaulding *et al.* (1986) reviewed a number of other similar small-scale or pilot studies.

These studies therefore show some promise, but the results are not yet impressive. There are considerable methodological problems associated with the measurement of subjective beliefs, and these have only just begun to be tackled (Shepherd, 1984b; Garety, 1985). There are perhaps even greater technical problems in finding psychological techniques which are actually capable of producing generalized and enduring changes in underlying cognitions where medication has failed. Thus, although this research shows promise, in my view other lines may be more fruitful.

Before leaving this area, it is worth considering briefly another cognitive strategy which has been suggested for improving generalization and maintenance. This is the teaching of 'problem-solving' skills. Clearly, if patients could learn general strategies for solving interpersonal difficulties, then they should be able to transfer these from one situation to another. Again, problem-solving methods now have a well-established place in modern cognitive psychology (D'Zurilla and Goldfried, 1971) and there has been considerable interest in applying these techniques to chronic patient populations (Spivack *et al.*, 1976; Spratt, 1984; Bedell and Michael, 1985).

However, there have actually been very few controlled studies. Whether or not these techniques have anything to offer therefore remains an open question. My own view is that, like the attempts to change underlying attitudes and beliefs, these attempts to improve problem solving skills are likely to meet with limited success.

A NEW APPROACH TO SKILLS TRAINING

The 'generalization problem' is thus an extremely difficult one to solve. Indeed everywhere in psychology—with the possible exception of language acquisition—one sees examples of the specificity, rather than the generality of learning. Given the kinds of cognitive impairments that we know are often associated with schizophrenia, we might expect that this would be even more relevant here. So, how can we use a skills training model while recognizing the likely specificity of its effects? The key to this question is to change the point from which we define a person's needs in terms of life skills. We have already seen that the traditional skills model is 'prescriptive' in the sense that it attempts to specify in advance the skills that are needed. It then teaches them, and looks for evidence that they have generalized to functioning in key social roles. Perhaps a better way to proceed is by looking with the individual at his/her life situation, identifying the skills they actually need and which they think are important in order to function. If they are found lacking, we can then work out a technology for learning them. This approach, which begins with a 'criterion-oriented' assessment (Shapiro, 1970) is therefore built around a careful consideration of individual needs and it points to new directions for skills training in the future.

First, it defines the location of treatment. For, if the emphasis is on developing the skills the individual actually needs in his or her life situation, assessment and treatment must take place directly in the settings where he or she must function. This is the principle underlying the 'radical' community approach of workers such as Stein and Test (1978, 1985) and Hoult and Reynolds (1984). Help must be delivered *where* it is needed, *when* it is needed, and for *as long* as it is needed.

It is important to realize that these principles do not merely apply to radical community programmes. If my analysis of the failure of traditional skills training approaches is correct, the arguments also apply to much rehabilitation carried out in traditional hospital settings. This implies a shift away from assessment and training carried out in a setting different from that where the new skills are meant to be used. Instead, it suggests that a minimum of time be spent on prior assessment and training, and that the bulk of the effort be directed towards developing skills *in vivo* wherever the individual is likely to end up living and working.

In this way, we can ensure that personally relevant skills are learned. At an interpersonal level, it is the *only* way that relevant skills are likely to be identified since, as indicated earlier, it is not until faced with a specific role situation (i.e. as a specific employer/flatmate/fellow worker) that skills deficits are likely to be apparent. The same applies to instrumental skills, although perhaps to a lesser extent. It is when the individual is actually in the criterion setting—when the generalization problem has already been solved, so to speak—that skills training is really needed.

An emphasis on developing skills *in vivo* also raises the question of the effectiveness of structured learning approaches compared with simply giving people the opportunity to practise normal role skills in a fairly normal setting. It will be recalled that the evidence for the effectiveness of SST over and above that of active alternatives is rather weak. Nevertheless, proponents of the skills training approach argue that while socialization programmes (e.g. Stein and Test, 1978) can lead to skills acquisition: 'they do not harness social learning and reinforcement techniques that may be required to promote the acquisition, generalisation, and durability of skills needed in interpersonal situations' (Anthony and Liberman, 1986). This seems an important proposition and well-worth testing.

An emphasis on individually-relevant skills also suggests new directions for assessment. Skills training becomes something that you do *with* the person, not *to* them. This is very much in line with the rehabilitation counselling approach described by Anthony (1979) and Anthony *et al.* (1982, 1984), and an interesting paper illustrating this approach has recently been reported by McCarthy *et al.* (1986). They investigated task motivation and problem appraisal in a sample of long-term day attenders, about half of whom had received a diagnosis of schizophrenia. Subjects were asked to rate a variety of domestic and everyday tasks (shopping, cooking, household chores, budgeting, etc.) according to whether or not they had performed them in the last year, how important they felt them to be, how difficult they felt them to be, and how successful they felt in performing them. They were also asked to describe their current major problems, how upsetting they found these, what strategies they used to cope with them, and how successful these were. Staff were asked a number of similar questions. The results indicated generally good agreement between staff and patients regarding whether or not the tasks had been performed. The authors noted that on many occasions patients had more accurate and up-to-date information than staff and therefore any discrepancies may have reflected unreliable reports from staff rather than from patients. The data concerning perceived difficulty and perceived importance indicated that about half the tasks were seen as important and about half as unimportant. Only about 30% were seen as important *and* difficult—these are the ones the authors speculated are most likely to benefit from skills training. In about 20% of instances, tasks were seen as important and easy, but were still not performed. This was usually due to 'environmental constraints', e.g. 'My mother wouldn't let me' or 'My social worker is sorting it out'. Where tasks are perceived as unimportant, there are clearly motivational problems that would need to be addressed before mounting a skills training intervention (of course, they may *really* be unimportant, in which case skills training might be irrelevant).

This study illustrates how simply asking patients what skills they think are important may change the nature of an intervention. The patients also reported a number of current major problems, of a social and psychological kind that were not currently being attended to by staff, including poor social skills. There were also certain life stresses, such as shortage of money, lack of employment or chronic physical illness in the family, which it would be difficult for staff to modify. Although they complained about the distressing effects of some psychiatric symptoms (e.g. depressed mood, insomnia, concentration and memory difficulties) they did not acknowledge that 'negative' deficits such as neglect of appearance, slowness and sleeping during the day were problematic. This is important, as these are the types of problems that relatives find most difficult to cope with (Creer and Wing, 1975). In general, McCarthy *et al.* noted the poverty of patients' coping strategies, and suggest that this is an area where treatment interventions might focus in the future.

There has, in fact, already been some preliminary research. Thus,

Falloon and Talbot (1981) presented data from interviews with 40 schizophrenic patients who experienced persistent auditory hallucinations despite phenothiazine medication. They reported a variety of coping strategies, including changes in interpersonal contacts, changes in activity levels, 'attentional' strategies, and attempts to manipulate physiological levels of arousal.

A similar study has been reported by Breier and Strauss (1983), based on interviews with 20 psychotic patients with a variety of diagnoses. Again, they noted a range of coping strategies which they grouped under three main headings: (1) self-talk/self-instruction, e.g. 'act like an adult', 'be responsible'; (2) reduced involvement in activity, e.g. go for a walk, try to relax, withdraw from social contact; and (3) increased involvement in activity, e.g. keep busy, work hard, etc. The patients used these strategies in response to changes in their mood or behaviour which they saw as possible precursors to a psychotic relapse. Breier and Strauss noted that while this process of self-monitoring and self-control was clearly important in the avoidance of relapse, it was not always successful. What is striking about both these studies is the degree of individual variation. Thus, different individuals use totally contrasting coping strategies to deal with apparently identical changes in symptomatology (e.g. increasing activity levels versus decreasing activity levels). Once again, the importance of an individually-centred strategy is underlined.

These studies therefore suggest another new direction for skills training. Instead of starting with some abstract set of skills, formulated *a priori* and without proper regard to individual differences, we may use the technology of skills training—and related techniques like self-instructional training (Meichenbaum and Cameron, 1975)—to help strengthen and develop existing cognitive skills and thus improve the monitoring of symptoms and the 'early warning' signs of relapse. Whether these procedures can actually help *prevent* relapse is, of course, another matter, but controlled trials have already appeared using these kinds of approaches in the attempt to reduce the dosage of long-term maintenance medication (Herz *et al.*, 1982; Carpenter and Heinrichs, 1983). We ourselves are currently planning investigations into the feasibility of developing coping strategies in chronic patients in a series of single-case studies. Further research in this area would be very useful.

This turning of the skills training model upside down has further implications. It suggests not only a change in emphasis from assessment and training towards placement and support, but also a different model of service delivery. Current models tend to be serially progressive, with different levels of support distributed around the system in a series of fixed 'slots'. Patients are supposed to move through the system as they gradually gain in independence (the so-called 'car-wash' model). This is based on a model of recovery following physical trauma with a gradual and progressive return of strength. But recovery in psychiatry seldom follows such a course. In schizophrenia, functioning fluctuates and different aspects of functioning recover at different rates in different individuals (Jong *et al.*, 1985). Systems of service delivery should therefore reflect these patterns of individual variation hence indicating the use of special workers or peripatetic teams whose aim is to provide support and develop skills *in vivo* according to individual needs. Examples of this kind of service are the support team run by the Community Psychiatry Research Unit in Hackney, London (Lomas, 1984) and the Transitional Employment programmes run by Fountain House in New York (Beard *et al.*, 1982).

This is not to say that assessment and training are a waste of time. Some kind of prior assessment will usually be necessary in order to make the initial decisions. However, given the difficulties of making predictions on the basis of even good functional assessments, and given the demonstrable problems in generalizing most skills training programmes, some shift in emphasis towards support and skills training *in vivo* does seem required.

DELIVERING SKILLS TRAINING

So, how can we incorporate some of these ideas into routine models of service delivery? This brings us to the area of 'Quality of care', i.e. how can we ensure that the services we provide for schizophrenic patients are of the highest quality? This is a complex question. Quality of care is a difficult concept with a number of possible levels of interpretation (Shepherd, 1984c; Lavender, 1985). As Lavender noted, the central problem is that people with different theoretical viewpoints have varying conceptions of what constitutes good quality service. For example, behaviourists will want to look at the reinforcement contingencies, analysts at the nature of the relationships between staff and patients, 'normalizers' will want to examine the degree of access to socially valued settings, and so on. The only way of resolving such theoretical disputes is to collect data to determine how the presence or absence of these features affects outcome. This is what we need to do now. Lavender (1987) provided an illustration of an attempt to do this within an experimental framework, and Wing and Brown's (1970) original research provides an alternative paradigm which is more longitudinal and naturalistic. Both kinds of studies would be useful. There is now a set of principles regarding the organization of services which most people would agree constitute good quality care (e.g. establishment of individual care plans; a 'personalized' environment, reduced distance between staff and patients). What we must do is to examine how variations in the care provided across settings and agencies is reflected in outcome. Given the current proliferation of the settings and agencies providing care for people with serious and long-term disorders, this seems an urgent priority.

A specific example of this concerns day care. There is still considerable confusion regarding the aims and functions of different kinds of day services (Vaughan, 1983; Shepherd, 1988, and there has been virtually no attempt to identify interactions between programme and client characteristics. Thus, what *kind* of day service is most beneficial for people with schizophrenia? To my knowledge, there has been only one study that has tried to address this question directly, carried out by Linn *et al.* (1979). This was a large scale, multicentre study involving over 150 patients with a diagnosis of schizophrenia from 10 different centres. Outcome was assessed in terms of community tenure, social functioning and ratings of symptomatology, and the patients were followed up for a period of 2 years. The centres with the poorest outcome tended to have the highest rates of patient turnover, used more intensive treatment (e.g. group psychotherapy) and had greater professional input (including more psychology time!). The centres with better outcomes tended to treat schizophrenics more often, offered more recreational time and occupational therapy, and had more part-time staff. Linn *et al.* thus suggested that for a chronic schizophrenic population: 'it is possible that the less intensively personal and more object focussed activity of occupational therapy produced better outcomes than the intensive interpersonal stimulation often encountered in group therapy'. This would be consistent with other work in this area, including that of Wing and Brown (1970). Similar studies in the UK would be very valuable.

THE MANAGEMENT OF STAFF

Finally, I would like to say a few words about staff. Despite all the progress that has been made in the treatment and management of schizophrenia in recent years, everyone acknowledges that there is still a hard 'core' of untreatable disability in some cases. In these cases, supportive or 'prosthetic' environments are required which will maintain functioning at as high a level as possible, despite the presence of disabilities (Watts and Bennett, 1983; Anthony and Liberman, 1986). This is difficult and frustrating work, and the maintenance of such settings demands people who understand the nature of the disorder, its problems and possible limitations, and ways in which adverse consequences can be ameliorated. It also demands people who can remain optimistic, yet realistic, in the face of all this. In recent years the need to provide information, education and support for families who have to cope with this task has become increasingly and appropriately recognized. However, we have heard very little about 'high EE' *staff* or what affects staff's morale, enthusiasm and effectiveness. In these days of management efficiency, staff support seems a luxury, or, at any rate, something that requires no particular skill and is certainly not worth formally evaluating. I disagree. I would welcome studies similar to those conducted with families, to examine how information about schizophrenia, methods of coping, and so on, might best be communicated to care staff, both inside and outside the hospital, and what effects this might have. It is a truism that unless we are able to provide effective support to carers, in whatever setting, we cannot expect patients to receive good care. Nevertheless, we have hardly begun to examine in a scientific way how this might be achieved.

REFERENCES

Anthony W, A. (1979). *Principles of Psychiatric Rehabilitation*. Baltimore: University Park Press.

Anthony W. A., Cohen M. R., Cohen B. F (1984). Psychiatric rehabilitation. In: *The Chronic Mental Patient: Five Years Later* (Talbott J. A., ed.), pp. 137–152. Orlando, Florida: Grune and Stratton.

Anthony W. A., Cohen M., Farkas M. (1982). A psychiatric rehabilitation program: can I recognise one if I see one? *Community Mental Health Journal*; 18: 83–96.

Anthony W. A, Liberman R. P. (1986). The practice of psychiatric rehabilitation: historical, conceptual and research base. *Schizophrenia Bulletin*; 12: 542–59.

Argyle M. (1967). *The Psychology of Interpersonal Behaviour*. Harmondsworth: Penguin.

Ayllon T., Azrin N. H. (1965). The measurement and reinforcement of behaviour of psychotics. *Journal of the Experimental Analysis of Behaviour*; 8: 357–83.

Baker R., Hall J. N., Hutchinson K. (1974). A token economy project with chronic schizophrenic patients. *British Journal of Psychiatry*; 124: 367–84.

Baker R., Hall J. N., Hutchinson K., Bridge G. (1977). Symptom changes in chronic schizophrenic patients on a token economy: a controlled experiment. *British Journal of Psychiatry*; 131: 381–93.

Beard J. A., Propst R. N., Malamud T. J. (1982). The Fountain House model of psychiatric rehabilitation. *Psychosocial Rehabilitation Journal*; 5: 47–59.

Beck A. T., Rush A. J., Shaw B. F., Emery G. (1979). *Cognitive Therapy of Depression*. New York: Guilford Press.

Bedell J. R., Michael D. D. (1985). Teaching problem-solving skills to chronic psychiatric patients. In: *Handbook of Behavioural Group Therapy* (Upper D., Ross S. M., eds.), pp. 83–118. New York: Plenum Press.

Bennett D. H. (1983). The historical development of rehabilitation services. In: *Theory and Practice of Psychiatric Rehabilitation* (Watts F. N., Bennett D. H., eds.). Chichester: John Wiley.

Bockoven J. S. (1963). *Moral Treatment in Psychiatry*. New York: Springer Publications.

Breier A., Strauss J. S. (1983). Self-control in psychotic disorders. *Archives of General Psychiatry*; 40: 1141–5.

Brown G. W., Birley J. L. T. (1968). Crises and life changes and the onset of schizophrenia. *Journal of Health and Social Behaviour*; 9: 203–14.

Brown G. W., Birley J. L. T., Wing J. K. (1972). Influence of family life on the course of schizophrenic disorders: a replication. *British Journal of Psychiatry*; 121: 241–58.

Brown G. W., Monck E. M., Carstairs G. M., Wing J. K. (1962). The influence of family life on the course of schizophrenic illness. *British Journal of Preventive and Social Medicine*; 16: 55–68.

Carpenter W. T., Heinrichs D. W. (1983). Early intervention, time-limited, targeted pharmacotherapy of schizophrenia. *Schizophrenia Bulletin*; 9: 533–42.

Creer C., Wing J. K. (1975). *Schizophrenia at Home*. National Schizophrenia Fellowship, 79 Victoria Road, Surbiton, Surrey KT6 4JT.

240   *Schizophrenia: The major issues*

Curran J. P. (1977). Skills training as an approach to the treatment of heterosexual-social anxiety: a review. *Psychological Bulletin*; **84**: 140–57.

Digby A. (1985). *Madness, Morality and Medicine : A Study of the York Retreat, 1796–1914.* Cambridge: Cambridge University Press.

D'Zurilla, T. J., Goldfried M. R. (1971). Problem solving and behaviour modification. *Journal of Abnormal Psychology*; **78**: 107–26.

Elliot P. A., Barlow F., Hooper A., Kingerlee P. E. (1979). Maintaining patients' improvements in a token economy. *Behaviour Research and Therapy*; **17**: 355–67.

Engel G. L. (1977). The need for a new medical model: a challenge for biomedicine. *Science*; **196**: 129–36.

Engel G. L. (1980). The clinical application of the biopsychosocial model. *American Journal of Psychiatry*; **137**: 535–44.

Falloon I. R. H., Talbot R. E. (1981). Persistent auditory hallucinations: coping mechanisms and implications for management. *Psychological Medicine*; **11**: 329–39.

Garety P. A. (1985). 'Delusions': problems in definition and measurement. *British Journal of Medical Psychology*; **58**: 25–34.

Gibbons J. (1983). *Care of Schizophrenic Patients in the Community, 1981–3, Third Annual Report*, Department of Psychiatry, Royal South Hants Hospital, Southampton, S09 4PE.

Hall J. (1983). Ward-based rehabilitation programmes. In: *Theory and Practice of Psychiatric Rehabilitation* (Watts F. N., Bennett, D. H., eds.), pp. 131–50. Chichester: John Wiley.

Hall J. N., Baker R. D., Hutchinson K. (1977). A controlled evaluation of token economy procedures with chronic schizophrenic patients. *Behaviour Research and Therapy*; **15**: 261–83.

Hemsley D. R. (1985). Schizophrenia. In: *Psychological Applications in Psychiatry* (Bradley B. P., Thompson C., eds.), pp. 95–117. Chichester: John Wiley.

Hersen M. (1979). Modification of skills deficits in psychiatric patients. In: *Research and Practice in Social Skills Training* (Bellack A. S., Hersen M. eds.), pp. 82–98. New York: Plenum Press.

Hersen M., Bellack, A. S. (1976). Social skills training for chronic psychiatric patients: rationale, research and future directions. *Comprehensive Psychiatry*; **17**: 559–80.

Herz M. I., Szymanski H. V., Simon J. C. (1982). Intermittent medication for stable schizophrenic outpatients. *American Journal of Psychiatry*; **139**: 918–22.

Hoult J. E., Reynolds I. (1984). Schizophrenia—a comparative trial of community oriented and hospital orientated psychiatric care. *Acta Psychiatrica Scandinavica*; **69**: 359–72.

Jacobs S., Myers J. (1976). Recent life events and acute schizophrenic psychosis: a controlled study. *Journal of Nervous and Mental Disease*; **162**: 75–87.

Jones K. (1972). *A History of the Mental Health Services*. London: Routledge & Kegan Paul.

Jong A. de, Giel R., Slooff C. J., Wiersma D. (1986). Relationship between symptomatology and social disability: empirical evidence from a follow-up study of schizophrenic patients. *Social Psychiatry*; **21**: 200–5.

Kelly J. A., Laughlin C., Clairborne M., Patterson, J. (1979). A group procedure for teaching job interview skills to formerly hospitalised psychiatric patients. *Behaviour Therapy*; **10**: 299–310.

Lavender A. (1985). Quality of care and staff practices in long-stay practices in long-stay settings. In: *New Developments in Clinical Psychology* (Watts F. N., ed.), pp. 70 83. British Psychological Society. Chichester: John Wiley.

Lavender A. (1987). Improving the quality of care on psychiatric hospital rehabilitation wards: a controlled evaluation. *British Journal of Psychiatry*; **150**: 476–81.

Liberman R. P., Jacobs H. E., Boone S. E. *et al.* (1987). Skills training for the community adaptation of schizophrenia. In: *Psychosocial Treatment of Schizophrenia* (Strauss J. S., Boker W., Brenner H. D., eds.), pp. 94–109. Toronto: Hans Huber.

Liberman R. P., McCann M. J., Wallace C. J. (1976). Generalisation of behaviour therapy with psychotics. *British Journal of Psychiatry*; **129**: 490–6.

Lindsley O. R. (1956). Operant conditioning methods applied to research in chronic schizophrenia. *Psychiatric Research Reports*; **5**: 118–53.

Linn M. W., Caffey E. M., Klett J., Hogarty G. E., Lamb H. R. (1979). Day treatment and psychotropic drugs in the aftercare of schizophrenic patients. *Archives of General Psychiatry*; **36**: 1055–66.

Lomas G. (1984). The gentle touch: principles for progress. In: *Psychiatric Services in the Community* (Reed J., Lomas G., eds.), pp. 128–136. London: Croom Helm.

MacCarthy B., Benson J., Brewin C. R. (1986). Task motivation and problem appraisal in long-term psychiatric patients. *Psychological Medicine*; **16**: 431–8.

Mahoney M. J. (1977). Reflections on the cognitive learning trend in psychotherapy. *American Psychologist*; **32**: 5–13.

Marholin D., Touchette P. E. (1979). The role of stimulus control and response consequences. In: *Maximising Treatment Gains* (Goldstein A. P., Kanfer F. H., eds.), pp. 27–51. New York: Academic Press.

Marzillier J. (1978). Outcome studies of skills training: a review. In: *Social Skills and Mental Health* (Trower P., Bryant B., Argyle M., eds.), pp. 103–130. London: Methuen.

Matson J. L. (1980). Behaviour modification procedures for training chronically institutionalised schizophrenics. In: *Progress in Behaviour Modification* (Hersen M., Eisler R. M., Miller P. M., eds.), pp.37–61. London: Academic Press.

Meichenbaum D. H., Cameron R. (1975). Training schizophrenics to talk to themselves: a means of developing attentional controls. *Behaviour Therapy*; **4**: 515–34.

Myerson A. (1939). Theory and principles of the 'total push' method in the treatment of chronic schizophrenia. *American Journal of Psychiatry;* **95**: 1197–204.

Paul G. L., Lentz R. J. (1977). *Psychosocial Treatment of Chronic Mental Patients: Milieu versus Social-learning Programs.* Cambridge, Mass.: Harvard University Press.

Scott R. R., Himadi W., Keane T. M. (1983). A review of generalisation in social skills training: suggestions for future research. In: *Progress in Behaviour Modification: vol. 15* (Eisler R. M., Miller P. M., eds.), pp. 110–132. New York: Academic Press.

Shapiro M. B. (1970). Intensive assessment of the single case. In: *The Psychological Assessment of Mental and Physical Handicaps* (Mittler P., ed.). London: Methuen.

Shepherd G. (1980). The treatment of social difficulties in special environments. In: *Psychological Problems: The Social Context* (Feldman P., Orford J., eds.), pp. 249–278. Chichester: John Wiley.

Shepherd G. (1983). Social skills training with adults. In: *Developments in Social Skills Training* (Spence S., Shepherd G., eds.), pp. 21–30. London: Academic Press.

Shepherd G. (1984a). Studies in the assessment and treatment of social difficulties in long-term psychiatric patients. *Unpublished doctoral dissertation*, London University: Institute of Psychiatry.

Shepherd G. (1984b). Assessment of cognitions in social skills training. In: *Radical Approaches to Social Skills Training* (Trower P., ed.), pp. 261–283. London: Croom Helm.

Shepherd G. (1984c). Quality of care. In: *Institutional Care and Rehabilitation*, Chapter 4. London: Longmans.

Shepherd G. (1986). Social skills training and schizophrenia. In: *Handbook of Social Skills Training: vol. 2* (Hollin C. R., Trower P., eds.), pp. 9–37. London: Pergamon Press.

Shepherd G. (1988). Day treatment and care. In: *Community Psychiatry* (Freeman H. L., Bennett D. H., eds.). London: Churchill Livingstone (in press).

Spaulding W. D., Storms, L., Goodrich V., Sullivan M. (1986). Applications of experimental psychopathology in psychiatric rehabilitation. *Schizophrenia Bulletin*; **12**: 560–77.

Spivack G., Platt J., Shure M. (1976). *The Problem Solving Approach to Adjustment*. Washington, DC: Jossey Bass.

Spratt G. (1984). A skills training approach to facilitate social behaviours in long-term psychiatric patients: models, principles and techniques. Unpublished manuscript, Prestwich Hospital, Manchester, England.

Stein L. I., Test M. A. (eds.) (1978). An alternative to mental hospital treatment. In: *Alternatives to Mental Hospital Treatment*, pp. 43–55. New York: Plenum Press.

Stein L. I., Test M. A. (1985). *The Training in Community Living Model: A Decade of Experience*. San Francisco, Jossey-Bass.

Strauss J. S., Carpenter W. T. (1972). The prediction of outcome in schizophrenia: I. characteristics of outcome. *Archives of General Psychiatry*; **27**: 739–46.

Strauss J. S., Carpenter W. T. (1974). The prediction of outcome in schizophrenia: II. relationships between predictor and outcome variables. *Archives of General Psychiatry*; **31**: 37–42.

Strauss J. S., Carpenter W. T. (1977). The prediction of outcome in schizophrenia: III. five-year outcome and its predictors. *Archives of General Psychiatry*; **34**: 159–63.

Strauss J. S., Carpenter W. T. (1981). *Schizophrenia*. New York: Plenum Press.

Strauss J. S., Klorman R., Kokes R. F. (1977). Premorbid adjustment in schizophrenia: part V: the implications of findings for understanding research and application. *Schizophrenia Bulletin*; **3**: 240–4.

Trower P. (1984). *Radical Approaches to Social Skills Training*. London: Croom Helm.

Vaughan P. J. (1983). The disordered development of day care in psychiatry. *Health Trends*; **15**: 91–4.

Vaughan P. J. (1985). Developments in psychiatric day care. *British Journal of Psychiatry*; **147**: 1–4.

Vaughn C. E., Leff J. P. (1976). The influence of family and social factors on the course of psychiatric illness. *British Journal of Psychiatry*; **129**: 125–38.

Wallace C. J., Nelson C. J., Liberman R. P. *et al.* (1980). A review and critique of social skills training with schizophrenic patients. *Schizophrenia Bulletin*; 6: 42–62.

Watts F. N., Bennett D. H. (1983). Introduction: the concept of rehabilitation. In: *Theory and Practice of Psychiatric Rehabilitation* (Watts F. N., Bennett D. H., eds.), pp. 3–14. Chichester: John Wiley.

Watts F. N., Powell G. E., Austin S. V. (1973). The modification of abnormal beliefs. *British Journal of Medical Psychology*; 46: 359–63.

Wing J. K., Brown G. W. (1970). *Institutionalism and Schizophrenia*. London: Cambridge University Press.

Wolpe J. (1969). *The Practice of Behaviour Therapy*. New York: Pergamon Press.

World Health Organisation (1979). *Schizophrenia: an International Follow-up Study*. Chichester: John Wiley.

17 *Special needs and their assessment*

J. LEFF

In this chapter, the initiation of an evaluative study of the closure of Friern and Claybury Hospitals is described. A main focus of the research is on non-demented patients who have been in hospital for at least one year. Patients discharged to district care are matched with patients likely to remain in the hospital for a further year and both are followed up one year later. One thousand patients in the two hospitals form the study population, of which the great majority suffer from schizophrenia.

The assessment techniques are described in detail and involve the use of seven schedules: personal data and psychiatric history; present state examination; physical health index; social behaviour schedule; patient attitude questionnaire; environmental index; and social network schedule. The rationale for each instrument and the reasons for any modifications introduced are discussed.

The process of translation of disabilities and dysfunction into the need for services is considered, as well as the problematic issue of the relationship between the research team and the providers of services.

SPECIAL NEEDS AND ASSESSMENTS

The team for the assessment of psychiatric services (TAPS) was set up by the North East Thames Regional Health Authority (NETRHA) in May 1985 to evaluate the policy of transferring psychiatric care from Friern and Claybury Hospitals to local health districts. The initial task of the team was to assess the patients currently in the two hospitals. A census of patients had been carried out by the staff in Friern Hospital in 1983 and provided useful information, but more detail was necessary for research needs. The census revealed that 23% of patients suffered from dementia, 53% from schizophrenia, and 11% from affective illness. TAPS decided that its first priority was to concentrate on the long–stay non–demented patients, since they were to be the first group to move out of the hospital. Long stay was defined arbitrarily as a continuous stay in the hospital of one year or more. Thus defined, length of stay in this group varied between one year and over 60 years (five patients). The group comprised 450 patients in Friern Hospital and 550 in Claybury hospital.

These numbers can only be approximate as a number of patients admitted originally with the diagnosis of a functional illness have grown old in the hospital, and have developed dementia. Some of these have been transferred to psychogeriatric wards, while others remain on long-stay non-geriatric wards. Others have suffered from a functional psychosis, such as schizophrenia, for decades and are so impaired cognitively by the illness, or institutionalism, or both, that communication is virtually impossible. Hence, the question of whether they should be grouped with the demented patients is very difficult to answer. It remains possible, as some have speculated, that years of suffering from schizophrenia lead to a form of dementia resulting from a cerebral deterioration. Thus the boundary between dementia and long-standing functional illness is indistinct, and estimates of numbers must remain imprecise. We are planning a study of cognitive impairment in demented patients, long-stay schizophrenic patients, and cases of uncertain classification, in the hope of clarifying this issue.

In the 1983 census of Friern, it was found that of patients with a duration of stay between one and 5 years, one-third suffered from schizophrenia, whereas this diagnosis was given to three-quarters of those staying more than 5 years. In a number of patients admitted decades previously, a diagnosis was difficult to establish from the case records, partly because of the quality of the original notes and partly because of the current absence of any florid psychotic symptoms. Thus the diagnostic categories to which patients were assigned in the census were necessarily tentative, but the bulk of patients suffered from schizophrenia.

The research questions to be answered sounded deceptively simple: would patients' clinical state improve after transfer to district care, and would their quality of life be better? However, they proved very difficult to tackle. Each of the seven schedules used for assessment is discussed in some detail as they relate to those two questions. The selection and development of the schedules was mainly undertaken by Dr C. O'Driscoll in conjunction with the present author.

Personal data and psychiatric history schedule (PDPH)

The outcome of schizophrenia has been found consistently to be linked with age, sex and marital status; early age of onset, male sex and single status being associated with a poor outcome. It is quite likely that these factors also influence patients' ability to adjust to life outside a psychiatric hospital. Therefore they are collected routinely with the PDPH as well as the borough and health district of the patient's permanent address, if any, and the composition of the household from which he was admitted. After some discussion we also decided to include a question about the patient's ethnic origin. We recognized that this was a delicate issue, but felt that it was of considerable importance in influencing the acceptance of the patient by the local community. We deliberated over the method of assigning

246 Schizophrenia: The major issues

individuals to an ethnic group—what is the ethnicity of second and third generation immigrants? Is Judaism a religious or ethnic description?—and decided to ask each patient to which ethnic group they considered themselves to belong.

Various items from the patient's history were also recorded, including number of previous admissions, total time in hospital, length of current admission, legal status, reason for admission and for continued stay, forensic involvement either as offender or victim, psychiatric diagnosis, both current and on first presentation, medication and day-time activity. With the exception of ethnic origin, all data are obtained from the case notes.

Present state examination (PSE)

In assessing the current psychiatric state of the study patients, we have found that a substantial proportion respond negatively to enquiries about the whole range of psychiatric symptoms. This could mean that they were entirely healthy, or that they were concealing their symptoms, or that the interview is not sensitive to the deficits of chronically hospitalized patients. It is well recognized that negative symptoms are prominent in chronic schizophrenia, so that in selecting our assessment schedules we hoped to find one that was sensitive to these phenomena. We began by using the Krawiecka scale (Krawiecka et al., 1977) which includes ratings based on observations of incoherence of speech, flattening of affect, and psychomotor retardation. Unfortunately, this did not prove to be reliable in our hands in a pilot study, and we decided to replace it with the present state examination (PSE), although recognizing that the latter instrument is restricted in its coverage of negative symptoms. The PSE has the advantage of including 32 items that record behaviour observed on examination, which can be rated for patients who do not respond to probes about symptoms because of being mute, uncooperative, incoherent or unable to speak English.

In our view a satisfactory instrument that assesses the range of negative symptoms does not exist. Some of the symptoms are not appropriately evaluated in an hour's interview, e.g. lack of initiative and motivation. Others are difficult to distinguish from similar phenomena with a different aetiology, e.g. the distinction between flattening of affect and a parkinsonian facies resulting from neuroleptic drugs. Leff and Abberton (1981) suggested that voice analysis using a laryngograph might be used to monitor blunting of affect, as this measure was not influenced by neuroleptic medication. It seems likely that a range of assessment techniques is required to measure negative symptoms adequately. This should probably include the performance of standardized tasks, and laryngographic recordings. These have obvious practical disadvantages compared with an interview technique, but almost certainly entail greater validity.

The question of concealment of symptoms is awkward to accommodate.

There is no doubt that long-term patients learn to deny their psychotic experiences because of the negative consequences of revealing them, e.g. increased medication, more restrictions on freedom of movement. I am responsible for 12 long-term male patients in Villa 2 at Friern Hospital. Most of them deny hearing voices when I ask them directly in my regular reviews of their condition. Some of them even assert that they have not heard voices for years. Yet, since my research hut is a few paces from Villa 2, I have plenty of opportunities to hear the very same men talking, shouting and laughing at their voices day in and day out.

A similar problem arises with respect to delusions. With the passage of time a proportion of schizophrenic patients develop an encapsulated delusional system which may not be elicited by relatively general questions of the type included in the PSE. For example, the probe 'Is there anything the matter with your body?' (item 90) may well be answered negatively, while the idiosyncratic question, 'Is Percy still living in your stomach?' will produce a wealth of delusional material.

We have attempted to deal with these problems by the addition of two extra questions to the PSE. The interviewer is instructed to scrutinize the case notes and to question the nursing staff in order to determine whether there are specific delusions of the type exemplified above, and whether the patient is believed to be actively hallucinated. Furthermore, the interviewer records whether there is evidence for delusions and hallucinations during the interview even though the patient denies any. The additional items are formulated as follows:

Item 141: Expression of delusions and hallucinations

0. Patient denies delusions and hallucinations (go on to next item).
1. Patient expresses delusions and hallucinations only in response to pointed questions.
2. Patients freely expresses delusions and hallucinations without prompting.

Item 142: If denies delusions and hallucination

0. No ancillary evidence of delusions and hallucination.
1. Evidence from staff of delusions and hallucinations but not in interview.
2. Evidence during interview of delusions and hallucinations.

Physical health index (PHI)

The average age of the long-stay patients in Friern and Claybury Hospitals is above 60 years. They are therefore subject to all the diseases of an ageing population, including heart failure, obstructive airways disease, diabetes, renal insufficiency, and impairment of vision and hearing. These physical ailments are supervised carefully by nursing and medical staff in the hospitals. In fact, the psychiatric registrars act as general practitioners to the patients. There have been considerable problems in arranging general practitioner (GP) care for long-stay patients transferred to the districts. Some GPs have been reluctant to accept patients on to their lists through anxiety about the additional work-load. The psychiatric staff see the problem in a different light. Their dilemma is whether to encourage patients to choose their own GP on an individual basis, as any normal member of the public would do, or to make a special arrangement to attach a GP to each unit of sheltered accommodation, a more institutional approach. The advantage of the latter is that the GP would regularly review the physical health of the residents, whereas with the former arrangement residents may well neglect their physical complaints and avoid visiting their GP.

Whatever is decided, and it will inevitably vary from one facility to another, there is concern that patients' physical health may not receive the level of care currently provided in psychiatric hospitals. Therefore we felt impelled to make an assessment of the physical health of our sample in order to record its progress after one year. It was out of the question to examine each patient, since we lacked the medical personnel and time required. Instead we used the case notes, supplemented by information from the nursing staff, to record any problems with physical health that had been observed. The questionnaire is organized around bodily systems, e.g. cardiovascular, respiratory, locomotor, to accommodate the style in which information is normally obtained by ward doctors. Each problem is listed under the appropriate system, and the level of physical disability, mild, moderate or severe, is noted.

In addition to noting the physical problems of the patients, we wished to ascertain the level of service provided in the hospital, in order to determine whether this would be maintained after discharge. Here we encounter the problem of translating disability and dysfunction into the need for a service. I will expand on this important topic later. In this instance, we introduced a hierarchical system which requires the rater to indicate the highest level of care currently received.

0. Needs no medical or nursing attention for this problem.
1. Takes daily medication without supervision.
2. Has regular appointments with GP.
3. Has regular appointments with hospital specialist.
4. Takes daily medication with supervision.
5. Has regular but less than daily care from a nursing or paramedical service.
6. Has daily nursing care.
7. Has daily medical care.

Social behaviour schedule (SBS)

Schizophrenia often has a profoundly disturbing effect on a person's ability to form relationships with other people and to function in society. The resulting problems range from poor hygiene, through difficulty in shopping, to inability to hold the simplest conversation. For any one individual, the difficulties are usually very patchy across the wide range of behaviours expected from a member of society. Indeed, the expectations of society cannot be ignored in assessing patients' difficulties. There is some evidence that the better outcome for schizophrenia in Third World countries is partly attributable to a greater tolerance by family members (Leff *et al.*, 1987). However, the deficiencies in social behaviour that characterize long-stay patients are sufficiently pronounced for them to be recognized as problematic in any social setting.

We adopted the social behaviour schedule, which has been refined and tested over several years in the social psychiatry unit. The most recent version has been validated and found to be reliable by Sturt and Wykes (1986). It is completed by a research worker on the basis of information provided by a senior member of the care staff. The data can be reduced to a single figure, which represents the number of areas of social performance in which the patient's disability exceeds a certain threshold of severity. However, in assessing ability to adjust to life in the community, it may be more informative to look at the patterns of dysfunction as they affect the range of social behaviour.

Our study involves the follow-up of patients after their discharge into the community. Whereas the PDPH, PSE, and PHI are equally applicable in hospital and community settings, this is not true of the SBS. In some environments, patients are not given the opportunity to perform certain activities independently, and hence it is not possible to assess their competence. For example, shopping and the preparation of food are undertaken rarely by patients in hospital, but commonly in the community. The areas of personal hygiene, clothing, toiletting and compliance with medication are usually so closely supervised in hospital as to limit the patient's ability to demonstrate competence. For this reason, we felt it necessary to construct an additional instrument, the adaptive behaviour scale (Margolius), which covers certain areas of social behaviour in more detail than the SBS, and requires the rater to make a judgement of the opportunity for independence afforded the patient in each area.

Patient attitude questionnaire (PAQ)

The long-stay patients are the clients of the new service, and ought to be consulted about their views of what needs to be provided. Otherwise the paternalistic attitudes associated with custodial practices will be carried over into district-based care. Previous studies have demonstrated that the longer patients remain in hospital, the less inclined they are to want to leave. Nevertheless, it seemed worthwhile to ask a range of questions about their attitudes to the services provided for them. The PAQ involves asking patients why they are in their present accommodation, whether they know of any plans to change, what they like and dislike about where they live, and whether they would like to remain or live elsewhere. Different questions about future arrangements are then asked of those who wish to stay and those who would prefer to leave. Further questions probe whether patients would take their doctor's advice about a move, and whether or not they have found any medication or formal day care provision helpful.

Information can only be obtained from the patients themselves, so that data are incomplete for patients who are mute, incoherent, unable to speak fluent English or unwilling to cooperate. We observe strict confidentiality for the data on patient attitudes, and reassure each respondent on this point. It is natural for doubts to arise about the ability of long-stay patients to convey consistent attitudes towards their social and physical environment, particularly when they are deluded or hallucinating. We therefore decided to examine the test–retest reliability of the PAQ, in addition to the checks on inter-rater reliability which we conduct routinely on all the interview schedules.

The PAQ was used to re-interview a group of 40 patients from both hospitals who had been assessed previously and who had remained in hospital subsequently. It was necessary to determine for each patient whether there had been changes in their care over the intervening period, such as an alteration in medication or discussion of an alternative placement, which might be reflected in their attitudes. Of the items in the PAQ, 13 are considered to be attitude indicators, giving a total of 520 paired responses from the 40 subjects. The range of identical responses varied from 2 to 11 per patient, with a median value of 9 in the Friern patients and 8 in the Claybury patients, suggesting that attitudes were equally consistent in both hospitals. In all, 66% of the 520 responses were identical on the two occasions of questioning. Of the altered responses nearly half were due to changes in specificity and only 21% (7% of the total) were due to a reversal of attitude. To give an example, only three out of the 40 respondents changed their mind about wanting to stay in hospital or leave. One patient from Friern changed to wanting to remain in hospital, which the staff had always felt to be appropriate, while two Claybury patients decided that they now wanted to leave.

The findings indicate that the PAQ has a reasonably high test-retest reliability over 6 months, and gives us confidence in treating the responses to this interview as valid indicators of patients' attitudes to the services they are receiving.

Environmental index (EI)

One of the major forces behind the policy of deinstitutionalization has been the critique of institutional practices by sociologists such as Goffman (1961). Therefore it is important to compare the new environments to which patients are transferred with that in the psychiatric hospitals, on the degree of autonomy available to an individual. This is one aspect of that elusive concept, quality of life. Another concerns the amenities available to a person. Therefore the EI explores the degree of choice open to patients in a variety of circumstances, but also contains a section on the amenities of the physical environment. This inquires into the accessibility of shopping facilities, a pub, cafe, day centre, social club, park or common, cinema and laundrette. There are two supplementary questions about crime rates in the neighbourhood, since ex-patients in the USA have become victimized by criminals. We determine from the local police whether the rates of offences against the person and against property within the district of residence are higher, lower, or the same as the national average.

Social network schedule (SNS)

Our interest in this area stems from two concerns: to discover whether regional policy of moving patients together with their important social contacts is implemented, and to determine whether patients in the community develop social contacts with non-professional people. Patients who have lived in a psychiatric hospital for decades have social networks almost entirely composed of professional staff and other patients. If moving into the community means more than extruding an encapsulated fragment of the institution, patients should forge social links with healthy members of the public. The major problem in investigating this area is in recognizing social behaviour that is of significance for long-term patients. We cannot apply our own concepts of meaningful relationships to a population in which social interaction occurs at a minimal level. In this milieu non-verbal interactions may well be of much greater importance in cementing relationships than verbal ones. A new assessment instrument was devised, since existing measures were mostly aimed at neurotic patients, whose social activity is not different in kind from that of healthy individuals.

The SNS begins by eliciting from the patient the number of people whose name he knows. Where a name is not known, a social contact can be identified by his role, e.g. sister's husband. This questioning proceeds in the context of constructing a time budget of the previous week. Further probes are used for contacts seen less than weekly or corresponded with. The list of people named or otherwise identified constitutes the social universe of the patient, within which various degrees of social bonding exist. To distinguish between these, questions are asked about the frequency of contact—daily, weekly, monthly, less than monthly—and about the nature of the relationship—would the patient visit them after discharge, would they miss them, do they consider them a friend, would they confide in them? Social activity between the patient and the identified contact is also characterized as passive, intermediate or active, depending on whether they just sit together, do things for each other, or engage in conversation. We recognize that there is an assumption built in to these distinctions that verbal interaction is more 'active' than non-verbal. However, we do not assume that it is more influential in establishing and maintaining social bonds in this long-stay population. In fact, we have initiated an observational study of non-verbal interactions in the patients' club at Friern to investigate this issue.

Some of the most severely disabled patients are unable or unwilling to cooperate with the administration of the SNS. In these instances we interview nursing staff with the schedule. However, it has become apparent that nurses overestimate the number of significant social contacts the patient has on the ward, and have little or no idea about social activity off the ward. Therefore we have to accept that data from the SNS from sources other than the patient are almost certainly unreliable.

The batch of seven schedules was piloted in a study of 30 long-stay patients on admission wards in the London borough of Hackney and 30 clients of community psychiatric nurses (CPN) in Haringey (Burford, 1988). The performance of the SNS in this pilot study was of particular interest since it was the only completely novel instrument. Burford's findings throw some light on the structure of the schedule. His 30 respondents reported that they spoke at least once a month to a total of 415 individuals. Of these, the respondents said they would miss 339, would expect to visit 235, regarded 131 as friends, but would confide in only 97. These data seem to establish a hierarchy of social intimacy, but before giving this any weight, another sample would need to be investigated. The data we are accumulating on the long-stay patients in the two hospitals already look different in one respect. Whereas the CPN clients named an average of 25 social contacts, the hospital patients are averaging five or six. The follow-up of those patients discharged to district-based care will reveal whether these restricted social networks expand to include ordinary citizens.

THE TRANSLATION OF DISABILITIES AND DYSFUNCTION INTO NEEDS

While NETRHA decided on the policy of closure of the two psychiatric hospitals, the regional health authority did not issue any blueprints for the replacement services to be developed in the health districts concerned. Planning teams were set up in the health districts, but had very little to go on since no model service existed in the UK. The Worcester Project, which had been running for 10 years, had generated some useful data, but the sociodemographic differences between a semi-rural area and deprived inner London boroughs were too great for the findings to be applicable to the Friern and Claybury catchment areas. The process of designing services to meet the needs of long-stay psychiatric patients is currently in its infancy, and is too often dominated by political and economic considerations.

In an attempt to provide a more client-oriented approach, researchers in the social psychiatry unit have developed Needs Schedules (Brewin *et al.*, 1987) as part of the Camberwell High Contact Study. The aim is to translate the disabilities and dysfunctions of patients into needs for 'ideal-type' interventions which collectively may form the total service requirement for an individual patient. Needs include the areas of symptoms, behavioural problems and social skills deficits, accommodation, occupation, leisure, and material welfare. Identified needs are classified as currently being met, still unmet, or likely to emerge in the foreseeable future. These are matched with the professional or voluntary agent who is believed to provide the minimum effective therapeutic intervention. This judgement clearly requires a broad view of potential interventions and an opinion about their effectiveness for particular disabilities.

The decisions made on this basis build up a profile of the types of agents each client needs currently or is likely to need in the foreseeable future. The agents are then grouped into agencies as they are constituted at present, e.g. a need for frequent interventions by a psychiatrist, occupational therapist, nurse, etc. indicates the need for day hospital rather than day centre care. In some cases the total needs for service for a client may not be catered for by existing agencies. In these instances, the team is required to make a judgement of what new types of provision would be appropriate. Hence the schedule includes a stimulus to innovatory thinking.

The delineation of an 'ideal-type' service is only one stage of the planning process, which then has to enter the phase of implementation. The sociopolitical activities which are involved in planning and implementation are studied as part of the TAPS research.

THE RELATIONSHIP BETWEEN PLANNERS AND RESEARCHERS

Our research on behalf of NETRHA has raised a problematic issue that is common to studies of health services. From a purist stance, we should remain separate from the providers of services in order to retain our objectivity. Yet the information we are collecting is seen by the planners of services to be of great value to them. Initially, we thought this issue might not surface because of differences in the time scale of planning and evaluation. Planning should theoretically have begun shortly after the announcement of the policy decision by the Regional Medical Officer in July 1983. TAPS was set up as late as May 1985 and it was anticipated that it would take at least 18 months to complete baseline assessments on the 1000 long-stay non-demented patients. We believed that most of the detailed planning for this group would be completed well before the end of 1986. We were wrong on both counts. The baseline assessments have taken much longer than estimated, partly because of the amount of work involved, partly because of lack of research personnel initially, and partly because the consultant psychiatrists at Claybury refused access by research workers to their patients until January 1986. Our revised deadline for completion of the baseline assessments was September 1987. Detailed planning took several years to emerge and is still proceeding for a large section of this patient group. The first patients to move into newly planned accommodation left Friern Hospital in November 1986, 3.5 years after the closure plan was first announced. As a consequence, our data collection on the long-stay patients and the planning for these same clients are moving along in parallel.

Repeated demands have been made on us by the planning teams to provide data on individual patients. We had to decide how to handle these early on in the study. We considered that we could not respond with a blanket refusal and still retain the cooperation of the care staff in the hospitals and the districts, on whom much of our data collection depended. As a compromise, we decided to release data on individual patients which were accessible to care staff as part of routine clinical practice. Thus, we prepared clinical summaries on each patient which comprised a digest of data from the PDPH (abstracted from case notes), the SBS (obtained from care staff), and the PSE. The clinical summaries are sent to the ward staff concerned, and are accessible to planners at their discretion. We withheld data from the PAQ and SNS as we considered that to be confidential.

However, one health district pressed strongly for data from the SNS, on the grounds that without them they could not fulfil the regional policy of moving patients together with their key social contacts. After much discussion, we agreed to train members of the district planning team in the use of the SNS, so that they could obtain the desired data themselves under different conditions of confidentiality than those we established with our respondents.

When we have completed analysis of the baseline data and the first year follow-up, we intend to make our findings public. We hope that at that stage they *will* have an impact on the process we are studying. But until then, we trust that the compromises we have felt impelled to make have not undermined our objectivity. Problems of this nature that beset health services research heighten our awareness of a universal dilemma: by observing a phenomenon we inevitably alter its nature.

REFERENCES

Brewin C., Wing J. K., Mangen S. P., Brugha T. S., Maccarthy B. (1987). Principles and practice of measuring needs in the long term mentally ill: the MRC needs for care assessment. *Psychological Medicine*; 17: 971–81.

Burford C. (1988). A survey of clients of a community psychiatric nursing service. *British Journal of Psychiatry*; (in press).

Goffman E. (1961). *Asylums: Essays on the Social Situation of Mental Patients and Other Inmates*. New York: Doubleday.

Krawiecka M., Goldberg D., Vaughan M. (1977). A standardised psychiatric assessment schedule for rating psychotic patients. *Acta Psychiatrica Scandinavica*; 55: 299–308.

Leff J., Abberton E. (1981). Voice pitch measurements in schizophrenia and depression. *Psychological Medicine*; 11: 849–52.

Leff J., Wig N. N., Ghosh A. *et al.* (1987). Expressed emotion and schizophrenia in North India. III. Influence of relatives' expressed emotion on the course of schizophrenia in Chandigarh. *British Journal of Psychiatry*; 151: 166–73.

Sturt E., Wykes T. (1986). The measurement of social behaviour in psychiatric patients: an assessment of the reliability and validity of the SBS schedule. *British Journal of Psychiatry*; 148: 1–11.

Index